Paul, the apostle of Jesus Christ, his life and work his epistles and his doctrine

A contribution to the critical history of primitive Christianity

(Volume I)

Ferdinand Christian Baur

Alpha Editions

This edition published in 2020

ISBN : 9789354007750

Design and Setting By
Alpha Editions
email - alphaedis@gmail.com

As per information held with us this book is in Public Domain. This book is a reproduction of an important historical work. Alpha Editions uses the best technology to reproduce historical work in the same manner it was first published to preserve its original nature. Any marks or number seen are left intentionally to preserve its true form.

Prospectus of the
THEOLOGICAL TRANSLATION FUND.

As it is important that the best results of recent theological investigations on the Continent, conducted without reference to doctrinal considerations, and with the sole purpose of arriving at truth, should be placed within the reach of English readers, it is proposed to collect, by Subscriptions and Donations, a Fund which shall be employed for the promotion of this object. A good deal has been already effected in the way of translating foreign theological literature, a series of works from the pens of Hengstenberg, Haevernick, Delitzsch, Keil, and others of the same school, having of late years been published in English; but—as the names of the authors just mentioned will at once suggest to those who are conversant with the subject—the tendency of these works is for the most part conservative. It is a theological literature of a more independent character, less biassed by dogmatical prepossessions, a literature which is represented by such works as those of Ewald, Hupfeld, F. C. Baur, Zeller, Rothe, Keim, Schrader, Hausrath, Nöldeke, Pfleiderer, &c., in Germany, and by those of Kuenen, Scholten, and others, in Holland, that it is desirable to render accessible to English readers who are not familiar with the languages of the Continent. The demand for works of this description is not as yet so widely extended among either the clergy or the laity of Great Britain as to render it practicable for publishers to bring them out in any considerable numbers at their own risk. And for this reason the publication of treatises of this description can only be secured by obtaining the co-operation of the friends of free and unbiassed theological inquiry.

It is hoped that at least such a number of Subscribers of *One Guinea Annually* may be obtained as may render it practicable for the Publishers, as soon as the scheme is fairly set on foot, to bring out every year *three 8vo volumes*, which each Subscriber of the above amount would be entitled to receive gratis. But as it will be necessary to obtain, and to remunerate, the services of a responsible Editor, and in general, if not invariably, to pay the translators, it would conduce materially to the speedy success of the design, if free donations were also made to the Fund; or if contributors were to subscribe for more than one copy of the works to be published.

If you approve of this scheme, you are requested to communicate with Messrs. Williams and Norgate, 14, Henrietta Street, Covent Garden, London, and to state whether you are willing to subscribe; and if you are disposed to assist further, what would be the amount of your donation, or the number of additional copies of the publications which you would take.

We are, your obedient servants,

JOHN TULLOCH,	H. J. S. SMITH,
H. B. WILSON,	H. SIDGWICK,
B. JOWETT,	JAMES HEYWOOD,
A. P. STANLEY,	C. KEGAN PAUL,
W. G. CLARK,	J. ALLANSON PICTON,
S. DAVIDSON,	ROBT. WALLACE,
JAMES MARTINEAU,	LEWIS CAMPBELL,
JOHN CAIRD,	RUSSELL MARTINEAU,
EDWARD CAIRD,	T. K. CHEYNE,
JAMES DONALDSON,	J. MUIR.

A Committee selected from the signataries of the original Prospectus agreed upon the works to commence the series. Of these, the following were published in

The *First* Year (1873): 3 vols., 21s.

1. KEIM (TH.), HISTORY OF JESUS OF NAZARA. Considered in its connection with the National Life of Israel, and related in detail. Second Edition, re-translated by Arthur Ransom. Vol. I. Introduction; Survey of Sources; Sacred and Political Groundwork; Religious Groundwork.

2. BAUR (F. C.), PAUL, THE APOSTLE OF JESUS CHRIST, his Life and Work, his Epistles and Doctrine. A Contribution to a Critical History of Primitive Christianity. Second Edition, by Rev. Allan Menzies. Vol. I.

3. KUENEN (A.), THE RELIGION OF ISRAEL TO THE FALL OF THE JEWISH STATE. Translated by A. H. May. Vol. I.

The *Second* Year (1874): 3 vols., 21*s*.
4. KUENEN'S RELIGION OF ISRAEL. Vol. II. Translated by A. H. May.
5. BLEEK'S LECTURES ON THE APOCALYPSE. Edited by the Rev. Dr. S. Davidson.
6. BAUR'S PAUL; the second and concluding volume. Translated by the Rev. Allan Menzies.

The *Third* Year (1875): 3 vols., 21*s*.
7. KUENEN'S RELIGION OF ISRAEL; the third and concluding volume.
8. ZELLER, THE ACTS OF THE APOSTLES CRITICALLY EXAMINED. To which is prefixed, Overbeck's Introduction from De Wette's Handbook, translated by Joseph Dare, B.A. Vol. I.
9. EWALD'S COMMENTARY ON THE PROPHETS OF THE OLD TESTAMENT. Translated by the Rev. J. Frederick Smith. Vol. I. General Introduction; Yoel, Amos, Hosea, and Zakharya 9—11.

The *Fourth* Year (1876): 3 vols., 21*s*.
10. ZELLER'S ACTS OF THE APOSTLES. Vol. II. and last.
11. KEIM'S HISTORY OF JESUS OF NAZARA. Vol. II. Translated by the Rev. E. M. Geldart. The Sacred Youth; Self-recognition; Decision.
12. EWALD'S PROPHETS OF THE OLD TESTAMENT. Vol. II. Yesaya, Obadya, Mikha.

The *Fifth* Year (1877): 3 vols., 21*s*.
13. PAULINISM: a Contribution to the History of Primitive Christian
15. Theology. By Professor O. Pfleiderer, of Jena. Translated by E. Peters. 2 vols.
14. KEIM'S HISTORY OF JESUS OF NAZARA. Translated by A. Ransom. Vol. III. The First Preaching; the Works of Jesus; the Disciples; and the Apostolic Mission.

The *Sixth* Year (1878): 3 vols., 21*s*.
16. BAUR'S (F. C.), CHURCH HISTORY OF THE FIRST THREE CENTURIES. Translated from the third German Edition. Edited by the Rev. Allan Menzies (in 2 vols.). Vol. I.
17. HAUSRATH'S HISTORY OF THE NEW TESTAMENT TIMES. The Time of Jesus. Translated by the Revds. C. T. Poynting and P. Quenzer (in 2 vols.). Vol. I.
18. EWALD'S COMMENTARY ON THE PROPHETS OF THE OLD TESTAMENT. Translated by the Rev. J. Frederick Smith. Vol. III. Nahum, Ssephanya, Habaqquq, Zakharya 12—14, Yeremya.

The *Seventh* Year (1879): 3 vols., 21s.
19. KEIM'S HISTORY OF JESUS OF NAZARA. Vol. IV. The Galilean Storms; Signs of the approaching Fall; Recognition of the Messiah.
20. BAUR'S CHURCH HISTORY. Vol. II. and last.
21. EWALD'S COMMENTARY ON THE PROPHETS. Vol. IV. Hezeqiel, Yesaya xl.—lxvi.

The *Eighth* Year (1880): 3 vols., 21s.
22. HAUSRATH'S NEW TESTAMENT TIMES. The Time of Jesus. Vol. II. and last.
23. EWALD'S COMMENTARY ON THE PSALMS. Translated by the Rev.
24. E. Johnson, M.A. 2 vols.

The *Ninth* Year (1881): 3 vols., 21s.
25. KEIM'S HISTORY OF JESUS OF NAZARA. Vol. V. The Messianic Progress to Jerusalem.
26. EWALD'S COMMENTARY ON THE PROPHETS. Vol. V. and last. Haggai, Zakharya, Malaki, Yona, Barukh, Daniel.
27. A PROTESTANT COMMENTARY ON THE BOOKS OF THE NEW TESTAMENT: with General and Special Introductions. Edited by Professors P. W. Schmidt and F. von Holzendorff. Translated from the Third German Edition by the Rev. F. H. Jones, B.A. (in 3 vols.). Vol. I. Matthew to Acts.

The *Tenth* Year (1882): 3 vols., 21s.
28. EWALD'S COMMENTARY ON THE BOOK OF JOB. Translated by the Rev. J. Frederick Smith (in 1 vol.).
29. PROTESTANT COMMENTARY. Vol. II. The Pauline Epistles to Galatians.
30. KEIM'S HISTORY OF JESUS OF NAZARA. Vol. VI. and last.

The *Eleventh* Year (1883-84): 3 vols., 21s.
31. PROTESTANT COMMENTARY. Vol. III. and last.
32. REVILLE (Professor ALB., D.D.) PROLEGOMENA OF THE HISTORY OF RELIGIONS. Translated by A. S. Squire. With an Introduction by Professor Max Müller.
33. SCHRADER (Professor E., D.D.) THE CUNEIFORM INSCRIPTIONS AND THE OLD TESTAMENT. Translated by Professor Owen C. Whitehouse. Vol. I. Map.

The *Twelfth* Year (1885-86):
34. PFLEIDERER (Professor O.) THE PHILOSOPHY OF RELIGION ON THE BASIS OF ITS HISTORY. Translated by the Rev. Alex. Stewart and the Rev. Allan Menzies. Vol. I. Spinoza to Schleiermacher.

Beyond these, the following Works are in the hands of Translators, and will be included in the next years' Subscriptions:

SCHRADER (Professor E.) THE OLD TESTAMENT AND CUNEIFORM INSCRIPTIONS. Vol. II.

PFLEIDERER'S PHILOSOPHY OF RELIGION. Translated by the Rev. Alexander Stewart, of Dundee, and the Rev. Allan Menzies Vols. II.—IV.

CONTENTS OF THE
THEOLOGICAL TRANSLATION FUND LIBRARY.

A Selection of Six or more volumes may be had on direct application to the Publishers, at 7s. per volume.

1. **Baur (F. C.) Church History of the First Three Centuries.** Translated from the Third German Edition. Edited by the Rev. Allan Menzies. 2 vols. 8vo. 21s.
2. **Baur (F. C.) Paul, the Apostle of Jesus Christ, his Life and Work, his Epistles and Doctrine.** A Contribution to a Critical History of Primitive Christianity. Second Edition. By the Rev. Allan Menzies. 2 vols. 21s.
3. **Bleek's Lectures on the Apocalypse.** Edited by the Rev. Dr. S. Davidson. 10s. 6d.
4. **Ewald (H.) Commentary on the Prophets of the** Old Testament. Vol. I. Yoel, Amos, Hosea, Zakharya, c. 9—12. Vol. II. Yesaya, Obadya, Mikha. Vol. III. Nahum, Ssephanya, Habaqquq, Zakharya, c. 12—14, Yeremya. Vol. IV. Hezeqiel, Yesaya, c. 40—66. Vol. V. Anonymous Pieces, Haggai, Zakharya, Malaki, Yona, Barukh, Daniel, Index. Translated by the Rev. J. Frederick Smith. 5 vols. 8vo. Each 10s. 6d.
5. **Ewald (H.) Commentary on the Psalms.** Translated by the Rev. E. Johnson, M.A. 2 vols. 8vo. Each 10s. 6d.
6. **Ewald (H.) Commentary on the Book of Job,** with Translation by Professor H. Ewald. Translated from the German by the Rev. J. Frederick Smith. 1 vol. 8vo. 10s. 6d.
7. **Hausrath (Professor A.) History of the New Testament Times. The Time of Jesus.** By Dr. A. Hausrath, Professor of Theology, Heidelberg. Translated, with the Author's sanction, from the Second German Edition, by the Revs. C. T. Poynting and P. Quenzer. 2 vols. 8vo. 21s.
8. **Keim (Th.) History of Jesus of Nazara.** Considered in its connection with the National Life of Israel, and related in detail. Vol. I. Survey of Sources, Paul, Gospels, the Sacred Groundwork. Vol. II. The Sacred Youth, Self-recognition, and Decision. Vol. III. The Galilean Springtime. Vol. IV. The Galilean Storms, Recognition of the Messiah. Vol. V. The Messianic Progress to Jerusalem, the Decisive Struggle, the Farewell, the Last Supper. Vol. VI. The Messianic Death, Burial and Resurrection, the Messianic Place in History. Translated by Arthur Ransom and the Rev. E. M. Geldart. 6 vols. 8vo. Each 10s. 6d.

9. **Kuenen (A.) The Religion of Israel to the Fall of the Jewish State.** Translated by A. H. May. 3 vols. 8vo. 31s. 6d.

10. **Pfleiderer (Professor O.) Paulinism:** a Contribution to the History of Primitive Christian Theology. Translated by E. Peters. 2 vols. 21s.

11. **Pfleiderer (Professor O.) The Philosophy of Religion** on the Basis of its History. I. History of the Philosophy of Religion from Spinoza to the present Day. Vol. I. Spinoza to Schleiermacher. Translated by the Rev. Allan Menzies and the Rev. Alex. Stewart, of Dundee. 10s. 6d. (Vol. II. in the Press.)

12. **Protestant Commentary on the New Testament;** with General and Special Introductions to the Books, by Lipsius, Holsten, Lang, Pfleiderer, Holtzmann, Hilgenfeld, and others. Vol. I. Introduction, the Gospels, the Acts. Vol. II. Epistles to the Romans, Corinthians, Galatians. Vol. III. Ephesians, Philippians, Colossians, Thessalonians, Pastoral Epistles, Revelations. Translated by the Rev. F. H. Jones. 3 vols. 8vo. 31s. 6d.

13. **Reville (Rev. Dr.) Prolegomena of the History of** Religion, with Introduction by Professor Max Müller. 10s. 6d.

14. **Schrader (Professor E.) The Old Testament and** the Cuneiform Inscriptions. Translated by the Rev. Owen C. Whitehouse. (In 2 vols.) Vol. I. Map. 10s. 6d. (Vol. II. in the Press.)

15. **Zeller (E.) The Acts of the Apostles Critically** Examined. To which is prefixed Overbeck's Introduction from De Wette's Handbook. Translated by Joseph Dare. 2 vols. 8vo. 21s.

The price of the Works to Subscribers, 7s. per vol.

Works in the Press:

Pfleiderer (Professor O.) The Philosophy of Religion. Translated by the Rev. Alexander Stewart, of Dundee, and the Rev. Allan Menzies. Vols. II.—IV.

Schrader's Old Testament and Cuneiform Inscriptions, Vol. II.

All new Subscribers may purchase any of the previous volumes at 7s. instead of 10s. 6d. per volume. A selection of six or more volumes may also be had at the Subscriber's price, or 7s. per volume, upon direct application to the Publishers.

THE HIBBERT LECTURES.

1886.—**Professor J. Rhys. Lectures on the Origin and** Growth of Religion as illustrated in Celtic Heathendom. 8vo, cloth. 10s. 6d.

1885.—**Professor O. Pfleiderer. Lectures on the Influence** of the Apostle Paul on the Development of Christianity. Translated by the Rev. J. F. Smith. 8vo, cloth. 10s. 6d.

1884.—**Professor Albert Reville. Lectures on the Ancient** Religions of Mexico and Peru. 8vo, cloth. 10s. 6d.

1883.—**The Rev. Charles Beard. Lectures on the Reformation** of the Sixteenth Century in its Relation to Modern Thought and Knowledge. 8vo, cloth. 10s. 6d. (Cheap Edition, 4s. 6d.)

1882.—**Professor Kuenen. Lectures on National Religions** and Universal Religions. 8vo, cloth. 10s. 6d.

1881.—**T. W. Rhys Davids. Lectures on the Origin and** Growth of Religion as illustrated by some Points in the History of Indian Buddhism. 8vo, cloth. 10s. 6d.

1880.—**M. Ernest Renan. On the Influence of the Institutions,** Thought and Culture of Rome on Christianity, and the Development of the Catholic Church. Translated by the Rev. Charles Beard. 8vo, cloth. 10s. 6d. (Cheap Edition, 2s. 6d.)

1879.—**P. Le Page Renouf. Lectures on the Origin and** Growth of Religion as illustrated by the Religion of Ancient Egypt. Second Edition. 8vo, cloth. 10s. 6d.

1878.—**Professor Max Müller. Lectures on the Origin** and Growth of Religion as illustrated by the Religions of India. 8vo, cloth. 10s. 6d.

Works published by the Hibbert Trustees.

Illustrations of the History of Medieval Thought in the Departments of Theology and Ecclesiastical Politics. By REGINALD LANE POOLE, M.A., Balliol College, Oxford, Ph.D. Leipzig. 8vo, cloth. 10s. 6d.

The Objectivity of Truth. By GEORGE J. STOKES, B.A., Senior Moderator and Gold Medallist, Trinity College, Dublin; late Hibbert Travelling Scholar. 8vo, cloth. 5s.

An Essay on Assyriology. By GEORGE EVANS, M.A., Hibbert Fellow. With an Assyrian Tablet in Cuneiform Type. 8vo, cloth. 5s.

The Development from Kant to Hegel, with Chapters on the Philosophy of Religion. By ANDREW SETH, Assistant to the Professor of Logic and Metaphysics, Edinburgh University. 8vo, cloth. 5s.

Kantian Ethics and the Ethics of Evolution. A Critical Study by J. GOULD SCHURMAN, M.A., D.Sc., Professor of Logic and Metaphysics in Acadia College, Nova Scotia. 8vo, cloth. 5s.

The Resurrection of Jesus Christ. An Essay, in Three Chapters. By REGINALD W. MACAN, Christ Church, Oxford. 8vo, cloth. 5s.

The Ecclesiastical Institutions of Holland, treated with Special Reference to the Position and Prospects of the Modern School of Theology. By the Rev. P. H. WICKSTEED, M.A. 8vo. 1s.

WILLIAMS AND NORGATE,
14, HENRIETTA STREET, COVENT GARDEN, LONDON;
AND 20, SOUTH FREDERICK STREET, EDINBURGH.

THEOLOGICAL
TRANSLATION FUND LIBRARY.

PAUL
HIS LIFE AND WORKS.
By F. C. BAUR.

VOL. I.

PAUL

THE APOSTLE OF JESUS CHRIST,

HIS LIFE AND WORK, HIS EPISTLES AND HIS DOCTRINE.

A CONTRIBUTION
TO A
CRITICAL HISTORY OF PRIMITIVE CHRISTIANITY.

BY

DR. FERDINAND CHRISTIAN BAUR,
PROFESSOR OF THEOLOGY IN THE UNIVERSITY OF TUBINGEN.

TRANSLATED FROM THE SECOND GERMAN EDITION,
EDITED AFTER THE DEATH OF THE AUTHOR BY
DR. EDUARD ZELLER.

VOL. I.

SECOND EDITION.

REVISED BY REV. A. MENZIES.

WILLIAMS AND NORGATE,
14 HENRIETTA STREET, COVENT GARDEN, LONDON;
AND 20 SOUTH FREDERICK STREET, EDINBURGH.
1876.

PREFACE TO THE FIRST EDITION (1845).

FOR a considerable number of years I have been engaged in critical investigations chiefly of the Pauline Epistles and the Acts, with a view to a better understanding of the life and work of the Apostle Paul, and of his historical position and importance. The first fruits of these studies appeared in the year 1831, in the Tübinger Zeitschrift für Theologie, 1831, p. 4, and was an essay entitled "The Christ-party in the Corinthian Church, the opposition of Petrine and Pauline Christianity in the Primitive Church, the Apostle Peter in Rome." In this paper I advanced the assertion which I have since maintained and furnished with additional evidence, that the harmonious relation which is commonly assumed to have existed between the Apostle Paul and the Jewish Christians with the older Apostles at their head, is unhistorical, and that the conflict of the two parties whom we have to recognise upon this field entered more deeply into the life of the early Church than has been hitherto supposed. Many points of this essay were noticed by Neander in the first edition of his " Planting and Training of the Christian Church by the Apostles," which appeared soon afterwards, in 1832 ; and it certainly did something to bring about a better understanding of several questions of early Church History. The road which had thus been opened soon led me to further results, which I laid before the world in my work on the Pastoral Epistles, 1835, and in the essay on the Epistle to the Romans, Tub. Ztschr. für Theol. 1836, Part 3.

I have long meant to republish the two essays which appeared in our Magazine here, uniting them into a connected work with other cognate discussions. This is what the reader now has before him; in fact the greatly extended compass of the present work entitles it to the position of a monograph on the Apostle Paul. It may also claim to be a special examination of a movement in the early development of Christianity, the proper understanding of which is certainly surrounded with great difficulties, but is nevertheless indispensable for the solution of the great question of our time, what Christianity originally was, and essentially is.

I may assume that my method of historical criticism is well known. The doubtful honour has lately been paid me of being called the founder and master of a new critical school; against which, even if I thought the compliment was seriously intended, I could do nothing but protest. It would be a poor account of former criticism, if the principles I have followed could with justice be called new ones. It cannot be the novelty of the principles that has given offence; it must be the results to which they lead when well applied, which have caused the criticism of the new school to be called negative and destructive. What do these formidable epithets amount to? What would criticism be if denuded of the right to deny and to destroy? The question can only be, what is denied, what is destroyed, and if there is good reason for doing it. And is not that criticism, which is held to be nothing but negative and destructive, really in the best sense conservative? Does it not proceed on the simple principle that every man is to get and to keep what belongs to him, and nothing but what belongs to him? To this limitation the conservative principle is essentially subject, and feeling this, I can have no wish to acknowledge claims which are indefensible, to defend traditional opinions which are unfounded and untrue, or to ignore contradictions which are evident and palpable. There are distinctions and differences which require to be clearly set forth, if the matter in hand is to be understood at all; and I cannot be a party to smoothing them over and obliterating them, in order to keep things comfortable on the surface, and save the labour of thought. If this negative and destructive road has led me to results which conflict with the ordinary conceptions, let it be shown that they are wrong; let them be examined and refuted, if that is possible, let them be denied and destroyed by the power of facts and arguments, if any one feels that he can do so!

There is no limit to controversy on points of detail. The abstract possibility of this and that detail can never be disproved: but this is not the way to dispose of a comprehensive historical theory. Such a theory appeals to its broad general truth, to which details are subordinate, and on which they depend: to the logical coherence of the whole, the preponderating inner probability and necessity of the case, as it impresses itself quietly upon the thoughtful mind; and against this the party interests of the day will sooner or later cease to assert themselves. In this conviction I leave this work to make its own way.

TABLE OF CONTENTS.

PAGE

INTRODUCTION.—The Standpoint of the Inquiry—The Acts of the Apostles as the source of the Apostle Paul's History—Division of the whole subject, . 1

First Part.

THE LIFE AND WORK OF THE APOSTLE PAUL.

CHAPTER I.

The Church at Jerusalem before the Apostle's Conversion (Acts of the Apostles iii.-v.), . . . 15

CHAPTER II.

Stephen the Predecessor of the Apostle Paul (Acts of the Apostles vi. vii.), ... 42

CHAPTER III.

The Conversion of the Apostle Paul (Acts of the Apostles ix., xxii., xxvi.), ... 61

Chapter IV.

The First Missionary Journey of the Apostle (Acts of the Apostles xiii. xiv.), . . . 90

Chapter V.

The Transactions between the Apostle Paul and the elder Apostles at Jerusalem (Acts of the Apostles xv., Galatians ii.), . . . 105

Chapter VI.

The Second Missionary Journey of the Apostle (Acts of the Apostles xvi.), . . . 146

Chapter VII.

The Apostle in Athens, Corinth, Ephesus—His Journey to Jerusalem by Miletus (Acts of the Apostles xvii.-xx.) . . . 168

Chapter VIII.

The Arrest of the Apostle in Jerusalem (Acts of the Apostles xxi.), . . . 195

Chapter IX.

The Apostle in Rome—His Imprisonment and Martyrdom, 216

Second Part.

THE EPISTLES OF THE APOSTLE PAUL.

Introduction, . . 245

FIRST CLASS OF PAULINE EPISTLES.

The Epistles to the Galatians, the Corinthians, and the Romans.

CHAPTER I.

The Epistle to the Galatians, . . . 250

CHAPTER II.

The two Epistles to the Corinthians, ... 258

CHAPTER III.

The Epistle to the Romans, . . . 308

INTRODUCTION.

THE STANDPOINT OF THE INQUIRY—THE ACTS OF THE APOSTLES AS THE SOURCE OF THE APOSTLE PAUL'S HISTORY—DIVISION OF THE WHOLE SUBJECT.

CRITICAL inquiry into the primitive history of Christianity, its origin and first development, as they lie before us in the series of writings which form our New Testament Canon, is one of the great wants of our time; the interests and tendencies of this age earnestly demand a solution of this great problem. It may be justly said of the present age that its prevailing tendency is critical, and that its task is not so much to shape a world still growing, as to grasp one already grown and present, and to understand by what steps and processes it has come to be what it is. The principal efforts of the age in the higher walks of science are critical and historical in their nature; everything that seeks to assert a position in the world is asked for its warrant in history; everything found existing is examined down to the very foundation; it is sought to go back to the beginning, to the first elements in which the germs of the whole process lay, in order to arrive at a clear insight into the whole from the discovered relations of the individual parts. Thought has now, after the laborious toil of many centuries, emancipated itself and cast away its crutches, and it naturally turns its gaze back into the Past. The spirit, at rest in itself in the assurance of its own self-consciousness, stands for the first time on a vantage-ground, from which it can look back upon the paths along which it has passed, as circumstances shaped its course; it retraces those paths not as at first, when it yielded unconsciously to surrounding influences, but recognising the inner necessity in obedience to which it has grown up to its present form. If in so many walks of human knowledge this critical labour is the necessary process through which the consciousness of the Present finds out its own relation to the Past, where can it be of greater importance than where the Present is linked with the Past by the strictest and closest ties, and where this union has its roots in the deepest interests of our spiritual being? Christianity is on the one hand the great spiritual power which determines all the belief and thought of the present age, the absolute principle on which the self-consciousness of the spirit is supported and maintained, so that, unless it were essentially Christian, it would have no stability or firmness in itself at all. On the other hand, the essential nature of Christianity is a purely historical question, whose solution lies only in that Past in which Christianity itself had its origin; it is a problem which can only be solved by that critical attitude of thought which the consciousness of the present age assumes towards the Past. As soon as the separate elements of the problem which had been long preparing, independently of each other, were gathered together into one view and expressed systematically, the importance of the subject could not fail to appear: and this was done by Strauss in his critical Life of Jesus. The strength of this criticism consisted in little more than this, that it drew necessary deductions from premises which had long been in existence; yet it took the public by surprise with the negative character of its results, and produced a painful impression which sought relief in crude and hasty refutations. How far these were successful, and in what way the public mind has been affected by this great critical agitation, we need not here inquire; but it is clear that, in spite of all possible results, the criticism was amply warranted on scientific grounds. It must be recognised as a service which the education of the age distinctly called for, and the result of what is said in so many quarters against the work of Strauss is simply to demonstrate the necessity of going still deeper and more thoroughly into the critical process which he began.

The criticism of the gospel history, inasmuch as it immediately concerns the life of the Founder of Christianity, and brings us in contact with so many other momentous questions, will long remain the most important object of the critical labours of our time. The inquiry which ranks next to it in point of interest is concerned with the question how Christianity, which was at one time so closely interwoven with Judaism, broke loose from it and entered on its sphere of world-wide historical importance. The great historical interest of the Life of Jesus is that we see there the consciousness of the idea of Christianity and of its principle, which he first expressed and exemplified by the entire devotion of his whole being; this is the great result of the Evangelical history. But when we proceed from the Evangelical history to that of the time of the Apostles, it is the practical realisation of that idea which becomes the object of historical research. And this practical realisation of the idea of Christianity first became a question when, in consequence of the death and resurrection of Jesus, that idea passed into the actual consciousness of men, and became part of them and a living power in them, and when it found in the bounds of the national Judaism the chief obstacle to its reaching the position in the world which was its due, as we can now perceive. How these bounds were broken through, how Christianity, instead of remaining a mere form of Judaism, and being ultimately absorbed in it, asserted itself as a separate, independent principle, broke loose from it and took its stand as a new form of religious thought and life, essentially differing from Judaism, and freed from all its national exclusiveness, is the point of next greatest importance in the primitive history of one Christianity. Here also, as in the Gospel history, the historico-critical inquiry finds itself engaged with the person and character of one man. That Christianity, in the universal historical importance which it achieved, was the work of the Apostle Paul is undeniably a matter of historical fact; but in what manner he brought this about, how we are to conceive of his relations with the elder

Apostles, whether it was in harmony with them or in contradiction and opposition to them, that he carried out these principles and opinions which he was the first to ennunciate, this still requires a more thorough and searching inquiry. As in the Gospel history, historical criticism has here two accounts before it, which differ from each other and must be weighed and compared, in order to get from them what purely historical matter they may contain. These are the accounts given in the Acts of the Apostles and the historical data to be found in the Apostle's own Epistles. It would appear natural to suppose that in all the cases where the accounts in the Acts do not altogether agree with the statements of the Apostle, the latter must have such a decided claim to be considered authentic truth that the contradictions in the Acts would scarcely be worth attention, but this rule, which the very nature of the case might seem to have required, has not up to this time been so much followed as it ought. Proceeding on the assumption of the thorough identity of the statements in the Acts of the Apostles and the personal declarations of the Apostle in his Epistles, writers have held that the existing discrepancies, even when they cannot be denied, are too slight and unimportant to need serious consideration, and in some cases the statements of the Acts have been believed, though contrary to the clear assertions of the Apostle. Thus not only is historical truth shorn of its own clear light, but we fall far short of that justice and impartiality which are due to the Apostle in judging of his life and labours. In order to show that his relations to the other Apostles were not disturbed by any serious differences, scholars have not hesitated to ascribe to him in many cases a course of action which, if it really was such as is stated, throws a very equivocal light on his character. A discussion of this part of the primitive history of Christianity, undertaken on the foundation of strict historical criticism, will therefore be at the same time an apology for the Apostle. Neander's History of the Apostolic Age is by no means free from this one-sided manner of treatment; it makes a point of bringing the whole historical material into apparent harmony, and in this way it has done much to distort and obscure the view of the chief events of this period of the development of Christianity.

The Acts of the Apostles first presents itself as the chief source of the history of the apostolic life and labours of the Apostle Paul. But the historian cannot take his stand on this work without first making himself acquainted with the relation in which it stands to its historical materials. Between the Acts of the Apostles and the Pauline Epistles, as far as the historical contents of the latter can be compared with the former, there will be found in general the same relation as that between the Gospel of John and the Synoptical Gospels. The comparison of these two sources leads us to the conclusion that, considering the great difference between the two statements, historical truth must be entirely on one side or entirely on the other. To which it does belong can only be decided by applying the undisputed historical canon that the statement which has the greatest claim to historical truth is that which apppears most unprejudiced and nowhere betrays a desire to subordinate its historical material to any special subjective aim. For the history of the Apostolic Age the Pauline Epistles must in any case take precedence of all the other New Testament writings as an authentic source. On this account alone, if this were all, the Acts must take a secondary place; but there is also the further consideration that the same rule which defines the relation of the Synoptical Gospels to the Gospel of John finds its application in the case of the Acts of the Apostles. The opinion which I have here to express on the Acts of the Apostles, in order to indicate the standpoint of the following inquiry, is that the facts with which it deals do not appear to be narrated simply and directly, but to be modified by certain subjective aims which the writer had in view. And here I am very glad to be able to refer to a critical investigation which I have no scruple in following, its results being in fact what I had myself arrived at some time ago in a different way.[1] Schnecken-

---

[1] Schneckenburger "Ueber den Zweck der Apostelgeschichte," Berne, 1841. See my review of this Essay in the Jahrbücher für wissenschaftliche Kritik, March, 1841. No. 46.

burger designated the aim of the Acts of the Apostles as apologetic. According to the results of his inquiry, we have to consider this work as a defence of the Apostle Paul in his apostolic dignity and his personal and apostolic conduct, especially in the matter of the Gentiles, as against the attacks and accusations of the Judaizing party. The idea that runs through the whole is that of a parallel between the two Apostles Peter and Paul, and pervades each of the two great sections into which the work is divided[1] (chapters i. to xii., and xiii. to the end). The unity of the work consists in this idea; its chief tendency is to represent the difference between Peter and Paul as unessential and trifling. To this end Paul is made in the second part to appear as much as possible like Peter, and Peter in the first part as much as possible like Paul. Thus it is sought to bring the two as near to each other as possible, so that the one may be, as it were, answerable for the other; and the author being undoubtedly a Paulinist, this has been done in the interests of Paul. Hence, as Schneckenburger points out, the second part omits no possible proof of Paul's righteousness according to the law (such as zealous keeping of feasts, frequent journeys to the Temple, private asceticism, and circumcision); and, on the other hand, there is no trace of that side of Pauline religion which was a protest against legalism. The same Judaizing tendency which meets us in the personal conduct of Paul is also evident in the account of his official labours. Paul pays all due consideration not only to the elder Apostles, who are completely at one with him (chapter xv.), but also to the Jewish people. In one point this is especially insisted on; we are told again and again, as often as the occasion requires, that wherever he went, he first proclaimed the Gospel to the Jews, and that only when they rejected him and his Gospel did he turn to the Gentiles. Schneckenburger, with much acuteness, further endeavours to prove that all the important omissions in the Pauline history are to be accounted for by this apologetic tendency of the

---

[1] This idea, and the view of the aims of the Acts of the Apostles depending on it, I first enunciated in my treatise Ueber den Ursprung des Episcopats, Tübingen Zeitschrift für Theologie, 1838, pt. 3, p. 142.

Acts. They refer to persons or events, the mention or description of which would have involved an essentially different picture of Paul from that suggested by the story as it stands. They save the writer, in fact, from mentioning the prejudices and misrepresentations of the Judaizers which we hear of in the Pauline Epistles. The most remarkable instance of this kind is the utter silence of the Acts of the Apostles with regard to the scene related in the Epistle to the Galatians between Peter and Paul at Antioch; and with this may be connected the omission of the name of Titus in the Acts. The first part of the Acts is constructed in accordance with the same apologetic aim. The Jewish opponents of the Apostle Paul, as we see especially in the Second Epistle to the Corinthians, would not allow that the visions which he claimed for himself were any proof of his apostolic mission. In this view the vision ascribed to Peter (chapter x.), and its acknowledgment by the Primitive Church, is of importance as an indirect legitimation of the Pauline visions. But this vision has reference to the conversion of the first Gentile, Cornelius. If therefore the Judaizers complained that the Apostle Paul devoted himself to the conversion of the Gentiles, whilst the children of the Covenant were still for the most part unconverted, the first part shows that Gentiles had been baptised long before Paul's time, baptised by Peter himself, the head of the Judaizers. Thus the whole question of the admission of the Gentiles had been decided by a divine vision, by the assent of the Primitive Church, and by the most distinct expressions and acts of the Apostles. Paul therefore had only to tread in the footsteps of the older Apostles. In particular, a comparison of the passages (xv. 7, 14) shows an unmistakable design to claim for Peter the earliest labour among the Gentiles, and through this precedent to impress on the activity of Paul, so blamed by some, the seal of legitimacy given by the whole Primitive Church. Everything shows how desirous the author of the Acts of the Apostles is to prove that Peter began the conversion of the Gentiles. He did this by divine command after the indifference of the Jews in general had been proved by experience.

Schneckenburger rightly finds another great proof of this

apologetic tendency of the Acts of the Apostles in the fact that whilst the second part makes Paul believe and speak as much as possible in conformity with the demands of the Judaizing party, the same principles of equal participation by Jews and Gentiles in the Messianic salvation which Paul develops at length in the Epistle to the Romans are laid down and carried out in practice by the Judæo-Christian Apostles in the first part. The universalism of Christianity and the propriety of preaching to the Gentiles were so distinctly recognised by Peter that no doubt can be entertained that the narrator intended the words of Jesus (i. 8) to convey an intimation of this doctrine.

Schneckenburger has incontestably proved that the Acts of the Apostles is to be understood from this apologetic point of view. It might indeed be asked whether it was written exclusively in this apologetic interest, whether it does not also contain passages which cannot be so easily reconciled with such a purpose, and in which the aim seems to be the general one of furnishing a historical narrative. But the great aim of the work is perfectly clear, and we need not give it up even though there should be some passages of such a kind. The second part, which is occupied exclusively with the Apostle Paul, offers no difficulty in this respect, for although the narrative of the Apostle's travels might seem to contain more personal and special details than the apologetic aim required, still it is clear that this very narrative is coloured throughout in accordance with that aim. In the first part indeed the purely historical interest would seem to predominate over the apologetic one, if we did not take into consideration that the author had first of all to secure his historical basis for the parallel which he has in view, and also that his apologetic aim was forwarded, indirectly at least, to a considerable extent, by the care and accuracy which he employs in his account of the circumstances and arrangements of the first Christian Church. His description of the early church was the part of his work which would appeal most to the Judaists, and by dwelling on it at some length he secured a good introduction for his main theme, the apology of the Apostle Paul, which thus appeared in the form of a simple historical narrative. In reality, however, we ought not to set the apologetic in such direct opposition to the historical interest; they are not inconsistent with each other: the first may be established in such a way as to leave ample room for the second: indeed the apologetic aim cannot be carried out without a proper historical foundation on which to proceed. Another and much more important question here suggests itself, namely, how the supposition of the apologetic aim of the Acts of the Apostles which we have indicated affects the historical trustworthiness of the work and the authorship of Luke? Schneckenburger takes great pains to show that the book need not suffer in these particulars, though his results be true. He is anxious to refute the opinions of those who differ from him in casting suspicion on the historical trustworthiness of the Acts, and pronounces repeatedly and decidedly in favour of the traditional view that Luke was the author. But it is not possible for him to carry out his view of the aim of the Acts without sometimes granting more than seems to be compatible with the supposition of its being the work of an author standing in so close a connection with the Apostle. In this point of view, how suspicious are such admissions as the following: "Luke's plan evidently did not suggest to him a complete historical picture of Paul, but as brilliant a one as possible. He may not have incorporated in his work any unhistorical feature, yet the picture is obviously incomplete, wanting, as it does, the chief features of the Pauline character which meet us in his own writings" (p. 58). "The picture it presents of Paul and his labours is a partial one, not always nor in every detail in conformity with the description he gives of himself in the Epistles, and is one that could not have been drawn by a Paulinist writing without any apologetic aim" (p. 92). "There may be really some difficulty in reconciling the later historical fact of the Judaizing of Peter with the Paulinist teachings and labours which are attributed to Peter in the first part; and on the other hand Paul seems in the second part to have accommodated himself more to Jewish wishes and prejudices than we could have expected; to say the least, the characteristic Pauline decisiveness nowhere appears either in teaching or action" (p. 210). That in speaking of the Apostle's journey to Jerusalem the author has not only forborne to mention the collection, for the sake of which we know that it was undertaken, but even given a different reason for the journey in order to fill up the gap thus made (p. 113); that the objective succession of events is internally improbable (p. 145); that he has permitted himself to use an unhistorical exaggeration (p. 182), etc. etc.;—all this Schneckenburger cannot deny, however lightly he passes over such points, and careful though he is throughout to prevent any suspicion of historical fiction from attaching to the author of the Acts of the Apostles. In spite of all he thinks the historical credibility of the work stands unshaken; but after admissions like these this is no longer possible.

This silence of itself, and the distortion of facts which it involves, is enough to show that the writer was not too truthful or too conscientious even to deny the truth of history when he found it his interest to do so. If we go through the whole series of particulars in which Schneckenburger traces the parallel which the writer sought to draw between the two Apostles, and then carefully consider how analogous the one is to the other, who can believe that the author took all this only from the history lying before him, and did nothing but select what suited him? This remarkable fact is just what leads us to the assumption of a special aim, in the light of which the work is to be read. But supposing Schneckenburger's view of the author's trustworthiness to be the true one, what the better are we? The phenomenon before us remains unexplained: if the facts occurred as they are here narrated, then our writer need have been nothing more than a mere chronicler, and it becomes extremely doubtful if he did follow the apologetic aim which is imputed to him, a thing which he himself nowhere mentions. The more clearly we trace an apologetic aim in his narrative, the more questionable must it appear whether what he gives us is a purely historical narrative; and it cannot be denied that possibly, if not probably, he has in many cases altered the true history, not only negatively, by ignoring actions and circumstances which bear essentially on his subject-matter, but also positively.

The most weighty reason for this opinion is, that the Paul of the Acts is manifestly quite a different person from the Paul of the Epistles. "Evidently," says Schneckenburger himself (p. 150), "we do not here get a full and entire account of Paul's relation to the law, but a one-sided one, and there is really nothing laid before us to explain how the other side of that relation is to be reconciled with this one. When we consider how this view of Paul's relation to the law is here embodied in a historical narrative, and how, when the writer comes to discuss the charge brought against Paul of unfaithfulness to the law, he simply, and without any explanation, makes him perform an act of legal conformity in order to prove that charge a slander (Acts xxi. 20 *sq.*) (Paul himself makes good his position (Rom. iii. 31), νόμον οὐ καταργοῦμεν διὰ τῆς πίστεως, ἀλλὰ νόμον ἱστῶμεν, in a different way, by force of the keenest dialectic), the conjecture is surely allowable that a special purpose is to be served in presenting Paul to the readers of the Acts in this particular light." The two views which are to be taken together to make one Paul are, in fact, so divergent and heterogeneous that the connection that is necessary to harmonise them is anything but self-evident. If the writer of the Acts be, after all, a faithful reporter of history, then the means for harmonising the two representations must be sought for in the Apostle himself; that is to say, the historical character of the author can only be maintained at the cost of the moral character of the Apostle. When the whole bearing of the case is considered, as Schneckenburger's investigation has demonstrated it, it is impossible for us to remain within the limits which he sets to himself, and which appear to us to be completely arbitrary; the results of his inquiries draw us on from the mere supposition of an apologetic aim to a much further point, where the question as to the aim of the Acts of the Apostles and its author must be put in a different form. If we start from the idea of an unquestionable apologetic interest, then the question follows unavoidably—What can have decided the author to sacrifice historical truth to this bias? That this can only have been done on very weighty grounds is certainly a natural supposition; but further it is natural to suppose that these grounds are not personal to the Apostle, nor drawn from the circumstances by which he himself was surrounded. Surely the best apology of all, if the Apostle needed an apology, would have been found in an open statement of his apostolic life and labours, and of the manner and principles of his actions, as these had been dictated by his apostolic calling. The reasons for the mode of treatment really pursued can only be sought for in circumstances in which the general good of the Church called for such concession on the part of the disciple of Paul. These circumstances took place at a time when, in consequence of all those efforts of his Judæo-Christian opponents, of which his own Epistles show us the by no means trivial beginnings, Paulinism was so far overcome that it could only maintain itself in the way of concession, by modifying the hardness and directness of its opposition to the law and Judaism; when it was reduced to come to an understanding with the powerful Jewish-Christian party by which it was opposed, so as to harmonise conflicting views and interests, and form a unity on a new basis. Little though we can follow the course of these circumstances, we find it undeniable that such relations did exist, that they extended far into the second century, and that they were powerful enough during that period, when the Church was taking form and preparing to appear out of the conflict of heterogeneous elements, to produce other literary results of a similar tendency. If we carefully consider these relations and the order in which they must have arisen, and remember that not for some time could they acquire such importance, we shall be carried on by them to a point when we can no longer maintain the authorship of Luke for the Acts of the Apostles, at least in the form in which we possess the work. Still, it may not be impossible that sketches, collections, narratives, chronicles, especially those concerning the last journey of the Apostle, from the hand of Luke, may have formed the foundation of the Acts. That the name of Luke has been prefixed to it only shows how it was thought probable that, as it treats mainly of the life and labours of the Apostle Paul, and is evidently written in his interest, the work can only have proceeded from one of his intimate friends. Was not this in the mind of the author, when, in the passages marked by the use of "We," he presents himself as an eye-witness and fellow-traveller? Who is it that speaks of himself in this way? He calls himself by no name—the name of Luke nowhere occurs in the Acts of the Apostles; but as Luke is represented in Colossians iv. 14 as standing in close relations with Paul, may not the author have meant by the use of "we" to put himself in the place of Luke, and to identify himself with him? Perhaps there was in existence an account of the journey from the hand of Luke which suggested this. In such passages the author is very willing to be considered as one person with Luke; but he did not venture to declare himself in the character of Luke as the writer of the Acts of the Apostles, for he was well aware of the difference in dates, and could not so completely escape from his own identity. The apologetic interest of his statement does not altogether destroy its historical character, but only limits and modifies it. Unhistorical as it appears in many points, on which we can bring to bear proofs from the Apostle's own writings, it is, on the other hand, in agreement in many instances with the history of that time as we know it from other sources. The Acts of the Apostles, therefore, although our verdict, with regard to its author, its aim, and the time of its production, differs widely from the ordinary one, remains a highly-important source of the history of the Apostolic Age. It is, however, a source which needs strict historical criticism before it can be held to yield a trustworthy historical picture of the persons and circumstances of which it treats.

The foregoing remarks may suffice for the present to indicate generally the standpoint from which we have to start in conducting our historical examination of the life and labours of the Apostle Paul. Our verdict on the historical value and character of the Acts of the Apostles depends chiefly on the answer we may give to the question—How does it stand related to the historical contents of the Pauline Epistles? and thus requires to be sought for by a careful inquiry into the principal features of the Apostle's personal history. This inquiry into the life and labours of the Apostle, proceeding on the criticism of the Acts of the Apostles, is what has first of all to be undertaken in our attempt to form an estimate of his life and work. The results of this inquiry will enable us to assign to the Epistles their proper place in the history, and to judge how far the Epistles ascribed to the Apostle are to be held as genuine. From this it will appear how only those of the Epistles which are accepted as genuine can be employed in our discussion of the Pauline doctrine. The whole subject thus divides itself into three closely-connected parts :—1. The life and work of the Apostle; 2. The historical position and meaning of his Epistles ; 3. The contents and connection of his doctrine.

FIRST PART.

THE LIFE AND WORK OF THE APOSTLE PAUL.

CHAPTER I.

THE CHURCH AT JERUSALEM BEFORE THE APOSTLE'S CONVERSION.

THE conversion of the Apostle Paul to Christianity is an event of such peculiar importance in the history of the nascent Church that it can scarcely be understood aright without taking into consideration the condition in which the Church had been during the short time of its existence. But the only thing of which we have any certainty during this earliest period is that which is so closely connected with the name of the Apostle Paul, and to which he himself bears witness (Galatians i. 13, 23 ; 1 Corinthians xv. 9), namely, that he became a Christian and an Apostle from being a persecutor of the Christian Church. Thus even in the earliest times persecutions had fallen on the Church at Jerusalem. Persecutions are spoken of in the Acts of the Apostles, but in such a manner that historical criticism must assert its right of doubt and denial with regard to the statement.

When after its weak beginnings the Christian Church had organised itself in the way we all know and into which we will not here further inquire, first inwardly by the power of the Spirit imparted to it as the principle of a new consciousness[1] which animated it henceforward and then outwardly after the rapid increase of its numbers, by the first institutions of its social life, a series of measures was taken against the Apostles by the Jewish rulers, induced by a miracle of healing wrought on a man lame from his birth by the Apostles Peter and John on their way to the Temple. The description of this first persecution of the Apostles is characterised by the same idealising tendency which is apparent in the whole description of the progress of the primitive Church. In the statement as a whole, as well as in its individual features, a design is evident which makes it impossible to believe that we have the natural historical sequence of events before us. What is intended is, in a word, that the Apostles should appear in their full glory. This exaltation of the Apostles is the aim of the narrative from the beginning, and both the main event and the particular circumstances attending it subserve that aim. The greatness and grandeur of the Apostles, whose glorification is the object in view, are put in a still clearer light, and are brought all the more prominently forward by the humiliating position in which their adversaries are exhibited; all that serves to glorify the Apostles serves also to confound and humble their adversaries, who in fact draw down disgrace upon themselves with all the means at their command and in the most public manner possible. The whole proceedings are of a formal and public nature, so as to attract attention. As soon as the Apostles were seized in consequence of the miracle and of the discourse delivered after its performance, preparation was made to treat the affair as one of the utmost gravity, and with all due formality. Early on the next morning (for there was no time left for such a meeting on the evening of the day before, chapter iv. 3) all the members of the Sanhedrim, the Elders and Scribes, Annas and Caiaphas the High Priests, who are known to us from the history of the condemnation of Jesus, and

---

[1] Compare, with respect to the occurrences at Pentecost, my treatise in the Theol. Studien und Kritiken, 1838, p. 618; Critical review of recent researches on the γλώσσαις λαλεῖν in the early Christian Church.

CHAP. I.]   THE CHURCH AT JERUSALEM.   17

all those who belonged to their party, came together. No one whose name was of any importance must be wanting. Even those members of the Sanhedrim who, from various circumstances, were not present in Jerusalem, were obliged to return in all haste to the capital[1] in order to take part in the proceedings. And what resulted from all this? Nothing more than that the whole assembled Sanhedrim allowed itself to be told by the two Apostles under examination that the cause of this judicial inquiry against them was a good deed wrought on a suffering man, and that the worker of this miracle was Jesus Christ of Nazareth, by them crucified and slain, and to whose saving name this miracle of healing gave irrefragable evidence. In order to heighten still further the effect which this must have produced on the Sanhedrim, we are carefully shown how much that court had been mistaken in its estimate of the Apostles. It had taken them for uneducated persons of low rank, for the same men, in fact, who at the condemnation of Jesus had given so many proofs of their weakness and timidity, but now it could not but wonder at them for the fearlessness and courage with which they behaved, iv. 13. This change in the Apostles is mentioned as now perceived for the first time by the members of the Sanhedrim and to their great astonishment,[2] although those occurrences in the Temple, which had so roused their attention, must already have shown them with what kind of men they had to deal. This incomprehensible want of perception on the part of the Sanhedrim adds lustre to the appearance of the Apostles who have been brought before them. Even this is not enough: the greatest difficulty which the Sanhedrim had to contend with, and which indeed made them appear completely routed and disarmed, was the presence of the lame man who had been healed, which afforded incontestable evidence of the Apostles' assertions. If it is asked how the lame man who had

[1] So must the words, iv. 6, be taken: συναχθῆναι—εἰς Ἱερουσαλὴμ, where εἰς is not equivalent to ἐν; it would be unmeaning to remark that the dwellers in Jerusalem had assembled in Jerusalem.

[2] The words, iv. 13, ἐπεγίνωσκόν τε αὐτοὺς ὅτι σὺν τῷ Ἰησοῦ ἦσαν, express a recollection which only then, during the progress of the trial, dawned upon them.

VOL. I.   B

been healed came to be present at this trial, the narrative says only, iv. 14: τὸν δὲ ἄνθρωπον βλέποντες σὺν αὐτοῖς ἑστῶτα τὸν τεθεραπευμένον, οὐδὲν εἶχον ἀντειπεῖν, and the commentators have nothing to say in explanation of this certainly remarkable circumstance. Had he, as at first would appear, been summoned by the Sanhedrim itself, or had he, since the author remarks, iii. 11, that he never left the Apostles' side from the time when the cure was wrought on him, followed them to prison and from prison to the judgment hall? In either case, if the members of the Sanhedrim lost self-command at the presence of this man (which they must certainly have themselves permitted, if not ordered) to such an extent that they were completely silenced with regard to the chief point of the prosecution, though a point which they could hardly fail to have foreseen and provided for, then they showed a want of forethought unexampled in such a court. In fact the members of the Sanhedrim did not know what they wanted; the points which they ought to have well considered and settled beforehand, they first thought of only after they had assembled—what had been plainly seen by all Jerusalem then first flashed on their blinded eyes. If this miracle was such a public one (iv. 16), they could not have been in ignorance of it—they must surely have come to an understanding on the subject with each other beforehand, and determined in what manner they were to meet the assertion of the Apostles. That the matter had no further result before such blind and weak-minded judges as these members of the Sanhedrim are made to appear throughout the whole narrative, is the only thing about which no wonder can be felt. And yet we do wonder how the writer could have thought that he had accounted for the failure of the whole process, which had no result but to throw discredit on the Sanhedrim, by the remark that nothing could be done for fear of the people, iv. 21. If the people had been so much to be feared, the rulers would never have dared to seize the Apostles (iv. 3) in the midst of their discourse to the crowd which had assembled round them, and was filled with wonder at the miracle, nor to carry them off to prison. All this could only be disregarded by taking a standpoint, from which the Apostles were thought to be the more glorified the more the ill deeds of their enemies turned to their humiliation and confusion.

This is, however, only the first part of this story, which is carried forward almost dramatically, not exactly in direct development, but in the same strain. A second part follows, which is a mere repetition of the first with this important difference, that in it everything is on a larger scale. This appears in the fact that not merely one, but a great many miracles had now been worked, not only on one suffering man, but on sick and suffering people of all kinds; and the attention of their enemies was again directed to the Apostles, because people flocked to them, not only from Jerusalem, but also from the neighbouring towns. As in the first instance it was the two Apostles Peter and John who were seized and thrown into prison, and then brought before the Sanhedrim, now it is the whole number of the Apostles who are so treated.[1] The first time their enemies kept their hold of the two Apostles, at least so far as to detain them in prison through the night and to be able to produce them the next morning before the Sanhedrim. On this occasion, however, the Apostles who were in prison were freed in the night by an angel of the Lord, who led them out of the prison and commanded them to preach before the people in the Temple; and when the Sanhedrim assembled next morning in full and solemn conclave, and caused the Apostles to be summoned before them by their officers, they were astounded by the news that the gates of the prison had been found most carefully closed and the guard standing before the door, but that on opening the prison no one was found in it. In the difficulty in which the Sanhedrim was now involved, they accidentally received tidings that the men who had been put in prison were in the Temple preaching to the people. The Apostles allowed themselves to be entreated with gentle words to present themselves

[1] We now hear simply of οἱ ἀπόστολοι, v. 18, 29, 40; the signs and wonders which gave cause to the prosecution διὰ τῶν χειρῶν τῶν ἀποστόλων ἐγένετο, v. 12; and immediately after this ἅπαντες, sc. ἀπόστολοι, are spoken of.

again before the Sanhedrim. Force would not have availed, as the people, though it had suffered the arrest of the Apostles on the previous day, was now in such a mood that it would have stoned the Temple-keeper and his servants. But when the Apostles repeated their former declaration that they ought to obey God rather than man, and that God the Father had raised the crucified Jesus from the dead, the same scene was repeated. Great as the exasperation was, and though it seemed that the most serious consequences could scarcely be avoided, yet the result actually attained formed on this occasion also the most striking contrast to the plans and arrangements which the Apostles' enemies had made; and the slight punishment with which, in addition to an utterly futile prohibition, the Apostles were dismissed, served but to increase the satisfaction which they felt: ὅτι ὑπὲρ τοῦ ὀνόματος αὐτοῦ κατηξιώθησαν, ἀτιμασθῆναι, v. 41.

In all this, who can see anything else than an enhanced and exaggerated repetition of the narrative already related, devised with the one idea of setting forth the Apostles in their full greatness and dignity, in the glorified light of the higher power under whose protection and guidance they stood? If we can see no natural connection and progress of events in the circumstances as they were related in the first instance, how great does the improbability become when the same occurrences are represented as happening for the second time as if outbidding themselves? The simple enumeration of the separate points through which the story moves cannot possibly make any other impression on an unprejudiced mind. It is self-evident that if we are to pronounce a well-digested judgment on the probability or improbability of the whole, all the points of the narrative ought to be taken together and considered in their relation to each other. The affair, however, appears in a totally different light in the statement given by Neander, as follows: "Meanwhile the great work which the Apostles had performed before the eyes of the people (the healing of the lame man), the power of the word of Peter, and the fruitless trial of force, resulted in increasing the number of the disciples to two thousand.[1] As the Apostles, without troubling themselves about the command of the Sanhedrim, laboured (as they declared openly they would do) more and more with word and deed to spread the Gospel, it could not be otherwise than that they should again be brought before the Sanhedrim as contumacious. When the president of the Sanhedrim reproved them for their disobedience, Peter renewed his former protest (v. 29). The words of Peter had already excited the rage of the Sadducees and fanatics, and the voices of many were raised for the death of the Apostles; but among the crowd of angry men one voice of moderating wisdom made itself heard. The word of Gamaliel prevailed; no heavier punishment than scourging was laid upon the Apostles for their disobedience, and they were dismissed after the former prohibition had been repeated."[2]

Represented in this light, the whole affair assumes a different aspect; but is this representation a correct one? By what right does it ignore the miraculous release of the Apostles from prison, which is so large a feature in this part of the narrative, and which, if it be considered to be a miracle, must surely for that reason count for something more than a mere chance detail? If the silence on this point is due to a feeling that the narrative would be simpler, more natural, and more probable without it, it would also seem to give room for a doubt which would change the whole aspect of this section of the Acts, and which on this account must not be admitted in silence, but considered with all due attention. If we have a right to doubt this part of the narrative, then we may also doubt another portion, and thus inevitably arises the question, what in the whole section is historical and what unhistorical? But to omit everything which does not suit the theory entertained, and to use the rest of the materials with the modifications which such omissions render necessary—to interpolate now this supposi-

---

[1] The conversion of the two thousand is, however, reported before the trial of force—iv. 4.

[2] Geschichte der Pflanzung und Leitung der Christl. Kirche durch die Apostel. Ed. 1841, vol. i. p. 62, Bohn's Transl. i. 46.

tion and now that, in order to make the whole hang well together and appear probable,[1] and then to present the results of this omission and addition, as the undoubtedly genuine historical contents of the narrative that has been subjected to this treatment, this is nothing else than the acknowledged rationalistic method, which makes its own arbitrary history. And if this method does not carry out its rationalistic principles consistently, but at one time sets miracle aside, and at another adopts it and treats it as an essential factor of a narrative of events on their objective side, yet it is easy to see where such a method of treatment must lead, and by what necessity we are shut up to the alternatives, either to confine ourselves to a simple, literally exact narrative of the facts, or to allow historical criticism (if we cannot altogether ignore its existence) full scope to exercise its functions.

The manner in which the chief event is narrated betrays the tendency of the whole passage; but that tendency is no less apparent in the minor details of the story, in some of them indeed even more clearly and unmistakably. The Apostles are throughout represented as exalted, superhuman beings, who affect all around them by their indwelling, supernatural, miraculous power, who, with imposing mien, sway the assembled crowds, and draw to themselves with irresistible power all who listen to their preaching. How clearly is this expressed when we are told that great fear fell upon the whole Church, and upon all who heard these

[1] Neander allows himself to make use of such an aid, page 45, in reference to iv. 1-22, when he conjectures thus: "Perhaps also the secret (if not absolutely declared) friends whom the cause of Christ possessed from the first among the members of the Sanhedrim used their influence in favour of the accused." Secret friends of the cause of Christ among the members of the Sanhedrim! How far is this idea removed from the whole spirit of the Acts! What has led to such a completely arbitrary and improbable hypothesis? Manifestly the fact that the course and the issue of the affair have appeared unintelligible. But this hypothesis granted, is the problem even then solved? So little is this the case, that another difficulty is raised, which is artfully concealed and as much as possible ignored. There is nothing more blameable than a method of treating history, which instead of looking freely, openly, and impartially at the facts as they are and sifting them thoroughly, sets its own arbitrary ideas and imaginations in the place of historical truth.

things, in consequence of the miracles which were performed, v. 11. How suggestively is the impression that their greatness made brought before us when we hear that when they, *i.e.* the Apostles, were all together in the Porch of Solomon, where a large crowd usually gathered, they formed an isolated group, which no man dared to approach. The high estimation in which they were held is suggested by the fact that the people kept at a certain distance from them, holding them to be superior, superhuman, perhaps magical beings, whom no man ought to approach too nearly.[1] The idealistic view of the Apostles, which underlies the whole account, is here clearly and decidedly expressed.

The bright light which is shed over the assembled Apostles centres itself in its richest glory in the person of the Apostle Peter, who stands at the head of the twelve. In the first division of the section (chap. iii.-v.) the Apostle John shares this pre-eminence with the Apostle Peter—but in the rest of the narrative it is only the Apostle Peter who is raised above his fellow-apostles in the same proportion in which they are raised above other men. Whilst the Apostles collectively perform signs and wonders in great numbers, the Apostle Peter's very shadow brings about these miraculous results, and while at the first trial John is mentioned as being with Peter, iv. 19, at the second Peter alone is spoken of, and represented as being the spokesman of the rest. But the most brilliant passage of the apostolic activity of Peter is the miracle which was worked on Ananias and Sapphira. It may be assumed that there was good reason for these two names being interwoven with the history of the early Church. They may have exhibited a course of thought and action directly opposed to the example of self-sacrifice and unselfishness given by Barnabas, who

[1] ἅπαντες, v. 12, is commonly taken as referring not merely to the Apostle but to Christians generally. Zeller also, "Acts of the Apostles," T. T. F. L., p. 215, prefers this rendering, as the Church was constantly assembled, ii. 42, 44, 46. But v. 12 has to do with the μεγαλύνειν of the Apostles, on account of the influence which proceeded from them, and as through this a φόβος seized the πᾶσα ἐκκλησία, the Christians also felt this awe and shrank from standing side by side with such superior beings (κολλᾶσθαι).

is placed in direct contrast with them; this may have caused their names to be so hated and despised that in their death, in whatever way it came about, men saw an evident act of divine retribution; but everything beyond this merely serves to enforce the writer's view of the πνεῦμα ἅγιον as the divine principle operating in the Apostles, and can only be explained in connection with that view. As the πνεῦμα ἅγιον, animating all Christians, is a divine principle, imparting to them an elevated and peculiar character, so it is bestowed in a special manner on the Apostles. Their human individuality stands in so secondary a place to this animating divine principle that they seem to be only the instruments and organs of it, and all that they do bears in itself the immediate stamp of divinity. In this sense must be taken the words of Peter, through whom as the first of the Apostles the πνεῦμα ἅγιον of course declared itself in all its force and significance when he said to Ananias, v. 4, οὐκ ἐψεύσω ἀνθρώποις, ἀλλὰ τῷ Θεῷ. But if a striking illustration were to be given of the activity of this principle dwelling in the Apostles and of the divine character imparted to them by it, how could this be better done than by narrating a case in which a doubt is cast on it, thereby putting the Holy Spirit itself to the proof? This was what Ananias and his wife Sapphira were held to have done, inasmuch as they had agreed together on a course of conduct which could succeed only on the supposition that the divine principle animating the Apostles did not bestow on them divine omniscience, which one would naturally have thought the most essential attribute of the πνεῦμα ἅγιον. What other result could follow from such a course of conduct than that the divine judgment should go forth upon the two in sudden death? For they had sinned not against man, but against the organs of the Divine Spirit, against God himself.

There would be no necessity to speak of the attempts to put a natural interpretation on this event, which have been made by Heinrichs and other interpreters, if this mode of explanation had not received fresh support and authority from Neander. For it is nothing else but an endeavour of this kind which Neander makes, when he says, page 28 : "If we reflect what Peter was in the eyes of Ananias : how the hypocritical, superstitious man must have been astonished and confounded at seeing his lie brought to light—how the reproving holy earnestness of a man, speaking to his conscience with such divine assurance must have worked on his terrified spirit and the fear of punishment from a holy God laid hold on him: then we do not find it so difficult to conceive how the words of the Apostle brought about so great an effect. The divine and the natural are here intimately bound up together."

According to this, we have to look at the death of Ananias as a natural event quite intelligible as such on psychological grounds. But even if such an event as sudden death might not impossibly be the direct psychological consequence of such a violent mental shock, the case before us cannot be considered from this standpoint. The rarer and more uncommon such a death is, the more unlikely is it to have happened two different times in the space of three hours. For the death of Sapphira must be attributed to the same cause, and Neander does not hesitate to give it the same psychological explanation: "When Sapphira entered the assembly three hours later, without suspecting what had happened" (this of course must be supposed on the naturalistic hypothesis, however it conflicts with verse 5),[1] "Peter first of all endeavoured, by questioning her, to arouse her conscience. But when, instead of being led to consider and repent, she persisted in her dissimulation, Peter accused her of having concerted with her husband to try the Spirit of God, whether or not it could be deceived by their hypocrisy. He then proceeded to threaten her with the divine punishment which had just overtaken her husband. The words of Peter were in this instance aided by the impression of her husband's fate, and striking the conscience of the hypocrite produced the same effect as on her husband." If such an event (granting that it really occurred once) is in the highest degree uncommon, its immediate recurrence deprives the story of all probability. We might of course disregard the improbability; but this is quite beside the mark : since the

[1] At v. 7 we read expressly, μὴ εἰδυῖα τὸ γεγονός.—*Editor's note.*

narrative of the author admits no interpretation but that a miracle was intended to be wrought, and was wrought. The speech of Peter to Ananias is spoken in so threatening a tone, that the death of Ananias immediately succeeding it can only appear as the execution of the threatened punishment. This is seen even more distinctly in the speech addressed to Sapphira: ἰδοὺ, οἱ πόδες τῶν θαψάντων τὸν ἄνδρα σου, ἐπὶ τῇ θύρᾳ, καὶ ἐξοίσουσί σε, v. 9. A death which follows immediately on such a clear declaration cannot be looked on as accidental, but as an intended and miraculously-procured event. If it be considered as a merely accidental, natural event which the Apostle did not expressly wish nor call for, a new doubt arises, namely, whether it would not have been the duty of the Apostle, when so shortly before he had seen so unexpected and fatal a result of his words, to endeavour rather to moderate than to enhance the impression which could not fail to be made on Sapphira. Except on the hypothesis of a miracle, the narrative must appear almost meaningless. But the natural explanation, as Neander gives it, is not meant to be carried out to its conclusions; it is intended merely to smooth the way for the reception of the miracle by one who is prejudiced against the supernatural. Such an one is to learn that the supernatural of the miracle is in fact natural, and so to be led round to the concession that natural as it is, it is yet supernatural. For not only does Neander speak here of a divine judgment which was necessary in order to preserve the first operations of the Holy Spirit from the admixture of the most dangerous poison, and to secure a proper respect for the apostolic authority, he remarks expressly that the Divine and the Natural appear here to be in the closest connection. How we are to understand this connection between the Divine and the Natural, Olshausen may inform us in his Commentary; on v. 1, *sq.*, he reminds us that "the absolute distinction between the natural and supernatural is in this case also mischievous. There is nothing to prevent us from giving a purely natural explanation of the death of Ananias; but by the adoption of this theory the miraculous character of the event is not set aside. The natural itself becomes miraculous through the relation which it bears to its circumstances and surroundings, and such is the case with this death, which, taken in connection with the sentence of the Apostle spoken in the power of the Spirit, and penetrating Ananias like a sword, to convict him of sin, was in reality a miracle ordered by a higher power." But what end does this irresolute way of thinking serve? The absolute distinction between the natural and supernatural is not mischievous, for the idea of miracle demands such a distinction; a miracle, if it is not something essentially or absolutely different from the natural, is not a miracle at all. But the illogical blending of two essentially different ideas is mischievous—the neutralising of natural and supernatural into an indifferent *tertium quid*, which on the one hand shall be as much natural as supernatural, but on the other hand neither supernatural nor natural, and thus is nothing whatever. Two views only can be taken of this event. The death of Ananias and Sapphira was either natural—the natural result of terror and the consequence of an apoplectic fit, and for that very reason no miracle, and not the result of the will or words of the Apostle—or it was a miracle, and then not the mere result of fear and apoplexy, for even if fear and apoplexy were the immediate cause of the death, they did not operate independently, or the death would have been no miracle; but they had this result, owing to the will of the Apostle and the divine miraculous power accompanying his words. It is therefore clear that if so great an importance is attached to the natural causes of Neander and Olshausen as to allow of a strictly natural construction being put on the death of Ananias and Sapphira, the true nature of the question is altogether lost sight of. The secondary intermediate cause is illogically regarded as the primary cause, and a middle cause neither primary nor secondary is introduced, of which the narrative says nothing, because the narrator is very far from intending that what he relates as miracle should be taken for an accidental natural event. If we are thus shut up to the miraculous theory of the event, the miracle remains in all its hardness, and the less this hardness is in unison with the rest of the New

Testament miracles, or vindicates itself on satisfactory grounds, the more justly will this miracle be reckoned as part of the evidence which tends to discredit the historical character of the whole passage to which it belongs.

We will here glance at the miracle which introduces the whole story. In this whole passage the glorification of the Apostles is the aim to which everything tends; they are to be contrasted with their enemies as high, super-human, unapproachable beings. The principal transaction narrated in the passage is unintelligible and disconnected, and obviously serves merely to work out the idea which underlies the whole narrative. These considerations must certainly determine to some extent our judgment on the occurrence which stands at the head of the story, and the fact of its being a miracle cannot make any difference. It is clear on the face of this miracle that it serves only to introduce, to show the occasion of, the events which follow. The object of the narrative being to enhance the glory of the Apostles, it was necessary to show the enemies of the cause of Jesus as taking fresh steps which could lead to nothing but their own shame and humiliation. For this end, something must of course take place to draw their attention to the Apostles, and compel them to take action. The cause of Jesus must win the sympathy of the people, the preaching of the Apostles must cause a very considerable increase in the number of believers. But results like these could not be imputed to the mere preaching of the Apostles; that preaching needed some new point to start from; the interest of the people must be aroused by some event of a palpable and striking nature. How could this be better effected than by a miracle worked by the Apostles? But it was not every miracle that would have served this purpose. It must not be one which would have a merely transitory effect, but one of such a nature as to continue to excite public attention, and evidence itself to the public eye, by its abiding results after the miraculous act was performed. No miracle could better fulfil these conditions than the healing of the man lame from his birth, who had never walked before, but who immediately used the power given to him in such a manner as to be a walking miracle which no one could help observing. The narrative itself represents the miracle in this light. As soon as it is performed, the lame man springs up, walks about, accompanies the Apostles to the Temple, walking and leaping and praising God, and publishing what had happened to him, so that all the people saw him, and were filled with wonder and astonishment at the change, iii. 8-10. He even remained an inseparable companion of the two Apostles, in order that, by the side of the workers of the miracle, he might bear witness to the miracle they had worked, iii. 11, and appear, in what way we are not told, with the Apostles at the judicial meeting of the Sanhedrim. Then the narrative points out again and again how notorious the miracle had become throughout Jerusalem, and how it had been the more recognised as a highly extraordinary event, because the lame man was known as a beggar, of more than forty years old, who sat daily at the gate of the Temple, iii. 2, 9, 14, 16, 21, 22. As soon as the dominant idea of the whole is rightly understood, how clearly does the relation appear in which each separate feature stands to the whole—how clearly do we see how the whole grew into the form in which we find it! And if the historical character of the chief occurrence must be doubted, how little can we hold as historical facts the individual minor circumstances, which merely lead up to and prepare for what is to follow. In every individual trait do we not trace the internal connection by which the writer strove to bind the whole together, in order that the end he had in view might be advanced?

This peculiar idealising tendency of the whole passage is not, however, limited to the Apostles; the glorifying ray of the same light shines also on the whole Church of the believers. The glory which falls to the share of the Apostles is indeed the tribute due to the Holy Spirit which dwelt in and animated them; and it is the same Spirit with which all the believers are filled. In them also there is a divine principle, which raises them above the level of common men, and sheds a more than earthly light around them. In this light they are represented in both the short sections—ii. 42-47, iv.

32-37—in which the aim of the author is to give a general description of the state of the early Church. That which is reported of the Apostles, namely, that they enjoyed the admiration, reverence, and love of the whole population of Jerusalem, is extended to the Church as a distinction which belonged to it as well: ἐγένετο δὲ πάσῃ ψυχῇ φόβος, ii. 43; ἔχοντες χάριν πρὸς ὅλον τὸν λαόν, ii. 47; χάρις τε μεγάλη ἦν ἐπὶ πάντας αὐτούς, iv. 33. It is evident how little the persecution of the Christians, which broke out so soon afterwards, confirms this account. Such a conception of the relations of the first Christian Church to the whole people must be set down to the gradual embellishment of legend, and other features in the narrative confirm this view. What enabled the Church to make such a favourable impression on the people and to engage their good-will and confidence to such a marked degree must have been, more than any of its other features, that spirit of unity and harmony which animated all the members of the body. This spirit bound them together, and showed itself especially in their social arrangements, in that general community of goods which they introduced among themselves, and before which all distinctions of private property disappeared. We should expect to find this a genuine historical report of the social relations of the Primitive Church; but that this is by no means the case is allowed even by those who have the highest opinion of the historical credibility of the Acts of the Apostles. "In the narrative of the Acts itself," remarks Neander, p. 34 (Bohn, p. 25), "there is a great deal which contradicts the idea of such a community of goods. Peter expressly says to Ananias that it lay with himself whether to keep the piece of ground or to sell it; and that even after it was sold he was at liberty to do what he chose with the proceeds, v. 4. What we find in the sixth chapter of the Acts is a regulated division of alms to widows, but nothing of the nature of a common purse for the use of the whole church. We find, xii. 12, that Mary possessed a house of her own at Jerusalem, which, accordingly, she had not sold for the benefit of the common purse. These instances show clearly that we are not to imagine an entire suspension of the rights of property in the case of the early Church."

But this, and nothing but this, is what the author explicitly declares. If the contradiction between his description here and the facts he himself relates in other passages compels us "not to take that description literally," as Neander says, then we must acknowledge as a fact that other interests besides historical ones underlie the narrative. It is also incontestable that there is a desire manifested to represent this primitive Church in the beautiful light of a fellowship from which all that is disturbing and dividing in the social relations of humanity has been banished, and first of all, the distinction between rich and poor. But this state of things did not actually exist, in fact could not exist, from the very nature of the case; for how can we imagine that in a Church, which at that time, according to the declaration of the writer, iv. 4, consisted of 5000 members, all those who possessed houses and landed property sold them, iv. 34; and that not one individual in the whole Church possessed a house of his own? And if (let this be added to the other considerations) it was an established rule that every member should sell all that he possessed, and put the proceeds as a contribution in money into the common purse, why is it told, as a remarkable fact, iv. 36, that Joses Barnabas sold his land, and brought the price and laid it at the Apostles' feet? We must again conclude that what the writer represents as a general arrangement of the first Christian community did not take place so generally as is here represented. We may, perhaps, take this as the historical truth, that "a common purse was established, out of which the needs of the greater part of the poorer members of the Church were relieved; out of which, perhaps, the expenses which the Church body incurred (such as the preparations of the feasts) were defrayed, and that many sold their property in order to increase their contributions to this joint-purse. Thus there may have been a reproduction of the economical arrangements of that fellowship of men and women who attached themselves to Christ; the arrangement may have been similar to what generally obtained afterwards in the ordinary collections for the poor." (Neander, p. 36, Bohn, 26.) But this does not bear out the description of the Acts, and if no other data were at our disposal, we should not be at liberty to consider the element of truth in it to be so great, since a narrative to which historical credibility must be denied as a whole leaves us in total uncertainty as to the amount of truth which may yet lie at its foundation. All that can lead us in this case to suppose a substratum of historical fact is the general truth that unhistorical narratives are not usually altogether invented, but in most cases rise out of something in actual history. But in order to obtain the historical element which may be present in the two passages in question, though neither of them gives us much help to discover it, we must add to the particulars we possess what, according to Epiphanius (Haer. 30), the Ebionites said of themselves. This was, that the epithet "poor," which they gave themselves, and considered as an honourable distinction, they took on account of their having sold their possessions in the time of the Apostles, and laid the price at their feet. Thereby they took upon themselves poverty and renunciation, and on this account, they said, they were everywhere called "poor." The expression itself, "laid at the Apostles' feet," shows that this account is closely related to the two passages of the Acts; we cannot believe it to have been adopted from the Acts, a work which could have no authority for the Ebionites, owing to the well-known hatred of this sect to the Apostle Paul. Thus we have here a historical datum which tells us of a similar τιθέναι παρὰ τοὺς πόδας τῶν ἀποστόλων as a characteristic feature of the apostolic time. But we must not suppose the poverty of the Ebionites arose first of all from their having sold all their possessions. The supposition is much more natural that they were poor from the beginning, that they considered their poverty as something honourable and distinctive, and that they wished it to be considered as a thing they had voluntarily adopted. This naturally gave rise to the story that they had originally possessed property, but that they had sold it and laid the money realised by such sales at the Apostles' feet. What we may suppose to have been the historical truth in this instance, is not so much the action, as the disposition, the estimate of worldly goods, which the action would reveal; and as the disposition must prove itself in action, it is here translated into an action which vividly represents it. What the Acts of the Apostles states respecting the social relations and arrangements of the first Christian Church is not to be understood as referring to a real, total, and general community of goods, but only to the general willingness not merely felt, but also displayed in action by men like Barnabas, to sacrifice their riches and possessions for the sake of the cause of Jesus, devoting them to the public objects of the Church, and in this sense laying them at the Apostles' feet. But the general community of goods and actual renunciation of worldly possessions mentioned in the Acts of the Apostles only shows us in a remarkable manner the peculiar nature of mythic tradition. It prefers what is concrete, living, and capable of being represented in strong colours; mere disposition is too bald and empty; it must be realised in action, if it is to have any life and meaning of its own, and take its place as a subject fit to be handed down in tradition. This may also explain the following discrepancy, that while the Ebionites affirmed that they became poor through the $\tau\iota\theta\acute{\epsilon}\nu\alpha\iota\ \pi\alpha\rho\grave{\alpha}\ \tauο\grave{\upsilon}\varsigma\ \pi\acute{o}\delta\alpha\varsigma\ \tau\hat{\omega}\nu\ \mathring{\alpha}\pi o\sigma\tau\acute{o}\lambda\omega\nu$, the Acts of the Apostles declares that by the same process all poverty and need were banished from the Church. This, though it should perhaps be taken relatively, is yet distinctly expressed in the words $o\mathring{\upsilon}\delta\grave{\epsilon}\ \gamma\grave{\alpha}\rho\ \mathring{\epsilon}\nu\delta\epsilon\acute{\eta}\varsigma\ \tau\iota\varsigma\ \mathring{\upsilon}\pi\hat{\eta}\rho\chi\epsilon\nu\ \mathring{\epsilon}\nu\ \alpha\mathring{\upsilon}\tauο\hat{\iota}\varsigma$, etc. If the writer kept in his eye the disposition which prompted the renunciation of these worldly goods and possessions, he had to hold fast the idea of poverty; but when he proceeded to speak of the actual realisation of this disposition for the benefit of the community, he had to show that the wants of the community were actually relieved.

If it is asked what is the true historical residuum of the whole section, Acts iii.-v., the actual results are very small; the nature of the stories that are given seems to point to the fact that the early history of the Church was extremely uneventful. The fact that bears the most decided impress of historical reality, namely, the advice given by Gamaliel, seems to indicate that the enemies of Jesus troubled themselves very little about his disciples during the time immediately following his death. When they came to observe that instead of decaying the disciples were increasing and flourishing, and were obliged to take more notice of them, it did not seem worth while to take any very strict measures against them. Even the division between the two sects of the Pharisees and Sadducees, as it is represented in the different attitudes which Gamaliel and the members of the Sanhedrim take up with reference to the disciples of Jesus, can scarcely be taken as historical. It has been remarked with justice,[1] "Although the Sadducees had allied themselves for a common object with Caiaphas the High Priest, who had condemned Jesus, and afterwards endeavoured with special zeal to ruin the Apostles, we find no historical trace that Caiaphas himself was a Sadducee; the Sadducees first appear with true party bigotry against the Apostles on account of the resurrection of Jesus." It is exactly this which must make us suspicious about the part which the Sadducees are represented as playing in the matter; for it cannot but occur to us that, as their testimony to the resurrection of Jesus was the most important thing the Apostles had to preach about, the Sadducees, who were the declared enemies of the doctrine of the resurrection, must surely have been their bitterest and most decided opponents. The repeated and pointed observation that the Sadducees did most to stir up persecution against the disciples, iv. 1, v. 17, and principally from annoyance that they preached as a fact the resurrection of Jesus from the dead (διὰ τὸ καταγγέλλειν ἐν τῷ Ἰησοῦ τὴν ἀνάστασιν τὴν ἐκ νεκρῶν, iv. 2) has quite the appearance of such an *a priori* combination. But if the Sadducees were eager to procure the suppression of the disciples of Jesus, and if all the plans and measures which they took proved fruitless, what could have caused this failure but the influence of the opposite party, that of the Pharisees? It must have been a very weighty authority which could exert so much influence over the Sadducees, and still their rage; who else could have done this but the most prominent Pharisaic leader of that time, the renowned Gamaliel?

[1] Comp. Meyer, Apg. v. 17.

And yet Gamaliel does not seem quite fitted for the part assigned to him, or for the moderate and peaceful nature of the advice ascribed to him, when we call to mind that the most zealous persecutor of the Christian Church of that time, Saul, had been educated in his school and on his principles. Therefore we must give up the person of Gamaliel too, and reduce his celebrated advice to the mere opinion prevailing among the Jewish rulers at that time, that it might be the best way to leave the cause of Jesus to its fate, in the full assurance that its little importance would soon be made obvious.[1] During this period, in which the disciples of

[1] That Gamaliel cannot really have spoken the words as they are put into his mouth by the author of the Acts, v. 35, is shown by the striking chronological error in the appeal to the example of Theudas, who, according to Josephus (Antiq. xx. 8), first appeared as a false prophet and agitator about ten years later, under the procurator Cuspius Fadus. As Cuspius Fadus became procurator of Judea about the year 44 of the Christian era, the revolt of Theudas could not have occurred before that time. How little does the view expressed in the words of Gamaliel, Acts v. 38, agree with the statement of facts as related in the whole section comprising chapters iii.-v. If all these miracles were really performed as is here narrated, and in so authentic a manner that the Sanhedrim itself could not ignore them, nor bring forward anything against them—if the man lame from his birth was healed by the word of the Apostle, and if the Apostles themselves, without any human intervention, were freed from prison by an angel from heaven—how could Gamaliel, if he was a man such as is here described, unbiassed and thoughtful, resting his judgment on experience, express himself so problematically as he does here, and leave it to the future to decide whether this cause were or were not divine? If the miracles here related were really performed, so much must have been quite evident; they were publicly recognised, authentically witnessed matters of fact, on which no one could throw any doubt. For what could Gamaliel be waiting in order to give a decided opinion on the matter? For fresh miracles, which would not prove anything more than those already performed? Or for still greater additions to the number of adherents to the disciples from among the people? But even in this view everything had already occurred which could be expected to occur. Every discourse of the Apostles had been followed by the conversion of thousands; the whole people hung with awe and wonder on the preaching of the new faith, so that even the rulers did not dare to employ force for fear of being stoned. What stronger testimony to the popularity of the new doctrines could there well have been, and what danger must not the Sanhedrim have incurred by continuing its opposition to the universal inclination of the people? If, on the other hand, we suppose that Gamaliel could not deny the miracles that had been performed, but did not consider them as divine, even then we cannot understand why he should express himself so weakly and undecidedly, and vote for the cessation of any measures of interference. If

Jesus were not disturbed by their enemies, they had time to gain fresh confidence from their belief in the resurrection, and to strengthen themselves by winning new adherents to their cause. Jerusalem was the best place for making such accessions. No more momentous decision for the cause of Jesus could have been taken than that of the disciples to remain in Jerusalem. Here only could all the elements of union which were involved in believing in the risen One operate effectively to keep them all together; here only did a field of action open before them, rich in probable results. Not without reason does the Acts of the Apostles date back this resolve of the disciples to the command given by Jesus shortly before his departure, namely, that they should not leave Jerusalem, but remain there till the promise of the Holy Spirit should be fulfilled, through whose power they were to be his witnesses in Jerusalem, in all Judea, in Samaria, and even unto the ends of the earth, Acts i. 8. We must understand by this gift of the Spirit the confidence and boldness with which the disciples proclaimed the Gospel and endeavoured to work in its interest;[1] and the actual results show us the internal connection, founded on the nature of the case, which these two points bear to each other, the staying in Jerusalem, and the descent of the Holy Spirit which was represented as depending upon it. The same phenomenon which the history of the first development of Christianity presents

the miracles were looked at as having been performed, but not as being divine, how could there be any doubt that a still worse deceit was being carried on, the investigation and punishment of which ought to have been a highly important duty of the Court? If we conclude that the events took place as the narrative says they did, but as we can scarcely think they did, the advice of Gamaliel appears to be wanting in the prudence which the case required, as too much had already happened to allow such a movement to have its way undisturbed. Either the testimony of truth must have been recognised, or active steps taken against such a palpable deceit. But the two statements which here lie before us—on one side the nominal facts, on the other the wise measures counselled by Gamaliel—do not agree. Either the events took place as they are here narrated, and Gamaliel did not give such advice, or if he did give it, it did not hold the same relation to the facts of the case as is represented.

[1] Compare especially the passage, iv. 31: ἐπλήσθησαν ἅπαντες πνεύματος ἁγίου, καὶ ἐλάλουν τὸν λόγον τοῦ Θεοῦ μετὰ παρρησίας. Also vi. 5, 10.

to us, namely, that the larger cities, such as Antioch, Rome, Corinth, and Ephesus, became the first seats of Christianity, and the starting-points of its wider activity, meets us also in the fact that the first Christian Church was established in Jerusalem. But here we must work on a decidedly lower scale than that employed in the Acts of the Apostles, when it speaks of the conversion at one time of many thousands—indeed, we can scarcely accept the same number of hundreds. We have a remarkable instance of how little these numbers are to be relied on in Acts i. 15. We are there told that after the ascension of Jesus the disciples numbered altogether a hundred and twenty. But, on the other hand, the Apostle Paul, whose testimony is earlier and has a greater claim to credibility, speaks of five hundred brethren to whom Jesus appeared at once after his resurrection. If the small number be manifestly incorrect, the subsequent statement of much larger numbers (Acts ii. 41, iv. 4) is no more worthy of credit, and we must come to the conclusion that the lesser number precedes the greater, in order to give a more vivid impression of the speedy and remarkable growth of the Church. In addition to this, when we consider the persecution of Stephen, we cannot think of the Church at Jerusalem as so important and as consisting of such a number of believers, as we must suppose it to have done if we accept all the increase to it mentioned in these passages of the Acts, ii. 41, iv. 4, v. 14, vi. 1, 7. From all this there is strongly impressed upon us the conviction that if we wish to arrive at a proper conception of this earliest period, we must not place much weight on the different figures and the accounts of the different events here given us. This remark applies equally to the speeches contained in this part of the Acts of the Apostles which were delivered on various occasions by the Apostle Peter, and to the Christian hymn, iv. 24. They may be taken as fragmentary pictures of the circle of action and ideas in which this first Christian Church moved, and as interesting evidence how the first disciples of Jesus sought, both for themselves and for others, to harmonise Faith in Him, the Risen and Ascended One, with the Jewish standpoint on which they stood, by appealing to those passages in the Old Testament which were thought capable of a Messianic reference to Jesus. But however suitably these passages are interwoven with the historical narrative, they cannot make the historical sequence of events more probable, and we must consider their bearing on the facts to which they are thus applied as a very accidental and capricious one. The only question remaining after the preceding inquiry is whether in the unhistorical parts of this section the author composed freely at first hand, or followed a tradition which he found already existing. Doubtless both elements exist here in very close connection. Taking into consideration the theatre on which the events of the narrative are carried on, which is the sacred circle of the first Christian Church, we are disposed to assign no mean share to tradition; but a writer like the author of the Acts of the Apostles cannot deny himself the right to use even traditional materials in a free and independent manner.

So little do we here stand on firm historical ground, that even the fact that persecutions did arise against the Apostles and the early Church could scarcely be deemed to be proved beyond all question, if it rested on no other evidence than what this narrative supplies. What follows this ideal scene, however, the martyrdom of Stephen and the persecution of the Christians which was connected with it, wears the indubitable stamp of historical reality.

On the same day on which Stephen, the first martyr, fell a victim to his energetic activity in spreading the new doctrine, a great persecution broke out against the Church at Jerusalem. The Christians all left Jerusalem and scattered themselves in Judea and Samaria; only the Apostles, it is said, remained behind in Jerusalem, viii. 1. This may justly surprise us. We might imagine that they were made an exception from the rest simply because it seemed inconsistent with their dignity to fly before danger and leave the appointed scene of their labours; although the Apostle Peter, when placed in a similar position, does not seem to have had any such scruples, xii. 17. However, it cannot be doubted that they did remain behind in Jerusalem, where we immediately afterwards find them, viii. 14. But if they remained we cannot believe that they were the only ones who did so; we are rather led to suppose from the whole circumstances that the persecution, which was occasioned by the actions of the Hellenist Stephen, was directed chiefly against the Hellenistic part of the Church, which, with Stephen, had placed itself in open opposition to the existing Temple worship. But the Hebraistic part, which, with the Apostles, adhered to that worship even more closely than before (Luke xxiv. 53, Acts ii. 46, iii. 1, 11, iv. 1, v. 25), was not included in a persecution which was aimed at its enemies. Had all the Christians in Jerusalem left the city with the sole exception of the Apostles, something more would certainly have been said of the return of the fugitives to the Church, which we find maintaining itself in Jerusalem after that time. But nothing of this kind occurs; we are told merely that they were scattered widely abroad, and founded new churches in other places. One of the fugitives, Philip, remained in Cæsarea (viii. 40, xxi. 8) after he had preached the Gospel in Samaria; although, as he is named with Stephen as one of the seven deacons, we should certainly have expected that he would have returned to Jerusalem as soon as circumstances permitted. We must therefore suppose that this first persecution of the Christians produced this important result for the Church in Jerusalem; that the two elements composing it, the Hellenistic and Hebraistic, united hitherto, though in some respects differing, were now outwardly separated from each other. At that time the Church at Jerusalem became purely Hebraistic; as such it adhered closely to its strictly Judaizing character, and it developed at a later time a strenuous opposition to the freer Hellenistic Christianity. It would seem that the Church at Jerusalem was desirous even then, in order to further its Judaizing views, to bring the Christian Churches which were at a distance from Jerusalem into closer relations of dependence on itself, in order to prevent the free development of Hellenistic principles. This was probably the reason for the mission of the Apostles Peter and John into Samaria; the alleged reason that they might bestow on the Samaritans whom Philip had converted and baptised the gift of the Holy Spirit by laying on of hands, gives no clear idea of the case. This representation involves the notion of an outward communication of the Spirit bestowed by the Apostles as the immediate organ of the Holy Spirit, and accompanied by miraculous signs. In the same manner as Peter and John were sent into Samaria, Peter afterwards travelled into Judea, Samaria, and Galilee, and visited the churches established there (ix. 31, *sq.*), in the name, as appears from xi. 1, *sq.*, of the Church at Jerusalem, and in the interests of its fixed Judaistic principles; but there is nothing said here of imparting the Holy Spirit to the newly-converted by the hands of an Apostle. We might also suppose that when it was known in Jerusalem that the Christian faith was accepted in Antioch, Barnabas made a similar journey of visitation to that city. But this is very doubtful. Neander himself says (p. 139, Bohn 99): "Astonishment and mistrust seem to have been awakened in Jerusalem by the news that in Antioch a church of Gentile Christians was arising which did not hold the ceremonial law in observance." But if this were the case, Barnabas the Hellenist would scarcely have been selected for the visit to Antioch, as his liberal principles, so nearly allied to the Pauline standpoint (as was proved by the sequel), could not have been unknown at that time to the Church at Jerusalem. There is every indication that he did not undertake the journey to Antioch as an errand from the Church, for there is no trace of his being in any way dependent on the Church at Jerusalem. It even seems doubtful if he had been in Jerusalem before he went to Antioch, since his name (ix. 27) is associated with events which we will show can scarcely have happened in the manner related. Perhaps, therefore, after the persecution which followed the death of Stephen, he had left Jerusalem with the rest, and at last found with Paul in Antioch the sphere of action which promised greater freedom to his individuality. The actual division between the two elements of the Church, formerly allied together, became wider and wider, but it existed before this. The persecution itself shows that a distinction was drawn between the Hebraists and the Hellenists by the Jews at Jerusalem. We have probably to seek for the first germ of the dissension which arose between the two divisions of the Church in Jerusalem, in the facts related, Acts vi. 1, *sq.* We are here told of the neglect of the widows of the Hellenists in the apportioning of the daily gifts and of their openly-declared dissatisfaction against the Hebrews. That γογγυσμὸς of the Hellenists against the Hebrews brings us down at once from the ideal harmonious relations of the Primitive Church to the sphere of life's ordinary reality. It seems to have had deeper grounds in the dislike between the two parties, from which such disputes as these derived importance. The fact that such a grievance existed, and the means that were taken to remove it, namely, the institution of the office of deacon and the appointment of Hellenists, as it appears, to all the newly-created offices—all this shows us that the accessions the Church had gained had consisted chiefly of Hellenists. This of course enabled the liberal turn of thought which was exhibited by the Hellenists, as distinguished from the Hebrews, to have more scope. If these appointments were really made as is related, we shall have some indication of the spirit in which they were made, and of the previous condition of the Church, in the fact that Stephen, of whom we know something, was one of those who were then appointed.

CHAPTER II.

STEPHEN THE PREDECESSOR OF THE APOSTLE PAUL.

ACCORDING to the Acts of the Apostles, the first disciples of Jesus adhered as nearly as possible to the Jewish religion and to the national worship. The only thing that distinguished them from the rest of the Jews was the conviction at which they had arrived, that the promised Messiah had appeared in Jesus of Nazareth. They saw nothing antagonistic to their national consciousness in this belief in Jesus as the Messiah. Yet in this belief, simple and undeveloped as it was, a breach was introduced into their consciousness as Jews, which might seem insignificant at first, but could not fail to divide Judaism and Christianity further and further from each other. The persecution to which Stephen fell a victim shows us clearly that he was the first to express this antagonism between Christianity and Judaism as a thing clearly felt and not to be concealed. There is more doubt attendant on the statement made in the Acts of the Apostles as to the form in which he first gave decided expression to this antagonism. He is represented as having had disputes with the different Hellenistic communities in Jerusalem, to whom he had doubtless turned with especial confidence, that they, as Hellenists, would have understood the views and principles which he considered to be the essence of his Christian faith. As for the charge on which he was condemned, we hear merely that certain false witnesses stated that he had expressed himself in an irreligious manner against the Jewish Temple worship and the Mosaic law, and had proclaimed the impending destruction of the Mosaic religion through the teachings of Jesus of Nazareth. What was true and what false in those charges, the Acts of the Apostles does not say; whether founded or unfounded is left to be deduced from Stephen's speech in his own defence. To this speech, which, if it be the work of Stephen himself, is incontestably one of the most important documents of that period, we are accordingly referred. But the point of authorship is by no means settled. In order to pronounce upon it we have to examine the contents of the speech itself, for the latest commentators have failed to penetrate into its argument and internal arrangement; they have discovered no plan in it, but a bewildering variety of meanings.

The first and greatest difficulty is generally found in the fact that Stephen takes so little notice of the special accusation against which he is defending himself. But the truth is, that he takes up this subject not in its special bearing on himself, but in its wider scope; the application to himself and his own case comes in at the close as a natural deduction from this general view. The contents of the speech divide themselves into two parts running parallel to one another; on one side are enumerated the favours which from the earliest times God bestowed on His people, whilst on the other the behaviour of the people towards God is contrasted with them. Hence we find the prevailing idea of the speech to be that in proportion as the favours which God from the beginning bestowed on the people were great and extraordinary, the attitude of the people towards the Divine will was from the beginning unthankful and rebellious, so that where a thoroughly harmonious relation ought to have subsisted, the greatest antagonism prevailed, and in the same proportion in which God on the one hand had done everything to draw the people to Him and raise them to Himself, the people had turned away from God. Whilst the speaker takes up the relation of the people to God from this general point of view, it is clear how his own case is involved in it: this, however, comes prominently forward in one of the main points of the speech. Stephen was accused of having spoken irreverently, not only against the Mosaic law, but also against the Temple. In evident reference to this accusation, the Temple is one of the chief matters on which the argument turns. The Temple is the ultimate goal to which the promises tend, the focus of their fulfilment.[1] And so the peculiar spirit which had characterised the people from the beginning must, since God and the people stood thus opposed to each other, show itself in connection with the Temple.

The speaker thus reduced the accusation which had been raised against him, or rather the antagonism which the people displayed by this accusation against him and the Divine cause which he advocated, to the attitude which they had taken up towards God all along; and this of course implied that his speech took the form of a historical review. He began from the earliest times, and enumerated the whole series of events of which Jewish history consists, to which he indicated the present crisis had now to be added as a further development. These epochs, which are to be distinguished in the course of Jewish history, form the chief points of the speech.

The first part of the speech treats of the period from Abraham up to the time when the people had become a nation in Egypt, and when Moses appeared as their liberator. During this first period, the goodness of God to the people manifested itself in all its fulness, inasmuch as the promises given by God to his chosen Abraham were not confined to him alone, but extended to his descendants, and the people who should proceed from them. For the people's sake he was obliged to leave his home and kindred, and wander in the land where his people were at some future time to come to dwell, but where he himself was not to possess so much land as to set his foot on. The land was promised to the people; and although Abraham at that time had no child, yet all God's dealings with him had reference to his posterity, v. 5. The destiny of the people was foretold even at that time, and it was announced as the crowning point of all the promises that they should serve

---

[1] Acts vii. 7, cf. verse 46 *sq*. The τόπος of the seventh verse is the temple, which is also called ὁ ἅγιος τόπος, cf. xxi. 28.

God in the place where now the Temple stood. Circumcision was given as a token that all the promises to Abraham were to have reference to his posterity; by this token all the descendants of Abraham were to enter directly after their birth into their full right to the promises given to him. Hence everything having happened up to this time with a view to the posterity (οὕτως, vii. 8), this posterity now began to appear in Isaac. How little share the patriarchs themselves had in the land of promise, the spirit of the divine promise being rather to exclude them, was to be seen first in the history of Joseph, who was sold into Egypt, and then in that of the rest of the patriarchs who followed him there, after suffering the most extreme want in the land of promise. So little did they enjoy the promised land during their lifetime; and after their death it was still apparent how little the promise affected them. After their death in Egypt, their bones were indeed brought back to Palestine, and buried in the burial-place of Abraham; but, in the first place, Abraham had been obliged to buy this burial-place for a sum of money; and then it did not lie even in the actual promised land, but only in Sichem, in the country of the Samaritans, so hated by the Jews. Thus, even in death, they were not allowed to rest in peace in the land of promise.

The second part of the speech embraces the period extending from the residence of the people in Egypt and the appearance of Moses, to the times of David and Solomon (vii. 17-46). During the time treated of in the first part of the speech, the people did not yet exist; that section therefore dealt only with what God resolved to do for the people about to be formed. Of course there could be then no question of the relation of the people to God; but so much the more had this relation to be dealt with in the second part of the speech. For in the beginning of the second period, which the second part of the speech now proceeds to take up, the descendants of the patriarchs in Egypt had grown into a great nation; and as soon as this came to pass, God let nothing be wanting to bring about the fulfilment of the long-promised blessing of which the people was the proper object. But now how did the people behave?

First of all, they showed themselves incapable of understanding the deed which Moses—who had been so wonderfully preserved for his great work, and so carefully educated for it—performed for them as an earnest of greater deeds to come, vii. 25. They even broke out into open opposition against him, vii. 27. For these reasons Moses was obliged to flee out of Egypt from his own brethren. Notwithstanding this, God afterwards carried out, through him, the work he had determined on of saving the people from Egypt, by sending Moses, who had been rejected by his brethren, back to Egypt, as their leader and deliverer, to bring them out with signs and wonders. But against this Moses, from whom they had received the promise of a prophet like unto himself—this Moses who, in the solemn assembly at Sinai, was the Mediator between the people and God (or the angel who spoke with him in the place of God), and who received there the law as "lively oracles"—against this man the people committed an act of disobedience by which they turned back again to Egypt in their idolatrous hearts, and even forced Aaron to make for them a golden calf, as a symbol of the old gods whom they had seen worshipped there; and not content even with this one worship, they fell into all kinds of idolatry. Yet God did not on this account delay the fulfilment of what He had once promised. The ancient words of promise, λατρεύσουσί μοι ἐν τῷ τόπῳ τούτῳ, vii. 7, had not been fulfilled. The σκηνὴ τοῦ μαρτυρίου (of which the σκηνὴ of Moloch, vii. 43, was the idolatrous antitype, and with which the speaker therefore passes over to ver. 44) accompanied the Israelites as a mere movable tent through the wilderness, yet it was brought by them into the promised land and remained in the same form until the time of David. To realise the word of promise in this respect was reserved for the third period.

This third period, to which the third part of the speech refers, comprehends the age of David and Solomon. Instead of the movable tabernacle carried from place to place, David and Solomon established the Temple at Jerusalem as a permanent abode for the worship of God. But now the godless and carnal temper of the people manifested itself more openly, for they changed the general aspect of their religion with the change of the place where they worshipped. Now that they possessed a permanent Temple, their religion took the form of a Levitical worship attached to the Temple, and became a formalism composed of outward rites and ceremonies. For what did the Prophets who appeared from this time forward contend for, if not for a spiritual worship of God? What else was the cause of the suffering and persecutions which they underwent —of the martyr deaths which so many of them died, as forerunners of the coming Messiah—but this constant struggle against the people's merely external worship through which the adoration of God in spirit and in truth was completely superseded?

The last portion of the speech is undoubtedly to be understood in this way: the speaker draws the picture that is before his mind in a few bold strokes, and it is clearly evident how this conclusion of the speech is in agreement with its design as a whole, as well as with the apologetic aim of the speaker. This point, however, appears to me to need a more exact inquiry.

If we look at the conclusion of the speech in the way here indicated, the question may arise whether the speaker meant that the exclusive tendency of the people towards the outward and ceremonial, developed in the existing Temple worship, was to be considered as a fresh token of their perversity, or whether he did not intend to point out that the very building of a permanent Temple was to be considered a corruption. The question is by no means answered by the fact that it is said of David, after he had craved permission from God to build a "dwelling for the God of Jacob," that "he found favour before God." These words only mean that David laid his entreaty before God in the full confidence of possessing the grace of God which had been vouchsafed to him; but that the entreaty itself was the subject of divine favour is not here stated. Neither must we omit to mention that David is said to have wished merely to εὑρεῖν σκήνωμα τῷ Θεῷ 'Ιακώβ, but the building of a special οἶκος is ascribed to Solomon, of whose conduct in doing so nothing is said. Is not a disapproving sentence passed on the building of the Temple itself—in so far as it confined to a settled, narrow spot that worship of God which had hitherto regarded the great free Universe as his natural Temple? This sentence is surely implied in the direct contrast presented to the statement, Σολομὼν δὲ ᾠκοδόμησεν αὐτῷ οἶκον, by the words immediately following: "Albeit the Most High dwelleth not in temples made with hands—as saith the Prophet, Heaven is my throne, and earth is my footstool: what house will ye build me? saith the Lord, or where is the place of my rest? Hath not my hand made all these things?" The external, sensuous, ceremonial worship of the Jews may not have been the necessary consequence of the building of the Temple, yet it was open to the speaker so to consider it; and that he really does so consider it is clear not only from the antithesis present in the two verses, 47 and 48, but also in what he says of the "tabernacle of witness," in verse 44. For why should it have been here said that the "tabernacle of witness" was possessed by the fathers in the wilderness in the form in which Moses had been ordered to make it, "after the fashion he had seen," by the Being who spoke with him—God, or the angel standing in the place of God, ver. 30—if not with the view of calling attention to the great difference between the Ideal and the Real, and at the same time to the difference between a spiritual and sensuous worship of God? According to the opinion of the speaker as here indicated, the "tabernacle of witness," free, movable, wandering from place to place, bound to no particular spot, and therefore imparting its own movableness to the worship connected with it, fulfilled much better the aim of a spiritual service of God than the massive, stationary Temple, with the rigid fixed worship which it occasioned—in which the external, visible, and tangible machinery of worship assumed an overwhelming preponderance, and ceased to be a living and flexible expression of that invisible Ideal—the Heavenly "fashion" which Moses had seen. David, therefore, was truer to the idea which the σκηνὴ τοῦ μαρτυρίου represented: all that he wanted to do was to replace the σκηνὴ with a σκήνωμα. It was

Solomon whose reign was so marked a turning-point in this particular, who built an actual "house" for God. If this (as cannot be doubted) is the real and true sense which the speaker intended to express in the last part of his speech, we must not understand the former words of promise, λατρεύσουσί μοι ἐν τῷ τόπῳ τούτῳ, as referring immediately and exclusively to the Temple. The idea of the conclusion of the speech, viewed in the light of these words, must be this: "If by this place we understand the Temple only, then we are chargeable with that external and sensuous turn of thought which lies at the root of the Temple worship; this is just the error of the prevailing form of worship, that it is thought that God can be worshipped in no other place than in a temple raised to Him by the hands of men." In this way we see how the speech answers sufficiently the apologetic aim of the speaker, although it partakes so little of the nature of a defence in point of outward form. The denunciation of the Temple with which the speaker was charged had in fact been directed against the outward ceremonial service to which at that time the true essence of the Jewish religion had been perverted; and his protest proceeded from the same interest in the true spiritual worship of God which had animated the prophets. In giving utterance to these views the speaker gave all the defence he had to offer; but he cannot have concealed from himself that with such a defence he could have no expectation of inducing his judges to acknowledge the justice of his cause. The whole speech takes for granted that the defence cannot possibly be successful. He addresses himself to the task of contrasting the goodness and grace of God towards the people with the behaviour of the people towards God; he shows in the fairest light the goodness and grace of God, by showing how it was the fulfilment of promises that had been made to the people before they were a people, and could apply to none but them. But in dwelling upon this he is also exhibiting the grossness of the people's perversity; ingratitude and disobedience, with that overwhelming bias towards materialism which the people had

VOL. I. D

always manifested, must really have been their truest and most characteristic nature, because from the beginning—from the first moment in which they began to be a nation—they showed no other inclination. But what is so deeply rooted in the inmost being of an individual or of a nation as to be almost an innate and natural passion, must always exhibit itself outwardly in the occurrence of the same behaviour; it is an invincible tendency which it is at any time useless trouble to attack. This ruling idea of the speaker explains how from the beginning of his sketch, there is an obvious parallel between the earlier and later times, and the fate of Moses is typical of that of Christ. Moses appears as a deliverer (λυτρώτης, vii. 35); from him also do the people receive the words of life (λόγια ζῶντα, vii. 38); out of his mouth comes the promise (προφήτην ὑμῖν ἀναστήσει Κύριος ὁ Θεὸς ἐκ τῶν ἀδελφῶν ὑμῶν ὡς ἐμέ, vii. 37). How then can we wonder that this prophet like unto Moses had to endure what Moses endured, only in a greater degree, from the disposition of his people, so closed against all higher influence, so opposed to the divine? How can we wonder that if the prophets—the foretellers of the Coming One—were persecuted and slain, the Righteous One also, when He came, found betrayers and murderers? how wonder that the same fate still overtakes all those who seek to labour in the same spirit? With such accusers and such judges the speaker himself does not anticipate any better result from his defence. The people would have been false to their inmost nature if they had not sacrificed him to their own want of comprehension of a spiritual worship of God, and their consequent hatred of him. Therefore the feeling of the speaker, which up to this point was kept under and controlled as his historical treatment of his leading ideas demanded, breaks out at the close without further moderation or restraint, in the words: σκληροτράχηλοι καὶ ἀπερίτμητοι τῇ καρδίᾳ καὶ τοῖς ὠσίν, ὑμεῖς ἀεὶ τῷ πνεύματι τῷ ἁγίῳ ἀντιπίπτετε, ὡς οἱ πατέρες ὑμῶν καὶ ὑμεῖς. τίνα τῶν προφητῶν, etc. οἵτινες ἐλάβετε τὸν νόμον εἰς διαταγὰς ἀγγέλων, καὶ οὐκ ἐφυλάξατε, vii. 51. This it was, then, that the speaker had on his heart from the beginning, and now at last uttered freely and openly. The accusation brought against him of irreligion in regard to the τόπος ἅγιος and the νόμος, and the sentence of condemnation pronounced thereby on the Christian faith, fell back on his accusers and judges; but his own fate was at the same time sealed. The question which some interpreters have raised as to the conclusion of the speech, and which is commonly answered in the affirmative, finds here its answer, namely, whether Stephen was interrupted by his hearers; whether, therefore, his speech was not finished? In one sense it was interrupted; his passionate words must have provoked his hearers to a point at which it must have been out of the question to listen to him any longer. In another sense it was not interrupted; he had in reality said all that he had to say. What continuation does the plan and development of his speech admit of? He had laid bare to their deepest root the impure motives that lay at the foundation of the accusation raised against him; he had kept back nothing that could have been said directly or indirectly to expose the nature of his enemies' proceedings; he had carried on his speech to a point when the chief reproach which had been made against him about the τόπος ἅγιος received an exhaustive answer; and of what use could any further continuation of his speech have been? That he did not intend to say anything more about the time of the prophets, is shown by the comprehensive summary in which (vii. 49 and 52) he touches on this whole period; he had already left this period behind him, and could not well go back to it again. It might be thought that he had something further to say with regard to the charge brought against him with reference to the Mosaic law. But that is scarcely likely. The high respect with which he spoke of Moses would defend him from this part of the accusation; the manner in which he treats of the giving of the Law from Mount Sinai, and of the Law itself as "lively oracles," would serve to prove his recognition of the Divine origin and spiritual contents of the Mosaic law. And as he turns the charge concerning the τόπος ἅγιος back upon his enemies, so also does he deal with the other charge concerning the νόμος in his concluding words:

ἐλάβετε τὸν νόμον εἰς διαταγὰς ἀγγέλων, καὶ οὐκ ἐφυλάξατε. Was he then going to enlarge upon this οὐ φύλαττειν? But this οὐ φύλαττειν τὸν νόμον is sufficiently explained and justified by what he had already said in the former part of the speech regarding the disobedience of the people towards Moses, and their constant tendency towards idolatry. From whatever side we look at it, we find that the aim of the speaker was attained, and the main idea of the speech quite sufficiently carried out. And how can we think that the natural end of the speech had not been reached at the point where we find it ended, when we reflect how flat and superfluous anything that the speaker might have had to urge further in his own defence would necessarily have appeared after so emphatic and energetic an apostrophe against his enemies?

The more remarkable in contents and form this speech undeniably appears according to the foregoing analysis, the more does it appear that it must have been the work of a man possessing such a mind as that of Stephen, whose superior wisdom and spirit have already been expressly dwelt upon by the author, vi. 10. And if it be argued that a speech so carefully conceived, and so measured in design and execution, cannot be supposed to have been unpremeditated, as must necessarily have been the case if Stephen spoke in these circumstances, cf. vi. 12, we may still say that this scarcely applies to a speaker who had long had these ideas in his mind, and had already arranged them in some order by dint of repeated use; and in addition to this the historical form which the speech takes would make an unpremeditated one very easy. We must also remember how exactly the speech replies to the charge brought against Stephen. How telling and striking is all that is said in answer to the charge! How thoroughly the speaker goes into the matter in question, in order to attack the disposition of his enemies, which led them to prosecute him, at its very roots!

On the other hand there is very much to be said for the contrary view; it is impossible to suppose that we have here the speech of Stephen himself in its original form. This speech, which so well answered its purpose of refuting the charge of the accusers in the most complete and humiliating manner, and exposing the inward reason of its futility, is, for this very reason, of such a nature that the speaker of it must have felt it to be utterly useless for his own personal defence, and have seen that it could only exasperate his judges and make his condemnation the more assured. This, however, does not necessarily prove much, for Stephen did not belong to that class of men who think more of their own personal interests than of the universal cause of truth. A more serious difficulty is to be found in the improbability that his enemies, angry and irritated as they were, still had so much forbearance and patience as to listen to a defence of such length, and deferred the renewed outbreak of their passion until the speaker had completed his argument, and fully gained his purpose in speaking. The interruption takes place just when the speaker has worked out the idea of his speech; his opponents now discover to their extreme disgust that they have been listening to him in a mistaken expectation of what was to follow, and as it were in spite of themselves. (This trait is found also in connection with Paul's speech at Athens.) Does not all this look as if the writer had been looking for a fitting situation for a speech of this nature, and thought he had found it here? We must therefore carefully consider the circumstances under which Stephen delivered this speech. His case is represented as having been tried before the Sanhedrim, and the stoning which immediately followed the speech must be looked upon as a sentence of death carried out at the command of the Sanhedrim, or at least with its connivance. Now, it is well known that the Sanhedrim could not execute a capital sentence without the sanction of the Roman Governor. But there is nothing said of the concurrence of the Roman Governor in this case, and in fact it is impossible to assume that his concurrence was sought; the carrying out of the sentence followed so immediately on the trial before the Sanhedrim that we cannot interpose a step like this between the two. It is generally maintained, in view of this deviation from the legally established rule, that the stoning of Stephen could not have taken place before the year 36, as in that year Pilate, under whom it is thought that the Sanhedrim would certainly never have dared to act in such a high-handed way, was recalled from the Procuratorship of Judea. It is therefore asserted that the most correct date for the condemnation of Stephen is in the interval before the successor of Pilate, the new Procurator Marcellus, arrived, and when L. Vitellius, the Proconsul of Syria, who visited Jerusalem in the year 37, conferred many favours on the heads of the Jewish nation.[1] Others, as Neander, Olshausen, and Meyer, think that they can settle the difficulty which exists with reference to the relation of the Sanhedrim to the Roman Governor, by the remark that the whole of the proceedings against Stephen were of a very tumultuous character. "Perhaps," says Olshausen, "the Sanhedrim, in order to avoid a collision with the Roman magistrates, passed no formal sentence of condemnation; but connived at its execution, which was carried out by some fanatics." But in this case also the whole blame of the trial must be laid on the Sanhedrim. And what are we to think of this supreme spiritual tribunal, which surely must have had the fear of the Romans sufficiently before its eyes to make it pay some attention at least to legal form, if it allowed such an outburst of fury to take place under its own eyes, some of its own members even taking part in it (vi. 15, vii. 54, 57) before it came to pass sentence in its capacity as a court of justice—for that there was no time for this we must assume as certain? What natural consistency is there between the following facts: that Stephen was dragged before the Sanhedrim from a street riot, then dragged away again in a riotous manner to be stoned to death outside the city—and that these enraged enemies of his showed so much gentleness and forbearance that they could listen to a speech of such length and of such purport between these two outbursts of their fury? That Stephen was seized and stoned in a tumultuous insurrection is indisputably the fact which we have to regard as the nucleus of the story. Does not the fact that the proceedings against Stephen were of a riotous nature of itself make it improbable that there was any trial before the Sanhedrim at all? and how much more when we consider the

[1] Jos. Antiq. xviii. 6. 7.

additional difficulties mentioned above? If we dismiss all idea of the scene before the Sanhedrim, how natural and simple does the whole story become! What remains is then, that Stephen fell a sacrifice to a popular tumult which suddenly arose on account of his trenchant public utterances. Although the speech which he is said to have delivered may be perfectly characteristic of the man, though the religious theory it contains may have been actually his, handed down in traditions which the author of the Acts employed for his own purposes, still what is there to prevent our thinking that it is the composition of the historian himself? That he does not consider himself as overstepping the bounds of his licence as a historian by putting such speeches into the mouths of persons who appear as actors in his history, is shown by many other similar instances in the Acts of the Apostles. If he considered this to be part of his historical task, why should not this appear to him to be a good opportunity to represent a man who had appeared so prominently in the history of that period, and had drawn so much attention to himself by the religious opinions which he defended, and by the fate which he underwent, as actually speaking in public? If this was to be done, the speech must be delivered before the court to whose jurisdiction the case belonged. The circumstances which made such a trial before the Sanhedrim improbable assumed far less importance in the eyes of an author who looked at the relations and occurrences from a distance, than they do to us when we attempt to reproduce the actual events and sequences of the history. This is enough to explain to us in part how the author came to represent the case as tried before the Sanhedrim. But I think there is another point of view from which this circumstance may be regarded. It is clear that the dying Stephen is a reflection of the dying Saviour. As Jesus died with the prayer that the sins of his enemies might be forgiven, so the last words of the dying Stephen are Κύριε, μὴ στήσῃς αὐτοῖς τὴν ἁμαρτίαν ταύτην. And as Jesus yielded up his spirit to the Father, so did Stephen to the Lord Jesus.[1] To this parallel hovering before the writer's

[1] It is worthy of remark that both these expressions of Jesus adopted by Stephen

eye between the first martyr and the dying Saviour must be ascribed the fact that the scene before the Sanhedrim becomes for Stephen a scene of transfiguration. As the Saviour was raised to the glory of the Father through a similar death, so the radiant, divine light streaming around him as he sits on the Throne of the Godhead must also shine on the first of the martyrs who followed him. Nor was it enough that in this hour in which he was glorified by an end like that of Jesus, he should see the "heavens opened and the Son of Man standing at the right hand of God," ready to receive him.[1] Even before his trial by the Sanhedrim began, his judges saw " his face shine as though it had been the face of an angel." What can be more reasonable than to think that this parallel with Jesus, which is so unmistakably indicated here, coloured the statement of what occurred previous to the stoning?

are only found in the Gospel of Luke, xxiii. 34, 46. The three other Evangelists do not give them, as is well known. It is natural that the author of the Acts of the Apostles should adhere closely to the Gospel of Luke, but is it as natural that Stephen should have confined himself to these expressions of Jesus, which are found in Luke's Gospel?

[1] Only a modern critic could here ask the question, "How Stephen could have seen the Heavens opened in the room in which doubtless the sitting of the Sanhedrim was held?" Meyer answers the question as follows: "The Heavens may have been visible to him through the windows of the session chamber." Neander and Olshausen adopt without hesitation the theory (which Meyer also assumes) of an ecstasy, a prophetic spiritual intuition which Stephen had, and which took the form of a symbolical vision, so that when he looked up to the Heavens they seemed to open before his eyes. How paltry and arbitrary a thing does interpretation become when it tries to give an account of things which in themselves are very unimportant, and yet assume a fictitious importance when it is attempted to frame an idea, by means of them, of how the events occurred! We may dismiss Meyer's looking out of the window, but the ecstasy is also a mere hypothesis, and it is just as reasonable to suppose that what the author represents Stephen as having seen and said was simply his own view of the situation which he described as an actual occurrence. We may take the perfectly analogous example, vi. 15, ἀτενίσαντες εἰς αὐτὸν πάντες οἱ καθεζόμενοι ἐν τῷ συνεδρίῳ, εἶδον τὸ πρόσωπον αὐτοῦ ὡσεὶ πρόσωπον ἀγγέλου. It is said that Stephen was so transfigured that men thought they saw an angel in him. This view of Stephen can certainly only have been taken by his friends and adherents; it is perfectly clear that there is here only related the subjective Christian side of an objective phenomenon which involuntarily attracted the notice even of his opponents.

CHAP. II.] STEPHEN THE PREDECESSOR OF PAUL. 57

This appears all the more natural when we consider that the charge against Stephen was only a repetition of that already made against Jesus, that he had said δύναμαι καταλῦσαι τὸν ναὸν τοῦ Θεοῦ, Matt. xxvi. 61, Mark xiv. 58, with the addition τοῦτον τὸν χειροποίητον. That Stephen's attack on the existing temple worship was the cause of the outbreak of fury against him to which he fell a victim cannot be doubted. And as false witnesses were brought against Jesus with the same charge (Matt. xxvi. 60, etc.), false witnesses must not be wanting in this case (although there seems little reason why their testimony should have been a false one); and as the condemnation of Jesus took place before the Sanhedrim, so the same conditions must be fulfilled in this case. In short, everything in the whole matter must be exactly similar. People, priests, scribes, elders, and the whole Sanhedrim, must be set in motion,—Acts vi. 12, vii. 1, and Matt. xxvi. 57-59.

Notwithstanding all this it cannot be doubted that the attack of Stephen on the Jewish national worship was the cause of the outbreak of indignation to which he fell a victim. The author of the Acts of the Apostles states that the accusation brought against Stephen was the work of false witnesses; but the parallel charge brought against Jesus cannot be held as completely false. What was false in the testimony of the false witnesses may only have referred to the form in which they brought forward an accusation, which was substantially true; perhaps in the special mention of the Temple, a design to destroy which was, particularly after the event had actually come about, the pregnant and concrete expression of all hostility to the existing national worship, and could only be supposed to proceed from an inimical Gentile feeling. This charge, the same which had led to the condemnation of Jesus, was the outcome of the feeling which even then possessed the Jewish enemies of Christianity, and in which they were not deceived, that Christianity would make a great change upon their own religion. That the essence of true religion did not consist in outward ceremonials, connected with a temple service confined to one appointed spot,—this was the great idea, through which, even at that time, Judaism saw itself in danger of being superseded by Christianity. This inevitable rending asunder of Christianity from Judaism, whereby Judaism would cease to be considered an absolute religion, and by which its final extinction was threatened, had been clearly perceived and even expressed by Stephen; the high and free standpoint to which he felt himself raised by this discovery fostered in him the energetic zeal with which he laboured in the cause of Jesus—and in proportion to this was the earnestness of the opposition which he drew down on himself.

This spirit of Christianity, asserting itself all at once in its full power and true meaning in Stephen, is a startling phenomenon, as even the Apostles occupy much lower ground in comparison with him. But in this affair there is no mention made of the Apostles; it is Stephen alone who wages this fresh and so momentous battle against the enemy; and whilst he considers the Temple worship, with all its outward forms, as a thing already antiquated and in ruins, the Apostles always remain immovably true to their old adherence to the Temple. This relation of Stephen to his immediate surroundings is of itself enough to give us a high opinion of the man; but let us further consider the historical connection to which he belongs. The rise of distinctively Hellenistic Churches in Judea and the bordering countries, viii. 1-4, ix. 31, xv. 3, is to be traced to that persecution whose cause and victim he was; but more than this—we find that the Hellenists, who were scattered far and near, soon became impatient of the restrictions their connection with the Mother Church of Jerusalem tended to impose on them, and took the important step of preaching the Gospel not exclusively to the Jews, but to the Gentiles also. The first impulse to this course of action must certainly be looked for in the same Hellenistic circle of ideas in which Stephen worked; as soon as men felt, what Stephen had come to see, that they were no longer bound to the old cramping forms of Judaism, they also saw that the division which separated Jew and Gentile could no longer be considered an essential thing. So nearly do Stephen and Paul here approach each other, though when we see them first, at the martyr-death of the former, they appear to be as far as the poles asunder. The most violent persecutor of Stephen, and of the Hellenists who shared his opinions, soon after entered on the new path which Stephen had opened up for Christianity. And there can be little doubt that the new ideas of the Christian consciousness which Stephen first propounded were the means of that profound impression which changed a Saul into a Paul, and not only so, but from the very moment of his change caused his conversion to Christianity and his call to be the Apostle of the Gentiles to be inseparably identified with each other in his mind, Gal. i. 15, 16. Because in Stephen, whom he had persecuted, he had been confronted with the idea which to a Jew was most of all intolerable, which set aside the Jewish particularism, and substituted for it a universalism, in which Jew and Gentile stood with equal privileges side by side, he could now in the revulsion of his consciousness adopt without any further mediation the exact opposite of all that he had hitherto clung to with all a true Jew's feelings and instincts. If we took the ideas contained in the speech of Stephen as indisputably his own, we might easily establish a still closer connection between Paul and Stephen. If we are not quite entitled to do this, we cannot but think that the line of historical reflection taken in the speech is a very true suggestion of the mode in which a precursor of the Apostle, as Stephen must in any case be considered to have been, would first come in sight of the principles of Pauline Christianity. The chief logical difficulty for the convert from Judaism must have been how the Messiah could be rejected by the very people for whose behoof alone he had been appointed to that office. This could be explained only by the analogy of the fate of the prophets, and by the feeling and character of the people, which it had displayed not only now, but at every age of its past history. The Jews having by their crowning act of disobedience rejected the Messiah, it seemed to follow as a necessary consequence that the Messianic salvation was meant for the Gentiles. But it was impossible to stop short here. This result of the history of Jewish religion was a complete and glaring refutation and reversal of the lofty ideas the Jews entertained of the distinction with which God regarded their race; and the cause of the failure had to be sought not only in the character of the people, but in the nature of the Old Testament religious institutions themselves, in the essential nature of the law, and the impossibility, subjective, if not also objective, of attaining salvation by the law. If, as the whole story warrants us to assume, Stephen's religious consciousness had already broken loose from the Mosaic Law, he must have felt the necessity of defining in some way the relation the Law and Gospel bore to each other. The historical review of the Old Testament history which this speech puts in his mouth may very likely have formed part of his theory on this head. And we are thus perfectly justified in recognising him as the immediate precursor of the Apostle Paul, not only in the more obvious external features of his mission and experience, but in respect of the inner process by which his Christian consciousness was formed.[1]

[1] Schneckenburger, "Ueber den Zweck der Apg.," p. 184, says that this speech of Stephen's is in its main drift a preparation for the one with which Luke makes Paul conclude the Acts of the Apostles, xxviii. 25. The state of the case, he says, could not have been put more emphatically than was done by Stephen, that the Jews in general were altogether incapable, from their peculiar national disposition, of receiving the Messianic salvation. The general sentence on the Jewish nation to which the speech of Stephen leads up is thus just what their treatment of Christianity, as represented in the Acts, would seem to warrant, and there is no doubt that such a sweeping verdict could only have been reached at a later time on a review of the history of the case. We may here also see a further proof of the unhistorical character of the speech. The historical importance which Stephen must have possessed cannot on the other hand be understood except by placing his thought at the root of the collision between him and the Jews. Stephen's historical importance lies in his being the predecessor of Paul. How is it then explained, that in the writings of Paul himself there is not the slightest mention of such a predecessor? The answer can only be found in the breach with Judaism, which his conversion was; in the originality of his religious conceptions and the immediateness of the revelation—the directness of the manifestation made to him, Galatians i. 16. His conversion was of such a nature that he would never be led to inquire into the means by which the transition was brought about.

CHAPTER III.

THE CONVERSION OF THE APOSTLE PAUL.

ON the road to Damascus, whither Saul, breathing out threatenings and slaughter, was pursuing the Hellenists who had been scattered abroad by the fierce persecution raging in Jerusalem, that great change occurred by which he was so completely transformed. We possess three accounts of this occurrence which made such a marked turning-point in the life of the Apostle; the principal one in Acts ix. 1-25, and two others, Acts xxii. 1-12, and xxvi. 9-20. We must at once dissent from the view that the first of these accounts is by the historian, while the other two contain the narrative of the Apostle himself. We are not justified in ascribing to the speeches given in the Acts so authentic an origin as this; they have all passed through the hands of the writer of the Acts—a writer who, as we have seen by his report of the speech of Stephen, knows well how to use his literary licence. But if we grant, as Neander does, that the difference in the three accounts may be due to a want of accurate reporting of the speeches of Paul, this amounts to a virtual surrender of them as authentic speeches of Paul, since it cannot be known how far this want of accuracy goes, nor of any particular detail of the speeches whether it is accurately or inaccurately given.

A comparison of the three accounts shows several discrepancies. The point most worthy of remark is, that in ix. 7 the companions of Paul are made to hear the voice that spoke to him, but in xxii. 9 they do not hear it. It is generally thought that this difference is to be accounted for simply by supposing that the companions really did hear a sound—that of the thunder which accompanied the phenomenon, but not the articulate words which were spoken to Paul. But how unsatisfactory this is, when there is nothing said of any other φωνή except the φωνὴ τοῦ λαλοῦντος, whilst it is expressly stated on the one hand that the voice that spoke to Paul was heard by his companions as well, and on the other hand that it was not.[1]

That in the first account, ix. 7, the companions "saw no man," but in the two others, xxii. 9, xxvi. 16, they saw "the light" which shone round about them as well as Paul, is of course (as the appearance of the light is mentioned in the first passage as well as in the second as an objective matter of fact) no contradiction ; nor is the additional statement in the last passage that the voice spoke in the Hebrew tongue to be regarded as such. It is more striking, however, that according to the first account the companions of Paul remained standing, but according to the third they fell down with Paul, whilst the second has only the vague expression ἔμφοβοι ἐγένοντο. It is also remarkable that the instruction given by Christ in both the two first accounts to Ananias about the vocation of the Apostle, is in the third given by Christ to Paul himself, and this is a difference not to be easily passed over, at least by those who think that in these speeches they possess the Apostle's own authentic narrative of the occurrence. We might say with Olshausen, in order to set all these differences aside once for all, that we must accept the account as simply as it is given us ; that we certainly find variations in the narratives as we often do in the Gospels, but that they only concern unimportant minor points which affect the credibility of the event as a whole so little that they in reality tend to establish it ; but that the account given by Paul himself ought certainly to have the precedence over that of Luke, who relates the occurrence very shortly, and may easily have overlooked some

---

[1] τὴν φωνὴν οὐκ ἤκουσαν τοῦ λαλοῦντός μοι, is said xxii. 9, and on the contrary ix. 7 has ἀκούοντες τῆς φωνῆς. And this φωνή is certainly the φωνὴ λεγοῦσα αὐτῷ.

small details of an event of which he was not an eye-witness. But all this is in the highest degree arbitrary, and even thus an author whose authority in general stands so high that we give unquestioning belief to his accounts of miracles, stands convicted of a serious degree of inaccuracy and confusion; and if inaccuracy and confusion be in other cases a slur upon an author's credit, they cannot be taken in this instance as any proof of trustworthiness, but rather of the reverse. In reality these differences, which would scarcely be cited as an example of how different narrations may yet be easily harmonised, would be considerable enough to indicate a difference in the sources of tradition if it were not that they are found in the accounts of the same author, and if this author had not already given many proofs of the free manner in which he handles his historical materials.

Instead therefore of taking refuge in the usual manner in a forced and arbitrary reconciliation between accounts which simply contradict each other, such as the hearing and the not hearing, the standing upright and the falling down, we confine ourselves to the question, What led the author to relate the event in these different ways? As for the discrepancy between the expressions ἀκούειν and οὐκ ἀκούειν τὴν φωνὴν τοῦ λαλοῦντος, it is very probable that in the passage, ix. 7, the author thought it desirable to ascribe the ἀκούειν τῆς φωνῆς to the companions of the Apostle also, because by so doing he could best show the objectivity of the occurrence, the voice which the Apostle describes as having addressed itself specially to him having been heard by others also. But in both the other passages, especially in the second, in which it is expressly said that the companions did not hear the voice, it may have occurred to the author that as the Apostle himself is speaking, he would perhaps like to represent this voice as one addressed to him alone, belonging especially to him, and not heard by his companions. In furtherance of the aim which is apparent in these two speeches, it is essential that no doubt be felt as to the Apostle being the sole and especial object of this wonderful appearance. But its objectivity, on which no less stress must be laid, could be sufficiently provided for by the statement that the companions of the Apostle suddenly saw a light streaming down from heaven in the clear noon-day (this particular is stated here, as at xxvi. 13, as an additional piece of evidence). That the discrepancies of which we are treating are to be explained chiefly by such a design on the part of the author seems also to be confirmed by a peculiar remark made in the third passage, that the voice which talked with Paul spoke in the Hebrew tongue. In the first speech, which was delivered before the Jewish people (xxii.), and which we are expressly told was delivered in Hebrew (xxi. 40), this remark was not necessary; but as we must suppose that the third speech, which was delivered before the Roman Procurator Festus and the Jewish King Agrippa, was spoken in Greek, the remark might here appear to be called for, to save the audience from supposing that Jesus spoke to Paul in the very Greek words he repeated to them, the unlikelihood of which might have discredited the whole story to their minds.

It is also easily seen why in one of these two speeches of the Apostle the addition is made to the words addressed to him by Jesus, $\sigma\kappa\lambda\eta\rho\acute{o}\nu$ $\sigma o\iota$ $\pi\rho\grave{o}\varsigma$ $\kappa\acute{e}\nu\tau\rho a$ $\lambda a\kappa\tau\acute{\iota}\zeta\epsilon\iota\nu$, xxvi. 14, as this proverb expresses very happily the idea which the speaker seeks throughout to suggest, viz., that he was unavoidably constrained to take the step which was so distasteful to the Jews, by a power coming from without, which he could not resist. The narrative of the author himself, however, did not require to have the point brought out in this way. The discrepancy between the standing and falling of the companions is, like their hearing and not-hearing, a contradiction which can only be reconciled from the standpoint of the author. The most striking proof of the powerful impression made by the phenomenon was the throwing down of the Apostle and those who accompanied him; but if in the first passage the author described the impression made on them by the strong word $\dot{\epsilon}\nu\nu\epsilon o\grave{\iota}$, this was a sufficient compensation for the falling down; that they should remain standing suited the word $\dot{\epsilon}\nu\nu\epsilon o\grave{\iota}$ better than that they should fall down, and they must be represented as standing because they were to attest that they saw no one from whom the voice could have proceeded. And as for the difference in the words spoken by Jesus in calling the Apostle, it is perfectly evident that events which are kept separate in the first passage are in the third summarised and drawn together; and this is of no importance, as the words addressed to Ananias by Jesus are in fact only a continuation of his conversation with Paul; but it is just details like these that show us most distinctly the freedom with which the author used his materials.

Now we must remember that in these three passages we are merely comparing the different statements of the same author, and we cannot long compare them together without seeing that every detail of the narrative must not be taken as of the same value; those that are essential must be carefully separated from those of less importance. For the main event we have the Apostle Paul's own testimony in his Epistles. It was the most decided conviction of the Apostle that Jesus, after he had appeared to the Apostles and the other believers, so at last had visibly manifested himself to him, 1 Cor. xv. 8, ix. 1. But the Apostle does not give any explanation as to the way and manner in which this manifestation took place. He scarcely mentions or alludes to the event in his Epistles, a reserve which the two long and detailed speeches in the Acts would scarcely lead us to expect. The analogy which he insists on between the former appearances of the risen Jesus and the appearance to him would certainly suggest an outward objective occurrence: yet the expression he uses on the subject, Gal. i. 15, $\epsilon\dot{\upsilon}\delta\dot{o}\kappa\eta\sigma\epsilon\nu\ \dot{o}\ \Theta\epsilon\dot{o}\varsigma\ \dot{a}\pi o\kappa a\lambda\dot{\upsilon}\psi a\iota\ \tau\dot{o}\nu\ \upsilon\dot{\iota}\dot{o}\nu\ a\dot{\upsilon}\tau o\hat{\upsilon}\ \dot{\epsilon}\nu\ \dot{\epsilon}\mu o\dot{\iota}$, points to the subjective element of the occurrence in such a way as to prevent our laying too much stress on the outward appearance. We are the more justified on this account in trying to find out what is to be accepted in the narrative of the Acts of the Apostles and what is not. The chief point lies unquestionably in the inquiry, whether this appearance of Jesus is to be considered as an external or an internal occurrence? The whole representation in the Acts of the Apostles seems to suggest a material appearance; but it is decisive against this supposition that the companions of the Apostle are asserted to have seen a bright flash of light, but no person. The distinct expression, ix. 7, εἱστήκεισαν, μηδένα θεωροῦντες, is here of the more importance, since, as a matter of fact, there is nothing in the three narratives in the Acts of the Apostles to lead to the idea of a material, visible, objective appearance of the person of Jesus. Hence even Neander (p. 119, Bohn, p. 87) declares for a spiritual occurrence in the mind of Paul, a spiritual manifestation of Christ to his deeper self-consciousness; and by assuming this he is of opinion that we lose nothing of the real, divine part of the matter, as the external manifestation is only a means, and the material perception can give no greater certainty and reality than an occurrence in the region of the higher self-consciousness. But Neander (p. 122, Bohn, p. 88) feels obliged to return again to the idea of a real, visible appearance, since, according to him, the Apostle (1 Cor. xv. 8) places the appearance of Christ vouchsafed to himself on an equal footing with all the other appearances of the risen Christ; and this declaration, as he thinks, must have all the greater weight, because from 2 Cor. xii. 1 we see that the Apostle knew perfectly well how to distinguish between a state of ecstasy and a state of ordinary consciousness. As for the latter point, it follows, from the very pertinent reasons adduced by Neander himself (p. 121), that the appearance of Jesus which is here spoken of cannot have been an ecstatic vision, like that referred to in 2 Cor. xii. 1; but does it therefore follow that as an occurrence in the region, not of the normal, but of the higher self-consciousness, it can have had nothing in common with an ecstatic vision? This cannot be maintained, and although the Apostle places this appearance of Jesus and the other appearances of the risen Christ in one line, it does not follow, in the first place, that this appearance to him must have been an external one, for an internal appearance would perfectly justify the assertions of a ἑωρακέναι and ὀφθῆναι; and secondly, if the parallel were actually to imply an external appearance, the rule which Neander himself lays down (p. 97, Bohn, p. 70) in reference to Cornelius would apply here; and Paul, being the only witness for the objective reality of the appearance, could be accepted in evidence only of what he believed he saw. We cannot here get beyond the subjective element, as, according to the express declaration of the author, not one of the companions of the Apostle saw the form of Jesus,—a thing quite inconceivable in the case of an objective material appearance. However firmly the Apostle may have believed that he saw the form of Jesus actually and, as it were, externally before him, his testimony extends merely to what he believed he saw. Here we have arrived at a point from which the connection of the rest of the narrative may be perceived without difficulty. To the question whether the appearance of Jesus was really an outward and visible one, there is allied the further inquiry whether the words which Paul believed he heard from the Jesus who appeared to him were really audible. Had we only the testimony of the first passage on this point, the question would be answered immediately in the affirmative; but as the author is directly in contradiction to himself on the subject, our answer must come not from what is said on the point, but from the analogy of the whole. Now, with regard to the analogy, there can be no doubt that just as little as the appearance of Jesus was a real and outward one, so little could the words which Paul thought he heard have been outwardly audible. As he believed that he saw Jesus without an outward visible objective form of Jesus being there, so he might believe that he heard words which were for him only and not for others, that is to say, not outwardly and objectively audible. This connection between seeing and hearing can be very well explained on psychological grounds. If the Apostle was once convinced that Jesus had appeared to him, he must also have supposed that there was some decided reason for this appearance; and for what reason should Jesus appear to him, except to present himself to him, the persecutor, as the object of his persecution? And if the belief in such an appearance of Jesus could not possibly arise in the Apostle's mind until he passed from his former unbelief to a conviction of the higher dignity of Jesus, his belief in that appearance must necessarily have brought with it something more, namely, the resolve to become a preacher instead of a persecutor of the Christian cause.

So considered, what are the words which the Apostle thought that he heard proceeding from the form of Jesus, and which, if the apparition itself was only a spiritual fact, he must have heard from some spiritual voice,—what are they but the necessary explanation of the fact itself, and of the idea that was bound up with it? It is impossible to sever the union between words and ideas; the idea necessarily expresses and clothes itself in words. And here also the connection of one with the other is close and immediate; of the Seen and the Imagined with the Spoken and the Heard. In what we have now said we have remained entirely within the sphere of the Apostle's consciousness; but must we not step over the boundary which divides the inner from the outer, the subjective from the objective, when we endeavour to explain what the companions of the Apostle may at least have seen, even if they heard nothing? If they did not see the person of the being who manifested himself, they are at least reported to have seen the stream of heavenly light by which they and the Apostle were surrounded. The well-known modern hypothesis, so often repeated, that this light was a flash of lightning which suddenly struck the Apostle and laid him and his companions senseless on the ground, is really mere hypothesis; and as it not only has no foundation in the text, but is also in manifest contradiction with the meaning of the author, we shall make no further mention of it here. All the more, however, is the question forced upon us, whether or not this bright light is to be taken as an objective reality. The narrative clearly means it to be so taken, but it is another question whether this be not the point at which mythic tradition laid its hand upon the celebrated event of the conversion of the Apostle Paul. It must be borne in mind, in order that this appeal to the mythical may not appear as a completely arbitrary proceeding, that the essence of a myth consists in the outward objective expression of what was formerly subjective and contained in the region of thought. In cases where the transition from the subjective to the objective, from the inner to the outward, is logically necessary and direct, the idea of the mythical can scarcely be brought into play, although this is in truth the point at which the natural province of the myth begins. In this sense, even the necessary transformation already discussed of a direct, inexplicable, sudden impression into distinct ideas, and of the ideas into words, belongs to the province of the myth; here also there is an inward process which becomes an outward one, a transition from the subjective to the objective, the idea becomes expressed, it clothes itself in words and outward signs, and takes material shape and form. In this case we have a natural and necessary process of the human spirit; here the mythical appears in its direct, inner connection with the logical. The myth proper appears in a different case, where the transition from the subjective to the objective, from the inner to the outward, has no longer any inner logical necessity, but proceeds from a merely subjective need, and appears only as the accidental and more or less arbitrary investiture, in palpable and material form, of an abstract thought, or of a matter lying beyond the province of the senses. It is from this point of view that we must consider what appeared to the Apostle's companions. If once the fact was firmly established that the ascended, glorified Jesus had appeared to the Apostle Paul on the way to Damascus, tradition could not rest contented with conceiving the event to have transpired only inwardly, in the higher self-consciousness of the Apostle. The inner phenomenon must in some way become an outward one, if it was to keep its full importance and concrete truth in the traditions of the Church. But that the inner vision, present only to the mind of the Apostle, did not become an outward perception to those who accompanied him, in the visible form of Jesus appearing in his heavenly glory, this is to be explained by the fact that tradition, though transforming the facts as they originally happened, yet has its fixed boundaries which it does not arbitrarily overstep. The truth of the original fact was preserved in the form with which tradition invested the story, where it was still held that the appearance of Jesus had not been visible to any one but the Apostle himself. But if He had been actually visible, though it were only to the Apostle, could tradition do other than assume that the heavenly light, without which no divine appearance can be imagined, spread over all those who were near the Apostle at the time? Jesus could not really have appeared without some outward token of his nearness and presence. The strange brightness, surpassing that of the sun at mid-day, that suddenly shone round the Apostle and his companions, is accordingly nothing but the symbolical and mythical expression of the certainty of the real and immediate presence of the glorified and transfigured Jesus. As soon as the appearance of Jesus was conceived of in this manner, it followed that it must have brought about in all who witnessed it the effects which always resulted from heavenly phenomena of this kind; its overpowering influence threw them all on the ground, or at least riveted them to the earth in rigid astonishment.

The occurrences in Damascus form the second part of the miraculous narrative in the Acts of the Apostles. The adherents of the so-called natural mode of explanation have experienced as much difficulty about these as about the principal event itself.[1] Although the latter is said to have been very satisfactorily accounted for by the lucky hypothesis of a flash of lightning coming down out of the sky, the complicated events in Damascus cannot be explained in so simple and easy a manner. This is the weakest place in the naturalistic series of explanations, and the cold hands of the aged Ananias, the vivid delight of Paul at his appearance, the sudden stepping forth from the dark chamber to the light, and the three days' fasting, are only weak unskilful means of releasing the Apostle from the darkness of the cataract left on his eyes by the lightning flash. But how difficult it is even to bring Ananias and Paul naturally into such mutual relations as, according to the narrative in the Acts of the Apostles, must have existed between them. It may on the other hand be justly asked, Who can believe that these two visions, so exactly fitting into each other, Paul

---

[1] Neander gives no further explanation of the occurrences at Damascus.

learning through one that Ananias was coming to him to restore his sight, and Ananias receiving through the other the command to go to Paul and help him, came about merely by some lucky chance? Just as little can these visions be taken as miracles in the ordinary sense. With our author, visions are precisely the means employed to bring persons widely separated and unknown to each other into connection with each other. As in the history of the conversion of Cornelius, he and Peter are drawn together by two visions, so here Ananias and Paul; only the visions of the two latter are more exactly and directly complementary of each other. As Paul in his vision saw Ananias coming to him, so Ananias in the vision which he had was apprised of the nature of Paul's vision. It was natural to suppose that it was very difficult for Paul, after his arrival at Damascus, to find an introduction to, or to win the confidence of, the Christians residing there; and to understand how this came about, it was necessary to supply some great extraordinary preparation, and such a preparation must appear all the more necessary, as Paul, in the state of blindness in which he had been ever since the appearance of the light from Heaven on the way to Damascus, had been quite dependent on the help of others. Who would venture near a man who until now had been known as the bitterest enemy and persecutor of the Christian name? and how could he himself, a man so blinded and prostrate, commit himself to any unknown visitor that might profess kindly intentions? Here then Deity must himself step in and complete the work already begun. Ananias accordingly receives, in a divine vision, the command to go to Paul, and to afford him the help he needed, and to Paul himself Ananias is shown in a vision as the man destined to assist him. The charge which Ananias received lies in so close a connection with the miracle he wrought on Paul, that only from the miracle itself do we come to a right understanding of the vision which prepared the way for it. According to the narrative in the Acts of the Apostles, Paul had been blinded by the tremendous brightness of the appearance of the Lord. He came to Damascus blind, and remained there for several days in that condition until he was released from it by Ananias. But was this blindness an actual one? And was his release from it by Ananias an actual miracle? This question is suggested to us by the narrative itself, in which the close connection between the cure of the blindness and the laying on of hands and that which was the aim of the latter operation, namely, the gift of the Holy Ghost, deserves the most special attention. Ananias indeed received in his vision the command to go to Paul and lay his hands on him that he might receive his sight; and as soon as he had come to Paul and had laid his hands on him, bidding him receive his sight and be filled with the Holy Ghost, there fell from his eyes as it had been scales, and he "forthwith saw." Is not then the πλησθῆναι πνεύματος ἁγίου, which was wont to follow the laying on of hands, in itself a healing of blindness, an ἀναβλέπειν in a spiritual sense; and does not the expression, ix. 18, εὐθέως ἀπέπεσον ἀπὸ τῶν ὀφθαλμῶν αὐτοῦ ὡσεὶ λεπίδες seem to indicate that they were no real scales, that there was no real blindness, and no real cure? If we remember the condition to which the Apostle must have been reduced by the appearance of the Lord, how can we think of him in any other manner than with a downcast, introspective look, in a moody, preoccupied frame of mind, in deep earnest meditation on the guilt he had incurred by this recent course of action and which now weighed upon him so heavily? This dark night of his spiritual life was not broken till Christian baptism was administered to him, and with the sense of the forgiveness of sin which it brought, caused light to shine upon him so that he again saw clearly. The narrative itself points to such a state of mind, brooding on itself, closed to all outward impressions, entirely occupied with itself and struggling from darkness into light, by showing us Paul, after some days' residence in Damascus, as not only seeing nothing, but eating and drinking nothing, and only after receiving baptism taking food and returning to full vitality, ix. 9, 18. But if we look at the condition of the Apostle, not only immediately after this event, but before it, whilst he was still the strenuous Pharisaic zealot, jealous for the law, and the persecutor of all who turned away from it, how great a contrast does this first state present to the second in which we now find him? Is he not in the former case a blind man, who has to be cured of his blindness? Grotius has remarked on the words, ix. 8, ἀνεῳγμένων δὲ τῶν ὀφθαλμῶν αὐτοῦ, οὐδένα ἔβλεπε, "Ea fuit imago Pauli, qualis antehac fuerat, speciem habens hominis eruditi in lege, quum plane animo cæcus esset." And on ix. 18, ὡσεὶ λεπίδες, "adumbrantes velut illud, de quo agit Paulus, 2 Cor. iii. 14." Thus even Grotius remarked that these expressions yield themselves to a figurative interpretation, and are apt and significant when understood of the Apostle's spiritual condition. The author himself represents the Apostle as making use of similar figurative expressions. In his speech of chap. xxvi. he puts into his mouth the following words as having been addressed to him by Christ in appointing him his office: he was sent to the Gentiles, he is made to say, ἀνοῖξαι ὀφθαλμοὺς αὐτῶν, τοῦ ἐπιστρέψαι ἀπὸ σκότους εἰς φῶς, καὶ τῆς ἐξουσίας τοῦ σατανᾶ ἐπὶ τὸν Θεὸν, τοῦ λαβεῖν αὐτοὺς ἄφεσιν ἁμαρτιῶν, καὶ κλῆρον ἐν τοῖς ἡγιασμένοις, πίστει τῇ εἰς ἐμέ, ver. 18. May not the conversion of the Apostle itself be described in the same manner as a passage from a state of darkness and blindness to a state of light and vision with clear and open eyes? Taking all these points into consideration, does it not seem reasonable to consider as tradition what is related in the Acts of the Apostles of the blinding of the Apostle, and the wonderful cure of his blindness by Ananias? In none of his Epistles does the Apostle himself mention any of these occurrences in his life. The tradition doubtless arose from the expressions which, when properly interpreted, that is not strictly but figuratively, served to indicate the great change in the inner spiritual life of the Apostle, and the great contrast afforded by the Apostle's earlier and later attitude of mind and religious views. The ordinary process took place here, by which myth is formed out of tradition, viz.: that these figurative expressions came to be interpreted strictly and literally. Spiritual blindness thus became bodily blindness: the looking up in a spiritual sense became the falling off of scales which had covered the eyes. Then dates had to be fixed for the two states and for the change. No better opportunity for the blinding could be found than the moment when the Apostle had seen the dazzling appearance of light in which the Lord appeared. If, in order to represent to the fancy what occurred at the moment when the Lord appeared to the Apostle, tradition represented an extraordinary heavenly light as spreading all around, this could not happen according to the usual conditions of such heavenly phenomena, without leaving behind on the person for whom the vision was intended the mark of blindness. And if the condition in which the Apostle was after that appearance and the change which it produced on him, was necessarily a condition of perfect unconsciousness towards the outward world, then everything concurs to place that blindness which affected the Apostle before he had attained to the clear light of the Christian life, in the period between the appearance of the Lord to him, and the act of his reception into the Christian community. What had been miraculously produced must of course be miraculously removed, and the fittest time for the removal was when, after the crisis of the struggle into light was fully past, the Apostle became a new man by his actual reception into the Christian community. But the greater the change in the outward as well as the inward condition of the Apostle, the more fitting did it seem that this should have been effected by a special divine arrangement, and (as is the case also with the conversion of Cornelius) two visions corresponding with each other seemed to be the most likely means to have brought about the change. A special divine communication, such as could only be conveyed through a vision, must in this case appear to be all the more necessary, as without it the distinctive outward act of imparting the Holy Spirit to the Apostle, by the laying on of hands by Ananias, could not have been considered as valid, Ananias not being an Apostle. All these details of the fully formed tradition fit very closely into each other, nor is their connection with each other during the process of the formation of the tradition less satisfactory, when we have secured one point from which to trace it. If we are right in assuming that the blindness of the Apostle was no real physical blindness, then the miracle of healing is no longer needed; and if Ananias was not sent to Paul for this purpose (for it was to this end chiefly that he was desired to go, according to Acts ix. 17, ὁ Κύριος ἀπέσταλκέ με, ὅπως ἀναβλέψῃς), the statement also falls to the ground that Ananias received this charge in a divinely sent vision; and the whole matter takes a completely different complexion from that given to it in the Acts of the Apostles. It therefore remains doubtful whether Ananias really came into such close relations with the Apostle Paul during this critical period of his life—whether his name did not get mixed up in the account of the conversion in some accidental manner. In the speech of the Apostle delivered before the Jewish people, Ananias is described as an ἀνὴρ εὐσεβὴς κατὰ τὸν νόμον, μαρτυρούμενος ὑπὸ πάντων τῶν κατοικούντων Ἰουδαίων, xxii. 12. How easy it is to imagine that there was a particular interest at work in thus representing the Apostle Paul as from the beginning in close connection with a man who stood in such good repute with the Judaizing party, which was always so suspicious of the Apostle.

A historical and critical view of the narrative of the conversion of Paul, as given in the Acts of the Apostles, does not allow us to consider it as simply miraculous; and if we look at it from a psychological point of view, the supposition of a miracle appears neither necessary, nor indeed admissible. Who can venture to say that such a change in the religious and spiritual life of the Apostle may not have been developed from his inner life in a simply natural manner? or who will venture to make the assertion that even the most sudden transition from one extreme to another lies outside the pale of psychological possibility? or that if such a phenomenon must be held as contrary to nature, that which is contrary to nature could be brought about by a miracle? If there be any sphere in which the notion of miracle must be discarded, it is the psychological sphere, and especially in cases in which miracle would be nothing but a violent interruption of the natural development of the man's inward spiritual life. Hence Neander, although in examining and accounting for this occurrence he makes the miracle the ultimately determining factor, still in no way allows a magic influence to have been in operation on Paul, whereby he was carried away and changed against his will. There must, Neander holds, have been some point of application in his inner life, without which the most essential element of all, the inner revelation of Christ to his highest self-consciousness would not have been possible, without which no outward impression could have proved the means to introduce that revelation to his mind, without which any outward impression, however strong, would have been merely transitory. But if once the theory of an inward point of connection be allowed, is it anything else but an admission of the principle, by which the whole change is to be referred to natural causes? What remains, therefore, is simply a question for historical criticism to investigate: whether what in itself is possible did, in accordance with the statements before us, actually occur without the interposition of a miracle properly so called? So clear and simple does this seem that we can only wonder how even the modern commentators on the Acts of the Apostles here embrace the theory of miracle in its most exaggerated form. Proceeding on the words, xxvi. 14, σκληρόν σοι πρὸς κέντρα λακτίζειν,[1] Olshausen brings in, quite *mal à propos*, the Augustinian doctrine of "gratia irresistibilis," only with this difference, that, by the assertion that in *this* appearance of our

---

[1] According to Olshausen, the meaning of these words can be only as follows:—"Thy striving against the overpowering strength of grace helps thee not. Thou must yield to it, in spite of all." This meaning can only be forced from the words by an interpreter biassed in favour of the Augustinian dogmas. It is certainly most natural to take the words not as referring to the subjective, but to the objective, uselessness of striving. Their meaning therefore would be: "Thou persecutest me in the belief that I am not the true Messiah, but as thou must be now convinced that I am the true Messiah, how can thy undertaking be anything but vain, and redounding to thy own destruction?" This reading is illustrated and confirmed by the parallel in the speech of Gamaliel, v. 39, οὐ δύνασθε καταλῦσαι αὐτό, μήποτε καὶ θεομάχοι εὑρεθῆτε. "You will not effect anything by your reaction; the end will show on the contrary that you will draw on yourselves the worst consequences, for only the worst is to be expected from a direct opposition to God."

Lord the power of grace was irresistible, it is by no means sought to deny that there may have been times in the subsequent life of Paul when it was possible for him to forfeit by unfaithfulness the grace vouchsafed to him. This is the very worst modification of this doctrine of irresistible grace, as by it two completely different standpoints become confused with each other,—the ordinary theory of free-will, and its opposite, that of absolute dependence. The consequence, or rather the cause, of this illogical blending of heterogeneous theories is a theory of miracle which thoroughly destroys the continuity of the spiritual life, the arbitrary assertion that there are circumstances in the life of man in which (as Neander well puts it) "the individual is carried away and transformed by magic influence against his own will." In this view of the conversion of the Apostle Paul, miracle is of course assigned its full right, but this is the only advantage; and what is believed to be gained by it on one hand, in favour of the glorification of divine grace, is lost on the other by the sacrifice of the moral dignity of the Apostle.

The event of the conversion and calling of the Apostle must have been of the greatest importance to the author of the Acts in furthering his apologetic aim. Not only, therefore, is it related at length in chapter ix., it is also repeated with equal length and detail in the two speeches which are put into the mouth of the Apostle Paul himself, chapters xxii. and xxvi. We see from the epistles of the Apostle how his enemies always reproached him with not having been, as the other Apostles, a disciple of Jesus, and for not having been called to be an Apostle by Jesus himself during his earthly life. Against such a reproach and such an attack on the apostolic authority of Paul, it was necessary to insist upon a fact by which he was connected with Jesus by a relation not less direct than that which bound the rest of the Apostles to him. The Apostle himself maintains with the most decided emphasis that he also had seen Christ the Lord, 1 Cor. ix. 1, that Jesus had manifested himself to him as well as to the other Apostles; even if after the others, still really and truly, 1 Cor. xv. 8. And not only once did this happen, but by repeated ὀπτασίας καὶ ἀποκαλύψεις τοῦ Κυρίου, he claims for himself direct communion with the Lord: 2 Cor. xii. 1. But there still remained the great and essential difference between his calling and that of the other Apostles, that the reality of the former depended on a momentary appearance which he asserted to have taken place—on a vision—an ὅραμα, which could be known as real only in the sphere of his own subjective consciousness, and which therefore lay open to the suspicion that it might be the result of self-deception. And as together with his calling to the office of an Apostle he claimed to have received also a distinct commission to proclaim the Gospel to the Gentiles, so the whole question as to the participation of the Gentiles in the Messianic Salvation, which was a cause of so bitter dispute between the Apostle and the Jewish Christians, rests also on the truth and reality of the visionary appearance by which the Apostle believed himself to have been called. In proportion to the difficulty of this question of the apostolic authority would be the anxiety of a writer who has so decided an apologetic tendency as the author of the Acts to procure for his Apostle as strong a case as possible. The authority of Paul, according to the nature of the circumstances under which the Acts of the Apostles was composed, could be legitimized in no better manner than by the authority of Peter. If it could be shown as a precedent that Peter also saw a divinely sent vision in which he received an important charge, and if that charge concerned a no less weighty matter than the adoption of the Gentiles into the Messianic kingdom, so that the conversion of the Gentiles had been already begun by him, what objection could be taken to Paul's being called to the office of an Apostle among the Gentiles? According to the whole plan and economy of the Acts of the Apostles, it cannot surprise us that we really do find in it such a legitimation of the Apostle. It is contained in the account of the conversion of Cornelius, which the author of the Acts, chapters x. and xi., apparently places purposely between the conversion of the Apostle, chapter ix., and the actual commencement of his apostolic office among the Gentiles, xi. 25. The detailed and circumstantial manner in which this is related indicates how much importance the author attaches to it. If everything had taken place as it is here related, and as it is commonly believed to have done, there would be no need of saying anything about an especial apologetic aim of the author. But how is it possible to take such a series of miraculous transactions, all so artfully linked together, as a piece of actual history? If we remember that this is not a question of miraculous events occurring merely in the external world, but of influences from the higher world acting directly on the religious thought and the whole mental position of the persons concerned, so as to produce resolutions and opinions which could not have been reached at least for long in the ordinary way of religious and spiritual development, we find we cannot credit the account of such direct operations of a higher causality in the sphere of the spiritual life. The persons concerned would be passive organs for the proclamation of ideas which, according to the divine plan, were to be introduced to the world as a purely supernatural revelation. We must notice how little the persons here treated of betray any clear consciousness, or even any suspicion, of the results which these occurrences were meant to bring about. Cornelius indeed received instructions to summon Peter to come to him, but he did not know what end was to be answered by his coming, x. 33. Peter followed the summons sent to him without understanding what it meant, x. 21. In deference to the divine command contained in the vision, he suppressed the opinions which he had hitherto held regarding the relation of the Jews to the Gentiles (28), but he understood so little of the real meaning and aim of that command that the light flashed upon him for the first time through the surprising discovery of the exact correspondence of the two visions with each other. It was not of his own free conviction and decision that he determined on his course of action, but through the overpowering impression of miraculous events which burst upon him suddenly and unforeseen, and by which alone the destined result was obtained. Obviously Peter serves here as the mere organ of a higher agency, and we see clearly enough how external the relation was in which the religious ideas and convictions here introduced stood to his religious consciousness and the stage of religious development which he had reached.

The entire series of these events is wanting in historical connection; there is nothing to lead up to it in the previous history: it has no result at all commensurate with its greatness and seeming importance. The Church at Jerusalem indeed allowed its doubts to be hushed by the assurances of Peter; but how little these doubts were really removed, the narrative in chapter xv. shows us; and Peter himself, when obliged here to speak on the subject, mentions those events as a thing long out of date, xv. 7 ($ἀφ'$ $ἡμερῶν$ $ἀρχαίων$, etc.), about which nothing had been thought in the interval, and which now for the first time required to be remembered and considered. With what aim did all this happen, if it harmonised so little with the time and with the stage of development then attained by Peter? was it merely to furnish him later on with a support for his religious consciousness, at a time at which he could not any longer need such a support? Or must we think it all took place for the sake of Cornelius? How passive he himself is, however, in all the events that befall him! and how little does he appear to be the true object of all those wonders! The miracle is thus without any adequate motive; indeed, we may say more: that so studied and complicated a series of miraculous occurrences has but little in common with the miraculous character of the Gospel history. Such a narrative cannot be held, when we consider its essential character, to be even a mythical tradition. It is carefully studied throughout; the details are connected with each other as a whole in a way which only careful and apt manipulation and combination could secure; one vision corresponds to the other, and the effect to be produced by each happens at a certain moment and in a certain manner, so as to fit in with the complete and rounded whole. For this reason also the remark with which Neander prefaces his discussion of the passage, "that we are not justified in assuming that Cornelius was able to separate clearly the objective and actual from the subjective in his apprehension of that which appeared before him as an object of experience and cognition," is completely purposeless and useless; for we cannot conceive how anything in this series of details could be different from what it is called, or could be imagined to proceed from hallucination. If one of these details is put out of its place, or changed, the whole becomes disarranged and confused, and loses coherence and connection. Such combination and coherence as are here presented are foreign to a myth. Such a narrative cannot be looked upon as the casual product of mythical tradition, but as a free composition, originating in a certain design. From this point of view, the two visions which are so essential in the matter must be held to be the symbolical form selected by the writer to set forth his idea, as in the literature of the earliest Christian times visions frequently occur as mere symbolical and poetical media for the idea the writer wishes to convey. The chief idea which is to be enforced here is so prominent that we can scarcely avoid seeing that the persons and events which are placed before us are only meant to illustrate the idea of the whole, and bring it into visible form. As soon, therefore, as the action used for this purpose is sufficiently developed, the idea is at once released from the material husk which enveloped it; and now the full consciousness has dawned upon Peter of what the author makes him utter as the ruling idea of the whole, x. 34, that "there is no respect of persons with God; but in every nation he that feareth him and worketh righteousness is accepted with him." These words, as the recent commentators rightly remark, can only be taken, when we consider the connection in which they stand, as asserting, in opposition to the Jewish exclusiveness, that God receives into the Messianic kingdom those who believe in Jesus, not with any regard to whether or not they are descended from a special theocratic nation, but looking only to the moral worth and capacity of each separate individual. The speech of Peter immediately following seeks to remove any idea of exclusiveness from the labours of Jesus. The idea that is here insisted on could not, however, have been set forth more expressively and vividly than by the representation of the

Holy Ghost coming before the water, x. 44. How evidently was it thus shown that the Gentiles were not to be excluded from the reception of the Holy Spirit as the principle of Christian consciousness, how clearly is the conclusion drawn that the outward, the formula of admission, is not to be refused, when the inward, the desire of and fitness for the Holy Spirit, is present, this being the main point and all else merely accessory. Peter accordingly insists again and again on this idea as the outcome of the whole proceeding (x. 47, xi. 16, 17), that as the Gentiles had received the gift of the Holy Spirit in the same way as they, the born Jews, its reception and operation being attested by the same outward manifestations as those at the feast of Pentecost, namely, the λαλεῖν γλώσσαις and the μεγαλύνειν τὸν Θεὸν (x. 46), there could be no distinction between Jew and Gentile with regard to the Messianic kingdom. From this it followed as a thing of course that with respect to the adoption of the Gentiles into the community of the followers of Jesus as the Messiah, nothing could be demanded which would involve, as circumcision would have done, that in order to become Christians they must first become Jews. As the whole matter is embodied in visions, and visions tend to the figurative and symbolical, this thought also had to be presented in a symbolical form. The distinction between clean and unclean in the relation between Jews and Gentiles, is founded specially on the Mosaic laws of food, by which the Jews were forbidden to taste the flesh of certain animals which were held to be unclean. The Gentiles, to whom those kinds of food were not forbidden, became for that very reason unclean to the Jews, who had to be on their guard against defilement in their intercourse with the Gentiles when this involved eating and drinking together. The idea that the difference hitherto subsisting between Jews and Gentiles as the clean and the unclean was no longer to be upheld, is very strikingly exhibited by the figure of a vessel in which clean and unclean animals were contained promiscuously, and commanded to be used as food without any distinction. The sharp hunger which Peter had experienced just before the vision, is thus connected very closely with the aim and purpose of the vision, and is meant to signify how the prohibition against eating certain beasts which were destined for the food of man, and serve his wants as well as the rest, must have appeared to him as an unnatural restriction. The removal of the distinction between clean and unclean was expressed also by the symbolical vessel which in the first place presented no distinction between clean and unclean beasts, and in the second place was let down with all its contents from heaven. As the difference between clean and unclean with regard to the animal world rested on a certain dualistic view of the world, on the idea of a clean and unclean creation, so also with regard to the relations of Jew and Gentile, the wall of partition which, according to old custom and the prevailing view, existed between them could be removed in no better way than by the introduction of the thought that God was the God of the Gentiles as well as of the Jews. As from the divine standpoint there can be no unclean creation, and no man is to be considered "common or unclean" (x. 28, compare 15), so Jesus, as the Messiah, is the common Lord of all in the peace of his Gospel, πάντων κύριος (36), ordained of God to be the Judge of quick and dead (x. 42). The idea which all the details serve to enforce is a clear and definite one enough; and after what has been said it is unnecessary to dwell upon the circumstance that it is Peter in whose mind the idea first arises and is acknowledged to be true. There is another point closely connected with this, however, which we have still to notice, namely, the author's evident desire to show that the idea thus brought forward by Peter obtained the assent of the Church of Jerusalem. He expressly mentions the opposition which Peter's act of imparting the Gospel to the uncircumcised and unclean, met with from the Church at Jerusalem, and makes Peter relate circumstantially the whole course of the affair in his own vindication. The author would not have allowed himself this repetition if he had not attached great weight at this point of his narrative to the impression which the affair made on the Church at Jerusalem. Accordingly after hearing this vindication, the Church at Jerusalem expressed itself content with what was done, and glorified God in that he had extended his salvation to the Gentiles (xi. 1-18). The behaviour that the members of the Church exhibited in the sequel shows plainly enough that they cannot have taken up this attitude then. We cannot understand, in the first place, how Peter succeeded so easily in his vindication of a step calculated to give such grave offence. He is said to have done so by appealing to the fact that before he had ended his speech, ἐπέπεσε τὸ πνεῦμα τὸ ἅγιον ἐπ' αὐτούς, ὥσπερ καὶ ἐφ' ἡμᾶς ἐν ἀρχῇ, xi. 15. This refers to the feast of Pentecost and the miraculous γλώσσαις λαλεῖν which then took place. So undeniable and public a miracle was of course better calculated than anything else could have been to silence the doubts of the Church. But if the miracle of the λαλεῖν γλώσσαις be taken in the case of Cornelius and those baptised with him, as well as in the previous case, to have consisted (as Neander states, page 105) in their feeling themselves impelled to give vent to their feelings in impassioned praises of God, who in so miraculous a manner had led them to salvation, would even this appear to the Church at Jerusalem to be a sufficient vindication? Shall we, in order to make this vindication appear more substantial and more satisfactory, retract what we have seen to be a well-founded result of criticism with regard to the λαλεῖν γλώσσαις? Certainly not; it simply follows that this vindication before the Church at Jerusalem, and *a fortiori* the circumstances which occasioned it, cannot be held to have occurred as the letter of the narrative would have us believe.

However little such a narrative can lay claim to historical credibility, it suits very well the apologetic tendency with which the Acts of the Apostles is written. However we may decide on the traditional element which lies at the root of the history of the conversion of Cornelius, its adoption into the narrative, and the place assigned to it there, can only be accounted for by the apologetic interest of the author of the Acts of the Apostles. Paul must be represented as entering on his apostolic work among the Gentiles under the shield of the Apostle Peter, who himself converted the first Gentile; and the heavenly appearance on which alone Paul grounds the proof of his apostolic calling is legitimised in the most authentic manner by a similar vision sent to the Apostle Peter. We can well imagine how important this must have been to the writer in the pursuit of his apologetic aims, if we consider to what attacks the Apostle Paul was exposed, both at the commencement of his career and long afterwards from the Jewish-Christian party, on account of the peculiar nature of his call. In the pseudo-Clementine Homilies the principle is enunciated, with evident reference to the Apostle Paul, that those revelations only should be considered true and trustworthy which are attested by outward communication and instruction, and not merely by appearances and visions. This is one of the chief subjects of controversy between the persons who are represented as conversing in these Homilies; and the arguments adduced on each side are of great use in making us see clearly the importance this matter must have had to the Apostle and his party. "Thou hast boasted," objected Simon Magus to the Apostle Peter (Homily xvii. 13), "that thou hast entirely understood thy Teacher (the true prophet Christ) because thou hast personally seen him present, and hast listened to him, and that it would be impossible for any other man to have the like certainty by means of any appearance or vision ($\dot{o}\rho\acute{a}\mu a\tau\iota\ \mathring{\eta}\ \dot{o}\pi\tau a\sigma\acute{\iota}\dot{a}$). Now, that this is untrue, I will show thee. He who clearly hears what another says is not fully convinced by what is said. For he must think in his mind, 'Does he not lie, being to all appearance a mere man?' But a vision, when it is seen, affords to him who sees it the conviction that it is divine." To this Peter replies, "Thou maintainest that more can be learnt through a vision than through a real operating presence ($\mathring{\eta}\ \pi a\rho\grave{a}\ \tau\hat{\eta}s\ \dot{\epsilon}\nu\epsilon\rho\gamma\epsilon\acute{\iota}as$). On this account thou thinkest that thou art better informed about Jesus than I am. But the prophet deserves all belief, as we know him well beforehand that he is true, and he gives, as the learner wishes, an answer to questions asked him. But he who believes a vision, an appearance, or a dream, has no security, and knows not whom he believes; for he may be deceived by an evil demon, or a deceitful spirit, into believing what is not the case, and if he asks who it is that appears,[1] it can answer what it will. It stays as long as it pleases, and vanishes like a sudden flash of light, without giving the desired information to the inquirer. In a dream no one can ask what he desires to know, since the mind of the sleeper is not in his own power. For this very reason we ask many things we want to know in our dreams, or without asking learn what is of no interest to us, and when we awake we are discontented because we have neither heard nor made due inquiry about what we wanted to know." The Magus rejoins that even if belief is not to be conceded to all visions, still those visions and dreams which are sent by God cannot be false; that only the righteous can see a true vision, not the wicked; Peter answers that he cannot agree to this; pursuing his argument he says, " I know that many idolaters, carnal-minded men given over to all sorts of sins, see visions and true dreams, and some also have seen demoniacal appearances. I maintain that mortal eye cannot see the incorporeal form of the Father or of the Son, because they shine in purest light. It is therefore not out of jealousy that God does not allow himself to be seen by men who are fettered by their fleshly nature. For who can see the incorporeal form even of an angel, much more of the Son? But if any one sees a vision ($\dot{o}\pi\tau a\sigma i a$), he must remember that it may proceed from an evil demon: and that ungodly persons see visions and true dreams is certain, and I can prove this from the Scriptures." Then are adduced the instances of Abimelech, Genesis xx.; of Pharaoh, xli.; of Nebuchadnezzar, Daniel iii. 5. " All these were ungodly persons, and yet saw sights, and visions, and true dreams. It results from this that a man who sees visions, dreams, and appearances, need not be concluded to be necessarily a pious man. For the truth springs out of the pure mind indwelling in the pious man; it is not sought in dreams, but is bestowed on good men with consciousness and judgment. Thus the Son was revealed to me by the Father; I therefore know what is the meaning of the revelation ($\tau i s\ \delta \acute{v}\nu a\mu\iota s\ \dot{a}\pi o\kappa a\lambda \acute{v}\psi\epsilon\omega s$, i.e. what the essence of it is) from my own experience. For as soon

[1] As Paul asks, Acts ix. 5, $\tau i s\ \epsilon \hat{i},\ K \acute{v}\rho\iota\epsilon$;

as the Lord questioned me (Matthew xvi. 14), something rose in my heart, and I myself knew not what had happened to me, for I said, 'Thou art the Son of the living God.' He who on this occasion called me blessed, first told me that it was the Father who had revealed this to me. From that time I knew what revelation is: to become aware of a thing without outward instruction, without visions and dreams; and that is the case, for in the truth which God implanteth in us is contained the seed of all truth. This is either concealed from or revealed to us by the hand of God, for God acts to every man according as he sees his deserts to be. To receive communications from without by dreams and visions is not according to the nature of revelation, but is a token of divine wrath —for it is written in the Law that God being wroth with Moses and Aaron, said (Numbers xii. 6), 'If there be a prophet among you, I the Lord will make myself known unto him in a vision, and will speak unto him in a dream. My servant Moses is not so, for with him will I speak visibly (directly, $\dot{\epsilon}\nu$ $\epsilon\ddot{\iota}\delta\epsilon\iota$), as a man speaketh to a friend.' Thou seest how visions and dreams are tokens of wrath. But what is imparted to a friend goes from mouth to mouth direct, and not through figures and dreams and sights, which he uses in communicating with an enemy: so although our Jesus may also have appeared to thee, manifested himself to thee, and spoken to thee, he did so in wrath, as to an adversary, and for that reason he employed apparitions, and dreams, and other outward revelations. But can a man be instructed and ordained for the office of Teacher by means of a vision? If thou sayest this is quite possible, then I say, Why did the Teacher go about familiarly for a whole year with men not dreaming, but awake; and how can these believe that he revealed himself to thee? How can he have appeared to thee, who art not even in agreement with his doctrine? If thou really didst become an Apostle by his appearing to thee and instructing thee, if only for one hour, then repeat his sayings, declare what he said and did, love his Apostles, and dispute not with me who was with him; for thou hast striven against me as an adversary,—against me, the strong rock, the corner pillar of the Church. If thou hadst not been an adversary, thou wouldest not have so vilified and abused me and my preaching that men would not believe what I myself heard from the Lord when I was with him, as though I were worthy of condemnation, when I was really worthy of praise. Yea, verily, when thou callest me worthy of condemnation, Gal. ii. 11, thou accusest God who revealed Christ to me, thou attackest him who called me blessed for this revelation. If thou wishest in deed and truth to become a fellow-worker in the cause of truth, then learn from us as we have learnt from him, and if thou hast become a disciple of the truth, be a fellow-worker with us."

Such was the opinion prevailing on the Jewish-Christian side at the time the pseudo-Clementine Homilies were composed, with regard to the apostolic calling of Paul; and that we are not here exhibiting a mere extreme heretical opinion of a later date is testified by the Epistles of the Apostle himself, in which we find the same view. This opinion must indeed have been the general one of the hostile Jewish-Christian party. It may be that at the time of the author of these Homilies a section of the Jewish-Christians had already come to hold a less extreme view on the subject, and that Paul was allowed to be an Apostle, though still in a subordinate position to Peter, in which he had no advantage over Peter, and had to share with him the glory of being the Apostle to the Gentiles. But is not this the result of the efforts by which the Pauline party generally, and the author of the Acts of the Apostles especially, had striven to procure for Paul the acknowledgment of his apostolic dignity, if only to this limited extent? This could not have been brought about without concessions and accommodations of various kinds on the side of the Pauline party. The primacy of Peter, first of all, together with the principle on which it was based, must have been conceded to the Petrine party. The author of the Acts of the Apostles must have made up his mind to accept and embody in his narrative the criterion of the apostolic calling, which the Homilies present as the only one. On the election of the Apostle Matthias in the place of the traitor, Peter enunciates the principle, i. 21, 22, δεῖ οὖν τῶν συνελθόντων ἡμῖν ἀνδρῶν ἐν παντὶ χρόνῳ ἐν ᾧ εἰσῆλθε καὶ ἐξῆλθεν ἐφ' ἡμᾶς ὁ Κύριος Ἰησοῦς, ἀρξάμενος ἀπὸ τοῦ βαπτίσματος Ἰωάννου ἕως τῆς ἡμέρας ἧς ἀνελήφθη ἀφ' ἡμῶν, μάρτυρα τῆς ἀναστάσεως αὐτοῦ γενέσθαι σὺν ἡμῖν ἕνα τούτων. In the same sense, Peter says in his speech with regard to the conversion of Cornelius, x. 41, that they, the Apostles, are the μάρτυρες προκεχειροτονημένοι ὑπὸ τοῦ Θεοῦ, οἵτινες συνεφάγομεν καὶ συνεπίομεν αὐτῷ (the following words, μετὰ τὸ ἀναστῆναι αὐτὸν ἐκ νεκρῶν, are, as De Wette also says, obviously not to be taken with the words directly preceding, but with ἐμφανῆ γενέσθαι, 40). It cannot be denied that a certain design which betrays a special reason is evident in the express enunciation and enforcement of the principle that the witnesses of the risen Jesus could be none but those who through communion with him during his lifetime, through the constant coming and going along with the disciples, and eating and drinking with him, were specially destined by him for this purpose. This, indeed, seems to be recognised by the author of the Acts of the Apostles himself as a criterion of the apostolic calling, which might have been made use of against his Apostle. But the more he yields in a point like this to the Jewish-Christian party, the more does he expect from that side a willingness to make its Apostle do justice to his; and, provided only that the exclusive primacy were assured to the Apostle Peter, he seems to ask from the Jewish-Christians the concession that there might exist another mode of being called to the apostolic mission, namely, through apparitions and visions, especially as the Apostle Peter himself had, by special divine appointment, and in furtherance of the important aim of the conversion of the Gentiles, been the recipient of similar visitations.

CHAPTER IV.

THE FIRST MISSIONARY JOURNEY OF THE APOSTLE.—ACTS XIII. XIV.

BETWEEN the conversion of the Apostle and his actual entrance into the sphere of his apostolic work, there intervenes a period which we cannot discuss till we reach a later stage of this work, as the account of it in the Acts of the Apostles varies considerably from the Apostle's own statement. Generally speaking, however, we have to think of this as the period of his life in which he developed the powerful impression which he had received from his sudden conversion, into that unity of religious conviction which became afterwards the firm foundation of his apostolic labours. As there is nothing known of his outward actions during this interval, which he himself says (Gal. i. 18) lasted several years, it is all the more likely that the time was spent in self-contemplation, his introverted spirit growing familiar with his newly-won Christian consciousness. When we consider his whole individuality, as well as the manner of his conversion, which was so sudden and thorough a transformation of his inward man, we cannot but think that he did not pass through many various intermediate stages, but as soon as he was once settled and fixed in his own mind, became at once what we see him to have been afterwards. So soon, as he himself says (Gal. i. 16), as God had been pleased to reveal his Son in him, that he might preach his Gospel among the heathen, a new world rose upon his consciousness, and his own characteristic independence preserved him from such dependence on others as would have prevented his own individuality from having full scope. This much is certain, that though he grounded his whole apostolic work and influence entirely on the directness of his apostolic call, and as all that he was he wished to be only through Christ, who had been thus revealed to him, yet he did not neglect to institute inquiries into the history of the life of Christ. He who could speak so definitely and in such detail about matters of fact in the Gospel history as the Apostle does, 1 Cor. xi. 23, etc., xv. 8, could not have been unacquainted with the rest of its chief incidents.

The Apostle of the Gentiles first entered on his wide and successful career in Antioch, where before his coming a new metropolis of the Christian world had begun to arise, in consequence of the events already mentioned, which had so great importance in the history of the development of Christianity.[1] From thence, with Barnabas, his greatest friend, he undertook his first missionary journey, which was directed to Cyprus, and then to the countries of Asia Minor, Pamphylia, Pisidia, Lycaonia, and their cities, Perga, Antioch, Iconium, Lystra, and Derbe. The discourses of the two Apostles are said to have been accompanied by miracles, and

[1] As an indication of the important position which Antioch had assumed in the affairs of Christianity, we may take the remark in xi. 26, that the disciples were called Christians first in Antioch. This name must have been commonly current in the general public at the time when the Acts was written; this is the proper meaning of χρηματίζειν. The name Χριστιανοί occurs only in two other passages in the New Testament, Acts xxvi. 28, 1 Peter iv. 16, and in both of these passages it appears as a term used by the opponents of Christianity, as it was also used afterwards by the writers of the second century; but the opponents who gave the name must have been Gentiles, as Jews would not have so used the the sacred name of Χριστός. The Gentile origin of the name causes the author to connect it with the city of Antioch, which was the first Gentile site of Christianity. But whether it originated in Antioch is very doubtful, on account of its Latin form. The name Christiani is first mentioned by Roman writers, and as one in use among the people; it is used by Tacitus and Suetonius on the occasion of the incendiarism of Nero and the cruelties then practised against the Christians. "Nero," says Tacitus, Ann. xv. 44, "subdidit reos, et quæsitissimis pœnis affecit, quos per flagitia invisos vulgus Christianos appellabat. Auctor nominis ejus Christus." Compare Suetonius, Nero, xvi. Already, in Nero's time, the people had called the hated sect, "Christians." The author may have assigned the origin of this name to Antioch, because he thought that as a Gentile name it must have originated in the first Gentile city in which Christians existed.

to have secured a ready acceptance of the Gospel among the Gentiles, but for that very reason to have called down on them the bitter hostility of the Jews. In the whole account the apologetic tendency and the literary freedom of the author of the Acts of the Apostles are shown in a manner which throws great suspicion on its historical statements.

The miracles which the Apostle is reported to have performed in this first missionary journey in the company of Barnabas bear most undoubted tokens of the apologetic parallel with Peter. One of Peter's most celebrated apostolic actions was his victory over Simon Magus. According to the Acts of the Apostles, Peter met the sorcerer in Samaria, when the Apostle himself for the first time visited the region beyond Judea in his apostolic calling. Parallel with this is the meeting of the Apostle Paul with Elymas the sorcerer, in Cyprus, on his first missionary journey. With Paul, as with Peter, the first important act of his apostolic life in foreign lands is the conviction and punishment of the sorcerer. In both cases the apostolic insight shows itself in the instantaneous unveiling of the deep moral perversity which lay at the root of sorcery as it came into contact with Christianity. Although the sorcerer Elymas took up a different relation to Christianity from that occupied by Simon Magus, the main idea of the speech against the former is the same as in the speech of Peter, chap. viii. The speech, xiii. 10, etc., evidently refers to viii. 21, etc. The main idea in viii. 21, ἡ γὰρ καρδία σου οὐκ ἔστιν εὐθεῖα ἐνώπιον τοῦ Θεοῦ, is carried further in xiii. 8, etc., where the sorcerer is described as ζητῶν διαστρέψαι ἀπὸ τῆς πίστεως, πλήρης παντὸς δόλου καὶ πάσης ῥᾳδιουργίας, διαστρέφων τὰς ὁδοὺς Κυρίου τὰς εὐθείας. This is an example of how imitation generally supplies a want of originality by exaggeration. It seems by this that the sorcerer Elymas did not, like Simon Magus, endeavour to introduce himself into the Christian community by impure means, but set himself in direct opposition to Christianity, for which reason the speech against him contains still stronger expressions than that against Simon (especially in xiii. 10, υἱὲ διαβόλου). But the exaggerated copy is most evidently apparent in the fact, that whilst there is no punishment pronounced against Simon, and he is even commanded to pray to God for forgiveness of his sins, a miracle of punishment takes place in the case of Elymas. This punishment itself is nothing else than a figurative representation of the main idea by which the sorcerer, or rather sorcery itself, is characterised. As sorcery in contrast to the true religion is untrue, perverted, erroneous, and therefore gropes about in dim light, crouches in darkness, blind, seeing nothing, so this is symbolised in the punishment inflicted on the sorcerer, παραχρῆμα δὲ ἐπέπεσεν ἐπ᾽ αὐτὸν ἀχλὺς καὶ σκότος, καὶ περιάγων ἐζήτει χειραγωγούς, xiii. 11. How clearly the hand of the imitator has been at work here! for all these traits are only the carrying out of the οὐκ εὐθεῖα καρδία, viii. 21.

This first important apostolic act of Paul is also remarkable, because from this time the Acts of the Apostles gives him his own distinctive apostolic name, Paul, instead of Saul, the name used up to this point. Henceforth he is named not after, but before Barnabas. It cannot be doubted that this change of name here has some reference to the Roman Proconsul, Sergius Paulus, converted by the Apostle Paul, and that the explanation of Jerome, "Apostolus a primo ecclesiæ spolio, Proconsule Sergio Paulo, victoriæ suæ trophæa retulit erexitque vexillum ut Paulus ex Saulo vocaretur," is the true one—only the erection of these trophies is not to be ascribed to the Apostle himself, but merely to tradition which connected the change of name already adopted by the Apostle with an important act of his apostolic life. How could the arrival of the Apostle of the Gentiles at his full glory be better shown than by the conversion of a Roman Proconsul? The Roman form of the name hints also at the conversion of a Roman. The conversion of a Roman Proconsul was thus the great work by which the Apostle clearly proved his right to the name which he bore as the Apostle to the Gentiles. The Gentile name Paul is the proper name by which to denote the Apostle to the Gentiles. Looking in this way on the account of how the name was given, we have a parallel to the distinctively apostolic act of the Apostle Peter,

Matt. xvi. 16. As Peter then, through his declaration, steadfast as a rock, that Jesus was the Christ and the Son of God, bore witness to the true meaning of his name, and was no longer to be called Simon, but Peter, so Paul adopted, as a memorial, the name of the Roman Paul, whom he had converted, thus giving public evidence that, as an Apostle to the Gentiles, he had a right to bear that name.

Yet even the conversion of so distinguished a Roman was not a sufficient display of energy to signalise this period in the life of the Apostle; it had to be shown to be yet more important and rich in results by the victory it then won over formidable opposition, the struggle of the true divine faith with the false, magical, and demoniacal faith. For this reason, the point at which the name of Paul receives its new importance is the point when his address overwhelms the sorcerer, xiii. 9 : $Σαῦλος\ δὲ,\ ὁ\ καὶ\ Παῦλος,\ πλησθεὶς\ πνεύματος\ ἁγίου,\ καὶ\ ἀτενίσας\ εἰς\ αὐτὸν\ εἶπεν$, etc. So two different events in the life of Peter are joined in one, for it was necessary that Paul's first appearance as Apostle to the Gentiles should take place in some striking and distinctly apostolic act.

Such narratives as those of the two Sorcerers in Acts viii. and xiii. are no doubt commonly considered worthy of historical belief, because sorcerers and enchanters were frequently to be met with at that time, and received ready acceptance from men of the first standing. Of course this cannot be denied, and we see an example of the kind in Josephus (Antiq. xx. 7), where he mentions the sorcerer, Simon of Cyprus, as a man much thought of by Felix, the Roman Procurator of Judea; yet the more common certain phenomena of the age are, the more natural is it that tradition and poetry should borrow their materials from them. It is for this reason that if we wish to prove the truth of the narrative in the Acts of the Apostles, we must not appeal to Alexander of Abonoteichos, described by Lucian, whose prophecies were eagerly sought after by the most important men in Rome, and whose most zealous adherent was the Roman statesman Rutilianus.[1] It is clear that in this impostor Lucian does not intend to sketch any historical

---

[1] Neander, Gesch. der Pfl. p. 148, Bohn 107.

personage, but only a common type of character at the time. Nor does the fact that the Acts of the Apostles gives to the sorcerer the name of Bar-Jesus, and says of him that he was a Jewish false prophet, make anything for the truth of the narrative; his being a Jew would make him all the more fit to be brought forward in this manner as an adversary of the Apostle Paul. But the conversion of the Roman Proconsul has a very slight degree of probability. The Acts of the Apostles does not give us any further particulars on the subject, it does not mention baptism, but merely says that he "believed," and this was in consequence of the miracle wrought on the sorcerer, the questionableness of which we have already seen. And what are we to think of the conversion of a man in such a rank of life, where there was no weighty reason for the change, and no warrant that the impression produced would be more than merely transitory? If such minor circumstances cannot in any case be regarded as confirming the truth of the narrative, we come back to the general point of view from which such stories have to be considered, with reference to the nature of the historical record as a whole, of which they form the ingredients.

The Apostle Paul is said to have wrought a second miracle during the same missionary journey at Lystra in Lycaonia, on a man lame from his birth, xiv. 8, etc. This miracle also presents a duplicate to one wrought by Peter, and described iii. 1, 4. Here, as there, it is a χωλὸς ἐκ κοιλίας μητρὸς αὐτοῦ, iii. 2, xiv. 8. The position which the worker of the miracle takes up towards the lame man, is indicated in both places by the word ἀτενίζειν (ἀτενίσας αὐτῷ—εἶπε [Παῦλος] xiv. 9, ἀτενίσας δὲ Πέτρος εἰς αὐτὸν—εἶπε, iii. 4), and the miracle following is in both cases described by the same words, ἥλλετο καὶ περιεπάτει, xiv. 10, ἐξαλλόμενος ἔστη καὶ περιεπάτει, iii. 8. The first narrative, where the lame man is described as a beggar, presents several additional features; and the second draws attention to the πίστις τοῦ σωθῆναι of the lame man. As the two miracles are exactly the same cure, we might think the similarity of the two narratives to be very natural, if there were not visible in both cases a special design to have the miracle just such as would awaken great attention, and point out the Apostle unmistakably as a miracle-worker. This end could be best obtained by a cure wrought on a lame man who had never been seen to walk, but who now sprang at once to his feet, and walking and leaping among all the people, was a living proof of the miracle that had been wrought on him. This trait is much dwelt on at iii. 8, and in the same way at xiv. 10, the healed man mixes with the crowd, and to the same effect (ἥλλετο καὶ περιεπάτει, οἱ δὲ ὄχλοι ἰδόντες, etc.)[1] The leading

[1] Neander simply translates and refers here, as usual; he feels himself called on, however, to add a note: "No one will feel constrained to believe this (that the lame man rose and walked at the mere word of the Apostle), but those who recognise the new divine power which entered into humanity through Christ. But whoever is not entangled in mechanical views of nature, whoever recognises the might of spirit over nature, and a hidden dynamic connection between soul and body, will find nothing so incredible in the representation of divine strength working directly on the whole inner being of man, and bringing about effects of quite a different kind from those attainable by the general remedies of the ordinary powers of nature." In a historical-critical investigation of the narratives in the Acts of the Apostles, I hold it quite superfluous to go into the general dogmatic question as to whether miracles are possible, for in such an investigation it is not needed to inquire into the possibility of miracle, but only into their recognisableness, and in this idea are comprised all the questions with which criticism has to do. But when others, in evasion of the critical questions which as historians they should have investigated, give unqualified assent to every miracle which is related in any one of the New Testament writings, and think themselves obliged to call to their assistance a theory of miracles, without being able to adduce in its vindication any better argument than the accusation that those who do not embrace this view of miracle are wanting in true insight into Christianity and nature,—such persons must put up with this accusation being thrown back on themselves. The charge is made to take the place of positive grounds: which shows us how weak the latter must be. The accusation that he who does not believe a miracle in the Acts of the Apostles like the one in question, does not acknowledge the divine strength of life bestowed on man through Christ, gives a very dishonouring idea of Christianity, as it must necessarily follow that miracle belongs so essentially to Christianity, that everywhere, where Christianity is not accompanied by miracle, it does not manifest its divine life-giving power. As it is acknowledged that no miracle now takes place, at least none of the same kind as those now in question, unless we take the legends of the middle ages and of the modern missionary reports as such, and assert of this belief that those who do not share it must refuse to recognise the divine life-principle of Christianity, Christianity must long have been extinct. It is therefore only just to concede that Christianity contains divine vital powers apart from miracles which one may heartily believe in, even if one does not consider every one of the miracles

thought of the historian is, that Paul had wrought as great and astonishing a miracle as Peter had done, and that by the whole affair he also had made an impression on the Gentiles that could not possibly have been more powerful or more striking. In this thought the sequel of the narrative closely agrees with its beginning. In consequence of the miracle, Paul and Barnabas were held by the astonished people to be gods, who had come down from heaven to earth in the likeness of men. They called Paul Hermes, and Barnabas Zeus; and in this delusion preparations were

related in the New Testament as a real actual miracle, because the letter of the narrative so describes it. As for the charge of taking a mechanical view of nature, we may say that a mechanical view of nature is one which believes not in a living organism of nature, but in a purely external relation between cause and effect, and considers nature as a machine, set in motion from time to time by a force applied from without. This is, however, precisely the view of nature which lies at the root of the theory of miracles, for every miracle must be considered as an interruption of the natural connection, established by an immanent law, between cause and effect, which natural causes can do nothing to explain, and which must be produced by the impact of some external power. This is necessarily the theory of miracles, unless it be equally arbitrary with the mechanical theory of nature. It is not evident what the power of spirit over nature and the secret connection of soul and body has to do with the vindication of the theory of miracle. What Schleiermacher, in the well-known proposition in his "Glaubenslehre," has said in regard to the divine omnipotence, "that we no longer consider that the divine omnipotence shows itself greater in the interruption of the order of nature than in sustaining it in the usual course," applies with equal force to the power of spirit over nature. Spirit shows its power over nature, not in interruption and disturbance of the arrangements of nature, but, as its essence is conformity with law, through the fact that it is the immanent law of nature. In the sequel of the passage we are speaking of, however, the power of the spirit over nature and the hidden dynamic connection between soul and body seems to be called in with a view to the partial naturalising of the miracle. A miracle such as the one in question, viz., the healing of a man lame from his birth by a mere word, is supposed to become more credible, if we think of it, first, as the action of divine power on the whole inner being of the man, the healing itself being the direct result of the influence of this action, so that the healing results from the hidden but natural connection between soul and body. The miracle is thus to be explained psychologically; it happens in accordance with the dynamic connection between soul and body; the healing power works through the medium of the soul, which operates on the body according to its own laws. But how does the divine power itself affect the soul? In a natural or supernatural manner? If in a natural manner, then there is no miracle at all. And it must then be explained how the healing which resulted from it is, never-made by the priest of Zeus in Lystra for a solemn sacrifice to the supposed gods, when the two Apostles, who from ignorance of the language did not at once understand what was going on, saw how things were. They were just in time to prevent, with great difficulty, the completion of the hateful act which was already so far advanced. Even at first sight the affair has a very strange and romantic aspect, and we cannot avoid asking why, among all the miracles which the Apostle wrought, this should have had so remarkable a result? why this apotheosis should have taken place at Lystra of all places? why the people of this place should so suddenly have gone from one extreme to the other, that they chased with stones out of the city and left for dead the same Apostle to whom just before they had been willing to offer sacrifice as a god, merely on account of the insinuation of some Jews from Antioch? All that we can say on this subject is comprised in what Olshausen remarks, "The Gentiles took Paul and Barnabas for Mercury and Jupiter, as these gods were said to have once visited Philemon and Baucis, the ancient inhabitants of this very district. These occurrences are held to be

theless, represented as a miracle. If it affects the soul in a supernatural manner, the miracle remains, and it is not evident what is gained by showing that it is partly capable of a natural explanation. Where a miracle is accepted (unless we are playing with idle words), there must also be accepted an interruption and disturbance of the order of nature; but in accepting miracle, it is perfectly the same whether it is accepted at one point or another, and perfectly useless to try to conceal this interruption of the order of nature by speaking of the hidden dynamic connection between soul and body, thereby awakening suspicion that the interruption of the order of nature is felt to be a more serious matter than is allowed to appear. If we do not hesitate to heap miracle upon miracle, then we must not hesitate to confess without affectation or equivocation that we are always ready to break the thread of the order of nature on any occasion when it appears desirable to do so. Perhaps we may convince ourselves that the belief in miracles must at least be grounded on better reasons than are here used, and that it may not be so superfluous to inquire in each individual case whether the character of the miraculous narrative, I will not say obliges, but entitles, us to say that there is actually a miracle at the bottom of it. But as such things are generally treated, it can be no great task to defend any such legendary miracle with such phrases as "New divine life-power," "Mechanical view of nature," "Power of spirit over nature," "Hidden dynamic connection between soul and body," etc.

specially interesting, in so far as they show that the belief in the ancient gods still had deep root in the life of the people, for we must remember that this event took place in a small remote town where the philosophical enlightenment of the Augustan age had not yet penetrated." But if we appeal to the legend of Philemon and Baucis, what right have we to assume that it was not only the Greek and Roman poets who related that legend, and who placed its scene in Phrygia and the neighbouring districts (this locality being a favourite theatre for primitive mythical occurrences of this kind), but that the inhabitants of these places themselves entertained it as a native tradition, and still preserved the religious belief which it embodied? There is also unquestionably a very great difference between a fact such as is described here and what is spoken of by Homer, and very pathetically described by Neander as "a belief spread widely among the heathen from the most ancient times, springing from the depth of the human breast, from the undeniable feeling of the connection of the human race with God, a belief that the gods descend in human form in order to dispense benefits among men." Still less can we understand how, according to Neander's assertion, this belief was furthered by the religious ferment at that time existing. Religious ferment rather promotes doubt and unbelief, and although that age with its unbelief was still at the same time much addicted to a faith in a direct union with the higher supernatural world, still it was by no means the childlike faith of the Homeric world that was still cherished at that time, or to which men had recurred; but it was rather a belief in sorcery, uniting the natural and supernatural worlds, and supported on a belief in the power of demons. For this reason we should have thought it much more natural if the people, in their astonishment at the workers of the miracle, had taken them for sorcerers and magicians, instead of seeing in them an Homeric incarnation of the gods. This may be illustrated by an example lying near at hand. The same locality which is assigned to the tradition of the pious couple Philemon and Baucis, was also the home of the well-known soothsayer and miracle-worker, Apollonius of Tyana.[1] According to his biographer, Philostratus, he was supposed by the inhabitants of the country in which he was born to be a son of Zeus; but this is part of the exaggerations of Philostratus, and the truth is, that originally he held no higher place in the estimation of the people than that of a sorcerer. This narrative does not become more credible when it is seen to imply that the belief in the appearance of the gods of the Homeric and pre-Homeric age still flourished at the time when it was written. We are undoubtedly reminded by it of the old traditions of appearances of gods, especially of the tradition of Philemon and Baucis, but criticism, instead of taking such tradition as a confirmation of the historic truth of the fact here related, has rather to turn round and ask, whether the pretended fact itself is to be looked at as anything but a later formation on the model of the ancient mythical occurrence. The apologetic parallelism between the two Apostles gives here also the simple key to the explanation of the alleged fact, a fact which is all the more incredible that the miracle, with the reality of which it must stand or fall, is itself entirely incredible. It is stated in the narrative in the Acts of the Apostles, as a peculiar distinction of the elder Apostles, and especially of Peter, that they were honoured by the people with a positively religious veneration as superhuman beings. The Apostles collectively are thus depicted, v. 11, *sq.* The author of the Acts of the Apostles describes Peter in a very especial manner as being regarded by a Gentile in the light of a lofty superhuman being, when Cornelius, at the entrance of Peter into his house, fell with religious reverence at his feet (πεσὼν ἐπὶ τοὺς πόδας προσεκύνησεν, x. 25), and Peter taking him up, said, ἀνάστηθι, κἀγὼ αὐτὸς ἄνθρωπός εἰμι. Just in the same sense the two Apostles say to the Gentiles at Lystra, who were worshipping them as gods, ἄνδρες, τί ταῦτα ποιεῖτε; καὶ ἡμεῖς ὁμοιοπαθεῖς ἐσμεν ὑμῖν ἄνθρωποι (xiv. 15). If

---

[1] Ovid says, Metamorphoses viii. 719, after he has described the transformation of the aged couple into two trees entwining together,

"Ostendit adhuc Tyaneïus illic
Incola de gemina vicinos arbore truncos."

the author of the Acts of the Apostles wished to make his Apostle Paul participate in this reverence and glorification, resulting from a deep impression of his superhuman dignity, what better opportunity could be afforded than among the inhabitants of a country in which, according to tradition, it was believed from ancient times that the gods appeared in the likeness of men, and went about among them; until they were recognised and worshipped as gods by those who were awe-struck at the miracles they wrought.[1]

But will the speeches and sermons which the Apostle delivered during his first missionary journey give us a truer picture of his Apostolic activity? We might justly expect this to be the case. The more independently the Apostle entered on his path the more ought we to find him as he was, and no otherwise, in his words; the fresher he came to the work laid upon him, the more clearly ought he to display the Pauline spirit in his speeches. But in this point also we are deceived in our expectations. How little does the lengthy address with which the Apostle makes his first appearance in the synagogue at Antioch in Pisidia, bear a Pauline character? How striking, on the contrary, is the dependent relation in which it stands to the speeches contained in the preceding part of the Acts of the Apostles! The speech takes in its first part a purely historical character. It begins with an enumeration of the favours which God had shown from the earliest times to the Israelites, in that he chose their fathers, prospered their descendants in Egypt till they became a great people, led them out of Egypt by his miraculous power, accompanied them through the wilderness, and bestowed on them the

[1] That just the same two gods who are said to have appeared to Philemon and Baucis in the same district, viz., Hermes and Zeus (Jupiter huc specie mortali cumque parente venit Atlantiades positis caducifer alis—Ov. Met. viii. 626), here enter on the scene, seems to indicate that the author was thinking of this very tradition, or at least of one very similar. The appearance of these gods was at that time also accompanied by miracles which excited astonishment. The author of the Acts of the Apostles shows us elsewhere that he is an author of literary culture and of learning, and that he knows how to utilise his acquaintance with mythology to increase the interest of his narrative. Compare what he says, xix. 24, about the Ephesian Artemis, and, xvii., about the description of Athens.

Land of Canaan as their own possession, and especially in that he gave them David, the man after his own heart, for their king. Such a review of the favours and guidance of God, since the days of the patriarchs, is given in the speech of Stephen (vii.), only that his speech starts from a different point of view, and carries on into further details what is here given more compendiously. Both speeches dwell mostly on the time of the patriarchs, the period in which the people were growing up in Egypt, and that of King David. (Compare especially, xiii. 17, τὸν λαὸν ὕψωσεν with vii. 17, ηὔξησεν ὁ λαὸς καὶ ἐπληθύνθη ἐν Αἰγύπτῳ.) The next division of the speech, vv. 23-31, harmonises most with the two speeches of the Apostle Peter, x. 37-41 (John the Baptist is here also particularly mentioned) and iii. 13-17. Compare especially οἱ ἄρχοντες αὐτῶν, τοῦτον ἀγνοήσαντες, etc. etc., xiii. 27, and κατὰ ἄγνοιαν ἐπράξατε ὥσπερ καὶ οἱ ἄρχοντες ὑμῶν, iii. 17. Ὁ δὲ Θεὸς ἤγειρεν αὐτὸν ἐκ νεκρῶν—οἵτινες εἰσι μάρτυρες αὐτοῦ πρὸς τὸν λαὸν, xiii. 30, and ὃν ὁ Θεὸς ἤγειρεν ἐν νεκρῶν, οὗ ἡμεῖς μάρτυρες ἐσμεν, iii. 15. The succeeding section, vv. 32-37, follows Peter's speech, ii. 27, sq., where the same argument is drawn from the same passage of the Psalms, xvi. 10, which is here also the principal text appealed to. For the conclusion which follows, διὰ τούτου ὑμῖν ἄφεσις ἀμαρτιῶν καταγγέλλεται· καὶ ἀπὸ πάντων ὧν οὐκ ἠδυνήθητε ἐν τῷ νόμῳ Μωυσέως δικαιωθῆναι, ἐν τούτῳ πᾶς ὁ πιστεύων δικαιοῦται, xiii. 38, 39, no parallel can be traced with the earlier speech; but do not these concluding words give us the impression that the author may himself have felt, after he had made the Apostle Paul speak long enough in the manner of Peter, that he ought now to make him say something specially Pauline? If the most general thought in the Pauline doctrine of justification, as it is developed in the Epistles of the Apostle, were to be abstracted and stated by itself, this was the proper way to do so. But, consequently, how foreign is the relation in which this doctrine stands to the rest of the speech; how purposeless does it appear, thus introduced for the first time, and coming at the very end of the discourse! This part of the speech seems to have made a like impression on

Olshausen, for he remarks on xiii. 37, "In the light of the Christian consciousness of the later Church, it appears strange that the Apostle Paul here lays all the stress on the resurrection, and not on the death of the Lord, as does Peter also in the speeches in the first part of the Acts. Yes: Paul here connects, as it seems, the ἄφεσις ἁμαρτιῶν with the resurrection, though in his Epistles he presents the death of Christ as the source of the forgiveness of sins. Yet the Apostle's teaching becomes quite intelligible in this regard if we reflect that in the missionary speeches by which men were to be convinced for the first time that Jesus was the Messiah, he could not develop more closely the contents of the Gospel, but felt it of the most importance to lay the foundation of the belief in the Messiahship of Jesus. Now the death of Christ was an occasion of offence, and had therefore to be kept in the background; the resurrection, on the other hand, was the strongest part of the argument, and therefore it is made the principal subject of the speech." If the striking feature of this speech be explained by the occasion of offence which the death of Jesus was to the Jews, we must remember that this offence could never be avoided, that no speech of this kind could have been delivered without speaking of the death of Jesus. The object of the speaker cannot therefore have been to leave the death of Jesus in the background (in this speech it is by no means so left, xiii. 27-29), but, on the contrary, to place it in such a relation to the Gospel doctrine of salvation that it should appear as an essential element in it. This might be done in two ways: the death of Jesus could be treated in such a way as to lead up to the resurrection, or the death could be considered as the cause of the forgiveness of sins (though not, of course, apart from the resurrection). The first is the line taken in the speech of Peter; the other, the peculiar Pauline way of treatment. But if the peculiarities of this speech are said to consist in this, that there is not so much said about the death as about the resurrection, still nothing is explained, as we cannot perceive why there is nothing said about the forgiveness of sins through the death of Jesus, nor why the latter does not serve as an additional ground for the belief in the Messiahship of Jesus. The explanation amounts simply to a repetition of what is sought to be explained, namely, that the speech does not so much bear the stamp of Paul as that of Peter. It does not, however, bear this stamp only in the passage referred to by Olshausen, but also in the preceding one; and if the peculiar Pauline idea of the insufficiency of the law for justification is enunciated in xiii. 38-39, it by no means follows, as Olshausen thinks, that the authenticity of the speech is thus placed beyond question, for the way in which this is done serves, as we have already seen, only to make it more doubtful.

It results from all this that here, as elsewhere, we learn nothing more than what was the standpoint of the author, and only from that standpoint was it possible to give such a recapitulation of the earlier speeches of the Acts of the Apostles, as is here done; and to make the Apostle Paul deliver a speech so thoroughly characteristic of Peter that its Pauline conclusion seems to be provided simply to remind the reader of what he might have otherwise forgotten, namely, that it was not Peter but Paul who was speaking. The threat contained in the concluding words is evidently connected with what is afterwards related of the result of the speech, namely, that the Gospel was rejected in the most decided manner and with the greatest hatred against the Apostle, by the Jews at Antioch, xiii. 45. That which really afterwards happened is foreseen by the speaker, little as such a change in affairs could be expected after xiii. 42. A speech which indicates so clearly the joints at which its several component parts are put together, can have no great claim to Pauline originality. What then remains certain to us concerning this first missionary journey of the Apostle, during which Christian churches were founded and organised in several places? The history gives no further information about the churches in the places it names, and it will be shown in the sequel how much uncertainty rests on the principle, which the Apostle is said to have adopted at this time, to preach the Gospel to the Gentiles, only, however, after it had been offered to and refused by the Jews.

CHAPTER V.

THE TRANSACTIONS BETWEEN THE APOSTLE PAUL AND THE ELDER APOSTLES AT JERUSALEM.—ACTS XV., GALATIANS II.

WE now for the first time arrive at a point at which we can attain some positive result, as we can here compare with the story in the Acts of the Apostles, on which we can lay no great dependence, the testimony of the Apostle himself. But this result can only be attained by a criticism which works on different principles from the usual ones.

The two first chapters of the Epistle to the Galatians form a historical document of the greatest importance in our investigations into the true standpoint of the Apostle and his relations to the elder Apostles. But if these chapters are to be of any value in the interest of the truth of the history, we must first of all free ourselves from the arbitrary supposition which generally attends this inquiry, that the most complete harmony must necessarily prevail between the author of the Acts of the Apostles and the Apostle Paul, and that the one narrative can only be used in confirmation of the other. It is self-evident that as the Apostle appears as an eye-witness and an actor in his own personal affairs, his statement alone ought to be held as authentic. In this way an unfavourable light is certainly shed on the Acts of the Apostles, the narrative of which can only be regarded as intentionally deviating from historical truth in the interest of the special tendency which it represents. The results to which the foregoing inquiry has already conducted us, make it less remarkable that this should be the relation in which the Acts stand to the true history: yet even had we not learned this lesson, we should have to acknowledge that in the present instance we have simply an undeniable discrepancy between the two narratives. All attempts to reconcile the two accounts, such as are generally made by interpreters and critics, are but useless trouble; they not only result in forcing on the Apostle's words a sense they cannot bear, but also in concealing the truth of the historical facts, or at least placing them in a false light, and imputing to the Apostle what can only redound to the disadvantage of his character.

In order to make as much use as possible in the interest of historical truth of so original and trustworthy a narrative as that which the Apostle himself gives of the course of his Christian development, and his whole apostolic position in relation to the older Apostles, we must not overlook what he relates as to the events connected with his conversion. Here we meet at once with discrepancies between this account and that of the Acts of the Apostles, which show very clearly the want of historical truth in the latter. According to Acts ix. 22, the Apostle remained for some time in Damascus after he had been baptized by Ananias and received into the Christian community, and during this time he was zealously occupied in accordance with his newly-gained convictions in seeking to persuade the Jews in Damascus of the truth that Jesus was the Messiah. But as plots were laid against him by the Jews and his life endangered, he was obliged to leave Damascus, and went to Jerusalem, ix. 26. Now in the Epistle to the Galatians, i. 16, the Apostle himself says that immediately after his conversion he went not to Jerusalem but into Arabia, and from there again back to Damascus, and that only three years afterwards did he travel to Jerusalem. The cause of his leaving Damascus was undoubtedly the danger with which he was threatened by the Ethnarch of King Aretas in Damascus, and although this cause is not spoken of in the Epistle to the Galatians, it is mentioned by the Apostle himself (2 Corinthians xi. 32), and it cannot be placed in any other period than this. In this detail indeed the two accounts agree; in the rest the difference is great enough. Not only does the Acts pass over in complete silence the journey of the Apostle into Arabia, it speaks of his sojourn in Damascus as merely of some days' duration, whilst the Apostle himself says that years elapsed between his conversion and his journey to Jerusalem. Even if we put a wide construction on ἡμέρας ἱκανὰς, ix. 23, and place the journey to Arabia in this time, which we would be quite warranted to do, as Galatians i. 17 does not give us the length of the sojourn in Arabia, we must still confess that the expression ἡμέραι ἱκαναί is not a fit expression for a time extending over full three years. But should we be inclined to disregard the mere expression, we could only do so if the connection of this passage made it probable that ἡμέραι ἱκαναί had to be understood as a space of time comprising several years. This is not the case: indeed quite the contrary. What is said (ix. 26) about the return of the Apostle to Jerusalem, that he παραγενόμενος εἰς Ἱερουσαλὴμ, ἐπειρᾶτο κολλᾶσθαι τοῖς μαθηταῖς, καὶ πάντες ἐφοβοῦντο αὐτὸν, μὴ πιστεύοντες ὅτι ἐστὶ μαθητής, places us manifestly in a time which could not have been very distant from the conversion of the Apostle, a time still preserving the fresh impression of so unexpected and incredible an occurrence, and which is therefore reckoned by the author of the Acts of the Apostles not by years but by days. The Apostle endeavoured when he came to Jerusalem to ally himself with the disciples as one who belonged to them and was as one of them (we may compare on this meaning of κολλᾶσθαι, v. 13); but they were all shy of him; they would not come near their old enemy and persecutor, because they did not believe that he was a disciple. How could this have been possible, if at that time a period of more than three years had elapsed since the conversion of the Apostle? and if, during that time, he had laboured in the cause of the Gospel not merely in distant Arabia, where his sojourn perhaps did not last long, but in Damascus, which was not so far from Jerusalem, that the news of so remarkable an occurrence would not be at once transmitted from the one place to the other? The aim which the Apostle had in view in his journey to Damascus, Acts ix. 2, corroborates the supposition that there was frequent intercourse between the two cities; and Acts ix. 20 obliges us to think that during his residence in Damascus he was engaged in preaching, thus furnishing the most tangible proof of the change that had taken place in him.

In both the speeches in which the author of the Acts of the Apostles makes the Apostle himself tell the story of his conversion, his journey to Jerusalem is mentioned in direct connection with it, and without any indication of a long interval having elapsed between the two occurrences (xxii. 16, 17, xxvi. 20). It is true that in both these passages, especially the latter, the narrative is so condensed that by themselves they prove nothing, but simply serve to confirm the narrative of the earlier passage. But between this latter and the narrative in the Epistle to the Galatians there is a contradiction which cannot be got over, and which shows how impossible it is to think that the author had command of original sources when he drew up his narrative. But if this discrepancy to which we have drawn attention is not the most serious one, but merely one feature of a much deeper and more fatal contradiction, how futile is it to contend about minor points! The Apostle, in the Epistle to the Galatians, asserts in the most decided and solemn manner that he had not received his Gospel from man, but immediately through the fact that God had revealed his Son in him. Immediately after he had received from God the charge to declare the Gospel to the Gentiles, he "conferred not with flesh and blood," neither with men in general, nor especially with the Apostles who were connected with him by common national ties (this is the force of $\sigma \grave{a} \rho \xi \ \kappa a \grave{\iota} \ a \hat{\iota} \mu a$); he did not then go to Jerusalem to the elder Apostles, but into Arabia, and thence to Damascus, and only at the expiration of three years did he go to Jerusalem.

It is clear that here the Apostle does all in his power ($\grave{a} \ \delta \grave{e} \ \gamma \rho \acute{a} \phi \omega \ \acute{\upsilon} \mu \hat{\iota} \nu, \ \acute{\iota} \delta o \grave{\upsilon} \ \acute{e} \nu \acute{\omega} \pi \iota o \nu \ \tau o \hat{\upsilon} \ \Theta \epsilon o \hat{\upsilon} \ \ddot{o} \tau \iota \ o \mathring{\upsilon} \ \psi \epsilon \acute{\upsilon} \delta o \mu a \iota$, i. 20) to meet the assertion that during the time which immediately followed his conversion he stood in such a relation to the elder Apostles that his apostolic mission could be looked upon as a thing derived from their apostolic authority. He wishes to have it believed that he entered on his apostolic mission under the influence of a revelation vouchsafed to him alone, in a perfectly free and independent manner, unbiassed by any human interposition. It is with this view that he makes his statements so distinct as to the place where he spent the period immediately following his conversion; he says it was in Arabia and Damascus, not in Jerusalem, that is, not in any place where he could enter into near relations with the elder Apostles. Even when he went to Jerusalem at the expiration of three years— after a time, that is to say, in which his apostolic character, whatever it was to be, must have already declared and consolidated itself—his aim was by no means to get the elder Apostles to grant him authority to follow his calling, but only to make the acquaintance of Peter, who during their fifteen days' intercourse sufficiently showed that he had nothing to allege against Paul's apostolic call. If the Apostle had met the assembled Apostles, or even some of them, this intercourse might have lent probability to the view that he got them then to legitimise his apostolic calling. For this reason he lays peculiar stress on the circumstance that during that time he saw no apostle but Peter, for Peter could not have authorised him to assume the apostolic office without the express consent of the rest of the Apostles, although by his own behaviour towards Paul he gave the most valuable testimony that he fully recognised the apostolic mission of the latter. Every idea of the authorisation of the apostolic office of Paul by the other apostles during the period immediately succeeding, is done away with by the fact that Paul was in Syria and Cilicia, and did not come into contact with the churches in Judea at all. The chief point towards which these considerations tend is undoubtedly that declaration which is given by the Apostle in the most positive manner, that during the whole period treated of in chapter i. nothing took place between him and the other Apostles which could be taken as a sign of subordination or dependence on his part. He would not give up any of his independence, because the more dependent on the rest of the Apostles he appeared, the more might the independence of his call be called in question. But if we take into consideration that the opponents of the Apostle, as we see in his Epistles, made use of the authority of the other Apostles to his disadvantage in the churches, and represented his doctrine as opposed to that of the other Apostles, what a necessity was there not for his so insisting on the independence of his position? If he had ever acknowledged the relation of dependence on the rest of the Apostles, if he had not emphatically persisted in declaring that he was an Apostle not by means of them, but as directly as they themselves, then he must have submitted to their authority with regard to any difference in doctrine existing between himself and them; he would have had no principle to which to appeal in order to prove and to enforce that which he, in opposition to the other Apostles, asserted to be the essence of Christianity. The whole significance of his apostolic labours depended on the fact that he was a specially called Apostle, and independent of all the other Apostles. In this way only could he claim for his view of Christianity the authority which the other Apostles claimed for theirs; and it is perfectly clear how critical a point this was for Paul, and how much weight he attached to those appeals which he made with so much emphasis to the well-known facts of history as the sufficient confirmation of his right.

Now how does the statement in the Acts of the Apostles agree with this? What does the author say, when we compare his account with the direct assertion of the Apostle himself? Exactly the opposite of what the Apostle has asserted in the most decided and most solemn manner. In Acts ix. 27, the Apostle is represented as having passed some time in intimate fellowship with the Apostles at Jerusalem soon after his conversion. Should we decide to pass over the discrepancy on which we have before remarked, and assume that Acts ix. 27 speaks of the same residence of the Apostle in Jerusalem which he himself mentions, Gal. i. 17, it is nevertheless perfectly clear that the idea which the Apostle was most careful to guard against, namely, that he had received an authorisation of his apostolic office from the rest of the Apostles, is here directly suggested. It is stated, ix. 27, that Barnabas introduced him to the circle of the Apostles (for so must these words be taken in any case, ἤγαγε πρὸς τοὺς ἀποστόλους, even if one or other of the Apostles may have been absent), and laid before them an account of the occurrences on the road to Damascus as if for their decision and recognition. If this account be held as authentic, it would really make the Apostle a liar; and it is simply incredible that he should have given the assurance, ἃ δὲ γράφω ὑμῖν, ἰδοὺ ἐνώπιον τοῖ Θεοῦ ὅτι οὐ ψεύδομαι. We cannot, on the other hand, feel any surprise at the way in which the author of the Acts chooses to tell the story; the difference between him and the Apostle grows greater the more closely we consider it. What a striking contradiction lies in this, that the Acts of the Apostles represents the Apostle as preaching the Gospel at that time in Jerusalem as well as in Judea, whilst he himself, Galatians i. 22, says he was not personally known to the Christian churches in Judea, that they had only heard that their former persecutor was now preaching the faith which he formerly sought to destroy, and praised God on that account. How does this agree with the παρ-ρησιάζεσθαι ἐν τῷ ὀνόματι τοῦ Κυρίου Ἰησοῦ (ἐν Ἱερουσαλήμ), and with the assertion put into the mouth of the Apostle himself, xxvi. 20, τοῖς ἐν Δαμασκῷ πρῶτον καὶ Ἱεροσολύμοις εἰς, πᾶσάν τε τὴν χώραν τῆς Ἰουδαίας καὶ τοῖς ἔθνεσιν ἀπήγγελλον μετανοεῖν. At what period can this have taken place, if not, as the words clearly indicate, during that in which, according to the Apostle's own assurance it did not occur? for he never went afterwards with such an object to Jerusalem. If he had for a long while laboured with all boldness in proclaiming the Gospel in Jerusalem, he could not have been so unknown in the churches of Judea. The Acts of the Apostles gives a character of publicity to the residence of the Apostle in Jerusalem at that time, which, according to the description given of it by the Apostle himself, it could never have had. How can we think that in the short space of time in which he was occupied by what he tells us was his errand, namely, con-ferring with the Apostle Peter, he could have appeared in public

in such a manner as is described in the Acts? In connection with
the whole of this anomalous statement, the Acts of the Apostles
gives another cause for his departure from Jerusalem. In his zeal
for the Gospel he came into collision with the Hellenists, and
because they sought to put him to death, the brethren brought
him for safety to Cæsarea. Not mere Jews but Hellenists are
here named, apparently under the supposition that they must
have been specially enraged at him as a converted Hellenist, as
had already been the case with Stephen, Acts vi. 8, and because
afterwards the Hellenists showed themselves especially hostile to
Paul. The Apostle himself says nothing at all of this. We see
at once that in his journey to Jerusalem he did not intend to
remain long there, nor to open up there for himself a field for the
preaching of the Gospel. As he regarded himself from the very
first as destined to be an Apostle to the Gentiles, he wished to
enter on his appointed field of labour in Syria and Cilicia; but he
took Jerusalem on his way thither, in order, as was very natural,
to find what his relations with the elder Apostles were to be, now
that his mind had so far cleared and he was decided as to the
standpoint he should maintain.

Fourteen years after, whether after that journey which is spoken
of, Galatians i. 18, or after his conversion, at any rate after a
good number of years had elapsed, the Apostle again went to
Jerusalem. Even if we had not the Acts of the Apostles to refer
to, which describes his apostolic activity during this time, we
should be obliged to assume that he had carried out the purpose
with which he had left Jerusalem and gone into Gentile countries.
The Apostle was now labouring as an Apostle to the Gentiles;
he had converted many Gentiles, and founded many Christian
churches; but the greater the strides were which the Gospel
made among the Gentiles, the greater was the importance which
the Gentile Christians assumed in proportion to the Jewish Christians, the more doubtful did the Church in Jerusalem become
as to whether the Gentiles could directly participate in the
Messianic salvation without approaching it through Judaism.

The question which had led to no dispute on the occasion of the Apostle's first journey to Jerusalem, probably because the matter then lay in the far distance, was now of the most pressing practical importance. This question was, whether such a Gentile Christianity as the Pauline Christianity had now become, could be recognised and tolerated from a Jewish standpoint? It could not be denied that in Jerusalem and Judea a considerable party, if not indeed the whole, of the Jewish Christians, was against this recognition. According to Acts xv. 1, as soon as the zeal of the Apostle began to bring forth greatly increasing fruits in Gentile countries, steps began to be taken in Jerusalem in order to put hindrances in his way. It was therefore quite to be expected, from the nature of the case, that after a long interval the Apostle should resolve on a fresh journey to Jerusalem, if only in the interest of his apostolic office among the Gentiles. That this resolution to go to Jerusalem was considered by him to be inspired by an ἀποκάλυψις, a special divine command summoning him thither (Galatians ii. 2), does not in any way set aside the cause above assigned to the journey, but rather shows that this matter was then occupying his mind in a very vivid manner as a thing of pressing moment, and the reason of this must be sought in the position of affairs at that time. He accordingly resolved to journey to Jerusalem and to take counsel with the members of the Church there, and first of all, of course, with the Apostles who might be in the city, upon the principles which he followed in the promulgation of the Gospel, and in virtue of which he considered himself to be the Apostle to the Gentiles. He also resolved to lay his Gospel before them that they might express their opinion on it, and that by a public statement of his views and principles it might appear whether or not he could maintain them, although he himself was not in the slightest degree doubtful or uncertain on the point. For these reasons he made a fresh journey to Jerusalem. How this journey (Galatians ii. 1) stands related to the journeys to Jerusalem narrated in the Acts of the Apostles has been endlessly treated of in modern times, as if it were an absolute impossibility to come to a certain result on the subject. The Acts makes the Apostle, after the journey, ix. 26 (which must apparently at least be assumed to be the journey in Galatians i. 18), travel twice from Antioch to Jerusalem in company with Barnabas, xi. 30, xv. 2. The Apostle, Gal. ii. 1, seems to speak of a second journey after the first, i. 18 (although πάλιν is not so strong as δεύτερον), and here we seem shut up to the journey in Acts xi. 30. But in Acts xi. 30 not the slightest hint is given of such an aim of the journey as the Apostle himself speaks of, whilst that spoken of in xv. 2 may be said to have been taken for at least a similar purpose. If we are thus led to take the journey in Acts xv. 2 as being that referred to in Gal. ii. 1 rather than the journey in xi. 30, on the other hand, the possibility of going beyond Acts xi. 30 is cut off by the following argument : the Apostle could not, considering his argument in the passage, have passed over the journey mentioned in Acts xi. His object required that no communication with the Apostles which occurred between Gal. i. 18 and ii. 1 should be omitted, else the proof of his teaching being independent of the tuition of the rest of the Apostles, would be defective; he would have been concealing something which could be alleged against the independence he was asserting, and he would not have given a faithful account of the circumstances of his life affecting this independence. If the object of the Apostle (Gal. i. and ii.) be said to be nothing more than to show that he had learnt his doctrine from no man, not even from the Apostles, we might justly rejoin that he seeks to prove more than this—to show by an appeal to facts the independence and originality of his apostolic authority. For this reason it could not have been his intention merely to give a complete enumeration of his journeys to Jerusalem; he wished to render those events conspicuous which formed the most decided proofs of the independence of his apostolic authority. The first period of his apostolic labours was the only one with regard to which the assurance was necessary that he stood towards the elder Apostles in no such relations that his doctrine could be traced to them. If he had once taught and worked as an Apostle, independently of the other Apostles, it mattered little whether he was with them in Jerusalem at a later period or not (he might have received his doctrine from them indirectly); but the manner in which the rest of the Apostles acknowledged his principles became in this case of the greatest importance. It seems, then, clear that he does not call attention to his journey to Jerusalem (Gal. ii. 1) merely as following another journey before spoken of, but only for the sake of the particular transactions which took place in connection with it. But there still remains something behind all this which is not so easily disposed of. If we fairly consider the words, we must acknowledge (especially if we consider the force of the preposition διὰ used in Gal. ii. 1) the most probable view to be that the Apostle never went at all to Jerusalem during that interval. In Galatians i. 19 he is careful to make a certain exception; and he would not have expressed himself as he does here if he had gone to Jerusalem in the interval. The question then presents itself, whether it is of any special consequence to bring the journeys of which the Apostle here speaks so entirely into harmony with those mentioned in the Acts of the Apostles? What would be gained by taking the journey Gal. ii. 1 as identical with that in Acts xi. 30, or xv. 2? If we take it as identical with xi. 30, we have indeed this advantage, that the journey Gal. ii. 1 follows chronologically on the first, i. 18, just as the journey Acts xi. 30 follows the first, ix. 26; but this is all, and this external resemblance does not give us any real and substantial identity of the two journeys. Not only is there no further point of resemblance in regard to the cause and object of the journey, to which Acts xi. 30 assigns a completely different aim, but the question may be raised whether the journey Acts xi. 30 is not a mistake, a mere fiction, which is not so very unlikely a supposition in such a narrative as the Acts of the Apostles. If we suppose that the Apostle (Gal. ii. 1) must have been speaking of his second journey, still we do not know whether that is the one Acts xi. 30. But suppose, since we find that in regard to Acts xi. 30 everything is so uncertain and undefined, that the journey in the Galatians is not the same as this one, and that we must turn to that of Acts xv. 2. The external chronological facts and the internal relations of the affair certainly render this more probable; but what do we gain? It is alleged by those who uphold the identity of Gal. ii. 1 and Acts xi. 30, that though Gal. ii. 1 and Acts xv. 2 deal with the same question, yet the whole circumstances of the affair in Gal. ii. 1 do not so completely agree with the transactions in Acts xv. 2 that we are really justified in upholding the identity of the two journeys. And if the advantage of maintaining the authenticity of both of these journeys can only be secured by giving up Acts xi. 30, of what use is it to assume that what the Apostle says (Gal. ii. 1) regarding his journey to Jerusalem must exactly coincide with the account in Acts xv. 2, *sq.*? Reasoning from what we have hitherto observed, we have every cause to be distrustful of a statement like that of the Acts of the Apostles, which agrees so little with the Apostle's own account; and the only course possible for us is to ignore the notion of an identity which does not exist, and without further inquiring whether the discrepancies are great or small, to proceed to investigate what relation the two narratives bear to each other. If we endeavour from this point of view to get at the true historical facts by a comparison of the two statements, the following important points of difference appear, as to which no doubt can exist which side we ought to take.

We find in the Acts of the Apostles an account of a formal public meeting of such a description that its consultations and resolutions have from the earliest times been taken, not without reason, as the utterances of the first Christian Council. Not only were the Apostles and Elders of the Church at Jerusalem gathered together at it, xv. 6, but the members of the Church generally took part in the meeting, xv. 12, 22. There was a question before the assembly which was the subject of debate; speakers rose who introduced and explained their different views. The meeting was presided over by the head of the Church at Jerusalem, who we are led to suppose acted as president in virtue of that very office; he summed up the debate, suggested the course which was adopted, a formal resolution being passed, and the contents of it, together with some explanations in detail, being sent in a special letter, by men selected for the purpose, to the churches in Antioch, Syria, and Cilicia, as the mind of the Holy Spirit. Of all this the Apostle knows nothing at all; on the contrary, he says, as if to contradict such a view of the affair, $ἀνεθέμην$ $αὐτοῖς$ $τὸ$ $εὐαγγέλιον$ $ὃ$ $κηρύσσω$ $ἐν$ $τοῖς$ $ἔθνεσι,$ $κατ'$ $ἰδίαν$ $δὲ$ $τοῖς$ $δοκοῦσι.$ Neander has not left quite unnoticed the main point in this passage, which is often overlooked. He remarks, "As Paul in the Epistle to the Galatians speaks only of his private transactions ($κατ'$ $ἰδίαν$) with the three chief Apostles, this would at first sight seem to contradict completely the narrative in the Acts of the Apostles; and this contradiction would seem to indicate that the two narratives do not deal with the same facts." Neander, indeed, is also of opinion that "if we assume that before there was any public council in Jerusalem, there may have been many private consultations, the two accounts may thus be seen to supplement each other, as it is self-evident that, before the affair was spoken of in a large assembly, Paul must have come to an understanding with the Apostles with regard to the principles to be kept in view," p. 159, Bohn, 115. This is, of course, conceivable; but we should have expected to find some mention in the Epistle to the Galatians of such a large assembly. But nothing is said of it, and this is only a new proof of the arbitrary and uncritical nature of such an attempt to harmonise the two accounts. What right have we to suppose that the Apostle is speaking of committee meetings, and that he leaves quite without mention the large meeting which alone could decide the question at issue? It is quite impossible to take up this position. If we understand the words $ἀνεθέμην$ $αὐτοῖς$ $τὸ$ $εὐαγγέλιον$ as referring to the great meeting, yet it would be a thoroughly vague and inaccurate way of stating the fact, in which it would be impossible to find what, according to the Acts of the Apostles, we ought to find; and the chief difficulty would still remain, that, on this hypothesis, the principal meeting at which the Apostles must have been present, is put in the background, and these private conferences made the most important. But looking at the passage in the right light, we cannot find any such meaning in the words. They do not describe any formal meeting—they are only a vague expression followed immediately by the more definite κατ' ἰδίαν δὲ τοῖς δοκοῦσι. We must take the passage as follows: "I travelled to Jerusalem in order to lay my Gospel before the members of the churches there, and I applied (not as Neander says, to prepare the business by means of private conferences, but in order to go to the root of the matter at once, and take the shortest and directest way to a decision) to those who seemed to be the heads of the Church." For this reason the Apostles are here throughout called οἱ δοκοῦντες, because they were the highest authority in the eyes of the Church at Jerusalem (the Apostle carefully chooses an expression to suggest that they took this high position only in this relative sense, not absolutely, so that he was at full liberty to reject their authority), and therefore had to be considered in this matter as the chief personages, whose attention to any matter rendered further transactions superfluous. In this passage there is no mention of any other meetings than those with the δοκοῦντες, i.e. with James, the president of the church at Jerusalem, and the two Apostles, Peter and John. De Wette, who also finds two different conferences in Galatians ii. 2, can show no ground in the passage itself for his supposition. Had there been two different meetings, we might say that the Acts of the Apostles is silent on the private conference, in accordance with the peculiar characteristics of its manner of narration, which would lead it to deal with the affair as a public one. But as the Apostle himself could not have been silent on so important an event if the public assembly had really taken place as the Acts of the Apostles relates, it follows from his silence that the Acts of the Apostles first gave a prominence to the affair which, according to the Apostle's own report, it could never have possessed. It is only in the narrative of the Acts of the Apostles, and in the interest to which it is devoted, that these transactions take the character of a Synod, which reminds us of the formalities of later times.

But the most important point is, that the Acts of the Apostles represents the elder Apostles as agreeing with the Apostle Paul with regard to his views and principles in such a manner as we see from the Epistle to the Galatians could never have been the case. According to the Acts of the Apostles, it was merely some members of the Church of Jerusalem, who had been converted to the Christian faith from the sect of the Pharisees, who were not willing to receive Gentiles into the Christian community, except under the condition of their submitting to the Mosaic circumcision, xv. 5. But the Apostles themselves were very far from sharing in this view, and supported the proposal made by the Apostle Paul in the most obliging and appreciative manner. The Apostle Peter referred to the conversion of Cornelius, and declared that it was tempting God to lay a yoke on the necks of the disciples (not only be it observed on those of the Gentiles, but of Christians generally), which neither they nor their fathers were able to bear, because they believed that the grace of Christ was the only way of salvation. This then is the conviction expressed, that the Mosaic law was no longer binding as such on Christians, whether Jew or Gentile. The author of the Acts of the Apostles seems purposely to give precedence to the views of the Apostle Peter, as the freest and most advanced, in order to make James, the chief of the assembly and the leader of its deliberations, express a more modified view, which became the deliverance of the Court. For though James agrees essentially with the opinion of the Apostle Peter, and with a similar aim recalls the utterances of the Prophets, according to which the entrance of the Gentiles into the service of the true God was an essential part of the building again of the fallen theocracy of David, yet he expressly limited his proposal to the Gentiles who might be converted, and calls the observance of the Mosaic law a burdensome yoke only so far as they are concerned. Yet the Law is considered in the true Pauline spirit as a yoke (comp. Gal. v. 1), and if it were once recognised as too great a burden in the case of the Gentiles, no great step would be required to make it appear an unbearable yoke in its very nature. From this point of view it is considered by the Apostle Peter.[1] If we compare with this statement the narrative which the Apostle himself gives of the whole procedure, everything appears altered. The question was by no means first agitated merely by individual, Pharisaic-minded members of the Church at Jerusalem; we here see a conflict between the Pauline and the Jewish Christianity. The elder Apostles are by no means outside the conflict; they are placed at a standpoint from which they had seen and conceived nothing beyond Judaism. There is nothing clearer than that the dispute was concerned first of all with circumcision, with regard to which the Jewish Christian party

[1] As for the words γνωστὰ ἀπ' αἰῶνός ἐστι τῷ Θεῷ πάντα τὰ ἔργα αὐτοῦ, whether we take the concluding words ἐστι—αὐτοῦ for genuine or not (the explanation of the passage which they afford is in any case correct), they must be meant to give point to the argument drawn from the prophetic quotation. What Amos prophesied, James says, namely, that the worship of the true God is to be one day universal among mankind, can never really take place unless the Gentiles are freed from the Mosaic law. As the divine prophecy is infallible, it must be the will of God that the Gentile should be absolved from the law. About the sense of these words there cannot well be any doubt, but we are not quite so sure about the meaning of 21. Neander takes the passage, as do many interpreters, thus (p. 119, cf. Schneckenburger, "Über den Zweck der Apostelgesch.," p. 23): "As to believers from among the Jews, no such special injunction was needed for them: of these there was now no question; they knew what as Jews they ought to observe, for in every city where Jews dwelt, the Mosaic law was read every Sabbath in the synagogue." "These words," remarks Neander, "cannot possibly be understood as being intended to give a reason for the laws now given to the Gentiles. This assembly required no reason why they should impose so much, but only why they should impose no more, on the Gentile Christians, and these words do not in the very least supply a reason for this." But this reason does not lie so far from the sense of the words as Neander thinks, if we take them in this way; Moses, *i.e.* the Mosaic law, has already been long preached in the cities —has been read in the synagogues every Sabbath, but nevertheless there are very few who can bring themselves to accept the law. But now, as the worship of the true God without the fetters of that law is preached, many turn to it, and it is incontestable that the ceremonial law is the only hindrance to the universal spread of the true religion. This explanation is given by Giesler in his essay on Nazarites and Ebionites in Ständlin und Tzschirner's Archiv für Kirchengeschichte, vol. iv. 312. (And the author adopted it in the first edition of this work.—*Ed.*) But it is doubtless the most simple plan to understand 21 as supplying a reason for sending a letter to the Gentile Christians, and requiring such an ἀπέχεσθαι from them. Such a claim, James says, so ancient a worship as the Mosaic has a good right to make. The more generally and regularly the Mosaic law became known, the more clearly did its incontestable authority become manifest.

maintained that the Gentiles could not take part in the Messianic salvation, except on the condition that they would submit to circumcision. But circumcision included in itself the whole of Judaism—it was the hardest condition which could be laid on the Gentiles; by it they would be forced to abjure their heathenism and become Jews, and lay themselves under an obligation to observe all the requirements of Judaism. The question thus was whether the Gentiles could become Christians directly as Gentiles, or only through the mediation of Judaism, by first becoming Jews. The Apostle, in order to show the energy with which he opposed this demand, says that "even Titus had not been compelled to be circumcised," *i.e.* he was not actually obliged to be circumcised, though this compulsion was sought to be put upon him : the whole context shows that when the Apostle took him to Jerusalem, the great point was to resist the pressure that was put on him in this direction, and we cannot say with De Wette that this would imply that such a demand had been made by the Apostles, and would thus contradict both the apologetic aim of this narrative and the spirit of the transactions and resolutions in Acts xv. Gal. ii. cannot be interpreted in the light of Acts xv.; and as for the apologetic aim of the account, we cannot understand the great earnestness with which the Apostle here defends the cause of his Gospel, till we suppose that he had not to do merely with the $\pi\alpha\rho\epsilon\acute{\iota}\sigma\alpha\kappa\tau\sigma\iota$ $\psi\epsilon\upsilon\delta\acute{\alpha}\delta\epsilon\lambda\phi\sigma\iota$ but with the Apostles themselves. Why should he have gone to Jerusalem himself? why did he so especially wish to treat of the matter with the Apostles, if he had not had good grounds for supposing that the Apostles in Jerusalem were by no means ignorant of the attempts made by the $\pi\alpha\rho\epsilon\acute{\iota}\sigma\alpha\kappa\tau\sigma\iota$ $\psi\epsilon\upsilon\delta\acute{\alpha}\delta\epsilon\lambda\phi\sigma\iota$? The course of the transactions shows in what relation the Apostles stood with regard to the principles of these false brethren. They are themselves the opponents against whom the Apostle contends in refuting these principles. From his assertion that he did not submit to compulsion in regard to the circumcision of Titus, we see that the efforts at compulsion were concentrated upon this case, and the reason for this can only have been that he, an uncircumcised Gentile, was actually the companion of the Apostle. He was to be the first to be circumcised, and it seemed that this demand made in the midst of those who advocated circumcision could scarcely be withstood. But the Apostle seems to have taken Titus with him to Jerusalem, in order that a clear and definite case might be presented for the trial of the question; that the strife of principles might be viewed in its practical bearing, or that the Gentile Titus, being actually present, might give him an accurate measure of his power to withstand the Judæo-Christian demands. There is no trace in the Epistle to the Galatians of any compliance on the part of the Apostle, and that which, according to the Acts of the Apostles, was done with the most willing agreement of the elder Apostles, was, according to the assurances of the Apostle himself, the result of the most powerful opposition, the most energetic repulsion of the most decided pressure. Not for a moment even, says the Apostle, did I give place to them by the subjection required of me, in order that the truth of the Gospel, the principles of true Christianity as freed from Judaism, might be upheld and carried on in the churches founded by me.[1] The

[1] Nothing can be more absurd than the explanation given, not merely by a Tertullian, c. Marc. v. 3, but even by commentators of the most modern times, of the passage Galatians ii. 4, according to which περιετμήθη must be added to διὰ δέ—ψευδαδέλφους, and Titus therefore must have been circumcised, if not by compulsion, still out of tender regard to the false brethren. If Titus were circumcised for the sake of the false brethren, how can the Apostle say without the greatest contradiction that he "did not give place by subjection, no, not for an hour"? The affairs of the Gentile Christians could not be separated from those of the Jewish Christians; he would have surrendered his principles if Titus had been circumcised. That his resistance was one of principle is testified by the emphatic οὐδὲ, ii. 5. How can such passages as these be misunderstood? and how can the historical inquiry into Primitive Christianity be founded on such misapprehensions? The broken language employed by the Apostle, verse 4, is certainly hard to interpret; but as far as we can gather the sense, it is this:—it was the false brethren who raised this dispute about circumcision, and obliged me to take this decisive step towards the maintenance of my Gospel principles. The παρείσακτοι ψευδάδελφοι are those τίνες κατελθόντες ἀπὸ τῆς Ἰουδαίας of whom the Acts speaks, xv. 1. They were thus called by the Apostle because they came to Antioch as members of the church at Jerusalem, Gal. ii. 4, in order to investigate on the spot the report which had reached Jerusalem, that in Antioch the Mosaic law was completely shaken off, and then that they might

Apostles themselves wrought no change in my views and principles, least of all by confronting me as the δοκοῦντες εἶναί τι, as if this gave them an authority to which I as well as others was obliged humbly to bow and submit myself. "The question is not," says the Apostle, with a well-reasoned consciousness of his evangelical freedom, "what a man's outward position or personal authority is; even if he were an Apostle and chief of the church at Jerusalem, it makes no matter to me! A merely outward condition of this kind can be of no importance to me. God looketh not at the outward and personal. The point was simply what arguments they had to bring forward against me; but as little on this ground as on the other did I find any reason for deserting the principles on which I had acted up to that time. For they brought nothing against me that I was forced to concede to them, or that I could appropriate as a correction or addition to my views. So little was this the case, that on the contrary they were obliged to acknowledge how well grounded and reasonable my views and modes of action

immediately seek to enforce their own stringent Jewish principles. What the Apostle means by the insinuating nature of these people, which he expresses in the phrases παρείσακτοι ψευδάδ. and παρεισῆλθον, refers simply to their coming as Jewish Christians into a Gentile Christian Church like that of Antioch, in order to introduce into that Church certain principles which, until then, were unknown in it, and which seemed to be in opposition to Gospel truth. The whole point of view would be altered if, as is generally done by interpreters, we take the Apostle as having considered these persons to be παρεισ. ψευδάδ. not merely in reference to the church at Antioch, but to the Christian Church generally, because they were enemies of Christian freedom. The Christian freedom which they opposed existed only in Antioch; nothing was known of it in Jerusalem, where, on the contrary, the Mosaic law was held binding on Christians in all its force. Therefore it is not to be overlooked that these were interfering and false brethren only in their relation to the church at Antioch, but not to that at Jerusalem; to this latter they belonged, and in it their zeal for the law would only be reckoned as a proof of their orthodoxy. Here first in the history a decided difference presents itself between Jewish and Gentile Christianity; what was looked upon in Antioch as a servitude in direct opposition to the idea of Christian freedom, was considered in Jerusalem as true and genuine Christianity. We also see undoubtedly that this question was first touched upon in Jerusalem at this time. Therefore it is an incorrect remark of De Wette's, that "the Jewish-Christians who came to Antioch went later on to Jerusalem itself." Whence could they have come to Antioch if not from Jerusalem? and where else could the principles which they maintained have prevailed but at Jerusalem?

were. Instead, therefore, of my Gospel of Gentile Christianity being, as was imagined on the Judæo-Christian side, quite ungrounded and untenable as compared with Jewish Christianity, its independence was fully acknowledged." But this acknowledgment was by no means made at the beginning: the Apostle obtained it by means of argument, the chief points of which he shortly indicates, Gal. ii. 7, etc. His enemies came to be convinced that the Gospel of uncircumcision was confided to him, as that of circumcision had been to Peter, or, in other words, that there existed not only a Jewish Christianity, but also a Gentile Christianity, independent of Judaism. Thus they were brought to acknowledge that the Gentiles might have a share in the Messianic salvation directly, without first becoming Jews. In the complete self-assurance of his standpoint, the Apostle places himself in opposition to Peter, so that we have before us man against man, teacher against teacher, one Gospel against another, one apostolic office against another, and the argument on which the Apostle relies in this encounter is the decided actual success to which he is able to refer. The Apostle says (ii. 8, in the words ὁ γὰρ ἐνεργήσας Πέτρῳ εἰς ἀποστολὴν τῆς περιτομῆς ἐνήργησε καὶ ἐμοὶ εἰς τὰ ἔθνη), that he could not have accomplished so great a success as an Apostle among the Gentiles, if God, to whose operation this success must be referred, had not willed to establish by it the fact that there was in reality an εὐαγγέλιον τῆς ἀκροβυστίας. The reality of the animating principle is concluded teleologically from the reality of the consequences. The meaning of the Apostle's words is,—" I am in fact the Apostle of the Gentiles, and could never have converted the Gentiles to the Gospel if I had not grounded my Gospel on the foundation of freedom from the law; who then will maintain against me that this form of the Gospel has not an equal right of existence? indeed it could not have had any existence at all if it had not been the will of God that it should exist." In this manner the Apostle appeals to the results of his efforts in the cause of Christianity as a proof that he was a true and genuine Apostle of Christ. In the same sense he speaks in the following words of the grace given him, understanding by it the divine principle lying at the root of his apostolic activity, without which supposition these consequences themselves would be quite inexplicable. The Jewish Apostles could not but acknowledge this; they could not deny the facts, and neither could they see in them the operation of an ungodly, unchristian principle. They gave to him and Barnabas the right hand of fellowship, recognised them as equally accredited companions with themselves in the work of the Gospel; and by so doing promised to put no hindrance in their way, even if they continued as hitherto to spread the Gospel among the Gentiles without imposing the law on them. So far did the agreement then extend: yet it is not to be thought that a full reconciliation took place at this time between the opposing views and principles. The κοινωνία was a separation as well as an agreement; the agreement was simply that the one party should go εἰς τὰ ἔθνη, the other εἰς τὴν περιτομὴν, i.e. the Jewish Apostles could really allege nothing against the principles on which Paul founded his evangelical labours, and were obliged so far to recognise them; but this recognition was a mere outward one; they left it to him to work further on these principles in the cause of the Gospel among the Gentiles; but they would have nothing to do with these principles for themselves. The apostolic sphere of operation therefore became divided into two parts; there was an εὐαγγέλιον τῆς περιτομῆς, and an εὐαγγέλιον τῆς ἀκροβυστίας; an ἀποστολὴ εἰς τὴν περιτομὴν, and an ἀποστολὴ εἰς τὰ ἔθνη: in one the Mosaic law had force, in the other it had none, and these two systems simply co-existed without being in any way harmonised.[1]

[1] If we place before us the facts as they really took place, how striking does the conversion of Cornelius appear, to which Peter refers at the opening of his discourse at Jerusalem (Acts xv. 7). Peter is made to say, "Men and brethren, ye know how that a good while ago God made choice among us, that the Gentiles by my mouth should hear the word of the Gospel, and believe. And God, who knoweth the hearts, bare them witness, giving them the Holy Ghost, even as he did unto us; and put no difference between us and them, purifying their hearts by faith." Who can help detecting here a consistent adherence to a plan on the part of the author, and who can fail to see the necessity of meeting the statements in the Acts in the same logical sequence in which they are made? Just as little as Peter could have spoken at Jerusalem in so Pauline a manner as the author of the Acts of the Apostles represents him to have done, could he have appealed to the

The standpoint which the elder Apostles occupied over against Paul cannot be sufficiently kept before us. It is as clear as possible that at this time at least, fourteen years after the conversion of the Apostle Paul, their circle of vision did not extend beyond Judaism. They knew nothing at all of a direct Gentile Christianity, it existed without any co-operation from their side; they had still to be brought to recognise it by Paul, and their recognition appeared entirely as a concession forced from them. They could do no otherwise, for they were not in a condition to resist the strength of circumstances and the overpowering personal influence of Paul. But they only consented not to oppose the Pauline Christianity, which with regard to their principles they should in consistency have done; they stipulated also that they should be allowed to hold themselves passive towards it, or in one word to ignore it. As the matter then stood, only two alternatives presented themselves. Either the Jewish Apostles agreed with

transactions with Cornelius. The one cannot be separated from the other. But if he cannot have appealed to what took place with Cornelius, what security have we that the conversion of Cornelius, as the Acts of the Apostles relates it, really took place? Is it not clear that the same motive from which the author makes the Apostle Peter refer to such an occurrence, may have led him to insert the story in his work as he has done? He who represents Peter as saying what he could not under the circumstances have said, raises a prejudice against himself, and gives rise to the suspicion that in other points also the statement may not be very strictly historical. Peter is made to acknowledge that liberal view of the Mosaic law and the principles dependent on it, not only when the pressure of circumstances and the imposing presence of the Apostle Paul left him but little choice. He is made to do this long before, and in a manner which showed that he did so, not under the authority of any other man, but through the immediate impulse of the divine Spirit. In this way not only is Peter's apostolic independence secured, but those more liberal views on which the Pauline preaching of the Gospel was based are invested with divine sanction even before the Apostle Paul himself entered on the sphere of his labours. How thoroughly it is the intention of the author of the Acts of the Apostles to found upon the conversion of Cornelius, and to make the chief idea of Pauline Christianity appear to have been implied in it, is shown also in the thought contained in Acts xv. 9, "And put no difference between us and them, purifying our hearts by faith." That things held to be unclean might not be unclean, is set forth in the conversion of Cornelius and the vision accompanying it, and as already, x. 43, the participation in the forgiveness of sins is made to depend upon faith in Jesus, so, xv. 9, the Pauline πίστις is set up as the true principle of the relation which enjoys God's favour.

the Apostle Paul in the principles of his εὐαγγέλιον τῆς ἀκροβυστίας, or not. If they agreed with him, they ought to have considered it a duty to work with him for the conversion of the Gentiles, else they would not be carrying out their apostolic office to the full extent to which they knew it ought to be carried out; they would have recognised theoretically as true and right what by their practical behaviour they declared objectionable. If they did not agree with him, they ought not to have yielded as much as they really did; they could not consider it as a matter of no moment, that with regard to the Gentiles the principle should be promulgated that salvation could be obtained without Judaism, without the observance of the Mosaic law. They could not recognise this principle without also recognising an obligation to work not merely for the εὐαγγέλιον τῆς περιτομῆς, but also for the εὐαγγέλιον τῆς ἀκροβυστίας. They did not do this; and as we must hold them to have been sincere in the concession made to the Apostle Paul, we must conclude that they were in an unsettled state regarding these views and opinions, which necessarily involved them in contradictions and inconsequences. They could bring nothing forward in refutation of the principles and facts which the Apostle Paul made use of against them, and still they could not free themselves from the limited standpoint of Judaism on which they had hitherto stood. As they had now made a concession by giving the right hand of fellowship, nothing else remained than to assume as indifferent a position as possible towards Pauline Christianity. We have here presented to us, with tolerable clearness, the origin of those two sections of Jewish Christianity, with which we become more nearly acquainted in the history of the succeeding period. There grew up within Jewish Christianity itself a strict and a liberal party. The stricter one wished to impose on Gentile Christians also the general principle that there was no salvation apart from Judaism, which all Jewish Christians held alike, and this to its full significance and practical issues. This class of Jewish Christians could not remain indifferent to the Pauline Christianity, it was forced to fight against it, to insist that if the Gentiles were to be called to a participation in the salvation of the Messianic kingdom—and they could not object to this; it had in fact been done—it must be on the condition that they should not be pronounced free from the observance of the law. They saw perfectly well that if the necessity of the law was not recognised in the case of the Gentile Christians, the absolute importance of Judaism was at an end. They were therefore the declared opponents of the Apostle Paul, and introduced themselves into all the churches founded by him, that after he had accomplished their conversion to the Gospel they might follow with the condition without which, they represented, it never should have taken place, and must be perfectly fruitless, namely, the imposition of the law. The more liberal party was in principle in harmony with the stricter one,—only after the concessions made by the Jewish Apostles to the Apostle Paul, they could not oppose him practically in the same manner; they renounced the carrying out of their principles, which consistency might have demanded, and limited their operations to Judaism. We cannot but think that the Jewish Apostles were at the head of this party; but the other, which, as the strict and consistent one, felt itself in no way hampered as to its practical activity by any vagueness of opinion, must from the very nature of the case have been destined to grow into greater historical importance. In the period immediately succeeding these transactions at Jerusalem, it became apparent how the two parties were related to each other, and how one had got the upper hand of the other.

In the closest connection with these party relations stands that scene between Paul and Peter at Antioch, which from the earliest times bore such evil notoriety, and is so important in helping us to determine the standpoint of the two parties. If the elder Apostles had been firmly and clearly convinced of the merely relative value of the law and its worthlessness in comparison with the grace of the Gospel, how could Peter have been guilty of such double dealing towards the Gentile Christians in Antioch? He acted thus, as we learn, from a timid regard to the Jerusalem Jewish Christians who visited Antioch. That visit is of itself enough to show that this resolution at Jerusalem cannot have been taken as the Acts of the Apostles represents it to have been, with the general consent of the whole community. How could the same Peter have so acted whom the Acts of the Apostles had shown shortly before as speaking in so decidedly Pauline a manner, and this indeed in Jerusalem itself before the whole Church, a few members of which afterwards proved sufficient to excite anxious timidity in the Apostle's mind? How striking and abrupt is here the contrast between Paul and Peter! How open and unsparing is Paul's censure! How severe and vehement his speech! How keenly he exposes the contradiction in which Peter found himself involved through his irresolution! The Acts of the Apostles indeed says nothing of all this. In a representation deviating so much from the truth as this account of the transactions at Jerusalem, there could indeed be no place for a scene like this; and hence not only does this discrepancy between the Acts of the Apostles and the Epistle to the Galatians become more apparent, but it also becomes indubitable that the silence of the Acts of the Apostles with regard to so public an occurrence is an intentional one. Where we expect to find the dispute between Peter and Paul mentioned, the Acts of the Apostles only speaks of a παροξυσμὸς between Paul and Barnabas, and even this quarrel is assigned to another cause than that spoken of Gal. ii. 13. If this work feels it necessary to make some mention of a quarrel which happened at this time, why is it silent as to the chief cause of the quarrel from which certainly even this παροξυσμὸς arose? This is for the same reason for which it did not dare to mention the name of Titus, who was mixed up with these events, in the list of the friends and companions of the Apostle.[1]

[1] Instead of the uncircumcised Titus, the circumcised Timothy is spoken of again and again. That the same Paul who in Jerusalem resisted with all his might the proposal to circumcise Titus for the sake of the Jews and Jewish Christians, should soon after himself have caused Timothy to be circumcised from regard to the same persons, Acts xvi. 3, belongs undoubtedly to the simply incredible side of the Acts of the Apostles. This act would have been the very same denial of principle on the part of Paul. That Timothy had up to this time never

We see clearly that it wishes to throw a concealing veil over all these occurrences in Jerusalem and Antioch, and by the mention of the less important quarrel between Paul and Barnabas, to divert attention from the chief fact and chief subject of the dispute. Nothing could be more abhorrent to its apologetic and conciliatory tendency than the renewal of a subject which made the Apostle Paul appear in so unfavourable a light in the eyes of the Jewish Christians,—an event of which the offensive impression (as we gather from many quarters) operated for so long a period after its occurrence, that even at that time every effort must have been made to soften it as much as possible, and to cause the whole affair to be forgotten.[1] This treatment made it possible at

been circumcised, although his mother was a Jewess, would seem to indicate that he chose to be reckoned as a Gentile, like his father. If he were now circumcised as a Gentile, and by the wish of the Apostle, in order that he might not be any longer looked on as a Gentile, as his father was, Acts xvi. 3, what could either Jews or Gentiles think on the subject, but that it was a proof that circumcision was not so indifferent a thing in the Apostle's eyes as he had once considered it? This deed performed on Timothy stands in the most evident contradiction, not only to Gal. ii. 3, but to Gal. iii. 28 and v. 11. Even if the submission to circumcision on the part of Timothy was a completely voluntary act, as Olshausen takes care to maintain, the Apostle would never have allowed it to be performed on his companion, as by so doing he would have exposed himself to the merited reproach of want of principle, and inconsequence of reasoning. Whatever be the truth as to the circumcision of Timothy, the λαβὼν περιέτεμεν αὐτὸν, Acts xvi. 3, cannot be ascribed to the Apostle.

[1] How Paul is reproached in the pseudo-Clementine Homilies, 17, 18, for having said of Peter, Gal. ii. 11, that he was κατεγνωσμένος ! Εἰ κοτεγνωσμένον με λέγεις, Θεοῦ τοῦ ἀποκαλύψαντός μοι τὸν Χριστὸν κατηγορεῖς καὶ τοῦ ἐπὶ ἀποκαλύψει μακαρίσαντός με καταφέρεις. Peter says this to the Magus Simon; but that the Apostle Paul is meant, there is no doubt. In the writing from Peter to James, which stands at the head of the Homilies, it is said, Τινὲς ἀπὸ τῶν ἐθνῶν τὸ δι' ἐμοῦ νόμιμον ἀπεδοκίμασαν κήρυγμα, τοῦ ἐχθροῦ ἀνθρώπου ἄνομόν τινα καὶ φλυαρώδη προσηκάμενοι διδασκαλίαν. Καὶ ταῦτα ἔτι μου περιόντος ἐπεχείρησάν τινες ποικίλιας τισὶν ἑρμηνείαις τοὺς ἐμοὺς λόγους μετασχηματίζειν εἰς τὴν τοῦ νόμου κατάλυσιν. ὡς καὶ ἐμοῦ οὕτω μὲν φρονοῦντος μὴ ἐκ παρρησίας δὲ κηρύσσοντος, ὅπερ ἀπείη. This also refers to Gal. ii. 12, only the affair is reversed. Instead of the assertion of Paul, that Peter really agreed with his (Paul's) view of the Mosaic law, and that it had been a mere ὑπόκρισις in Peter to deny his true opinions out of fear of the Jewish Christians, we here find Peter protesting against the idea that for want of παρρησία he conceded more than his real opinions warranted in the way of the abolition of the law; this, he says, is a wilful perversion of his words.

any rate to excuse the harsh attitude of the Apostle towards Judaism, on the score that the event took place in the first period after his conversion, in which sense Tertullian says, c. Marc. I. 20, "Paulus adhuc in gratia rudis—ferventer, ut neophytus, adversus judaismum aliquid in conversatione reprehendendum existimavit." On the same grounds the modern interpreters, in their chronological discussions on the journey of the Apostle, Gal. ii. 1, place this at an earlier date, and take it as identical with the second journey in the Acts, that at xi. 30. They also appeal to the fact that the behaviour of the Apostle towards Judaism was afterwards much milder and more yielding. But what proof have we of this, if we do not get it from the Acts of the Apostles, whose contradiction of the Epistle to the Galatians is sufficiently evident? What the Apostle says, 1 Corinthians ix. 20, "that unto the Jews he became a Jew, that he might gain the Jews," can certainly not be taken in a sense which would involve his denying essential principles. He can only have been a Jew unto the Jews in the same manner in which he was a Gentile to the Gentiles. The most certain proof that the Apostle continued in later times to hold the same views, and to regard his relation to the elder Apostles in the same light, is given by the Epistle to the Galatians itself, for how else could he express what he thought of the occurrences at Antioch in such a manner, in a letter written not so short a time afterwards? Not the least word is said in mitigation of the impression which must have been made by the long dispute between the two Apostles, which we are bound to suppose still continued at the time when the Apostle wrote.

What the Acts of the Apostles mentions as the result of the apostolic conference in Jerusalem is also completely at variance with the Apostle's own accounts. On the motion of James it was resolved, as is related in the Acts, that the Gentiles should "abstain from eating flesh offered to idols, from blood, from things strangled, and from fornication." James, as has already been remarked, stood in a certain sense between the two chief parties, between the Pharisaic-minded zealots of the law on one side, and Barnabas,

Paul, and Peter on the other. His policy was that the Gentile Christians should neither be entirely freed from all regard to the Mosaic law, nor yet be subject to that which to those among them who were willing to accept Judaism always appeared as the heaviest burden of the law, and therefore must have been the chief obstacle, the greatest hindrance to the Gospel among the Gentiles, namely, circumcision. This resolution formally entered into by the whole assembly, was sent to the churches in Antioch, Syria, and Cilicia, in the shape of a missive drawn up in the name of the Apostles, presbyters, and brethren of the Church at Jerusalem, by the hands of delegates chosen from the midst of the Church at Jerusalem, accompanied to Antioch by Paul and Barnabas. The author of the Acts of the Apostles dwells purposely on the importance of this resolution. It was passed, say the letters, with a view of quieting men's minds, and chasing away the anxious fears which were spread abroad by some who clung to circumcision and the strict observance of the Mosaic law. On this account it is expressly remarked what lively joy was awakened in Antioch by the arrival of the resolutions and the agreement as reported by the delegates between the Church at Jerusalem and that at Antioch. The author of the Acts of the Apostles refers again with evident intention to the existence of this decree. When not long afterwards Paul and Silas entered on a second missionary journey and visited the churches founded during the first, they " delivered unto them," Acts xvi. 4, "the decrees ordained by the Apostles and Elders at Jerusalem, that they might thereby rule themselves" ($\pi\alpha\rho\epsilon\delta\iota\delta ouv$ $\alpha\dot{v}\tau o\hat{\iota}s$ $\phi v\lambda\acute{a}\sigma\sigma\epsilon\iota v$ $\tau\grave{a}$ $\delta\acute{o}\gamma\mu\alpha\tau a$ $\tau\grave{a}$ $\kappa\epsilon\kappa\rho\iota\mu\acute{\epsilon}\nu a$ $\dot{v}\pi\grave{o}$ $\tau\hat{\omega}\nu$ $\dot{a}\pi.$), and the consequence of this was that the "churches were established in the faith, and increased in number daily." So beneficially did this decree operate in the cause of the Gospel, so essentially did the further spread of the Gospel among the Gentiles depend on it. As the affair is here represented, the transactions at Jerusalem and the decree made there at that time, mark a very important epoch in the early history of Christianity : the critical question, whether Christianity should be subordinate to Judaism or not, came to demand a solution, and was decided in favour of Christianity. Should we not expect that the Apostle Paul would not have left so weighty a decree wholly unmentioned in his Epistle to the Galatians, when speaking of the very same transactions, and with reference to the question what understanding had been arrived at on each side? The condition of the κοινωνία was, ἵνα ἡμεῖς μὲν εἰς τὰ ἔθνη, αὐτοὶ δὲ εἰς τὴν περιτομὴν—would not this have been an opportunity of mentioning the elements of harmony and mutual understanding which existed between the ἀποστολὴ περιτομῆς and the ἀποστολὴ εἰς τὰ ἔθνη, instead of placing them in such harsh opposition as is done by the words above quoted? But we find in the Apostle's writings not the slightest indication that any such important decree had been made at that time, but rather the most decided assurances to the contrary. The Apostle says expressly, ii. 10, μόνον τῶν πτωχῶν ἵνα μνημονεύωμεν. The only condition which was attached to the independence of the Apostle in the sphere of his apostolic labours was then the μνημονεύειν τῶν πτωχῶν, which it is impossible to understand otherwise than as a conciliatory promise which the Apostle gave from love of peace, that he would engage to support the poor church at Jerusalem by contributions which he would collect in the churches of the Gentile Christians; and this, says the Apostle, he was "also forward to do," as we indeed find he was from his Epistles. But does not this μόνον exclude all other stipulations? And how comes the Apostle to assert this promise of contributing to the poor, which after all was quite beside the main object of these deliberations, to have been the only condition that was made, when far more important conditions were made which bore directly upon the great matter under discussion, namely, the obligation of the Mosaic law? Let it not be said that the κοινωνία spoken of here was merely one concluded between Paul and Barnabas on one side, and James, Peter, and John on the other, and that among all these, according to the Acts of the Apostles, no difference existed, so that there was no reason here for mentioning those other conditions which the Apostle must yet be held as implying: it has been already shown that one of the chief differences in the two accounts is that the parties who are described as engaged in the dispute are not the same. There can be no longer any idea of a reconciliation between the two accounts, but the difference already shown rather grows wider. We find a private conference instead of a public assembly, and a dispute between the Apostles themselves, instead of between the Apostles and the Pharisaic-minded members of the Church at Jerusalem; and now we cannot find the terms to the decree which, according to the Acts of the Apostles, was arrived at, and this for the natural reason that according to the Epistle to the Galatians such a decree never existed at all. That it is not accidentally omitted, with all that belongs to it, is incontestably shown in the Epistle to the Galatians, as also in the rest of the Apostle's Epistles. In the Epistle to the Galatians the Apostle contends with the Judaising opponents, who were desirous of imposing circumcision on the Galatian Church as a necessary condition of salvation, Gal. v. 1. In order to do this the Apostle explains his entire relation to the $\dot{a}\pi o\sigma\tau o\lambda\dot{\eta}$ $\tau\hat{\eta}s$ $\pi\epsilon\rho\iota\tau o\mu\hat{\eta}s$. What would forward this more than an appeal to the decree? How could these opponents be better refuted than by a decree made in Jerusalem itself, through which circumcision had been declared to be a burden as unbearable as it was unnecessary? We may even go so far as to say that if he referred to this transaction at all, it was incumbent on the Apostle not to leave such a decree entirely unnoticed in a case on which it so especially bore. He could not be silent on it without prejudicing the truth of his narrative as well as his case against his opponents, as his statement would then be chargeable with keeping back the very gist of the whole history. What influence then can such a decree, which must have been of so great importance for the Gentile Christians, ever have had, if no use at all was made of it in a case like this, in which it was so eminently fitted to maintain the ground already won? Just the same reasoning may be applied to the other provisions of this pretended decree.

The Apostle is silent in a perfectly inexplicable manner on

another point, where we might expect not only a mention, but an express application of the decree. It is known how often in his Epistles he speaks from various reasons of eating flesh offered to idols. The matter in itself is neither right nor wrong to him, but he insists on the obligation of abstaining out of regard to the weaker Christian brethren. So the Apostle declares especially in 1 Cor. viii. concerning the εἰδωλόθυτα, about which we can perceive he has been questioned by that part of the Corinthian Church to which his Epistle is specially addressed. This inquiry would not have been put, if, as the Acts of the Apostles implies, these decrees had been meant to be deposited in every church of Gentile Christians, and if their observance was to be the condition of the Christian communion existing between the Gentile and Jewish Christians. But the Apostle himself, although he might be indifferent to the question as to the eating of meat offered to idols on its own merits, and for his own person, could not have declared his indifference under such circumstances as these, because the observance of a positive command given for such a purpose could never have been a matter of indifference. It cannot be doubted that the Acts of the Apostles intends to convey the idea that all these commands were to be observed for the future in all the Gentile Christian churches. According to xv. 20 (compared with ver. 22 and with ver. 28, 29), ἐπιστεῖλαι αὐτοῖς (ἔθνεσι) τοῦ ἀπέχεσθαι ἀπὸ τῶν ἀλισγ., it was resolved that it was indispensable that these conditions should be submitted to. Neither can we say that they were made merely in reference to the churches in Antioch, Syria, and Cilicia, because they were troubled at the time by these Judaising zealots, for the express remark of the author, xvi. 4, that they were delivered for observance to the churches in Derbe and Lystra by Paul himself on his arrival at those places, evidently implies that the same course was to be followed in all the new churches. It was on the same journey, moreover, that Paul arrived at Corinth and founded the church there. Neander also finds it worthy of remark (p. 260), that in regard to the disputes in the Christian church at Corinth, about the eating of meat offered to idols, the Apostle did not appeal to the decree of the apostolic assembly at Jerusalem in order to establish the rules for the Gentile Christians with regard to this sacrificial meat. But with reference to this subject, as well as to the question of why he did not appeal to the authority of those decrees in dealing with the Jewish Christians who wished to enforce circumcision on the Gentiles, Neander explains, that it is characteristic of Paul that he does not appeal to a positive outward command, to a $\nu\acute{o}\mu o\varsigma$, but to the inner law in the conscience of the believer, to what the spirit of the Gospel itself demanded. Neander must himself have felt how unsatisfactory this explanation is, for he remarks further, "It seems, although the observance of this decree was firmly established by the Apostles in Palestine, that beyond Palestine it had but very little authority. As this decree depended on a mutual agreement, it must follow that as one of the parties, the Jewish Christians, did not fulfil the conditions, since they refused to acknowledge the uncircumcised as brethren, the agreement ceased to have any binding force for the Gentile Christians, who, through the observance of this decree, would have been brought into nearer communion with the Jewish Christians." Neander here grants so much, that from what he concedes we have simply to draw the obvious conclusion. How did it happen that these decrees were of so little weight out of Palestine, the district for which alone they were designed, that the Jewish Christians did not fulfil the conditions, and indeed never had fulfilled them from the beginning? For if those $\tau\iota\nu\grave{e}\varsigma$ $\dot{a}\pi\grave{o}$ $'I\alpha\kappa\acute{\omega}\beta o\nu$ could appear in such open and decided opposition to the decrees so soon after the council at Jerusalem, and that too at Antioch, in the very church for which the decrees were ordained, we can only conclude how little weight they had ever had at all. And if they depended on a mutual agreement, how comes it that there was never any remonstrance raised by the Gentile Christians, the party injured by the violation? If we conclude it to have been in favour of the Gentile Christians that the obligation to observe these decrees was removed, we cannot see what interest could ever have been served by concluding such an agreement.

The original state of the case was that each side looked at the law as it liked. But when the Jewish Christians wished to enforce circumcision on the Gentile Christians, this mediating agreement must have been concluded for the greater tranquillity of the Gentile Christians, who now saw themselves freed, with the consent of the Jewish Christians, from the observance of this burdensome part of the law. If, however, the Jewish Christians did not hold to their agreement, if they insisted afresh on circumcision, the tranquillity which the agreement had bestowed on the Gentile Christians would be disturbed, and they would find themselves plunged again into a restless state of uncertainty as to whether they could be saved without circumcision. But if now, so shortly after the agreement had been made, they found it possible to disregard it altogether, it may be fairly argued that they might have been tranquillised before without any such agreement at all, and we cannot avoid coming to the conclusion that laws which not only were never kept, but whose existence was not called for by any special need, can never have been made at all. It is true that Neander appeals to Acts xxi. 25 as a proof that the Apostles always held fast to the observance of these decrees in Palestine, but this passage only bears testimony to the interest which the author of the Acts of the Apostles had in calling to remembrance the decrees mentioned by him in a former place. There is no proof outside of the Acts of the observance of these decrees, and only such proof, if it were forthcoming, would be worthy of credit. It is not by any means likely that the Apostles even held fast to the authority of these decrees in Palestine. For why should they have done so? Only to compel the Jewish Christians to recognise the decrees in their relations with Gentile Christians. But if so little resulted from this exercise of their influence as the history shows, how powerless must the authority of the Apostles have been with the Jewish Christians!—is it not more likely that the recognition of these decrees was not enforced, or that the decrees never existed at all!

However small the probability that these decrees were observed, or even that they existed at that time, they certainly existed at a later period. Even Neander remarks, "It was later that these decrees received a more binding authority through the predominance of another tendency in the Church." Those latter conditions show us from what point of view we have to consider the agreement which the Acts refers to the earlier period; but one thing is certain, that history does not trace the validity which these arrangements subsequently took to their having had the force of law in the early Church. From the earliest date the Gentile and Jewish Christians had stood in opposition to each other with regard to circumcision; whilst the latter firmly adhered to it, the former in no way recognised any obligation to adopt it, but considered baptism to be its outward and perfectly sufficient substitute. The situation of affairs at that time is precisely indicated by what the Apostle Paul says in opposition to those zealots for the law who, as members of the Church of Palestine, or at least under its influence, maintained the necessity of circumcision in the churches founded by the Apostle out of Palestine. Galatians v. 2, compared with iii. 27 : Ἴδε ἐγὼ Παῦλος λέγω ὑμῖν, ὅτι ἐὰν περιτέμνησθε, Χριστὸς ὑμᾶς οὐδὲν ὠφελήσει· ὅσοι γὰρ εἰς Χριστὸν ἐβαπτίσθητε, Χριστὸν ἐνεδύσασθε, οὐκ ἔνι Ἰουδαῖος οὐδὲ Ἕλλην. The next step that was taken was the leaving off of circumcision by the Jewish Christians, not indeed in Palestine, where the Ebionites and Nazarenes still continued strong adherents to the Mosaic law, but amongst the foreign Jewish Christians, the Hellenists, who thus show in this point how important an element they were in the most ancient history of the Christian Church, as a reconciling medium between Jews and Gentiles, thus preparing the path which Christianity itself was to follow. How this took place is not distinctly evident, as there is a lack of information; still some hints are afforded which are worthy of consideration. It is striking to find with what contempt circumcision is treated in the Epistle of Barnabas, which if we do not take it as having been written by the Barnabas known to us, still must be considered to be a Hellenistic work, from its having the name Barnabas attached to it. "Now first," says the author, chap.

ix., in a series of allegorical interpretations by which he endeavours to elucidate the meaning of the Old Testament, " are our ears circumcised for the right understanding of the divine words. The circumcision on which they placed their trust is now recognised as null and void, for God intended no carnal circumcision, they fell into error, being deceived by an evil angel." Here we have circumcision as it was observed by the Jews as a law of Moses, even ascribed to demoniacal influence. In the Epistles of Ignatius there is a difference made in the same way between an outer and an inner circumcision, and a true and false Judaism.[1] Another remarkable sign of the change in the views and customs of the Hellenists with regard to circumcision is given us by the Clementine Homilies. There is no other memorial which so clearly testifies as does this document to the influence which Judaism extended over Christianity down to the second half of the second century. Although Judaism is so very predominant in it, there is not the least question of circumcision, but so much the more the importance of baptism and the new birth is held up as a means for the renunciation of heathenism (the $\dot{a}\phi\epsilon\lambda\lambda\eta\nu\iota\sigma\theta\hat{\eta}\nu\alpha\iota$, Hom. xiii. 9), and the command of James to the elders of the Church at Jerusalem not to yield up the discourses of Peter sent to him to any one but a circumcised believer, is the only trace of a reference to the ancient value attached to circumcision. Without doubt this rejection of circumcision had its ground in the conviction that the Gentiles could never be won over by any other means. How eager the Hellenistic Jewish Christians were for the supplanting of Paganism and the spread of the only true religion, is seen also in these Homilies by their making their Apostle Peter entirely an Apostle to the Gentiles. The Acts of the Apostles also takes up this point of view, when it makes the increase that the Christian Church received from the Gentiles entirely owing to the change. But the more that the Jew yielded to

---

[1] Epistle to the Philadelphians, c. 6. He who proclaims the one God of the Law and the Prophets, and denies that Christ is the Son of God, is a liar, καὶ ἔστιν ὁ τοιοῦτος τῆς κάτω περιτομῆς ψευδοιουδαῖος.

the Gentile with regard to circumcision, with the greater justice could the observance and consideration of the Mosaic law, wherever possible, be urged on the Gentile. The very points which are mentioned in the Acts as the conditions of release from the obligation of circumcision, we find, as far as we can learn, to be the standing rules of Christian conduct in the apostolic time. When the Apostle Paul wrote his first Epistle to the Corinthians there was still a doubt in regard to εἰδωλόθυτα. Yet even the Apostle advises their rejection, not only on account of the regard which ought to be paid to weaker Christians, but also because the enjoyment of them would be μετέχειν τραπέζης δαιμονίων, 1 Corinthians x. 21. This became afterwards the prevailing view. In this sense the Clementine Homilies, vii. 4, enjoin the ἀπέχεσθαι τραπέζης δαιμονίων, and it was especially urged against the Gnostics, as they were generally looked upon as partly heathens, that they declared εἰδωλόθυτα ἐσθίειν to be a thing indifferent and not defiling. In the period in which the Church first emerged as a whole out of heterogeneous elements, it held fast to the ἀπέχεσθαι τοῦ πνικτοῦ καὶ τοῦ αἵματος (from the flesh of beasts which were killed by strangling, which were strangled in their blood, and from blood generally[1]). All this is connected with the views which prevailed in the first Christian Churches about heathenism, founded on the Jewish representations of demons as being the gods of the heathen world, and indeed the originators of heathenism generally.[2] The most remarkable in the series of the apostolic ordinances is, however, the

---

[1] In the Epistle of the Gallic Churches of Paris and Vienna, in Eusebius, H.E. v. 1, it is said, in reference to the well-known reproach made against the Christians, πῶς ἄν παιδία φάγοιεν οἱ τοιοῦτοι, οἷς μηδὲ ἀλόγων ζώων αἷμα φαγεῖν ἐξόν.

[2] This connection is alluded to in Origen contra Celsum, viii. 30, τὸ μὲν γὰρ εἰδωλόθυτον θύεται δαιμονίοις καὶ οὐ χρὴ τὸν τοῦ Θεοῦ ἄνθρωπον κοινωνὸν τραπέζης δαιμονίων γίνεσθαι, τὰ δὲ πνικτὰ, τοῦ αἵματος μὴ ἐκκριθέντος ὅπερ φασὶν εἶναι τροφὴν δαιμόνων, τρεφομένων ταῖς ἀπ' αὐτοῦ ἀναθυμιάσεσιν ἀπαγορεύει ἁ λόγος ἵνα μὴ τραφῶμεν τροφῇ δαιμόνων, τάχα τινων τοιούτων πνευμάτων συντραφησομένων ἡμῖν ἐὰν μεταλαμβάνωμεν τῶν πνικτῶν· ἐκ δὲ τῶν εἰρημένων περὶ τῶν πνικτῶν σαφὲς εἶναι δύναται τὸ περὶ τῆς ἀποχῆς τοῦ αἵματος.

ἀπέχεσθαι τῆς πορνείας. Interpreters rightly find it very striking that, as Neander expresses it (p. 166, Bohn, 120), along with the disciplinary ordinances, which were appointed for a certain time and certain conditions, we should find the prohibition of uncleanness— a law for all times and dealing with matters of objective morality. Neander, however, is of opinion that "the connection in which this prohibition stands, gives the best explanation of the cause and relations of the mention of this particular: πορνεία is here only mentioned in the same reference as the foregoing points, on account of the close connection in which they seemed to the Jews to stand with the worship of idols; men were already accustomed from the writings of the Old Testament to associate idolatry with immorality; excesses of this sort are really bound up with many branches of idolatry, and in general a strict idea of chastity is very far removed from the standpoint of natural religions. There is no question here of any special moral precept of Christianity; had there been, the command would not have been given as a positive one in this isolated way, but would have been deduced from the whole connection of the Christian Faith and Life, as is done in the Epistles of the Apostle. All that comes before us here is the ancient Jewish hostility to anything which might appear to have any connection with idolatry, and this hostility passed over into the new Christian Churches." This explanation I cannot consider satisfactory. For how could a special prohibition against participation in the immorality which was bound up with the Gentile idolatry have seemed necessary to Christians if they did not need the inculcation of the prohibition in general? Only he who held immorality in general to be a thing indifferent, could hold it as a thing allowed when in connection with Gentile idolatry. But a prohibition against the immorality of the Gentile idolatry must have been the less necessary for Christians, as, with the prohibition of participation in the εἰδωλόθυτα, there fell away every occasion for the immorality bound up with it. If we take the πορνεία in the sense Neander does, we do not perceive why the ἀπέχεσθαι πορνείας should find a special place close to the ἀπέχεσθαι εἰδωλοθύτων, as it is included in it, and such a useless addition is not to be expected in formal definitions of this kind; we therefore see ourselves again reduced to the necessity of taking the πορνεία in a general sense, and the ἀπέχεσθαι πορνείας as a general moral precept; and this, as has been acknowledged, is highly unlikely. What Olshausen gives as the only true explanation is equally untenable, namely, "that we must bear in mind the much greater freedom in sexual relations among the Greeks and Romans, which was an abomination to the more serious Jews, and seemed to them even as refined fornication. By means of an expression which comprised not merely gross but refined errors of this kind, greater care and circumspection in their intercourse with the female sex were recommended to the Gentile Christians, in order that no cause of offence might be given to the Jewish Christians." But who can believe that all this is expressed in the word πορνεία? How vague and arbitrary would be the whole idea of this πορνεία, while such legal definitions ought to have a precise meaning and be applied to a precise object. As the rest of the ordinances related to special and definite circumstances, this must be assumed to be the case with the πορνεία as well. In this view the explanation of Gieseler (in the Abhandlung über die Naz. u. Eb. in Staüdl. u. Tzsch. Arch. f. K. G. p. 312) deserves preference over every other, and we cannot but wonder how Neander and Olshausen have left it entirely disregarded. Von Gieseler, following some older scholars, supposes that πορνεία here may mean incest, which deserved special mention, as among Gentile nations unions among blood relations were held admissible. This is the meaning the word πορνεία has at 1 Corinthians v. 1. When further we remember that in that period of the Christian Church, to which the most ancient post-apostolic memorials which have reached us belong, the contracting of second marriages was looked on as fornication and adultery, and was so designated by the oldest Christian authors, we can the less have any doubt that the word πορνεία here indicates marriage relations, which, according to the view prevailing at that time among Christians, were considered unlawful, and held to be tokens of an unchaste and carnal mind. This explanation suits very well with the context. For as partaking in the Gentile sacrifices and the eating of things strangled, and of blood, were looked on as a Gentile pollution, because through them men were brought into communion with demons, the gods of the Gentiles, so also did illicit marriage unions, and the contracting of second marriages, appear along with them to lead away from the true God, and to be in conflict with Monotheism. He who contracted so unchaste a union gave evidence by such an act that he, as the Clementine Homilies express it, had no monarchical soul, *i.e.* no soul capable of directing itself towards the highest unity. We must here remember the Old Testament representation of the chosen people, that they owed, as it were, marriage fidelity to God, and the New Testament idea of the union of Christ with the Church as his Bride, in the light of which, as Christian marriage is spoken of in the Epistle to the Ephesians, vi. 22, each union between man and wife becomes a symbol of that holy indissoluble relation. Hence it was required of the overseer of a Christian Church, in fact this is mentioned first among the qualifications of the ἐπίσκοπος, 1 Tim. iii. 2, that he should be μιᾶς γυναικὸς ἀνήρ. From this point of view, everything about married life which was not in harmony with the Christian standard could be designated as an idolatrous, Gentile πορνεία.

All these directions which are alleged to have been given at that early period in Jerusalem, bear unmistakably the impress of a time in which the relations of the Gentile Christians were thus defined, not indeed towards the Jewish Christians of Palestine, who would abate nothing of the strictness of the Mosaic law, and could not sanction such relaxations of its demands, but towards the more liberal-minded foreign Hellenists. Whilst there is not the least hint in the Pauline Epistles as to the agreement which, according to the Acts of the Apostles, was so formally arranged in Jerusalem (for in 1 Corinthians v. 1, if the matter dealt with there is connected with our subject, we find no such hint), in all the post-apostolic writers, on the other hand, all these points are represented as the existing fixed rules of the Christian life. How likely is it therefore that the author of the Acts of the Apostles himself belonged to this later time, that in this apostolic council at Jerusalem he carries back to the earlier apostolic period, and refers to a decree of the Apostles themselves, that which had now become the settled practice of the Christian life in the relations which Jewish and Gentile Christians held to each other? The pseudo-Clementine Homilies place us in just the same sphere of practical questions. When the Apostle Peter, in his character of Apostle to the Gentiles, organised the Gentile Churches founded by him in Tyre and Sidon, he gave them the following precepts, Hom. vii. 4, 8 :—Ἔστι δὲ τὰ ἀρέσκοντα τῷ Θεῷ—τραπέζης δαιμόνων ἀπέχεσθαι, νεκρᾶς μὴ γεύεσθαι σαρκὸς, μὴ ψαύειν αἵματος, ἐκ παντὸς ἀπολύεσθαι (or according to Cotelier's emendation, ἀπολούεσθαι), λύματος, τά δὲ λοιπὰ ἑνὶ λόγῳ, ὅσα Θεὸν σέβοντες ἤκουσαν Ἰουδαῖοι, καὶ ὑμεῖς ἀκούσατε ἅπαντες, ἐν πολλοῖς σώμασιν μίαν γνώμην ἀναλαβόντες. The Apostle left this precept behind him at Tyre, and when he went from thence to Sidon, he there gave a similar one : Ἡ δὲ ὑπ' αὐτοῦ (God) ὁρισθεῖσα θρησκεία ἐστιν· τὸ μόνον αὐτὸν σέβειν, καὶ τῷ τῆς ἀληθείας μόνῳ πιστεύειν προφήτῃ, καὶ εἰς ἄφεσιν ἁμαρτιῶν βαπτισθῆναι, καὶ οὕτω διὰ ἁγνοτάτης βαφῆς ἀναγεννηθῆναι Θεῷ διὰ τοῦ σώζοντος ὕδατος· τραπέζης δαιμόνων μὴ μεταλαμβάνειν, λέγω δὲ εἰδωλοθύτων, νεκρῶν, πνικτῶν θηριαλώτων, αἵματος, μὴ ἀκαθάρτως βιοῦν, ἀπὸ κοίτης γυναικὸς λούεσθαι, αὐτὰς μὲν καὶ ἄφεδρον φυλάττειν, πάντας δὲ σωφρονεῖν, εὐποιεῖν, μὴ ἀδικεῖν, etc. If we deduct from this what belongs especially to the Clementine view of Christianity, and if we take into consideration that baptism is here put in the place of the circumcision which had been abandoned, we have the four points presented to us in the Acts of the Apostles. For there can be no doubt that the μὴ ἀκαθάρτως βιοῦν, or the παντὸς ἀπολούεσθαι λύματος, corresponds to the ἀπέχεσθαι πορνείας, and includes in itself what is apparently to be understood by the πορνεία. No express prohibition of second marriages is to be found in the Clementine Homilies; but as πορνεία, or μοιχεία, is considered next to idolatry to be the greatest sin, and as the greatest stress is laid on the fact that everything in human life has a strict monarchical form and direction, we are entitled to assume that second marriages would scarcely need an express prohibition, because it would be thought self-evident that they were included under πορνεία, or μοιχεία.

In the passage first quoted it is clearly stated that the Jewish Christians considered the observance of the decrees in question as the essential condition by which alone they could unite in one society with the Gentile Christians. It was in this way of accommodation that the two heterogeneous elements first approached to a unity. But how far both sides still stand apart in that time in which we first clearly perceive that the difference exists!

CHAPTER VI.

THE SECOND MISSIONARY JOURNEY OF THE APOSTLE.—ACTS XVI.

It was one of the grandest moments in the life of the Apostle when, at this conference of Jerusalem, he defended the great cause of his Gospel and apostolic mission against the elder Apostles and the whole Church of Jerusalem, penetrated as he was with that deep consciousness of its truth, which is expressed in his Epistles. What had been at the time of his first journey to Jerusalem nothing more than an idea, was now become a positive reality, evident to all eyes. The Apostle gave utterance to a real, undeniable truth when he insisted that the cause of his Gospel was the cause of God. If this, on the part of the Apostle, was the most powerful evidence of its truth, on the other hand the great practical importance which the matter had assumed now made the opposition of its enemies more decided and energetic. As even Barnabas soon after the transactions at Jerusalem showed signs of failing courage, it was in fact the Apostle alone who had to wage the whole battle with the power of that Judaism which was still so closely interwoven with Christianity. After he had spent some time in Antioch, he undertook a new missionary journey, in the strength of the loftier self-consciousness which had been evolved by the events at Jerusalem and Antioch, and in the conviction which these had afresh confirmed, that the cause of his Gospel could never be crushed by merely human power, but that it contained in itself the whole future of the history of the development of Christianity. In this journey he not only revisited the countries in Asia Minor where he had before been, but took the more important step of carrying over the doctrine of the Gospel from Troas to Macedonia, and from thence spreading it further in the countries of Europe. It is quite in the spirit of classic antiquity (a spirit which is by no means strange to the author of the Acts of the Apostles) that so important an era, including so much of the future history of the cause of the Gospel, should be inaugurated by a vision of the night. In this vision a man from Macedonia appeared to the Apostle with a prayer that he would go over to Macedonia and help them (xvi. 9). As the author of the Acts of the Apostles loves to indicate, by various hints and signs, the inherent desire of the Gentile world for the salvation of the Gospel, so here, by this man of Macedonia, he symbolises the desire for salvation with which not only the people of Macedonia, but those of Europe generally, invoked the Apostle as the ambassador of the newly revealed salvation. We could scarcely complain of the author of the Acts of the Apostles indulging his literary tastes by such an embellishment of the history, if he did not introduce us immediately afterwards to a series of narratives in which we see the further events in the Apostle's life only by the magic light of miracle, and find a thick veil hiding from us the historical truth of them.

The occurrences which are said to have taken place during the Apostle's visit to Philippi, in Macedonia, belong to the most miraculous order of those which the Acts of the Apostles relates of him. Interpreters and critics indeed (not excepting Neander) pass over these suspicious passages with their accustomed facility, but it cannot be denied that there is very much in them to which we may make valid objection. The chief difficulty is in the narrative beginning chap. xvi. 20, but the one preceding it where the cause of what follows is related, is strange enough. Whilst Paul and Silas, it is stated, were spending some days in Philippi, they were followed, whenever they took their way to the Jewish Proseuche outside the city, by a damsel possessed with a spirit of divination, with the loud cry, "These men are the servants of the

Most High God, who show us the way of salvation." After the damsel had done this for many days, Paul at last turned angrily to her, and in the name of Jesus Christ commanded the spirit to come out of her. But as those persons whose slave she was lost the important gains which they were wont to obtain from her prophetic powers, they excited a popular tumult against Paul and Silas, on the charge of political intrigue, and accomplished the arrest of the Apostle and his companion. The attempts of modern interpreters to explain this matter more clearly only place its improbability in a stronger light. The πνεῦμα πύθωνος is a very peculiar phenomenon. The latest interpreters reject the theory of ventriloquism, which the expression πνεῦμα πύθωνος would imply, and which some earlier scholars held to be indicated here; but Olshausen and Neander are positive that they find the solution they desire in the phenomena of somnambulism. "In the recognition of the spiritual characteristics of the Apostle by the damsel," says Olshausen, "there may be perceived the same *clairvoyance*, of which such numerous examples are found in those Gospel histories which relate the healing of those possessed by demons." In the same sense Neander (page 176) speaks of the "phenomena of the somnambulistic state taking the form of convulsions,[1] in which the impression of what the damsel had before heard of Paul reacted on, and became mingled with, her own heathen ideas." According to this explanation there is suggested to us, to say the least, a doubt as to how the Apostle could have treated the damsel as one possessed by an evil spirit, if she had merely been in a state of somnambulism. Olshausen gives no explanation of this, but Neander says (page 177), "There is no ground for assuming that an error could not possibly exist in the light of the Apostle's

[1] We may observe by the way that there is not the least hint in the text of convulsions, or of a condition of ecstasy. I must likewise declare to be quite beside the mark the assertion derived from reports of missionaries, that persons who imparted oracles in an ecstatic condition, and under powerful convulsions, could never return to that condition after their conversion to Christianity, as there is not a single word said in the text on the chief point on which the assertion is based,—the conversion of the slave.

Christian consciousness on such a subject as this, which does not affect the truth of the Gospel, but belongs to a perfectly different and lower province, namely, the question whether this was to be taken as a phenomenon explicable from the nature of the human soul, from its natural powers, its connection with the corporeal organism, or as the consequence of possession by a personal evil spirit." It is very evident what dangerous consequences lie in this explanation for a standpoint like that of Neander. If, as Neander expressly says, the possibility of error on the part of the Apostle may be assumed in a case like the foregoing, why may not this assumption be permitted in other like cases? Even Olshausen has brought the demoniacs of the Gospel under the point of view of somnambulistic phenomena. May we, following the lead of Neander's assertion, suppose the possibility of error in the religious consciousness of Jesus himself? For the demoniacs of the Gospel are never described as being in a condition of somnambulism, but as being possessed by evil spirits. With what right, moreover, can it be maintained, that a question of this sort does not properly belong to the sphere of the truth of the Gospel? As long as the doctrine of demons holds its peculiar place in the series of truths of the Christian faith, the question of the influence of demons, and its extent, must undoubtedly have a real religious importance, and it cannot be concluded without inconsequence that an Apostle enlightened by the divine Spirit may have been in error on the question whether a certain case was one of demoniac influence or of natural disorder. If, however, we let such questions rest as they are, the supposition of a condition similar to the phenomena of somnambulism is in any case refuted in this passage. If the damsel was not really possessed by an evil spirit, how could the Apostle command the spirit with which she was afflicted to come out of her? What must we think of the change which took place in the damsel, if the Apostle was so much at fault respecting the cause of her disorder? Must we accept it as an operation of his miraculous power, in a case in which he did not even know the object with which it had to deal?

And how are we to explain the displeasure which the outcries of the damsel excited in the Apostle, and the reproving earnestness with which he treated them, if there was no evil spirit at work here at all? Neander seems to have this question before him, as he remarks (page 177), "The Apostle commanded the spirit which held her heart and reason in bondage to come out of her. If this was not a personal evil spirit, the work was that of an ungodly spirit. That which ought to be free in man, and to rule over all his natural impulses and powers, was made subservient to such a spirit as this. And through the divine might of him who restored peace and harmony to the distracted soul of the demoniacally-afflicted damsel, she found herself in a changed condition, freed from the power of the ungodly spirit, and lost from this moment the power of returning to that state." According to this, we are to suppose an ungodly spirit which is no personal evil spirit, a state of bondage to natural impulses and powers from which the patient cannot free herself, and yet, at the same time, a state into which she can enter by choice and freewill. But what is gained by such half measures in reasoning? To what purpose is such a rationalising of miracles, when in other places there is no hesitation in heaping miracle on miracle? Let it be openly confessed, therefore, as the letter of the text requires, that an evil spirit is here spoken of, and that from our present standpoint we have no right to draw distinctions between the fact and the Apostle's view of it, or the author's narrative of it. The displeasure of the Apostle and the miraculous act performed by him can therefore have no other reason than that, although the evil spirit unwillingly bore witness to the truth, the Apostle did not wish to see the acknowledgment of the truth promoted any longer by demoniacal help. But the demon who here asserted his existence is called $\pi\nu\epsilon\hat{\upsilon}\mu\alpha$ $\pi\acute{\upsilon}\theta\omega\nu o\varsigma$. If we grant that the expression does not exactly necessitate the idea of a spirit of the Pythian Apollo, yet it must be looked on in any case as something characteristic that it is here stated that the demon was "a spirit of divination." There existed then a special class of spirits of divination, though, according to the general Jewish Christian idea, demons generally possess not only the superior knowledge that pertained to their race, but also the power of prophesying. But does not this lead us back to the heathen view, which Plutarch (De def. Orac. 9.) reprobates as a piece of childishness and folly. "τὸν θεὸν αὐτὸν ὥσπερ τοὺς ἐγγαστριμύθους Εὐρυκλέας πάλαι, νυνὶ Πύθωνας προσαγορευομένους, ἐνδυόμενον εἰς τὰ σώματα τῶν προφητῶν ὑποφθέγγεσθαι, τοῖς ἐκείνων στόμασι καὶ φωναῖς χρώμενον ὀργάνοις." But if it is insisted that the demon as such was a spirit of divination, how can we think, how reconcile it with sound psychological ideas, that a demon, being a superior being, and taking possession of men, was at the same time so completely in the service of the person it possessed that the latter could make what use he pleased of the divining power of the demon, and could even make a trade of it? This in fact surpasses even all that is said in the Gospels concerning the relations of demons with those possessed by them, and shows clearly that those interpreters who have no doubt of the reality of demoniac possession, yet feel that here they must take another course; which clearly shows that no intelligible idea can be formed out of the occurrences related.

The chief difficulties, however, as we have said, are to be found in the later part of the narrative, to which this is merely the introduction. The story is shortly this: The masters of the slave, deprived of the gains which they made by her, by the expulsion of the spirit of divination, excited the people to an uproar by a charge of seditious innovations brought against Paul and Silas; the result of which was that the Duumviri of the city of Philippi caused the two Apostles to be scourged with rods, thrown into the deepest prison, and held in the strictest confinement. But at midnight Paul and Silas raised a loud hymn, heard by all the prisoners, which was followed immediately by a powerful earthquake, which caused the doors of the prison to be thrown open and the fetters of the prisoners to be loosed. At the sight of the open doors the jailer, thinking that the prisoners had escaped, was about to throw himself on his sword, when Paul called out to him with a loud voice that they were all there, and he, falling at the feet of Paul and Silas, asked, "What must I do to be saved?" The answer was, "Believe on the Lord Jesus Christ." The word of God was then declared to him and to all his household, and they received Christian baptism. The jailer made a supper that very night, in token of his joy.

Scarcely had the day broken when the Duumviri sent the command to release Paul and Silas. But Paul declared that since they were Roman citizens on whom this indignity had been inflicted, it was not fitting that they should be put out privily; that the Duumviri should come in person and take them out of prison. These magistrates, learning for the first time that the men against whom they had taken these proceedings were Roman citizens, actually came in person, led the Apostles out of prison, and prayed them with friendly words to leave the city.

This simple summary of the chief points in the narrative shows clearly enough how signally the whole course of the matter is destitute of any natural connection. This objection by no means applies merely to the miracle included in the account, the reality of which must be insisted on, since the interpretation which regards the earthquake as a merely natural and fortuitous circumstance, is in direct contradiction to the words and meaning of the author. Neander gives this turn to the passage (page 178): "At midnight Paul and Silas joined in praising God in prayer because an earthquake shook the foundations of the prison." I can only see in this interpretation a transposition which the text does not justify, as the author certainly does not intend to represent the earthquake as the cause of the prayer, but as the consequence and effect of it. How can we believe that not only were the doors of the prison opened by the earthquake, but that it even loosened the fetters of the prisoners? Let us leave the miracle as we find it, as it is the only thing which brings a certain kind of connection into this part of the narrative, and let us take into consideration the circumstances which followed.

Whilst the two Apostles were singing and praying so loudly that all their fellow-prisoners heard them, the keeper of the prison alone lay in a deep sleep. When at last (alarmed, as we must suppose, by the earthquake) he awoke and saw the doors of the prison open, the first thing he did was to draw his sword in order to kill himself, without seeing whether the prisoners were really fled, as he feared, or not, before he resolved on this desperate deed. He also apparently never thought that the earthquake which awakened him might possibly have been the cause of the doors standing open, in which case no blame would have fallen on him; and when Paul called to him with a loud voice that they were all there, he threw himself at the feet of Paul and Silas without any visible cause. How did he know that the convulsion of the earth, which he also took as miraculous, had happened expressly for the sake of the Apostles? and assuming (although the author does not say so) that Paul and Silas had informed him of this, what could have decided him to place such implicit confidence in them on so short an acquaintance, and how could the Apostles themselves have given the assurance they did so confidently (28) in the darkness (29), which any of their fellow-prisoners might easily have availed himself of for the purpose of flight? Then is it likely that the keeper of the prison, who just before was about to kill himself at once, because he feared he had betrayed his trust without knowing how, now so completely forgot this fear and its cause—the Duumviri—that he carried off the two prisoners with him to his house and entertained them at a festival, as if he now at once were freed from all responsibility, although he could have no ground for the assumption that the Duumviri had changed their views with regard to the prisoners, and would leave him unpunished if he violated the trust of his office, and contravened the express commands he had received? With the dawn of day the Duumviri, they who had the day before taken such harsh measures, and seemed about to take some still harsher, sent without any explanation the command to let the two prisoners go; but there is no connection to be seen here. If we say they may have acted so strictly on the preceding day merely on account of the people, this does not seem a very probable course of proceeding for Roman magistrates, and (xvi. 35) would rather give us to understand that they were not quite sure about their ground, and as the narrative undoubtedly tacitly implies, had been warned by the earthquake, of which they must have been aware, to act as they did.[1]

The improbabilities are not yet exhausted. The Duumviri now first perceive that they have violated the rights of Roman citizens, and in order to spare themselves further disagreeable consequences, they go in person to the prison to ask forgiveness of the prisoners, and try to induce them not to carry the affair any further. Can we imagine that Roman magistrates would conduct themselves in such a manner, and make so manifest an official blunder, which imperilled the whole dignity of their position? Either it was a common practice to ask those who were liable to punishment first of all whether or not they were Roman citizens, or else it was concluded that those who were to be punished would proclaim their citizenship, and avail themselves of its privileges, as we find in a like case, Acts xxii. 25. If the first was the case, the inquiry would not have been omitted, but if the latter, the Duumviri were relieved of all responsibility for what occurred. Paul and Silas had themselves to blame for not asserting their rights. But in any case, we can find no reason why they did not at the very first prevent the injustice about to be committed, as it was their duty to do, and as Paul did, Acts xxii. 25, when he was going to be beaten, when he said to the centurion, Εἰ ἄνθρωπον Ῥωμαῖον καὶ ἀκατάκριτον ἔξεστιν ὑμῖν μαστίζειν; In this case the Apostles did not say that they were Roman citizens till after they had received their punishment. Were they not themselves to blame for this? or could they reckon beforehand, that in a matter where they had in their own hands ample means of self-protection, God had resolved to effect their complete release by so striking a vindication? This

[1] That this warrant of discharge was sent by them in consequence of a report they had received from the jailer, as Neander supposes, is the less likely, as so important a circumstance would not possibly have been overlooked by a faithful author. The narrative evidently will not warrant any outward motive of that kind.

is really the idea that lies at the foundation of this miraculous narrative. From the first the most illegal measures were taken against the two Apostles, and in the harshest manner. They were not merely beaten with rods, but thrust into the darkest dungeon, and watched with the greatest strictness, without any one seeming to know exactly what great crime they had committed. No inquiry was instituted, no legal forms were observed, nothing was done which was customary in Roman tribunals, and all this evidently with a view that God should have the more opportunity to give a complete vindication. It is a kind of triumphal cry to which Paul gives utterance, when he says to the despairing keeper of the prison (xvi. 28), "Do thyself no harm, for we are all here!" as though he would say, "It is by no means the case that we have made use of this miracle which has taken place on our account, in order to set ourselves free. Ye must, however, now perceive whom ye have seized, and of how much ye are guilty against our honour." It is not enough that the keeper of the prison be converted in one moment; he must also directly prepare a festive meal, in order to show all honour to his distinguished prisoners. And all this—the conversion of the keeper of the prison and his whole household, their first instruction in Christianity, the baptism of the converted, the entertainment—happened during the same night, in the course of the few hours between midnight and morning. So powerful and enthralling was the impression made by the miracle, and in so august a light do the two Apostles appear! The Roman magistrates are now obliged to condescend so far as to repair to the prison in person in order to offer the fullest compensation to the two Apostles for the injustice they had endured. The question may well be raised here, whether such a grave claim for satisfaction, gratified after all by such a trifling outward formality, was thoroughly suitable to the character of the Apostle and worthy of him. Wetstein is the only one of the older interpreters who notices this question, which yet so naturally presents itself. "Hoc Paulus debebat sibi ipsi, si enim clam abiisset, paullo post rumor fuisset sparsus, effracto carcere ipsum aufugisse, quæ res famæ et auctoritati apostolicæ apud Philippenses et alios multum nocuisset." Yet the command sent by the Duumviri does not, when we look at it, order a secret dismissal; and although the Duumviri had set the Apostles free by a written order, and not led them out of prison personally, we do not see how it could have been reasonably inferred that Paul and Silas had gone away secretly. Everything was publicly conducted, and if the Apostles found it necessary to demand a special public recognition of their innocence, why did they insist on a vindication of their honour, thus laying themselves open to the charge of egotism and exaggerated sensitiveness about their personal dignity?

Wetstein says further, " Porro etiam jure civili et naturali tenebatur immunitatem suam et civitatem Romanam asserere; quid enim sunt immunitates et jura, si quis ea negligat, et sibi eripi patiatur? si alii omnes idem facerent, et qui nunc vivunt, et posteri ipsorum perpetuæ addicentur servituti et mancipiorum loco habebuntur. Boni autem civis est, facere ne sua negligentia alii, quibuscum vivit, cives, et præcipue liberi nepotesque deterioris fiant conditionis quam fuissent absque eo." All this is quite true; but we must all the more wonder why the Apostles did not make use of their Roman citizenship at first, as it was their clear duty to do, and protest against such unjust and insulting treatment. If they wished to claim the privilege afterwards, we cannot see any reason why it should have been done exactly in this form.[1] In one word, the result to be reached by the judicial inquiry instituted against the Apostles is that they shall come out of it with increased glory,

[1] Neander (p. 246, Bohn, 179) takes a peculiar way to vindicate the conduct of the Apostle. "If there had been any element of fanaticism in the enthusiasm with which Paul bore all shame and suffering in the cause of the Lord, he certainly would have done nothing to escape from the disgrace, to avoid which could not prejudice but would rather help his office, nor to receive the apology to his dignity which his citizenship entitled him to claim. This is far from what in later times the morality of the monkish spirit called humility." Of such humility we indeed see no trace; but the question is not now of this, but rather of the contrary; he who stands not far from one extreme, is for that very reason not free from the suspicion of standing too near the other. Olshausen thinks that he can remove all difficulty by the remark that the Apostle may have acted towards those without, according to the *jus talionis*, the only one they were in a condition to understand.

that they shall appear as lofty, unapproachable beings protected by Divine power.

This entire series of improbabilities, brought together with such evident design, must cast the gravest suspicion on the historical character of the narrative. It does not bear a mythical stamp; reflection and purpose are evident throughout. Even the circumstance that the scene is laid at Philippi is a mark of the writer's ingenuity. The whole tenor of the narrative tends to exhibit the disgrace of the opponents; they are themselves made to aid in this design, by interfering in a flagrant manner with the two preachers of the Gospel. Nothing less could be done to them with this view than to beat them with rods, to put them in chains, and to thrust them into the darkest dungeon. But if a fitting satisfaction for this were to be rendered, some point was necessary on their side on which they could insist with all the formality of law. To this end nothing could more naturally offer itself than the well-known fact that the Apostle Paul was in possession of Roman citizenship. But that he might make use of this right effectively he must have Roman magistrates before whom to urge it. Romans were needed to pay the due respect to Roman citizenship. Roman magistrates had therefore to be represented as taking illegal and unjust proceedings against the two Apostles. But Roman magistrates could only be had in a Roman municipal city, and such a city was Philippi as a Roman colony. Thus at the very first mention of the city of Philippi it is remarked that it was a Roman colony, and everything that is related of the residence of the two Apostles in Philippi seems only to be told as an introduction to

But is this the morality of Christian principle? Whither must such a moral declension to the lower standard of others lead, and in what direct contradiction does this *jus talionis* stand to the command of Jesus, Matthew v. 38, 39. Again, it must be taken into consideration, with regard to Silas, that all proof of Roman citizenship in his case is wanting. This of itself would prove nothing, and on the other hand we cannot blame Grotius when he says that Paul here speaks "communicativè," he ascribes only *per synecdochen*, the Roman citizenship to his companion Silas; but then it must be granted that the Romans would scarcely have been willing to allow such a synecdoche, which by its very nature could have no application to legal relations.

what afterwards took place between them and the Roman magistrates. They were obliged to pass many days at the house of Lydia, because the affair with the possessed damsel is represented as extending over many days,[1] and this occurrence was the cause of the more important events which followed. Everything is here introduced with this ulterior motive, to enhance the effect of the chief scene, the glorification of the Apostle and his companion. And what is the foundation of all this? The apologetic parallel between the Apostle Peter and the Apostle Paul. Twice was Peter released from prison by miraculous means. The first time when he had been thrown into a dungeon with the rest of the Apostles at the command of the Sanhedrim, v. 19; the second time when, after the execution of the elder James, king Herod destined the same fate for him, xii. 3. The Apostle Paul must not therefore fail to give a similar token of the divine miraculous power which watched over him. If according to the analogy of the characters of the Acts of the Apostles the Pauline miracle is only to be looked at as a reflex of the Petrine, then the question as to the actual reality of such miraculous narratives must be raised upon the first event, of which the latter is but a copy. The copy can only be understood from the original. It will therefore not be out of place, in the interest of the inquiry before us, if we look a little closer into the nature of this Petrine miracle which is here reflected in Paul.

The narrative of the hostile measures which king Herod Agrippa took against the Christian Church at Jerusalem (Acts xii.) stands very detached. There is nothing said about the cause which led the king to act all at once in so extremely harsh a manner towards the Apostles who had remained unmolested in Jerusalem during the first persecution, nor how the elder James, who is nowhere

[1] Not without reason does it seem specially indicated (xvi. 18) that the damsel acted in this manner during several days (17). This is evidently to be taken as the cause of the Apostle's annoyance (the διαπονεῖσθαι, cf. iv. 2). This "grief" is the immediate cause of the expulsion of the demon. The more cause the Apostle had for annoyance in the behaviour of the damsel, the more unjust appears what afterwards occurred.

else mentioned by name, had drawn particular attention upon himself. Neither is there any mention of similar attentions being paid to the Apostles in Jerusalem afterwards; and the whole proceeding is so much the more incomprehensible, as Josephus is not only completely silent on these events, but expressly praises the mild, beneficent mind of the king, who was in no way inclined to cruelty.[1] In one point only is there any contact between the Acts of the Apostles and the narrative of Josephus. According to Acts xii. 3, the king seems to have been actuated when he took these persecuting measures by his desire to render himself pleasing to the people. Josephus especially mentions this desire for popularity, and indeed connects it with a strong adherence to the national worship.[2] In this respect, what is stated in the Acts of the Apostles seems to be confirmed. The zeal of the king for the established national worship would have made him hate a sect which, however closely it might adhere to Judaism, still by holding up the name of Jesus, who had been condemned by the Jewish authorities, had excited against itself a suspicion of religious innovation. On the other hand we find no trace of the harsh measures against the Christian Church at Jerusalem being calculated to gain popularity; —indeed Josephus relates a case in which, judging by analogy, the contrary would appear more probable. I mean the well-known narrative in which, according to the received text, he relates the death of James the Just. He says, Antiq. xx. 9: Ὁ δὲ νεώτερος Ἄνανος, ὃν τὴν ἀρχιερωσύνην ἔφαμεν παρειληφέναι, θρασὺς ἦν τὸν τρόπον καὶ τολμητὴς διαφερόντως· αἵρεσιν δὲ μετῄει τὴν Σαδδουκαίων, οἵπερ εἰσὶ περὶ τὰς κρίσεις ὠμοὶ παρὰ πάντας τοὺς Ἰουδαίους καθὼς ἤδη δεδηλώκαμεν· ἅτε δὴ οὖν τοιοῦτος ὢν ὁ Ἄνανος, νομίσας ἔχειν καιρὸν ἐπιτήδειον, διὰ τὸ τεθνάναι μὲν Φῆστον, Ἀλβῖνον δὲ

---

[1] Antiq. xix. 7. 3 : Ἐπεφύκει δὲ ὁ βασιλεὺς αὐτὰς—ἡδόμενος τῷ χαρίζεσθαι καὶ τῷ βιοῦν ἐν εὐφημίᾳ χαίρων, κατ' οὐδὲν Ἡρώδῃ τῷ πρὸ ἑαυτοῦ βασιλεῖ τὸν τρόπον συμφερόμενος· ἐκείνῳ γὰρ πονηρὸν ἦν ἦθος ἐπὶ τιμωρίαν ἀπάτομον—πραΰς δὲ ὁ τρόπος Ἀγρίππα καὶ πρὸς πάντας τὰ εὐεργετικὰν ὅμοιον.
[2] Antiq. x. 7. 8 : Ἡδεῖα γοῦν αὐτῷ δίαιτα καὶ συνεχὴς ἐν τοῖς Ἱεροσολύμοις ἦν, καὶ τὰ πάτρια καθαρῶς ἐτήρει· διὰ πάσης γοῦν αὐτὸν ἦγεν ἁγνείας, οὐδὲ ἡμέρα τις παρώδευεν αὐτῷ, τῆς νομίμης χηρεύουσα θυσίας.

ἔτι κατὰ τὴν ὁδὸν ὑπάρχειν, καθίζει συνέδριον κριτῶν· καὶ παραγαγὼν εἰς αὐτὸ [τὸν ἀδελφὸν Ἰησοῦ τοῦ λεγομένου Χριστοῦ Ἰάκωβος ὄνομα αὐτῷ, καὶ] τινὰς [ἑτέρους], ὡς παρανομησάντων κατηγορίαν ποιησάμενος παρέδωκε λευσθησομένους. Ὅσοι δὲ ἐδόκουν ἐπιεικέστατοι τῶν κατὰ τὴν πόλιν εἶναι καὶ τὰ περὶ τοὺς νόμους ἀκριβεῖς, βαρέως ἤνεγκαν ἐπὶ τούτῳ, καὶ πέμπουσι πρὸς τὸν βασιλέα (the King Agrippa of Acts xxv. 13, the son of Herod Agrippa, Acts xii. 1), κρύφα παρακαλοῦντες αὐτὸν ἐπιστεῖλαι τῷ Ἀνάνῳ μηκέτι τοιαῦτα πράσσειν· μηδὲ γὰρ τὸ πρῶτον ὀρθῶς αὐτὸν πεποιηκέναι. Τινὲς δὲ αὐτῶν καὶ τὸν Ἀλβῖνον ὑπαντιάζουσιν ἀπὸ τῆς Ἀλεξανδρείας ὁδοιποροῦντα καὶ διδάσκουσιν ὡς οὐκ ἐξὸν ἦν Ἀνάνῳ χωρὶς τῆς ἐκείνου γνώμης καθίσαι συνέδριον. Ἀλβῖνος δὲ πεισθεὶς τοῖς λεγομένοις γράφει μετ' ὀργῆς τῷ Ἀνάνῳ, λήψεσθαι παρ' αὐτοῦ δίκας ἀπειλῶν, καὶ ὁ βασιλεὺς Ἀγρίππας διὰ τοῦτο τὴν ἀρχιερωσύνην ἀφελόμενος αὐτὸν, ἄρξαντα μῆνας τρεῖς, Ἰησοῦν τὸν τοῦ Δαμναίου κατέστησεν.

It is confessedly very doubtful whether Josephus really names the Apostle James in this place; the passage is in all probability to be read without the words here included in brackets, which seem to be only a Christian gloss. But at the same time scarcely anything else except Christians can be understood by that παρανομήσαντες. And, indeed, if the apocryphal sounding narrative of Hegesippus (Euseb. H. E. ii. 23) contains any truth regarding the death of James the Just, he must at that time have perished by some violent means or other. According to Hegesippus also, James the Just was stoned, and not at the instigation of the populace, but at that of the chiefs of the sect (τινὲς τῶν ἑπτὰ αἱρέσεων τῶν ἐν τῷ λαῷ (Eus., *ib.*), by which we understand the Pharisees to be meant, but not them alone, since mention is made at the same time of the denial of the resurrection as a distinguishing doctrine of these sects (αἱ δὲ αἱρέσεις αἱ προειρημέναι οὐκ ἐπίστευον οὔτε ἀνάστασιν, οὔτε ἐρχόμενον ἀποδοῦναι ἑκάστῳ κατὰ τὰ ἔργα αὐτοῦ).

If we now compare the case related by Josephus with that mentioned in the Acts of the Apostles, we can easily imagine that,

CHAP. VI.]   *HIS SECOND MISSIONARY JOURNEY.*   161

as at the time of which Josephus speaks, a deed of violence had been committed against some of the members of the Church at Jerusalem, and perhaps even against its chief, something similar may have been done by the earlier king Herod Agrippa. A high priest belonging to the sect of the Sadducees may have aided in the matter on the earlier as well as on the later occasion. At any rate, according to Josephus, Antiq. xix. 6. 4, the king stood in a very close connection with the then High Priest. That in any case an act of cruelty was committed against the Church by Herod Agrippa, and as the Acts of the Apostles relates, the elder James then died a violent death, receives still further confirmation from the Christian legend which arose on the subject of the death of this king, and which could scarcely have arisen as we find it, Acts xii. 19, from what Josephus narrates of the manner of his death, had there not been some circumstances specially affecting the Church to make it a matter of some interest.[1] But the above quotation from Josephus shows quite clearly how unpopular such persecuting measures were, and the conclusion is very obvious, that if the act of violence subsequently committed by the High Priest Ananus excited general displeasure among all the right-thinking, orderly inhabitants of Jerusalem, and occasioned the measures spoken of by Josephus, so that the Roman Procurator Albinus thought himself obliged to interfere, and King Agrippa on just the same ground deprived the

[1] If we compare the narrative of the death of the king (Acts xii. 19) with that in Josephus, Antiq. xix. 8. 2, we see a remarkable similarity running through all the differences which exist in the accounts. Josephus also places the sickness and death of the king in direct connection with the festivities of the day, and with the indecent honour which was shown to the king by the sycophantic people. The historical fact which lies at the root of both narratives, namely, the sudden death of the king, occurring shortly after the festival, allows of no doubt; and Josephus also seems to have considered it as a divinely sent punishment, or else he would not have placed it in such direct relation to the superhuman honours of which he speaks. Josephus indeed does not say anything of an angel of death, but speaks of an owl as the ominous prophet of death. Still less does Josephus say anything of the king's living body being devoured by worms; according to his narrative, the sickness was only a very severe pain in the bowels; but even this account of the sickness evidently shows a point of connection with the Christian legend. The piercing, gnawing, inwardly devouring pains—what are they when mythically presented but worms devouring the living

High Priest Ananus of his office, these steps cannot have been received with great favour by the people, when taken by Herod Agrippa, though individuals who exercised great influence over the king may have been of a different opinion in the matter. On this we need not hesitate in laying to the credit of his historical theorising, what the author of the Acts of the Apostles says regarding the satisfaction of the people at the proceedings of the king. This theorising is the more evident as the remark, verse 3, that it "pleased the people" stands in the closest connection with the subsequent narrative of the miracle and the chief occurrence in it, namely, the saving of Peter, ἐκ πάσης τῆς προσδοκίας τοῦ λαοῦ τῶν Ἰουδαίων, xii. 11. If we take this view of the narrative, which the history of the time certainly warrants us to do, we reach a certainly not improbable historical combination on what the Acts here tells us about Peter. The same fate threatened the Apostle Peter; he also was to be publicly executed, but the feast of the Passover, which occurred at the time, caused a delay. But the intention of the king was not carried into effect after the feast, and the Apostle Peter was released in a perfectly unexpected manner. According to the narrative in the Acts of the Apostles, this was owing to a miracle, but after what we have remarked above, how natural is it to suppose that the king himself desisted from his purpose, and very unexpectedly released the Apostle Peter, because in the interval he

body? But what inducement could there be to paint the disease from which the king died in such glaring colours as to attribute it as it were to the gnawing worms which torment the damned in hell? (Mark ix. 44, compare Isa. lxvi. 24.) We may answer this question if we call to mind that King Antiochus Epiphanes is reported to have died in the same manner, that king so hated by the Jews, the cruel persecutor of all true worshippers of God, the enemy of true religion, who with presumptuous audacity assumed a hostile attitude towards the Most High. Compare 2 Macc. ix. 5. This deadly enemy of the Jewish name, the tyrannical Antiochus Epiphanes, seems to exist again in the person of King Herod Agrippa, who persecuted the believing disciples, put to death the Apostle James, and intended the same fate for the Apostle Peter; the overbearing, ungodly adversary, who at last even usurped divine honours. How clearly we see here a legend formed in the Christian interest; and when we compare a Christian legend so purposely prepared with the narrative of Josephus, what light is thrown on the historical event out of which it arose!

had ascertained how unpopular his proceedings were, and how little the execution of the Apostle James had found that favour with the people which he had anticipated. If we can as little doubt the release of the Apostle from prison as his imprisonment, how can we explain it otherwise than by some such sudden turn in affairs; and this seems to be indicated by certain other circumstances spoken of both by the author of the Acts and by Josephus. According to Acts xii. 19, King Herod left Jerusalem directly after the release of the Apostle Peter and went to Cæsarea. Josephus agrees with this, and says at the same time the third year of his reign was completed.[1] As the beginning of his reign was coincident with the beginning of the reign of the Emperor Claudius, *i.e.* the end of January of the year 41 A.D., we are justified, according to Josephus, in placing the departure of the king to Cæsarea at the time in which it is placed by the Acts of the Apostles, directly after Easter, A.D. 44. This departure of the King, who, as Josephus says, was not in the habit of leaving Jerusalem for any length of time, must have been caused by some special reason which determined him to take this step. We must also take into consideration that, before mentioning the king's departure, Josephus says that he had deprived the High Priest Matthias of his office, Antiq. xix. 8. 1. This dismissal must have taken place for some special reason, as Matthias had been appointed High Priest by King Herod himself, under conditions which certainly implied friendly relations. (Antiq. xix. 6. 4.) After the execution of which Josephus speaks in the former place, and which perhaps is that of James the Less, the High Priest Ananus, as the instigator of the proceedings which had been so much disliked, was deprived of his office. In the case of which we are now speaking, may not the dismissal of the High Priest Matthias have been owing to the same cause?

Thus the Apostle Peter was actually released from prison in a perfectly unexpected manner after the affair of James the elder; but the miraculous way in which this was brought about by an

---

[1] Antiq. xix. 8. 2: τρίτον δὲ ἔτος βασιλεύοντι τῆς ὅλης Ἰουδαίας πεπλήρωται καὶ παρῆν εἰς πόλιν Καισάρειαν.

angel of the Lord is only a Christian legend or poem, which explains in its own manner the darkness which at that time enveloped the whole matter, and ascribes the happy issue to the direct operation of a higher causality. If the Apostle was unexpectedly set free, as soon as the release came to be represented as a miracle, it was a short step to represent the intentions of the enemy as having been frustrated in the most surprising manner. On this account not only is the wondering expectation with which all the people waited for the promised show of the public execution brought prominently forward, ver. 11, but it is also stated as a remarkable circumstance that the Apostle was released in the night which preceded his intended execution, ver. 6. Can we wonder that on the next morning when the affair was discovered the greatest commotion ensued, and that the king, thus humiliated before the eyes of the whole people, vented his anger on the soldiers to whose charge the prisoner had been consigned, and caused the death destined for the Apostle to be inflicted on them, ver. 19? In such a case as this, if once the legend takes this direction, everything is turned to account which can heighten the dramatic effect. And we have accordingly here a circumstantial narrative of the measures taken for the most careful watching of the prisoner. Four quaternions of soldiers were told off for the successive watches during the night, so that two soldiers were inside the prison, between whom the prisoner was bound by two chains, and two others stood outside the door, xii. 4, 6. It may be granted that this truly Roman proceeding was nothing extraordinary on the part of a king accustomed to Roman manners and customs, though at the same time heedful of national feelings; but then why are all these details of this strict watch given here, and not in chapter xvi., where one should expect to find them, as being customary in a Roman colony? Evidently because they would not have accorded with the scene with the keeper of the prison in chapter xvi., whereas in chapter xii. they do good service in showing how important this matter was considered, and what complete precautions were thought to have been taken in order to make the release of the Apostle from prison impossible. But was there any reason for such great fear and apprehension? No one could have expected a miracle—the Christians themselves did not think of one,[1] and if such an expectation had existed, the measures taken would have been thought perfectly useless. But this is just the peculiarity of the story; as though the enemy had a presentiment of what did really afterwards happen, they take every precaution to make themselves secure against it, and yet only to be the more astounded when they find that all their precautions have been vain. This is evidently a mode of proceeding which involves a peculiar irony in the contrast of the intention with the result, but an irony which can have been inspired only from a Christian standpoint. But if the affair really took place as is here stated, how impossible is it to represent it to ourselves. How badly the four soldiers, placed with such care on guard, must have fulfilled their duty, if so shortly before daybreak they allowed themselves to be so completely overcome with sleep that the Apostle could walk unchallenged through the midst of his keepers lying around in slumber. This must have been shortly before daybreak, because if it had been earlier, the escape would not have been left to be discovered in the morning (xii. 18), but must at the very latest have been detected when the third $\tau\epsilon\tau\rho\acute{a}\delta\iota o\nu$ was relieved, between the third and fourth night watches. This profound sleep of the keepers must therefore have been brought about in a miraculous manner, and in fact the miracle is carefully exhibited in a series of events which have every resemblance to the operations of magic. The Apostle, lying, like his guards, in a deep sleep, is awakened by a blow on the side, suddenly freed from the chains which fall from his hands, stands up, dresses himself, and goes out, without any hindrance, through gates and guards. And even after he has successfully passed through the gates and

---

[1] The Acts cannot picture strongly enough the great astonishment of the disciples at the Apostle's miraculous release from prison, xii. 13-16. And yet we cannot avoid asking, Why were they so much astonished? must they not rather have expected such a miracle, if one had already happened in a perfectly similar case, Acts v. 19?

guards of the prison, the iron gate leading into the city is made to spring open before him, as though not to miss this special theatrical effect, which is really a very striking one. The magical effect which a series of miracles so completely out of the sphere of reality must have produced is carefully indicated by the author, when he remarks that the Apostle thought he had seen a vision, and that only after he had again come to his full consciousness was he able to decide exactly between reality and vision—truth and fancy. But we cannot ignore the question how the Apostle, who alone can count here as a witness, could have been so certain that all this had been done by an angel, if he had not been more clearly conscious of what had happened. The miraculous narrative thus bears with it its own refutation.

If the historical fact to which the two miraculous narratives, Acts xii. and xvi. (as well as the earlier one, Acts v. 19, etc.), may be referred, is in itself very probably true, a further conclusion may be drawn as to the circumstances of the Christian Church at Jerusalem at that time. As the members of this Church still adhered strictly to the Jewish religion, observed its laws and customs, and only differed from the rest of the Jews in believing Jesus to be the Messiah who had appeared, it cannot be supposed that the Jews in Jerusalem found any great offence in them. They were willingly tolerated as long as they did not come to any such openly pronounced breach with the Jewish law as had been the case with Stephen and the Hellenists who were of his way of thinking. But it was otherwise with the chiefs of the Jewish nation. The continued existence of a sect whose Founder they had removed out of the way by a public sentence of death, must have been peculiarly obnoxious to them. It is therefore not improbable that persecutions of the Christians had taken place at an earlier date, and as, according to Josephus, those who held the highest offices were chiefly Sadducees, we may believe the author of the Acts of the Apostles when he says that such oppressive measures generally came from the party of the Sadducees. This party would undoubtedly have taken further steps of this kind if they had

had full liberty of action, and had they not been restrained partly by fear of the Roman procurator, and partly by the disposition of the people. But everything beyond this general indication of the position of affairs at the time is very uncertain. What we find in connection with this is a miraculous narrative, which must be placed to the account of tradition, or to the peculiar mode of statement employed by the author of the Acts of the Apostles. In any case we must look upon it as a peculiar feature in the Acts, that such important miracles as those we have been considering are always doubled in this work. Nothing extraordinary can happen to Peter which is not repeated in the case of Paul; and again, there is no distinguishing feature in Paul's history without the exact counterpart being reported of Peter. This general type on which the Acts is constructed is very obviously present in the miracle related in Acts xvi.

CHAPTER VII.

THE APOSTLE PAUL IN ATHENS, CORINTH, EPHESUS.—HIS JOURNEY TO JERUSALEM BY MILETUS.—ACTS XVII.-XX.

FROM Philippi the Apostle took his way with his two companions, Timotheus and Silas, to Thessalonica, and from there to Athens. After a short stay there, he went on to Corinth, where he found a better sphere for his activity, and remained a considerable time. During the year and a half of his stay there, he founded, under great difficulties, the first important Church in Greece. After a journey to Jerusalem and Antioch, the city of Ephesus became the chief seat of his labours; the results of which, in combating the demoniacal and magical powers of the old religion and its idolatrous worship, were, according to the Acts, so remarkable as to give rise to a public contest between the old and the new faiths. He travelled once more by Macedonia into Greece, and then after a residence of three months set out on that important journey to Jerusalem, which filled him even then with the most gloomy forebodings, which he expressed to the Ephesian elders whom he summoned to meet him at Miletus. According to the statement of the Acts, the most determined opposition was raised against the Apostle by the hatred of the Jews in every place where he dwelt, either for a long or a short space of time. Aquila, Priscilla, and Apollos are known to us in the Epistles of the Apostle as well as from the Acts, so that the two sources may here be compared with each other. He met Aquila, a Jew of Pontus, and his wife Priscilla, in Corinth, when he went there for the first time.

Apollos, a Jew of Alexandria, with whom Aquila and Priscilla became acquainted at Ephesus, went, when the Apostle took his way through Galatia and Phrygia to Ephesus, and from the latter place to Corinth, where church matters were at that time in a state of ferment, and his presence had a very peculiar influence. In this part of the Acts of the Apostles, as in the rest of that work, the life and work of the Apostle is presented to us partly in his speeches, partly in miracles, in both of which critical examination recognises, through the veil of much foreign matter, a very obscure reflection of the actual history.

The celebrated speech which the Apostle is said to have delivered at Athens is introduced by a narrative to which historical criticism must take as much exception as it does to the speech itself. The chief reason for this critical doubt is here as elsewhere the evident design and studied arrangement of the narrative. All the well-known characteristic traits of the Athenian character are cleverly and ingeniously pressed into the service, so that the contrast which must have been presented in this brilliant seat of Grecian culture, between Christianity and polytheistic heathenism, and between the Christian and a popular character such as the Athenian, may be brought forward as prominently as possible. How completely the historian carries on his narrative from this point of view is shown from its very commencement. The reigning idea to which all that follows bears reference, namely, the striking contrast between Christianity and heathenism, as the latter appeared in its most brilliant aspect in Athens, is ascribed to the Apostle himself, when the author represents him as moved by the most intense emotion at the first view of the city so "wholly given to idolatry." The Apostle is described here as acting differently from his usual custom. Instead of waiting for the way to be opened for the preaching of the Gospel to the Gentiles through the Jews and proselytes in the synagogue, the Apostle is made to seek an opportunity for religious conversation among those whom he met in the public places; he disputes with Epicurean and Stoic philosophers, adherents of the same philosophical sects which afterwards raised the greatest opposition against Christianity, and in all his intercourse with the Athenians they are represented as repeating the behaviour they had already shown on other similar occasions. How clear it is that when the author put these words into the mouths of the Athenians, ξένων δαιμονίων δοκεῖ καταγγελεὺς εἶναι, he had before his mind the charge which was brought against Socrates when he was indicted (Xenophon, Memorabil. 1. 1), οὓς μὲν ἡ πόλις νομίζει θεοὺς, οὐ νομίζων, ἕτερα δὲ καινὰ δαιμόνια εἰσφέρων : and what does the mocking speech of the Athenians mean, τί ἂν θέλοι ὁ σπερμολόγος οὗτος λέγειν ; but the light, airy, sophistical talk that serves Aristophanes in the "Clouds" as a pretext for bringing his wit and mockery to bear on the seriousness of the Socratic philosophy, whose founder also was in the eyes of the people a mere σπερμολόγος. How strikingly the author paints the known ironical popular wit in his sketch of the Athenian character, when he makes them combine Jesus and the ἀνάστασις as a pair of new gods according to the manner of polytheism.[1] If the historian wished, as is evidently his intention, to give a general view of the Athenian character, he could not omit their very characteristic irony any more than their equally peculiar curiosity, which he goes on to describe in almost the same words in which it is painted by the old authors themselves. It could therefore have been nothing but curiosity which awakened in the Athenians a certain interest in the Gospel preached by Paul, and which caused them to listen to a discourse of the Apostle delivered in the Areopagus. But even this appearance of the Apostle in the Areopagus throws a new and very curious light on the whole affair, and this is just the point from which we can see the connection of this narrative most distinctly. We must

[1] So must the words, xvii. 18, τὸν Ἰησοῦν καὶ τὴν ἀνάστασιν, undoubtedly be taken. Among the modern commentators on the Acts, Meyer in especial finds it very strange that the philosophers thought the Ἀνάστασις to be a goddess proclaimed by Paul. "If Luke had meant this in his explanatory note, he would have indicated it more decidedly ; and would the Athenian philosophers have been so ignorant ?" Of course the author did not mean it to appear as ignorance, but as irony : and then does not the author sufficiently indicate that this is the sense of the expression when he twice puts the article before the word ?

ask accordingly, why was it precisely in the Areopagus that the Apostle delivered his discourse? The most obvious answer undoubtedly is that to the Areopagitic court of justice was committed the care of matters of religion. The Apostle would be brought to the Areopagus for his legal defence since he was accused of introducing ξένα δαιμόνια. This is what Chrysostom supposes along with other old commentators; ἦγον αὐτὸν εἰς τὸν ἄρειον πάγον οὐχ ὥστε μαθεῖν ἀλλ' ὥστε κολάζειν, ἔνθα αἱ φονικαὶ δίκαι. But there is not the least hint of this; the manner in which the Apostle is treated and ultimately dismissed makes it perfectly clear that curiosity was the only motive which prompted the Athenians to lead him to the Areopagus, for they saw in him only a good-natured enthusiast, not a dangerous heretic. Hence we have been reminded, not without reason, that we must not think of the seat of the court of justice, but merely of the open space at the summit of the hill. In this case also we may suppose that the same irony is shown in the choice of a locality which is displayed in the whole treatment of the Apostle. The narrative represents the Athenians as taking up the affair with an ironical air and pretended gravity (δυνάμεθα γνῶναι, τίς ἡ καινὴ αὕτη ἡ ὑπὸ σοῦ λαλουμένη διδαχή; ξενίζοντα γάρ τινα εἰσφέρεις εἰς τὰς ἀκοὰς ἡμῶν· βουλόμεθα οὖν γνῶναι, τί ἂν θέλοι ταῦτα εἶναι, 19-20), and as they are anything rather than serious, so the scene is laid in the Areopagus, for the obvious purpose of contrasting the importance of the place with the evident insignificance of the subject. But just as little as there seems to be any doubt as to why the Apostle was led to the Areopagus, so much the more striking is it that the Dionysius converted by the Apostle should be called the Areopagite. This surname would seem to indicate that Dionysius, a member of the Court of Justice, had become acquainted with Christianity as a member of the Court of Justice, and had been converted to the Christian faith at the time when the Apostle delivered his speech before the assembled court. Why should the name be here expressly mentioned, if not to indicate the occasion of his conversion? Or can it be held as an accidental circumstance that when the Apostle was led to the Areopagus, one, among the few converted by him, was an Areopagite? But if he was converted as an Areopagite, then the Apostle must have appeared before the whole assembled Court of Justice. How shall we explain this ambiguity with regard to the occasion of the speech of the Apostle in the Areopagus? The explanation is, I believe, as follows :—Ecclesiastical tradition speaks of a Dionysius with the surname of Areopagite, who was the first Bishop of Athens. According to Eusebius (H. E. iv. 23), Bishop Dionysius of Corinth wrote an epistle to Athens, as he had done to other churches, in which he admonished the members of the Athenian Church to faith and to a Gospel manner of living, as since their Bishop Publius had died as a martyr in the persecutions of that period, they had become indifferent, and had almost fallen away from the Christian faith, until Quadratus, the successor of the martyr Publius, reanimated their faith by his zeal. Eusebius says that in the same epistle Dionysius mentions Dionysius the Areopagite as the first Bishop of Athens who was converted by the Apostle Paul. The commentators rightly observe on this passage in Eusebius, that if Publius, who died as a martyr under Marcus Aurelius, had been the immediate successor of Dionysius the Areopagite, the latter must have been Bishop of Athens for more than seventy years. There must then have been other Bishops between Dionysius and Publius, but tradition says nothing of them, it speaks only of the first Bishop, Dionysius the Areopagite. Must we look upon our passage in the Acts of the Apostles as the source of this tradition? We should certainly be obliged to assume this, if we had no other reason for doubting the historical trustworthiness of our narrative contained in it. But, as we have already seen, other reasons do exist, and thus we are warranted to turn the matter the other way and to assume that Dionysius the Areopagite was imported into our passage in the Acts of the Apostles from ecclesiastical tradition, and only on this supposition can the whole scene in the Areopagus be satisfactorily explained. An old ecclesiastical legend mentioned one Dionysius an Areopagite, as among the first who accepted the Christian faith in Athens; whether it be that he was really an Areopagite, or that he had only received that surname because it was thought that the man who was so ready to receive Christianity must have been a member of that honourable senate. But in order still further to show the reason of his conversion, his surname gave rise to the tradition that he was converted in the Areopagus itself, and what better occasion could be found for this conversion than when the Apostle came to Athens on his journey from Macedonia to Corinth? But there could be no doubt that the Apostle had made a public appearance in the Areopagus itself. Doubtless the legend, as the author of the Acts of the Apostles found it, gave no further account of the occasion which led to this. So much the more was he therefore at liberty to carry out the idea which the legend of the Areopagite Dionysius had suggested to him. The whole nature of the passage leads to no other supposition than that the author intended to describe, by the reception which the Apostle received in Athens, how Christianity was considered and judged at the time when the author lived, as well by educated people generally,—and the Athenians were the highest example of intellectual culture,—as by the principal philosophical sects, the Epicureans and the Stoics, whose chief seat was also at Athens. Judging from every indication that he gives, there was floating before his mind a time in which Christianity had indeed drawn on itself the observation of the educated and the philosophers, but when it was considered by them as a ridiculous folly and a dream of enthusiasts. The irony which at a later date took so cutting and bitter a tone in Lucian and Celsus, speaks also here, only in a milder and kinder spirit. It is a fact worthy of special remark, that the author makes the doctrine of the resurrection the chief point on which the whole conference between the Apostle and the Athenians turns. From the very beginning this doctrine is maintained against the Gentile opponents as the most characteristic of Christianity. Against it was especially directed the mocking scorn with which the Apostle was met, and as soon as it was introduced into his speech, it was enough to cause the audience to declare that they had had enough of him and of his preaching. Here we have exactly the objection which the Gentiles felt to this doctrine as soon as they began to be acquainted with Christianity, and the first persecutions gave occasion for a more distinct expression of the Christian hope of a resurrection, as a compensation for the sufferings they were called on to endure. To such a time as this we must look for the true explanation of this passage. The author of the Acts of the Apostles wished to depict the marked supercilious scorn with which the Gentiles treated Christianity when they had come to be familiar with it. Such a scene as this in Athens was especially suited to such an aim. The ironical inquisitive Athenians, treating all things, even the holiest, in a light and frivolous manner, were the worthiest representatives of this side of heathenism. The occurrence in the Areopagus, which the traditionally given name of the Areopagite Dionysius seemed to pre-suppose, may therefore not have been intended to be understood seriously, as the author's principal point of view was a completely different one. Many things are not to be taken literally in poetry and legend, and would need to be looked upon quite differently if considered as they really happened; and so the author had no scruple on this occasion in representing this solemn venerated spot as having been thrown open to a public, who had gathered together merely to satisfy their curiosity and indulge their love of ridicule.

The most striking point in the speech, after its carefully designed introduction, is the sudden turn with which, as soon as it arrives at its principal object, namely, the exhortation to accept Christianity, it passes to the doctrine of the resurrection. We see that this doctrine is purposely introduced at the earliest point at which it was possible to do so, and dwelt upon as the chief doctrine of Christianity, although the Apostle must have known from experience that it was precisely the point adapted to give the most offence to the Athenians. To what purpose then did the speech so studiously dwell upon the resurrection, when the subject might so easily have been avoided, or at least kept more in the background? This speech is commonly praised as a model of the Apostle's apologetic method, and of his wisdom as a teacher. But has it been also considered that these merits ought to appear in recommending the chief idea which the speaker was anxious to enforce? Is it then so remarkable a token of a discourse being to the purpose, that before the speaker has arrived at the exposition of his principal idea, the hearers should take so great offence at the contents of his speech as to go away? It would rather seem to follow that the Apostle, if he did not on this occasion altogether forget his usually admirable skill as a teacher, cannot have delivered this speech as we possess it. It is only the author who wishes to bring plainly before us the obstacle which this doctrine of the resurrection presented to educated Gentiles like the Athenians, in conformity with the main idea which he is carrying out in this passage. Even that part of the speech in which interpreters think they perceive most clearly the Apostle's renowned wisdom in teaching, presents a totally different aspect if we consider the doctrine of the resurrection, mentioned at the conclusion, to be the chief topic of the speech. It cannot be disputed that, as is alleged for the credit of the speech, the speaker conformed as nearly as possible to the religious opinions of his audience, placed himself as much as possible at the same standpoint with them, in order by these means more easily to win them over to his own views. Although the contents of this speech are so strictly monotheistic, it contains many propositions whose leading ideas are found in almost the same words in Greek and Roman authors. The speaker appeals, in support of one of the principal ideas of the speech, to the words of a Greek poet, thus showing how much he wished to find a common ground between himself and his hearers for mutual approximation. This being his aim, it was quite to be expected that he should represent the age of polytheism as a time of ignorance, which God was willing to overlook, provided that the Gentiles would now change their mind and turn to Him. The necessity of such a conversion is also deduced from an idea which lay within the religious circle of ideas of the Gentiles—the idea of a future retribution. Up to this point the speech proceeded as well as possible; and the result it aimed at was all but won, when, by a word dropped incautiously by the speaker, all was changed and he was cut short, it appears in the middle of the sentence he had begun. We can only accept this as the natural historical course of the affair, if it be credible that the characteristic Christian doctrine of the resurrection was even at that time as repugnant to the Gentile mind as is here represented, and that the Apostle was guilty of so striking an offence against apostolic wisdom in teaching. But as both these suppositions are equally improbable, we can only see in this speech an ingeniously introduced effect of the author. Though the points of resemblance which the author makes the Apostle point out between the religious consciousness of the Gentiles and his own monotheistic standpoint were true and manifold, yet the impression which the Christian doctrine of the resurrection made on the educated Gentiles was to appear harsh and offensive. The resurrection of Jesus, the fact which to Christians was the greatest evidence of their Christian faith, made the whole of Christianity appear to the Gentiles the most incredible thing in the world, and a ridiculous folly. To give a graphic picture of this side of the Gentile mode of regarding Christianity is the chief design of the author of the Acts of the Apostles in this passage. All the details of the episode serve this design, and the speech put into the mouth of the Apostle is especially intended to further it.

Among the individual features which show us the unhistorical character of this speech, as well as that of the whole passage, I think we must specify in particular "the Unknown God" of the Athenians. The fruitless trouble which interpreters have given themselves with regard to the historical identification of this "Unknown God" is well known. All that can be historically proved is that in Athens, as well as in other places in Greece, there were altars which were dedicated to unknown Gods—that is, to Gods whom men did not know how to name. As it admits of no denial that unknown Gods, in the plural, would not have fulfilled the aim of the Apostle's argument, some of the modern scholars have expressly postulated as a historical fact the existence of an "Unknown God" in

Athens. It is maintained that the ἀγνώστῳ θεῷ must be literally correct, or it would compromise Paul as a σπερμολόγος, and that it can hardly be imagined that the Apostle would, at the climax of his noble speech, have brought before the Athenians a deliberate falsehood.[1] Neander also has argued on this side : " If we investigate with care all the records of antiquity, and compare the various phases of polytheism, we can find no real foundation for any denial of the existence of such an altar, actually bearing the inscription to which Paul refers. Altars may indeed have been raised on some occasions and dedicated to an ' unknown God,' when it was not known which god had been provoked, and therefore was to be appeased" (page 190). Of course this is in itself not impossible, but criticism must not be content with mere possibility, but must endeavour to find out the probable. But as for the historical credibility of our passage, what right have we to assume as indubitable the very point which is in question ? What right have we to pay so little heed to the testimony of the ancients who only speak of the ἄγνωστοι θεοὶ, and not of an ἄγνωστος θεὸς, as to presuppose, in spite of their silence, the worship of an ἄγνωστος θεὸς as a historical fact ? Is not this supposition the more arbitrary, as it is very conceivable that the ἄγνωστος θεὸς of the Acts of the Apostles may have originated in the ἄγνωστοι θεοὶ of the ancients ? In reality no other theory can be accepted if we consider the matter carefully. Neander regards it as a proof of the Apostle's trustworthiness that the altar he refers to is not dedicated to the unknown God, but to *an*, unknown, indefinite, god, but this proves just the contrary. The unhistorical character of the whole passage is admitted, as it must be, when it is granted that the altar with the inscription ἀγνώστῳ θεῷ was not dedicated expressly to "the unknown God," but to one whose name was accidentally not known; in this case how can we overlook the fact that the Apostle must have been guilty of open violation of the truth if he declared this very God to be the One whom he preached, the true God, the Creator of heaven and earth ? If he were only " an unknown God," he would

[1] Compare Meyer on this passage.

not be distinguished from the rest of the known gods by his individual character, but only by the accidental circumstance that his name was not known, or that no special name had been given him; he would be one of the same class with the rest of the deities of the polytheistic faith, from whom the true God of monotheism is different in every essential point, and it is evident that there may quite as well be several unknown gods of this sort as one. If we look at the matter in this light we can see why, in the passages quoted from the ancients, the altars mentioned are always to "unknown gods," and never to "an unknown God." Polytheistic religion naturally implied this: it could nowhere rest in one God; on the same grounds on which it presumed there might be one unknown God, it also presumed that there might be several. In this worship of the nameless and unknown there is betrayed in a very remarkable manner the unsatisfying nature of polytheism, that innate misgiving that there does exist something of which the conscious knowledge and name are still wanting; in other words, that negative nature of its principles which prevents polytheism from being more than a step in the transition to monotheism. This thought, which is the true one for the Apostle's line of argument, and for which it would not matter whether he started from ἄγνωστοι θεοὶ in the plural, or from one ἄγνωστος θεὸς only, cannot be traced in the account in the Acts of the Apostles, where the chief point in the Apostle's argument undoubtedly lies in the unity of the ἄγνωστος θεὸς.[1] Such a confusion between the ἄγνωστοι θεοὶ, who can be found in history, and the ἄγνωστος θεὸς, who is so unhistorical and foreign to the nature of polytheism, could only have been ventured on

---

[1] When Neander (p. 263, Bohn 188) says, "Paul used this inscription, in order to attach a deeper meaning to it, as a point of connection, to indicate the higher but indistinct longing which lies at the root of polytheism," it must be remarked on the other hand that in any case—even assuming the theory of a deeper meaning, which the Athenians at any rate were scarcely in a condition to appreciate—there remains a striking incorrectness in identifying this "unknown God" with the God of the Old Testament; such an identification could have no probability except it were warranted by the inscription. As soon as we are obliged to argue from the unknown one to the unknown several, we see traces of design rather than of depth of reasoning.

by an author who stood at a distance from the events related, and had not before his eyes, as the Apostle Paul would certainly have had, the fear of being refuted there and then. It is easy to see that this stands in very close connection with the tendency in the speech to make the Apostle bring forward as much as possible those points on which the religious consciousness of the Athenians most nearly approached to Christianity. To this end the author made use of the fact of which he was aware, that in Athens unknown gods were worshipped. But at the same time he imagined that the only way for him to express the very true thought that was floating in his mind was to substitute ἄγνωστος for ἄγνωστοι, and as soon as the plural had given place to the singular, the expression thus ingeniously altered suggested that this ἄγνωστος θεὸς might be turned into the true God of the Jewish-Christian faith.

The second speech which we have here to consider, that farewell speech which the Apostle is said to have delivered to the Elders of the Ephesian Church whom he had summoned to Miletus before his last journey to Jerusalem, bears also the undoubted impress of a later time. How could the idea occur to the Apostle to deliver such a farewell speech and to summon the Ephesian Elders to Miletus for the express purpose? Could he at that time foresee with the definiteness and certainty expressed in the speech, that he stood at the goal of his apostolic course, that his work was ended, and that none of those amongst whom he had hitherto preached the kingdom of God would see his face again? Is this same feeling, this same view of his course as being already closed, exhibited by the Apostle later on? When he saw himself at Jerusalem in danger of falling into the hands of the Jews and of being offered up as a victim to their hatred, would he have appealed to Cæsar for any other reason than to escape the danger threatening him in Jerusalem, and to secure with the preservation of his life the continuation of his apostolic work by a just decision of his cause in Rome? Does not the Acts of the Apostles itself (xxiii. 11) represent the Apostle as cherishing, even after his imprisonment, the joyful confidence that he should yet bear witness to the cause of the Gospel not only at Jerusalem but also at Rome? What could warrant this confidence if, according to the express assertion in this speech, he saw in the imprisonment he suffered at Jerusalem the end of his apostolic work? And what completely different views as to his position and to the future awaiting him did the Apostle entertain not long before, when in writing the Epistle to the Romans he spoke in the most cheerful manner of the journey which he intended making to Jerusalem, and at the same time passed so lightly over the probable dangers, without, however, seeking to ignore them ($παρακαλῶ\ δὲ\ ὑμᾶς,\ ἀδελφοὶ—συναγωνίσασθαί\ μοι\ ἐν\ ταῖς\ προσευχαῖς\ ὑπὲρ\ ἐμοῦ\ πρὸς\ τὸν\ Θεόν.\ ἵνα\ ῥυσθῶ\ ἀπὸ\ τῶν\ ἀπειθούντων\ ἐν\ τῇ\ Ἰουδαίᾳ$, Romans xv. 30, 31), that he connected the fortunate completion of this journey, which he confidently hoped for, with the plan of a further journey into Spain and the West, Romans xv. 22-32. There is no trace whatever here of that utterly sorrowful picture of the future which floated before the mind of the Apostle in the farewell speech at Miletus: it is rather a clear, joyful, hopeful view which he takes of it; he hopes to return from Jerusalem, and visit the Roman Christians, $ἐν\ πληρώματι\ εὐλογίας\ τοῦ\ Χριστοῦ$ (29), $ἐν\ χαρᾷ$ (32), evidently quite a different $χαρά$ from that with which (Acts xx. 24) he is ready to $τελειῶσαι\ τὸν\ δρόμον—καὶ\ τὴν\ διακονίαν—διαμαρτύρασθαι\ τὸ\ εὐαγγέλιον$.[1] Can we imagine that the Apostle's position and frame of mind could have so completely changed in so short a space of time? It cannot be said that the words uttered by the Apostle in this farewell speech, with regard to the future that lay before him, were merely vague forebodings, the results of the temporarily depressed state of his feelings on that occasion, and that on that account they need not be too minutely compared with what actually followed. This cannot be maintained; for not only is the speech a farewell, not only does it quite come up to the idea of a final separation, but everything

---

[1] I abstain here from uttering my doubts as to the authenticity of this part of the Epistle to Romans, as in any case this argument, $κατ'\ ἄνθρωπον$, is quite to the point.

it indicates regarding the impending fate of the Apostle agrees so exactly with what actually occurred that it is impossible to look on the words as the expression of a vague, casual presentiment. The Apostle already sees himself bound in spirit on his way to Jerusalem. Every city through which his way led him brought Jerusalem before him, and awakened in him the thoughts of bonds and imprisonment. Although the several circumstances which led to his imprisonment at Jerusalem were of course still in the distance, yet the chief fact itself stood clearly before his mind exactly as it really afterwards occurred—the fact that with his arrival at Jerusalem a time of captivity would begin, which would set a limit to his free apostolic work for ever. How could he have foreseen this so distinctly then, or have been able so exactly to predict what did not take shape till four years afterwards, and even then, it is probable, in a manner totally unexpected by the Apostle? Must not this incline us to think that the speech was not really so delivered by the Apostle as we have it, but only put into his mouth by the author *post eventum*? This theory is supported also by some very trustworthy criteria, which point to a later date of composition. The πρεσβύτεροι τῆς ἐκκλησίας (17), the ἐπίσκοποι, whom τὸ Πνεῦμα τὸ Ἅγιον ἔθετο ποιμαίνειν τὴν ἐκκλησίαν τοῦ Κυρίου, ἣν περιεποιήσατο διὰ τοῦ αἵματος τοῦ ἰδίου (28), are here invested with an importance of which there is no trace in the genuine Epistles of the Apostle Paul. The more weight must be laid on this as it is connected with another point, which, as it was closely allied with it in reality, is also allied with it here. The exhortations to watchfulness and faithful care for the church which the departing Apostle here gives, were addressed especially to the πρεσβύτεροι, or ἐπίσκοποι, because, as the author represents him as saying to them, xx. 29, ἐλεύσονται μετὰ τὴν ἄφιξίν μου λύκοι βαρεῖς εἰς ὑμᾶς, μὴ φειδόμενοι τοῦ ποιμνίου· καὶ ἐξ ὑμῶν αὐτῶν ἀναστήσονται ἄνδρες λαλοῦντες διεστραμμένα, τοῦ ἀποσπᾶν τοὺς μαθητὰς ὀπίσω αὐτῶν. That by these dangerous wolves so destructive to the flock are meant false teachers there can be no doubt; but we cannot overlook the fact that they are such false teachers as arise in the midst of the Christian Church itself, and draw disciples after them by departure from orthodoxy. How distinctly the existence of sects of heretics is here indicated, as they existed certainly not before the close of the first century, but more probably at the beginning of the second, as if this had been a spreading evil in the Church at that time. But of all this we find no trace in the genuine Epistles of the Apostle, which only speak of other kinds of false teachers and opponents of the Apostle. Only in the so-called Pastoral Epistles of the Apostle is there somewhat of a parallel to this passage, but the less doubt there is of their being spurious, and of their date being far removed from the apostolic period, the more distinctly does their agreement with the Acts of the Apostles on this point prove that this speech also bears the stamp of a later period; and we are not surprised to find that the author himself could not entirely conceal the fact of the difference of date, as he delays the appearance of these dangerous heretics till after the departure of the Apostle ($\mu\epsilon\tau\grave{a}$ $\tau\grave{\eta}\nu$ $\ddot{a}\phi\iota\xi\acute{\iota}\nu$ $\mu o\upsilon$, 29). The conclusion is obvious that throughout this speech that which is represented as a prophetic seeing of the Future on the part of the Apostle, is really a *vaticinium post eventum*, of which he is represented as the speaker.

It is therefore clear that the author of the Acts of the Apostles fixed upon the time when the Apostle Paul, on his last journey to Jerusalem, came into the neighbourhood of the church in whose midst he had so long laboured, in order to make him deliver a formal and solemn farewell speech, and in it, before these witnesses, to give an account of his apostolic mission up to that time. This was a moment full of importance, a critical turning-point in the life of the Apostle: he was leaving the chief theatre of his apostolic activity to which he was bound by so many solemn ties of the Past and thoughts of the Future. His departure from this sphere of labour was at the same time his farewell to his apostolic career; he was now for the last time the Apostle, working free and uncontrolled, and immediately afterwards there was to begin for him a period of imprisonment from which, however long it lasted, he was never again to be free. In this solemn light did this occasion appear to the author of the Acts of the Apostles, when from his own standpoint he reviewed the course of the events which had followed in such close connection from one pregnant event; and he believed that it was his duty as a thoughtful author, following the development of events with all attention, to represent this crisis in its full significance and solemnity. But only from the standpoint of a later time could the affair be thus considered. However much the principles enunciated may be worthy of the Apostle,—though the feelings and thoughts he is made to express, and the whole scene presented to us may be beautiful, elevating, tender, and moving,—it is to the author, not to the Apostle, that all must be referred, and we must even hold it to be extremely doubtful whether anything corresponding to this scene ever occurred at all. The fact that only the elders and bishops were summoned by the Apostle as representatives of the Church over which they presided shows the spirit of a later time. If the speech was not really so delivered, the occurrences which followed at its conclusion (36-38) must share its fate. We have here a striking instance how well the author of the Acts of the Apostles understood how to paint in living colours a situation so full of emotion, but at the same time to what extent he thought himself warranted to avail himself of his literary freedom.

The parallel with the Apostle Peter, which is generally kept in view, is not directly apparent in the two speeches now under consideration; still they must be reckoned as apologetic. Such a picture of the Apostle's activity, showing how it went forth in every direction, and was everywhere more or less successful, such a description of the devotion and self-sacrifice with which he applied himself to his office,[1] can only tend to the renown of the

[1] A special passing reference to Peter may, however, be contained in the words, xx. 20, οὐδὲν ὑπεστειλάμην τῶν συμφερόντων, τοῦ μὴ ἀναγγεῖλαι ὑμῖν καὶ διδάξαι ὑμᾶς δημοσίᾳ καὶ κατ' οἴκους. Compare 27. It seems that that rectitude in the office of teacher, and freedom from all taint of hypocrisy, which the Jewish Christians claimed for their Peter in order to defend him from the reproach of the ὑποστέλλειν, Gal. ii. 12, is here claimed for the Apostle Paul as well.

Apostle, and to the dispersion of the prejudices conceived against him. But there is no question that we find the apologetic parallel between the two Apostles again, when in the same section of the Acts of the Apostles we turn from the speech to the miracles, and to other tokens of the apostolic activity.

The first narrative we have to deal with here, Acts xix. 1, is one of the most obscure and difficult parts of the Acts of the Apostles, and can only be rightly understood from the point of view of this parallel. The question is about disciples of John who had only been baptised with the baptism of John, but received baptism in the name of the Lord Jesus from the Apostle Paul. To this class belongs also the Alexandrine Apollos, mentioned xviii. 25, for it is said of him also that he had only known the baptism of John. What conception are we to form of these disciples of John? On one side these men are described as Christians, they are even called disciples, $\mu a\theta\eta\tau a\grave{\iota}$ (which expression cannot possibly be taken in any other sense than the general one, and must mean disciples of Jesus), ver. 1, and also believers, $\pi\iota\sigma\tau\epsilon\acute{\upsilon}\sigma a\nu\tau\epsilon\varsigma$, ver. 2 ; and it is said of Apollos, xviii. 25, not only that he was instructed in the doctrine of the Lord, but that he taught the things of the Lord, and enforced them with all the fervour of his spirit. On the other hand, we have indications that these men were not precisely Christians. They were baptised in the name of the Lord Jesus, because John, whose baptism alone they knew, had only baptised them into the faith of one who was to come after him. That this One who was to follow John had really now come seems to have been still unknown to these disciples of John. Although Apollos appears to have been acquainted not only with the doctrine, but with the person of the Lord ($\tau\grave{a}\ \pi\epsilon\rho\grave{\iota}\ \tau o\hat{\upsilon}\ K\upsilon\rho\acute{\iota}o\upsilon$, xviii. 25), yet his knowledge must have been very incomplete and imperfect, as Aquila and Priscilla undertook to instruct him more exactly in the divine doctrine. How can we believe both these statements and unite them in a coherent account? Olshausen holds that these disciples of John " formed a middle party between those adherents of John who, like the Apostles, had identified themselves unreservedly with the Church, and those who openly opposed Christianity, making the Baptist the Messiah, and who were afterwards known as Zabians. This middle party had indeed been led by the Baptist to Jesus as the Messiah, and had been warmed by his light, but they knew nothing further about him, probably owing to the journeys which they made into foreign lands before the outpouring of the Holy Spirit." But, in the first place, this is not very probable in itself, and in the second it does not meet the case of Apollos, of whom it is expressly said that he ἐλάλει καὶ ἐδίδασκεν ἀκριβῶς τὰ περὶ τοῦ Κυρίου. How could this be said of him, if he knew nothing more of Jesus than what John the Baptist hinted about him, and when he had at last an opportunity of learning τὴν ὁδὸν τοῦ Κυρίου, how could he remain unacquainted with the most important thing of all? Equally vague is the relation of these disciples of John to the Holy Spirit. According to Olshausen, the meaning of their words is that their notion of God was still that of a rigid, self-contained, incommunicable unity, and that they had no insight into the distinctive properties of Father, Son, and Holy Ghost, which arise out of the essential nature of Spirit, and without which God cannot be apprehended as a living God who communicates and reveals himself. But even as Jews they must have known of the Holy Spirit as the principle of divine revelation, while we find them affirming, xix. 2, ἀλλ' οὐδὲ εἰ Πνεῦμα ἅγιόν ἐστιν, ἠκούσαμεν. Undoubtedly these words can only be understood as referring to the imparting of the Holy Spirit as the peculiar principle of Christianity, but this explanation fails to give us a satisfactory and consistent notion of what happened, unless we take it that the signs of the Holy Spirit which we are to think of here are those manifestations which the Acts regards as the essential and characteristic token of his presence, namely, the λαλεῖν γλώσσαις and the προφητεύειν. It was of these that they knew nothing, and this is what distinguishes them as disciples of John from the Christian μαθηταί in the more restricted sense. The best illustration of the passage is to be found in xi. 15, where Peter says that as soon as he began to speak in the house of Cornelius, the Holy Ghost fell on Cornelius and on the Gentiles who were with him, in the same manner as it had done on them, the Apostles, at the beginning, and that he then remembered the words of the Lord:—'Ἰωάννης μὲν ἐβάπτισεν ὕδατι, ὑμεῖς δὲ βαπτισθήσεσθε ἐν Πνεύματι ἁγίῳ. Here we see distinctly what we have to understand when the Acts speaks of the βάπτισμα 'Ἰωάννου and the βάπτισμα εἰς τὸ ὄνομα Κυρίου 'Ἰησοῦ. As in the case of Cornelius and those who were baptised with him, the descent of the Holy Spirit was at once made known by the λαλεῖν γλώσσαις and the προφητεύειν, so also in the case of the disciples of John. Thus though a man may be acquainted with the doctrine of the Lord and a believer in him, yet if he has not yet experienced these operations of the Spirit he is merely at the stage of the baptism of John; he does not become a Christian in the fullest sense till he is baptised with the Holy Spirit as well. But this is not the whole of the explanation we require: we must seek for some clearer light on these disciples of John. The λαλεῖν γλώσσαις and the προφητεύειν, in the sense in which the author of the Acts unquestionably uses them in chap. ii., can only be held to be a mythical representation of the operation of the Holy Spirit. Now if in this case we try to substitute the thing itself for the mythical veil of it, we find that we have no characteristic mark that could serve to distinguish the disciples of John from other Christians. What are we to think of them, if they were Christians, but Christians on a lower level than the rest, in that the Christian inspiration did not manifest its presence in them in the same lively manner as in other Christians? This inferiority must have had its root in a defective Christian instruction and life, and how could this form a distinct criterion to mark them off from other Christians? At that time, as at every time, we may assume that Christians were divided into the less perfect and the more perfect,— into those who were moved in a deep and living way by the Christian principle and those who felt it much less profoundly. Thus everything depends on the sense in which the Acts speaks of λαλεῖν γλώσσαις and προφητεύειν, and only so far as we take these mythical symbols to have been actual realities, can we suppose that the disciples of John were a peculiar class of Christians. This appears unmistakably in the case of Apollos, who is associated with them. Let us read the description of him given us, xviii. 25, 26, without the words ἐπιστάμενος μόνον τὸ βάπτισμα Ἰωάννου, which are evidently intended merely to make the transition from Apollos to the disciples of John, who are spoken of immediately after, and to identify him with them as one of the same class; and does not the account of Apollos then become clear and consistent, without anything being lost? We then find Apollos to have been an Alexandrian who, as was to be expected, did not adhere to the strict Judaism of the Jerusalem party, but who had not yet become acquainted with Pauline Christianity, nearly as he approached it, and easy as it was for him to adopt it. This form of Christianity he first learned from Aquila and Priscilla, the intimate friends of the Apostle, and thus he left the peculiar isolated position he had hitherto held as a sort of intermediate party between the Jewish Apostles and the Apostle of the Gentiles, and attached himself to the Apostle Paul, as we see from the Epistles to the Corinthians. Is not this a perfectly clear and satisfactory account of him, and does not the βάπτισμα Ἰωάννου envelop him in obscurity? We cannot help thinking that the peculiar phenomenon which was found in the history of Apollos suggested to the writer his notion of the disciples of John: in the form in which they are here presented they cannot possibly have existed. As distinguished from the βάπτισμα Ἰωάννου, which is mentioned in the case of Apollos, the βάπτισμα εἰς τὸ ὄνομα τοῦ Κυρίου Ἰησοῦ has now assumed the form of a λαλεῖν γλώσσαις and a προφητεύειν, which manifest themselves in a special class of Christians. This recurrence of the speaking with tongues is, as we easily see, the point of the whole narrative; it is for this purpose that the disciples of John are brought upon the stage. Now, what is the author's object in thus bringing up once more the λαλεῖν γλώσσαις? It is evidently done for the sake of the Apostle Paul. It is the imposition of his hands that has this miraculous operation of the Holy Ghost for its immediate result. Thus in the case of Apollos, whose βάπτισμα

Ἰωάννου required to be supplemented by the βάπτισμα εἰς τὸ ὄνομα τοῦ Κυρίου Ἰησοῦ as well as that of the others, we read neither of baptism and imposition of hands nor of any λαλεῖν γλώσσαις or προφητεύειν, since Aquila and Priscilla could not represent the Apostle in these particulars. As it is only the Apostle whose laying on of hands produces such an effect, this is a clear proof of his genuine Apostolic character. This is what the author of the Acts wants to bring out, and for no other reason than that the Apostle Paul may not be found wanting in any distinction which the Apostle Peter enjoyed. The Acts represents that by the conversion of the first Gentile, Cornelius, Peter became an Apostle to the Gentiles, and had precedence of Paul, the special Apostle to the Gentiles in that capacity; and as the view of the Acts on the λαλεῖν γλώσσαις is that it occurred only where the Holy Ghost manifested its operations in a new class of converts to Christianity, a λαλεῖν γλώσσαις must have taken place in connection with what Peter did at the conversion of Cornelius. The conversion of Cornelius was, according to the Acts, one of the most brilliant episodes in the apostolical career of Peter, and the manifestation of the Holy Ghost in so conspicuous a manner upon that occasion was a principal element in his triumph. Now though Paul was placed second to Peter as an Apostle to the Gentiles, yet he was as much as possible to be made equal to him too; and so the λαλεῖν γλώσσαις had to be given to him as a direct operation of the Holy Ghost which accompanied and attested his Apostolic activity. But to what class of men was this fresh λαλεῖν γλώσσαις to be represented as having been imparted? The first occasion when it was bestowed was the first Pentecost, and those whom it then showed to be the organs of the Spirit given by the risen Jesus were converts from Judaism. On the second occasion, at the conversion of Cornelius, it had proved the same of the first-fruits of the Gentiles. Now if the λαλεῖν γλώσσαις was to have the same significance as on these two occasions, it had to be imparted to a new class of men, composed of neither Jews nor Gentiles. The disciples of John seemed to meet these conditions; they formed a peculiar third class of half-believers in addition to the class of unbelieving Jews and the class of unbelieving Gentiles. They were not Gentiles (for they were born Jews), nor Jews like other Jews (for they believed in Jesus), and yet they were not Christians, for the Holy Spirit had not yet manifested itself in them as in other Christians. They were thus a third class of men, half-Christians, who were now to be made full Christians by the λαλεῖν γλώσσαις. So simple is the solution of the strange enigma of these disciples of John when we refer the different elements of the problem to the ruling idea of the author, without remembering which all must be dark and unintelligible, namely, to make good the parallel between the two Apostles by a new and striking demonstration of the Apostle Paul's apostolic authority and power.

Besides Antioch, which was the Apostle's starting-point, and whither he returned from time to time as he also did to Jerusalem (xviii. 22), the Acts represents Corinth and Ephesus as the chief scenes of his activity. In each of these towns the Apostle spent a considerable time, ceasing altogether from travel. The city of Ephesus, however, was the scene of the Apostle's most brilliant and successful labours. Here, after he left Corinth, the Apostle took up his residence, and spent two whole years; here, as the farewell speech at Miletus shows, he found his true sphere of labour. Here, accordingly, the author of the Acts reports not only the λαλεῖν γλώσσαις of which we have spoken, but also a number of miracles and other effects accompanying the Apostle's preaching, which attest its splendid success, and contribute to the glorification of the Apostle in the same way as the wonderful works of Peter, narrated v. 15, *sq*. During the Apostle Paul's two years' residence at Ephesus, we are told all the dwellers in Asia, Jews and Greeks, heard the word of the Lord; and God worked miracles of no ordinary nature by the hands of Paul. Even handkerchiefs and other linen that had come in direct contact with the person of Paul were carried to sick persons, and their sicknesses departed from them and the evil spirits went out of them. How remarkable is the similarity between this description of the brilliant success of Paul and what we hear of the Apostle Peter in the passage v. 15. How closely analogous is the purely mythical trait; in the one case it was the shadow of Peter which cured the sick when it fell on them, here it is the handkerchiefs and linen of the Apostle that manifest an inherent miraculous power, like the relics of a later age. We have also a good instance here of how exaggeration is inseparable from imitation; the details here are so apocryphal that we might despair of finding any historical element in the story at all. Among the miraculous deeds of the Apostle Peter we find the expulsion of unclean spirits (v. 16). But in our passage the demons themselves work to promote the faith of Christ, by punishing the abuse of the name of Jesus, which certain Jewish exorcists had ventured on.[1] The demoniac, whose demon seven Jewish exorcists had endeavoured to cast out in the name of Jesus, was outraged at the impurity of their motives in what they did (for demons possess a higher intelligence), and fell upon the exorcists, treating them with such violence

[1] Even in the Gospels, demons are said to be cast out in the name of Jesus (cf. for example Mark xvi. 17), yet the power over demons here ascribed (Acts xix. 13) to the ὄνομα τοῦ Κυρίου Ἰησοῦ is such as we do not find till the post-apostolic age. Compare on this point Justin's Dialogue with the Jew Trypho, ch. 85. Christ, it is here said, is the κύριος τῶν δυνάμεων. ὡς καὶ νῦν ἐκ τῶν ὑπ᾽ ὄψιν γενομένων ῥᾷον ὑμᾶς πεισθῆναι, ἐὰν θέλητε. Κατὰ γὰρ τοῦ ὀνόματος αὐτοῦ τούτου, τοῦ υἱοῦ τοῦ Θεοῦ, καὶ πρωτοτόκου πάσης κτίσεως καὶ διὰ παρθένου γεννηθέντος καὶ παθητοῦ γενομένου ἀνθρώπου, καὶ σταυρωθέντος ἐπὶ Ποντίου Πιλάτου ὑπὸ τοῦ λαοῦ ὑμῶν, καὶ ἀποθανόντος καὶ ἀναστάντος ἐκ νεκρῶν, καὶ ἀναβάντος εἰς τὸν οὐρανὸν πᾶν δαιμόνιον ἐξορκιζόμενον νικᾶται καὶ ὑποτάσσεται. Origen, c. Cels., 1. 25, whilst he speaks of the occult importance of the name, adds: τῆς ὁμοίας ἔχεται περὶ ὀνομάτων φιλοσοφίας καὶ ὁ ἡμέτερος Ἰησοῦς οὗ τὸ ὄνομα μυρίους ἤδη ἐναργῶς ἑώραται δαίμονας ἐξελάσαι ψυχῶν καὶ σωμάτων, ἐνεργῆσαν εἰς ἐκείνους, ἀφ᾽ ὧν ἀπηλάθησαν. Is not this the idea of the passage in the Acts now under consideration? By the υἱοί Σκευᾶ Ἰουδαίου ἀρχιερέως ἑπτὰ are generally understood seven real sons of a Jewish High-Priest (Olshausen makes the ἀρχιερεὺς a chief Rabbi, who, perhaps, was the head of the Ephesian Jewish community), but without doubt the expression υἱός ought to be taken in the sense in which, according to the Jewish mode of writing, the scholars of a master were called his "sons." The High Priest Sceva may therefore have been held by these and other Jewish exorcists as a celebrated master in the art of sorcery. That they were seven is due to the idea that seven demons sometimes took possession of a man. Such a union of spirits was thought to require a similar league of opposing forces to withstand it.

that they fled naked and wounded; and when this was known to all the Jews and Gentiles dwelling in Ephesus, general fear prevailed, and the name of the Lord Jesus was greatly magnified. Many, who already believed, indeed, but who at the same time practised sorcery, now burnt all the books that contained their magic formulas in one enormous pile. Οὕτω κατὰ κράτος, says the Acts of the Apostles at the conclusion of this narrative, ὁ λόγος τοῦ Κυρίου ηὔξανε καὶ ἴσχυεν. This is accordingly the point of view from which the whole narrative is to be considered. It is to give us a striking picture of the all-conquering power with which Paul worked for the spread of the faith of Jesus; but it betrays too distinctly the stamp of a later post-apostolic period. Let it be granted that the circumstances which caused these results really occurred as related (and this can only be granted on the unhistorical supposition of the reality of these demoniacal possessions), and even then we cannot suppose that the Apostle, who was in the habit of judging the result of his work only by the inner operations of the spirit, would have set any value on a propagation of the faith of Christ, however widely extended, which was carried on by such means as the demoniac, or rather the demon himself, employed. If the believers in Ephesus gave up the sorcery which still mingled with their Christianity, only because they deduced from such experiences the lesson that it was not safe to trifle with demons in the insincere manner that the exorcists had done, what was their Christianity but the exchange of one form of superstition for another? And yet the verdict of the author of the Acts on the occurrence is: οὕτω κατὰ κράτος ὁ λόγος τοῦ Κυρίου ηὔξανε καὶ ἴσχυεν. Such an expression of opinion is so unworthy of a companion of an Apostle, and is so much in harmony with the views of a later time, that it leaves us in no doubt about its origin. At the same time we cannot ignore the fact that the narrative, 13-20, as well as that which follows, 21-40, seem to have originated only in an *a priori* abstraction. The intention of the author, as we have already said, was to give as brilliant a picture as possible of the labours of the Apostle at Ephesus. To this end the Paganism that was opposed to Christianity, and required to be overcome by it, had to be clearly portrayed. Now Ephesus was celebrated for two things: for its magic and for its worship of Artemis. The great progress of the cause of the Gospel through the labours of the Apostle had therefore to be demonstrated in relation to those two particulars. That Ephesus was a notorious seat of magic, was clear from the universally known 'Εφέσια γράμματα. From the nature of the case, magic involved, wherever it prevailed, the worship of demons. He who renounced magic had also to renounce demon-worship. Here the demons themselves were made to co-operate to this end; since as intelligent spirits who could penetrate into the inner nature of things, they abhorred a syncretism in which Christianity was so impurely blended, partly with Judaism and partly with heathenism. From such data was the narrative 13-20 constructed.

If the author meant to represent here the victory which the Gospel obtained through Paul, over heathenism in the form in which it then existed at Ephesus, he could not forbear to speak of the celebrated temple-worship of the Ephesian Artemis. Could there be any greater proof of the extent to which the Gospel was prevailing, than that the great Artemis of the Ephesians was losing her worshippers, that the renowned silver shrines could no longer find purchasers, and that the whole guild of silversmiths employed in making them were in danger of losing their occupation, and very naturally broke out into open riot against the man who was the sole cause of this great change of affairs? The connection in which the story of the tumult of Demetrius appears in the Acts at once suggests that it can only be regarded as an ideal picture of the success of the Apostle's labours. We have no security for the truth of the individual statements; and in several points they fail to suggest to us any clear idea of what happened. We thus conclude that the historical result of the whole passage, xix. 10-40, adds nothing to the Apostle's own simple statement, 1 Cor. xvi. 9, about his residence at Ephesus, θύρα γάρ μοι ἀνέῳγε μεγάλη καὶ ἐνεργής, καὶ ἀντικείμενοι πολλοὶ (cf. xv. 32). In fact we see very plainly on comparing v. 15, *sq.*, and xix. 11, *sq.*, that the author had the example of Peter before his eyes; and the picture of the Apostle Paul's operations had to be made to answer to the parallel.

I am disposed to place the story of the youth who fell down from an open window on the third floor during the Apostle's evening discourse at Troas, and whom he brought to life again (Acts xx. 7, *sq.*), under the same point of view. It is certainly probable that the young man was not dead at all, and the whole occurrence admits of a very simple explanation, just as it is told here, without the supposition of any miracle. On the other hand, the historian's expression leaves it equally open to suppose that a miracle was wrought. That the Apostle hastened to the youth and laid himself upon him, proves nothing against the supposition of a miracle: secondary means of this kind were often employed in miraculous acts, though in no way necessary to the miracle. The words ἡ γὰρ ψυχὴ αὐτοῦ ἐν αὐτῷ ἐστιν may indeed signify "his life is still in him;" but how can it be said that Calvin's remark, "non negat fuisse mortuum quia miraculi gloriam hoc modo extingueret—sed sensus est, vitam illi redditam esse Dei gratiâ," is only a strange evasion, as Meyer, among the recent commentators, expresses it? How, we cannot but ask, could the author say, xx. 9, simply, ἤρθη νεκρὸς, if he did not really mean the reader to understand that the youth was dead? The whole occurrence may have happened in a perfectly natural manner; yet the writer must have considered it to have been a miracle, and must have designed to represent it as such. What led him to do this, if not the idea that Paul must not be left behind the other apostles in respect of miracles, and especially that he must be shown to be on a level with Peter, who among his other miracles had raised a dead person to life (ix. 36-43)?[1]

[1] In the narrative of the miracles performed by the Apostle Peter at Lydda and Joppa (Acts ix. 33, *sqq.*), the different miracles of Jesus, as reported in the Gospels, are summarised and transferred to Peter. Thus besides the cure of a paralytic (ix. 33-35 cf. Mark ii. 1, *sq.*), we have a raising from the dead, 36-43. As the raising of the young man at Nain, Luke vii. 12, was specially called for by the fact that the youth was the only son of his mother, and that she was a widow,

An occurrence which in itself had been perfectly fortuitous and natural could easily be utilised for this purpose. The narrative xxviii. 8-10 may probably be regarded in the same way; in which the Apostle appears as a miracle-worker, but which does not strictly require the hypothesis of miracle to explain it.

so a special reason is alleged here. It is very naturally drawn from the alms-giving and good works on which the writer has been enlarging. A life that has been spent in so many good works,—this idea is most pathetically represented by the widows who stand round weeping and displaying the clothes and garments which the dead woman had made for them,—such a life should not be taken from the world, or should be restored to the world again. On this account the act of restoring to the friends is specially dwelt on here as well as in the gospel of Luke. As it is said in Luke, καὶ ἔδωκεν αὐτὸν τῇ μητρὶ αὐτοῦ, so here, ix. 41, φωνήσας δὲ τοὺς ἁγίους καὶ τὰς χήρας παρέστησεν αὐτὴν ζῶσαν. For the rest the narrative closely follows that of the three Evangelists, Matthew ix. 18, sq., 23-26; Mark v. 22, sq.; Luke viii. 41, especially that of Mark. We may compare Mark v. 40, ἐκβαλὼν ἅπαντας καὶ κρατήσας τῆς χειρὸς τοῦ παιδίου, λέγει αὐτῇ Ταλιθά, κοῦμι· ... καὶ εὐθέως ἀνέστη τὸ κοράσιον, with Acts ix. 40, ἐκβαλὼν δὲ ἔξω πάντας ὁ Πέτρος, εἶπε· Ταβιθά, ἀνάστηθι: ἡ δὲ ... ἀνεκάθισε (compare Luke vii. 14, εἶπε νεανίσκε, σοὶ λέγω ἐγέρθητι· καὶ ἀνεκάθισεν ὁ νεανίας)· δοὺς δὲ αὐτῇ χεῖρα ἀνέστησεν αὐτήν. The supposition, however, is very obvious that the name of the woman Ταβιθά is only borrowed from the Ταλιθά κοῦμι of Mark. The name Ταβιθά, Roe-deer or Gazelle in Hebrew and Syriac, means the same as Ταλιθά, with which it is interchangeable by Paronomasia, namely maiden; and as Mark (v. 41) adds ὅ ἐστι μεθερμηνευόμενον τὸ κοράσιον, the author of the Acts follows with ἡ διερμη-νευομένη λέγεται Δορκάς.

CHAPTER VIII.

THE APOSTLE'S ARREST AT JERUSALEM.—ACTS XXI., *sq.*

THE sad and gloomy forebodings with which, according to the Acts of the Apostles, the Apostle Paul set out on his journey to Jerusalem, and which he expressed in his farewell speech at Miletus, were too well grounded to admit of their fulfilment being long delayed. Scarcely had the Apostle arrived at Jerusalem when a series of events occurred, the result of which was that he found himself in the hands of the Roman magistrate at Jerusalem. After an imprisonment of two years at Cæsarea, he was removed to Rome as a Roman prisoner to await the further decision of his fate by the Emperor, to whom, as a Roman citizen, he had appealed. Here, if anywhere, in this so famous passage of the Apostle's life, we might expect from the Acts a narrative which we might implicitly receive as true. But we are deceived in this expectation. The false position which the Acts makes the Apostle take up towards Judaism could not fail to modify the narrative of the final catastrophe which occurred at Jerusalem. It cannot, indeed, be doubted that that catastrophe was brought on by the hatred which the Jews had all along cherished against the Apostle as an apostate from and enemy to the national religion. This preparation for it is not wanting in the Acts, throughout which the Jews appear as the Apostle's bitterest enemies, who not only resist with all their might his preaching of the Gospel, but also attempt in every way to wreak their hatred on his person. But when we inquire for the precise cause of this hatred which the Jews bore to the Apostle, the Acts provides us with no adequate explanation: the apologetic tendency of that work called imperatively for the concealment of the Apostle's true relation to the Jews as well as to the Jewish-Christians. This is the only possible way of accounting for the fact that the Acts gives a totally different picture of the occurrences at Jerusalem and Antioch from that which we find in the Apostle's own Epistles. He is made to accommodate himself to Judaism in a way to which he could not have consented without utterly deserting his principles. On this point we have already remarked how little credit is due to the assertion of the Acts, that Timothy allowed himself to be circumcised at the Apostle's suggestion. Our verdict must be the same with regard to those actions ascribed by the Acts to the Apostle, which show a similar leaning to the usages and institutions of Judaism. If these be not directly inconsistent with his well-known principles, they at least do not increase our confidence in him. Twice does the Acts draw attention to the fact that he did not neglect the customary visits to Jerusalem at the times of the festivals. He is represented as saying, xviii. 21, $\Delta\epsilon\hat{\iota}\ \mu\epsilon\ \pi\acute{a}\nu\tau\omega\varsigma\ \tau\grave{\eta}\nu\ \dot{\epsilon}o\rho\tau\grave{\eta}\nu\ \tau\grave{\eta}\nu\ \dot{\epsilon}\rho\chi o\mu\acute{\epsilon}\nu\eta\nu\ \pi o\iota\hat{\eta}\sigma a\iota\ \epsilon\dot{\iota}\varsigma\ \mathrm{`I}\epsilon\rho o\sigma\acute{o}\lambda\upsilon\mu a$. He began this same journey, moreover, with taking a vow, of which the undoubtedly Jewish practice of shaving the head was a feature.[1] He did not wish to be detained on his last journey, because, as we are told, Acts xx. 16, he hasted $\epsilon\dot{\iota}\ \delta\upsilon\nu a\tau\grave{o}\nu\ \hat{\eta}\nu\ a\dot{\upsilon}\tau\hat{\omega},\ \tau\grave{\eta}\nu\ \dot{\eta}\mu\acute{\epsilon}\rho a\nu\ \tau\hat{\eta}\varsigma\ \pi\epsilon\nu\tau\eta\kappa o\sigma\tau\hat{\eta}\varsigma\ \gamma\epsilon\nu\acute{\epsilon}\sigma\theta a\iota\ \epsilon\dot{\iota}\varsigma\ \mathrm{`I}\epsilon\rho o\sigma\acute{o}\lambda\upsilon\mu a$. The Apostle himself says very simply, Romans xv. 25, in speaking of this journey, that he is going to Jerusalem, $\delta\iota a\kappa o\nu\hat{\omega}\nu\ \tau o\hat{\iota}\varsigma\ \dot{a}\gamma\acute{\iota}o\iota\varsigma$, in order to convey thither the contributions collected in Macedonia and Achaia. In any case this must have been the chief object of the journey, as we see from 2 Cor. viii. and ix., where these contributions are spoken of as a thing to which the Apostle attached great importance. The Acts says nothing of this, but on the other hand it dwells largely on the festival journey, on which the Apostle is entirely silent; and this

[1] Most commentators take the $\kappa\epsilon\iota\rho\acute{a}\mu\epsilon\nu o\varsigma$, Acts xviii. 18, as relating to the Apostle. Perhaps this is meant to prepare us for his readiness to undertake the Nazarite offering, xxi. 24.

is evidently done with a view to making the Apostle appear as a faithful adherent of the Jewish national worship. But if the Apostle always showed such an adherence to the ancient religion of his fathers—an adherence which was not invalidated by his denial of the necessity of circumcision,—how are we to explain the great collision into which he came with his brethren in the faith, and the irreconcilable hate with which they followed him? His faith in Jesus as the Messiah cannot have been the cause of this hatred, or it would have been directed equally against the Jewish-Christians who lived among the Jews in Jerusalem. It can only be explained by his teaching on the subject of the law, and nothing is more natural than that the Jews should consider him a deadly enemy to their religion, if, on the one hand, he was desirous of making the Gentiles Jews, by allowing them to partake of the Messianic salvation, which was ordained for the Jews alone, and on the other hand of relieving them from the necessity of circumcision, which the Jews regarded as the only portal through which they could enter to participate in the blessings of Judaism. As soon as circumcision ceased to be the specific mark of Judaism, the essential difference between Jew and Gentile, and with it the absolute importance of Judaism, disappeared. Thus a teaching which insisted more than anything on the assertion that circumcision was no longer necessary, was obviously the most direct contradiction of the very principle of Judaism. But however clearly this may explain the enmity of the Jews to the Apostle, yet it remains as inexplicable as ever, how, if we believe the Acts, the hatred of the Jews was directed exclusively against Paul, and not against the older Apostles, who on the subject of circumcision were entirely agreed with him. But if, as the Epistle to the Galatians leads us to assume, the elder Apostles were not agreed with him on this point, but, on the contrary, were at one with the Jewish-Christian party generally in upholding the necessity of circumcision, then we naturally conclude that the attack made on the Apostle on account of his doctrine of freedom from the law did not proceed only from the Jews, but that the Jewish-Christians took part in it as well. And what can we expect from a narrative which misrepresents the position of affairs in such essential particulars as this? Must it not misrepresent the events which followed, and if it cannot pass over the real facts of the case in complete silence, must it not fall into contradiction with itself? We have to keep this in mind in considering the narrative of the Apostle's arrest at Jerusalem with the events which led to it and accompanied it. We meet here with difficulties and contradictions which are nothing but the natural collision which must ensue, when a historian who has from the first taken up such a false attitude towards the facts of history, finds afterwards that he must treat in some way or other the events in which the sequel of the history is developed.

This view suggests itself irresistibly in regard to the first point with which the Acts of the Apostles begins the narrative of these last occurrences in Jerusalem. The Apostle went, on his arrival in Jerusalem, to James, the head of the Church at Jerusalem. In an assembly of the collected Elders, he gave a detailed account of the results of his apostolic labours among the Gentiles up to that time. All that he had to say on this subject was received with the most sympathetic recognition, but at the same time he was told that it was publicly known in Jerusalem that his teaching had been opposed to circumcision. In order, therefore, to allay the hostility which his appearance in Jerusalem would excite, he was advised to join himself to four men, doubtless members of the Christian Church in Jerusalem, who had just undertaken a Nazarite vow, and to defray their charges in carrying out their vow, as was often done. Thus every one would see that there was nothing in the accusation which had been brought against him, but that he was an exact observer of the law. This advice the Apostle followed. Now it is not inconceivable that he should have gone into a course of action which, without any sacrifice of principle on his part, might have the effect of dispelling a prejudice which many had conceived against him, and of lessening the hostility of his enemies. But we must consider well the design which this act was intended to serve. The Apostle was accused of having preached to the Jews in foreign countries that they should forsake Moses, asserting that they should not circumcise their children, nor observe the law (xxi. 21). This accusation was not in itself untrue; it is a matter of fact that the Apostle preached among Jews and Gentiles a doctrine which could not but lead to the discontinuance of circumcision. He made the custom appear to be totally useless for the purpose for which it had hitherto been held necessary. Now we read that the Apostle was recommended to perform an action which was intended to impress his opponents with the idea that he still adhered strictly to the law (στοιχεῖς καὶ αὐτὸς τὸν νομον φυλάσσων, i.e. as well as others), and that what was said of him was false (ὧν κατήχηνται περὶ σοῦ οὐδέν ἐστι); false, then, that he was an opponent of circumcision. But how could James, the brother of the Lord, recommend such an act to be done from such a motive, and how could Paul demean himself to do it? What should we think of the character of these men, if we supposed them capable of such a mode of action? The author of the Acts felt this himself, hence he takes care to limit the διδάσκειν ἀποστασίαν ἀπὸ Μωυσέως to the Jews who lived among the Gentiles (21 cf. 25), and the accusation is put in such a form as to imply the most direct hostility to circumcision and the Mosaic Law (λέγων μὴ περιτέμνειν αὐτοὺς τὰ τέκνα, μηδὲ τοῖς ἔθεσι περιπατεῖν, 21). Ver. 25 also bears reference to this. The meaning of this verse is, that the freedom of the Gentile-Christians is not to be curtailed; it is still to be the case that nothing further is exacted from them than the φυλάσσεσθαι . . . τό τε εἰδωλόθυτον, etc.: thus circumcision is not exacted from them. But how could the Apostle uphold the necessity of circumcision for the Jews if he denied it for the Gentiles? The reference to the transactions of Acts xv., an event which cannot have taken place as is here implied, simply shows that the author wished to represent matters in such a way as if in all his preaching on the subject of the law the Apostle had never said anything affecting Judaism in the very least. The commentators on the Acts hold it therefore to be inconceivable that the Apostle Paul ever directly attacked the observance of the law; what he attacked as unchristian, they say, was merely the making salvation depend on the observance of the law.[1] But even in this he was most distinctly controverting the Jewish-Christian view of the necessity of observing the law, and could by no means escape the charge that his whole doctrine aimed at the subversion of the law. On the other side of the question the commentators find no difficulty in believing that by his example, and by the spirit of his whole life and work, the Apostle led many Jewish-Christians to give up the observance of the Mosaic law altogether, and that with a good conscience. How weak, then, and how unworthy of an Apostle is the evasion to which it is necessary to resort in order to justify the assertion ὧν κατήχηνται περὶ σοῦ οὐδέν ἐστιν, ἀλλὰ στοιχεῖς καὶ αὐτὸς τὸν νόμον φυλάσσων. It was certainly very far from the Apostle's intention to pretend to such an observance of the law. In his own Epistles he states in the frankest manner that he is an opponent of circumcision, and considers adherence to it to be quite inconsistent with the principles of his teaching. Here again we find the Epistle to the Galatians maintaining a consistent and irreconcilable contradiction to the Acts of the Apostles. "Behold, I Paul say unto you," the Apostle unreservedly declares, Gal. v. 2, 3, 6, 11, 13, "that if ye be circumcised, Christ shall profit you nothing. For I testify again to every man that is circumcised, that he is a debtor to do the whole law." "For in Christ Jesus neither circumcision availeth anything nor uncircumcision; but faith which worketh by love." "And I, brethren, if I yet preach circumcision, why do I yet suffer persecution? then is the offence of the cross ceased." "Ye have been

---

[1] Thus Olshausen on Acts xxi. 17-26; cf. also Neander, p. 425, Bohn, 302. "Paul combated the outward observance of Judaism only so far as the justification and sanctification of men were made to depend on it." What Neander says against me in this passage does not in the least alter the case. The Apostle does express the opinion (1 Cor. vii. 18-20) that Jews should remain Jews after their conversion, that Christianity does not require any one to change in these outward things;—these are merely outward things, and being such, may remain as they are. But this is evidently quite a new way of looking on these things, and it must have been perfectly evident that if circumcision was no longer necessary to salvation, its mere outward retention could be of no value, and must come to an end sooner or later, even for the Jews themselves.

called unto liberty." Let it not be said that the Apostle speaks in this manner only to the Gentile-Christians of Galatia. When he declares in the same Epistle, "Ye are the children of God by faith in Christ Jesus, for as many of you as have been baptised into Christ have put on Christ; there is neither Jew nor Greek," he expressly asserts the principle that no difference can be acknowledged between Jew and Gentile. With what appearance of truth could he then come before the Jews with the statement, "In all that you have heard of me there is not a particle of truth. I am an adherent and an observer of the law as well as you!" Would this have been a less contemptible $\dot{\upsilon}\pi\acute{o}\kappa\rho\iota\sigma\iota\varsigma$ than that which the Apostle himself so unreservedly condemned in Peter? It is impossible that the Apostle should have resolved on such a course of action on the grounds given by the author of the Acts; and if the motive disappears from which a certain course of action is said to have proceeded, how doubtful does the action itself become! And what reasonable ground could be imagined for such a course of action as the Apostle was recommended to adopt? The result showed at once, and unmistakably, how vain and useless the advice and its adoption were. We conclude then that it is simply the author of the Acts who wishes to represent the Apostle as a faithful adherent to, and observer of the Mosaic law; here, as well as everywhere (especially in xxviii. 17), he slurs over, or rather entirely ignores, the real difference between him and the Jewish-Christian party; he desires, in one word, to represent the Apostle of the Gentiles at any cost as an Apostle of the Jews, which he certainly neither was, nor, according to his own express declaration, ever wished to be considered.

The advice thus given to the Apostle is founded on the alleged fact that there were so many tens of thousands of believing Jews in Jerusalem who were all strict zealots for the law (xxi. 20). But here also we meet with an insoluble difficulty. We must ask, how the Church of Jerusalem, which according to all accounts was not a considerable body, comes now to reckon as her members all those thousands of believing Jews? The Jewish inhabitants of Jerusalem in general might be correctly described as "many tens of thousands," and it seems very natural to suppose that the words τῶν πεπιστευκότων after Ἰουδαίων are spurious. I have expressed this view before, and the objection has been raised to it that the statement thus made to Paul that there were in Jerusalem many thousands of Jews who were all zealous observers of the law, would have been self-evident and meaningless. I remark, however, that the statement was not made to Paul by way of giving him information, but merely as appealing to a fact with which he was well acquainted, in favour of the cautious policy which he ought to pursue. But this correction of one mistake can do but little to restore credit to a narrative in which the grounds of critical objection lie so deep. If, comforted by Neander's remark, that this number need not be taken as an exact estimate,[1] we pass over the many "tens of thousands," there still remain the "believing Jews" of whom the Apostle was warned, Jewish-Christians, that is to say, of the very same church in which we have just seen that the brethren gave the Apostle so friendly a reception. These same brethren are now described to him as zealots for the law, from whom he had to fear the worst on account of the accusation which had been brought against him of preaching apostasy from the Mosaic law. How can we possibly harmonise these two statements? We might suppose that the members of the Church at Jerusalem were not all equally prejudiced and hostile to the Apostle, yet how trifling a proportion must the few brethren who were the exception have been to the general mass of the Jewish-Christians, who regarded the Apostle simply as the worst enemy of the law.[2] For we cannot help seeing that the description

[1] A writer who at first makes thousands upon thousands be converted by every sermon of the Apostles, need not surely make much difficulty about tens of thousands at this stage!

[2] Kuinöel appreciates this difficulty, and remarks quite frankly on ἀδελφοί (17), "Apostoli et presbyteri, nam coetus non favebat Paulo." He is taken to task, however, by Meyer, who thinks his remark strange, "as if ver. 20 spoke of a bigoted hostility to which there were no exceptions, and which went so far as not even to allow of a friendly reception." But is not this undeniably the meaning of what follows? The prejudice against the Apostle was so great that he was

of the temper of these zealots for the law is meant to depict to us that same hatred of the Apostle which soon afterwards broke out in so threatening a manner in spite of the advice which, though well-meant, could yet, from the nature of the case, scarcely avert the danger.[1] And why should we hesitate to believe in such a disposition against the Apostle among the Jewish-Christian inhabitants of Jerusalem, as well as among the Jewish inhabitants; are not those who came from James described to us as his declared foes and opponents? Does not this statement about the great apprehension for the Apostle, awakened at that time by the zeal for the law cherished by those inhabitants of Jerusalem, agree completely with what we know of the feeling which was afterwards entertained against the Apostle Paul by the Ebionites, who were so nearly allied to the Jewish-Christians of Jerusalem? We can only wonder how a writer who has hitherto taken the greatest pains to conceal, as much as possible, the true relation in which the Apostle stood to the Jewish-Christians, should have here come forward for once with the bare naked truth, and this too in a connection in which the matter in hand had so great a practical importance, and by its results must have tended to bring the

not recognised as a brother in the faith, but regarded only as an apostate. Thus it requires to be explained how in the Church of Jerusalem, a Church which was under the immediate guidance of the Apostles, such a difference had arisen between these ἀδελφοὶ πεπιστευκότες and the ἀδελφοὶ. Neander is completely silent on this point. Though, as Zeller remarks (Apostel. Gesch. p. 281), the words of ver. 21 need not involve more than a suspicion, the case is not much altered. Suspicion would be enough to fan a considerable blaze of fanaticism in zealots such as these.

[1] The writer himself suggests the connection between this temper of the Jewish-Christians and the scenes which took place afterwards. See ver. 22. Though the words πάντως δεῖ πλῆθος συνελθεῖν should be understood not of a tumult but merely of a concourse of the curious, how would that help us? A multitude which has flocked together from curiosity because an apostate and preacher of apostasy, of whom much has been heard, has ventured to appear in the streets of Jerusalem, cannot be credited with the kindest intentions. In such a case the merest accident might serve as an occasion for the smouldering hatred to burst out into open violence. This συνελθεῖν, then, is not different from the συνδρομὴ τοῦ λαοῦ of ver. 30. It is also evident that οὗτός ἐστιν . . . πάντας πανταχοῦ διδάσκων in ver. 28 refers to ver. 21, ἀποστασίαν διδάσκεις.

Jewish-Christians into disrepute. But the clear literal meaning of his words can leave us in no doubt on the matter, and even if, as the πόσαι μυριάδες seems to indicate, the Jewish-Christians of Jerusalem had become confused in his mind with the general body of the Jewish inhabitants of the city (for there cannot have been a very great difference between the Jews and the Jewish-Christians of Jerusalem),[1] what he has once said cannot be unsaid, and his testimony is of all the more value, as it must be looked on as wrung from him against his will by the might of historical truth. The result then is that, according to the statement of the author of the Acts of the Apostles himself, the Jewish-Christians in Jerusalem saw in the Apostle Paul an apostate from the law, and a preacher of this apostasy among both Jews and Gentiles. If they held this opinion of him, no one can be blamed for thinking that they cannot have been so indifferent and uninterested as is generally supposed, in events which, like the scenes that immediately ensued, were undeniably the natural outcome of views and opinions such as theirs.

What actually happened after this point was doubtless that the Apostle's appearance in Jerusalem led to tumults in which he was saved from the passion of the Jews by the military force of the Romans, but thus became a prisoner in their hands. The Acts tells us this; and it tells us in reality nothing more that we can implicitly believe. What it says of the occurrences which led to this result is all coloured through and through with the apologetic tendency which dominates the work. It is in pursuance of this tendency that the Apostle is made to take the advice that had been offered him. He absolved himself thereby from the charge that had been brought against him; the groundlessness and unreasonableness of the hatred which burst out against him as an apostate became perfectly clear. This idea is the thread which

---

[1] Ἰουδαῖοι οἱ πεπιστευκότες are therefore faithful adherents of the law in general—orthodox Jews, whether they are believing or unbelieving Jews in reference to Christianity. The expression is evidently used by the author in this sense as concerning Judaism merely.

runs through the series of public trials which followed the Apostle's imprisonment. We have here an artistically constructed plot, which, however, is by no means calculated to give us a clear or natural idea of what actually happened. If we turn to the chief scene of the narrative, which is certainly developed with some amount of dramatic interest, namely, the trial of the Apostle before the Sanhedrim, xxiii. 1-10, how unlikely and unintelligible, how unworthy of the Apostle even, does everything appear! Most of all are we struck with the artifice which the Apostle is represented as employing in order to involve the two parties composing the Sanhedrim, namely, the Sadducees and the Pharisees, in a quarrel with each other, so as not only to avert the attention and passion of the Sanhedrim from himself, but to gain for himself the good-will of one of the parties. After the violent outburst of passion from both sides which had interrupted the Apostle's discourse at its very outset, he commenced with the bold declaration, in which he had in view the difference which divided the two parties of the Sadducees and Pharisees, "I am a Pharisee, the son of a Pharisee; of the hope and resurrection of the dead I am called in question." This one word is represented as having had the immediate result not only of setting the Sadducees and Pharisees at violent strife with each other, but of bringing over the Pharisees to the Apostle's side, and making them declare openly that they found no fault in him. Here the first question that arises is whether the Apostle's statement of the difference between himself and his opponents was strictly true. He might agree with the Pharisees in believing in a resurrection, but he could scarcely say with truth that the reason why he stood before that court was that he had preached Jesus as the one through whom the people of Israel's hope of a resurrection was to be fulfilled. For if we take the sense of the Apostle's words, περὶ ἐλπίδος καὶ ἀναστάσεως νεκρῶν ἐγὼ κρίνομαι, as Neander takes it (Bohn, 307), it at once becomes clear that the question raised between him and his opponents was not that of the resurrection of the dead generally, but the question whether or not Jesus had risen from the dead. But this fact could be denied without prejudice to the general doctrine of a resurrection. And although the Apostle agreed with the Pharisees on this point, he at once differed from them with regard to a fact, without the recognition of which the belief in a resurrection could have no value or meaning for him. Here then it was simply useless for him to insist on this point of agreement, which included the bare possibility of the resurrection of Jesus, and at once suggested the great chasm there was between the possible and the actual. Thus it was only very superficially true that he stood for judgment as a Pharisee, on account of a belief which he held in common with the Pharisees. But the Apostle asserted expressly that he was being judged as a Pharisee. Even in this assertion we have a shifty and ambiguous way of evading the question at issue. And the same applies to the statement that the whole difference between the Apostle and his opponents could be reduced to the doctrine of the resurrection. The Apostle must have known perfectly well that the doctrine of the resurrection was not in dispute here at all; in regard to it he was in exactly the same case as the Jewish-Christians of Jerusalem who believed in the resurrection of Jesus and were not molested on that account.

The real cause of offence was that which distinguished him from the Jewish-Christians, namely, his doctrine about the law. Here then we find a second evasion of the real question at issue which does not agree with the Apostle's frank love of truth; and the remark of Grotius on ver. 6, "non deerat Paulo humana etiam prudentia, qua in bonum evangelii utens columbæ serpentem utiliter miscebat et inimicorum dissidiis fruebatur," is a very accurate description of the case, but on that account by no means a vindication of the Apostle. But setting aside these moral difficulties, we can scarcely imagine that a single expression casually let fall by the Apostle regarding the resurrection could at once have kindled so fierce a fire. Parties which differed from each other on such essential points, and yet came in contact with each other so constantly in ordinary life, must long have come to an understanding about the points on which they differed. In the Sanhedrim they were united as members of one and the same tribunal, and we cannot believe that their doctrinal differences could on any occasion break out in passionate conflict; least of all in a case like this where the defence of the accused was so palpable a stratagem. Here, however, we have both parties disputing with a fury and a passion which blinded them to their own interests as much as if they had been quarrelling about these opposing doctrines for the first time. The intention of the author of the Acts of the Apostles in this narrative appears all the more clearly from the absence in it of any historical probability. The Acts makes the Apostle Paul stand throughout in as close a relation as possible to Judaism; his real, essential opposition to it is concealed and ignored, and in place of it that side of the Apostle's teaching and conduct is presented to us on which he has some small agreement with Judaism. In doing this the author evidently wishes on the one hand to remove the prejudices which the Jewish-Christians may have felt against the Apostle as an opponent of the law, and on the other to show how groundless the hatred of the Jews against the Apostle had really been. As the Apostle stands here before the Sanhedrim, which was composed of Pharisees and Sadducees alike, and held the belief in a resurrection in common with the Pharisees, the author had an opportunity of making it appear that the Pharisees had not been so much the enemies of the Apostle as the Sadducees. The Apostle was thus the victim of the partisan hatred of a mere sect. The author allows us to see the train of thought which led him to give this version of the story, when he remarks, xxiii. 8, on the doctrinal differences between the Pharisees and the Sadducees. The reader is already well acquainted with these parties and even with their distinctive tenets (ver. 34), and what leads the writer to enlarge on this subject once more? If he were only relating a matter of fact in a simple and careful way, it would never have occurred to him to make special mention of a fact which is taken for granted all through the Gospels as a thing that everybody knew. The position in which he was to place the Apostle in regard to the Pharisees and Sadducees must have led him to dwell in this way on their doctrinal difference. He seems to have constructed his account of the Apostle's behaviour before the Sanhedrim out of his knowledge of this difference between the two parties. So far is he misled by the efforts which he makes to represent the cause of the Apostle as a party affair of the Pharisees, that he almost makes the Pharisees into Christians. It is not enough that he finds a point of contact in the doctrine of the resurrection: the other peculiarity of the Pharisees, their belief in angels and spirits, is also pressed into the same service. Whilst the Pharisees, acknowledging the Apostle's cause as their own, declare openly that they can find no fault with this man, they go so far as to add (ver. 9), εἰ δὲ πνεῦμα ἐλάλησεν αὐτῷ ἢ ἄγγελος, etc. This refers to what the Apostle had said in his speech to the people, xxii. 6-18, of the appearance of the risen Jesus, and the Pharisees seem prepared actually to concede to the Apostle the reality of these appearances; but in the very moment in which they seem to be about to acknowledge this openly, the author makes them suddenly suppress their declaration, as though they shrank back from so great a concession. We may say with Neander (p. 432, Bohn, 307) that "the concluding words of the interrupted speech, μὴ θεομαχῶμεν, are certainly a gloss, and a gloss disturbing the sense, because this was assuredly more than the Pharisees from their standpoint could ever have thought of saying." But the speech of the Pharisees requires to be completed in some way, and it matters little what words we supply; it is clear that even what goes before expresses far more than the Pharisees from their standpoint could ever have thought of saying. Those who were prepared to grant so much could have no objection of any weight to urge against the Christian faith. And how can we think that the Pharisees, seated in the Sanhedrim to judge the Apostle, could appear as champions of his cause, and that, blinded by a mere appearance of similarity between his faith and theirs, they could deem those features of his teaching which were offensive to them as Pharisees, and the great charge brought against him of profaning the temple, and undermining the authority of the law, to be unimportant matters which called for no further discussion? All this is in the highest degree improbable, and shows clearly that this whole trial before the Sanhedrim is, in the form in which we have it, a scene arranged by the author of the Acts, in which he does not even take pains to sustain the dignity of the Apostle's character. We need not scruple to say that the quarrel between the Apostle and the High Priest, which forms the prelude to this disorderly assize, is so unworthy of the Apostle that thanks are due to any criticism which, on sufficient reasons, would free him from this blot upon his character. The author of the Acts of the Apostles has here in his mind—a thing that tells against rather than in favour of the historical character of his narrative—the trial of Jesus before the Sanhedrim; but how unlike does the Apostle appear to the image of him who "lived in him." " Ubi est illa patientia Salvatoris qui quasi agnus ductus ad victimam non aperuit os suum, sed clementer loquitur verberanti; ' Si male locutus, argue de malo, si autem bene, quid me cædis?'" This is Jerome's sentence on this passage (contra Pelag. iii. init.), and the impression left by these words is not effaced when he adds, "Non Apostolo detrahimus, sed gloriam Domini prædicamus, qui in carne passus carnis injuriam superat et fragilitatem." Even Olshausen does not hesitate to say that it appears unworthy of the Apostle to have spoken so abusively; that by such behaviour he transgressed the decorum due to the supreme court of justice, and, confounding the office with the person, gave passionate vent to his feelings with regard to the man, where only the office was concerned.[1] Neander indeed is of opinion that these passionate words contained the truth, and that the Apostle, when it was pointed out to him that it was the High Priest whom he had thus vilified, at once retracted his words, saying that he had

[1] It is really incomprehensible how Olshausen from his standpoint could have committed himself to such an opinion on the behaviour of the Apostle. If the letter is worth so much, and leaves no room to doubt that the Apostle really behaved as is represented, and if it be also certain that the Apostles must, as direct organs of the Holy Spirit, be considered infallible authorities on every subject, then we ought not to judge the behaviour of the Apostle according to our human standard of morality, but rather to arrange our standard of morality according to the behaviour of the Apostle.

not reflected that it was the High Priest to whom he was speaking, and to whom, of course, according to law, reverence was due. But this can scarcely stand, for the simple reason that the words οὐκ ᾔδειν cannot mean "non reputabam." They can only mean "I did not know." Now the Apostle could not say in earnest that he did not know him : he can only have said, " I did not know that he was the High Priest," in an ironical sense. If the words are to be taken in this sense, they show how little he thought of retracting. The same is shown by the stratagem to which he immediately afterwards resorted in order to embarrass the Sadducees, his real enemies, who had the High Priest Ananias at their head, by ranging himself on the side of the Pharisees, and making common cause with the latter against them. The same tone and character run through the whole of the Apostle's behaviour at this trial. I cannot agree with the opinion which Neander expresses on this passage (p. 421, Bohn, 306), "The manner in which the Apostle conducted himself here shows him to have been a man who knew how to control the ebullitions of feeling with Christian self-control, and to avail himself of circumstances with Christian prudence without any compromise of truth." I can see here neither any " Christian repression of passion " nor any Christian "turning circumstances to account without prejudice to truth ;" and I consider it unjust that the picture of the Apostle's character which we gain from his Epistles should be distorted by the misrepresentations of an author who lived long after the Apostolic period, and wrote in the interests of a party.

If we have formed a true estimate of the passages, xxi. 17-26 and xxiii. 1-10, we are led to the conclusion that we are not entitled to regard the narrative of which they form a part as a piece of actual history : even though historical criticism should not be able to demonstrate in every particular the truth of the suspicion at which it has thus arrived. After our examination of the passage xxiii. 1, *sq.*, it must appear doubtful whether the Apostle's case was ever heard before the Sanhedrim at all. If this is doubtful, what security have we that the two speeches said to be delivered by the Apostle—one, in chap. xxii., before the Jewish people, the other, chap. xxvi., before King Agrippa—were really delivered as the author tells us? The first at any rate must have been delivered under circumstances which were scarcely suitable for such a discourse. Is it likely that the Roman tribune, who had arrested the Apostle in the midst of a wild tumult, should have given permission to a prisoner whom he held to be an incendiary of the most dangerous kind, and about whom he knew nothing except what he heard from his own mouth—that he was a Jew of Tarsus in Cilicia, to deliver a public address when he was in the act of being removed to the castle; it being impossible to foresee what effect the speech would have on the people, who were already excited to such an alarming degree? Is it likely that in the excited state they were in, the people would have listened so long with patience to a man whom they hated, and of whom they were already convinced that he was worthy of death? At any rate we must again draw attention to the curious circumstance which marks this speech as well as the speech of Stephen, and that delivered by the Apostle in the Areopagus. It is arranged in such a way that when the speaker arrives at a certain point he is interrupted. The point in this case is where he begins to speak of his mission to the Gentiles, and this reminds the people of their special reason for hating him. This point, however, is not reached until he has worked out his main thesis as far as he could mean to do so under such circumstances. Both speeches, chaps. xxii. and xxvi., have a thoroughly apologetic tendency. The chief idea which the Apostle dwells on is this: the vocation to which he had hitherto devoted himself among the Gentiles was by no means arbitrarily chosen, or the accidental result of a resolution arrived at in his own mind without being influenced from without; he had merely followed a call that had been addressed to him from above, he had been forced to take the step by an objective external agency, which operated on him so powerfully that he could not resist it. Of course, such an apology seems not inappropriate to the aim which the Apostle is supposed to have had in view in delivering the two speeches, but it also suits in a remarkable manner the apologetic tendency which the author of the Acts of the Apostles generally sets himself to further. The question therefore arises from it whether, when at other times he found it necessary to vindicate his position, the Apostle was in the habit of referring to the fact on which this apology is based. But this is not the case: in none of the Apostle's Epistles, in which he certainly had occasion to defend his position against opponents of various kinds, is there any distinct reference in such a spirit and for such a purpose to the outward matter of fact which he is here reported to have made the chief subject of important discourses on two separate occasions. But such an apology is, strictly considered, not at all suited to the situation in which the Apostle found himself, at least in chap. xxii. We must not here forget that the true cause of the hatred of the Jews against the Apostle was not so much his faith in Christ as his attack upon the law. As long as he did not vindicate himself on this last subject, any apologetic attempt must have been in vain; but the whole of the speech contains no reference to this, and we cannot suppose the reason to have been that he was interrupted, or that he would have spoken on the subject if the speech had been continued. In the second speech also, in which the Apostle was at full liberty to express himself fully and in detail, nothing is said on this point.

In fact the Acts of the Apostles purposely avoids it as if Paul did not differ in this respect from the other Apostles. In the then position of the Apostle such an apology could not have been of much use; but things would appear differently to a writer who had to vindicate the Apostle not merely in respect of his attitude towards the Mosaic law, but generally in respect of his Apostolic authority. What stronger evidence could be brought forward for such a purpose, than the repeated and circumstantial narrative of the extraordinary event by which, against his own intentions, and even against his will, he had been placed in the career in which he had been working as an Apostle?

If these two speeches, especially the first, can scarcely be thought to have been actually delivered, then we can scarcely help thinking, with regard to this part of the Acts which deals with the Apostle's arrest, that the course of affairs was in reality much simpler than we have it here. The simple original fact has been made up into quite a number of public trials, each of which, however, is merely a repetition of one and the same scene. The same idea, also, is present in them all, namely, to have the Apostle's innocence proclaimed, now by himself, and now by others whose verdict might appear to be entitled to respect. This is the intention of the Apostle's speech before the people : it was not indeed possible for him to convince them of his innocence, yet it was something to set up the objective point of view from which his case must, in justice, be decided. The proceedings before the Sanhedrim were instituted by the Roman tribune, to whom the true cause of the tumultuous popular riot against the Apostle was still unknown, in order γνῶναι τὸ ἀσφαλὲς, τὸ τί κατηγορεῖται παρὰ τῶν Ἰουδαίων (xxii. 30). As the Apostle succeeded in drawing the party of the Pharisees over to his interest, and received from them the declaration, οὐδὲν κακὸν εὑρίσκομεν ἐν τῷ ἀνθρώπῳ τούτῳ (xxiii. 9), how striking a public recognition of his innocence and of the justness of his cause was thus achieved! The mild, indulgent treatment of the Apostle by the Roman tribune was, as the Acts regards it, the result of the favourable issue of the trial before the Sanhedrim. The new trial which was instituted by the Roman Procurator Felix, in the form of a Roman process, gave the Apostle a fresh opportunity not only of proving the injustice of the accusation brought against him, but also of exhibiting his orthodoxy as a Jew, in such a way as to make the point on which he differs from his opponents appear to be a very trifling affair indeed. But here also we cannot see how the Apostle could say with a clear conscience, ὁμολογῶ δὲ τοῦτό σοι, ὅτι κατὰ τὴν ὁδὸν ἣν λέγουσιν αἵρεσιν, οὕτω λατρεύω τῷ πατρῴῳ Θεῷ, πιστεύων πᾶσι τοῖς κατὰ τὸν νόμον καὶ τοῖς ἐν τοῖς προφήταις γεγραμμένοις (*inter alia*, then the commandment, Genesis xvii. 14), ἐλπίδα ἔχων εἰς τὸν Θεὸν, ἣν καὶ αὐτοὶ οὗτοι προσδέχονται, ἀνάστασιν μέλλειν ἔσεσθαι νεκρῶν, δικαίων τε καὶ ἀδίκων· ἢ αὐτοὶ οὗτοι εἰπάτωσαν, τί εὗρον ἐν ἐμοὶ ἀδίκημα, στάντος μου ἐπὶ τοῦ συνεδρίου· ἢ περὶ μιᾶς ταύτης φωνῆς, ἧς ἔκραξα ἑστὼς ἐν αὐτοῖς, ὅτι περὶ ἀναστάσεως νεκρῶν ἐγὼ κρίνομαι σήμερον ὑφ' ὑμῶν (xxiv. 14, *sqq.*). The case of the Apostle is here again placed in a very equivocal light, but he is so far successful that the Procurator Felix not only does not decide against him, but treats him with attention and forbearance. Under the successor of Felix, the new Procurator Porcius Festus, a new and somewhat splendid trial took place, at which the Jewish King Agrippa and his sister Bernice were present. The Procurator was convinced of the Apostle's innocence as his predecessor had been, yet his compliant attitude towards the Jews made it necessary for the Apostle to appeal to the Emperor. This trial is said to have been held as a compliment to the king; another reason is given afterwards, that the Procurator wished to have the king's opinion on the case, he being a Jew (yet this opinion could only be founded on the *ex parte* statement of the Apostle himself), in order that he might have something definite to report to Rome. The Apostle accordingly relates afresh before this august assembly the history of his conversion, not without repeated assurances of his orthodoxy as a Jew, though at the same time evading the real point of the accusation against him. The result of this scene is the unanimous decision of the whole assembly: ὅτι οὐδὲν θανάτου ἄξιον ἢ δεσμῶν πράσσει ὁ ἄνθρωπος οὗτος with the additional declaration of Agrippa to Festus, ἀπολελύσθαι ἐδύνατο ὁ ἄνθρωπος οὗτος, εἰ μὴ ἐπεκέκλητο Καίσαρα. This was the result to which the author of the Acts wished to lead his reader, and he does not neglect to point out the importance of such an opinion from the mouth of one who was so well acquainted with all the customs and religious controversies of the Jews, and who also knew something of the history of Jesus (xxvi. 3). The question directly put to the King by the Apostle (verse 27), πιστεύεις βασιλεῦ Ἀγρίππα τοῖς προφήταις ; with the confident answer given by the Apostle himself, οἶδα ὅτι πιστεύεις, what purpose do they serve but to increase the importance of the King's decision, by this assurance of his orthodoxy? But it can scarcely be imagined that the decision of a King whose morals were not of the most respectable, could have possessed such value in the Apostle's eyes ; nor that he prized so highly the opportunity afforded him of pleading his cause before the King, as the author of the Acts of the Apostles represents him to have said at the outset of his speech, xxvi. 2.

CHAPTER IX.

THE APOSTLE PAUL IN ROME—HIS IMPRISONMENT AND MARTYRDOM.

IN consequence of the Apostle's appeal to the Emperor, the Procurator Festus ordered him to be removed from Cæsarea to Rome. He travelled with some other prisoners under the escort of a Roman centurion, whose humane treatment of him is warmly spoken of in the Acts. The detailed narrative of this journey, apparently taken from an account of it by Luke, though betraying another hand here and there, is yet the most authentic information that the Acts gives us on the Apostle's life ; for the history of his apostolic labours, however, it contains little of importance. But as soon as he arrives in Rome we see him plunged into a controversy with the Jews, the results of which demand our study and attention. The most important statement bearing on the Apostle's life which this part of the Acts contains, is that given at the close of the work, that the Apostle remained two whole years in Rome, and held free intercourse with all that came to him, working unhindered for the kingdom of God by the preaching of the gospel of Christ. What makes this concluding remark, which has been so much discussed, so enigmatical, is that in speaking of a period of two years, it suggests that at the expiration of this period there was a change in the Apostle's circumstances, and that some definite event then took place. But what could this have been ? If the appeal of the Apostle to the Emperor was decided after this long delay, and the Apostle consequently set at liberty, it does not seem conceivable that the author of the Acts of the Apostles should pass over in utter silence an event for which the reader is prepared by all that goes before, and which would have been in such striking accordance with the apologetic tendency of his work.[1] The general assumption is that at the end of these two years the Apostle was set at liberty, either in consequence of the verdict of the Emperor, or in some other way; that he then made several journeys, especially one to Spain, but that he afterwards underwent a second imprisonment at Rome, and at last suffered martyrdom along with the Apostle Peter. A second Roman imprisonment is first spoken of by Eusebius, but the idea had already become traditional in his time, and is based upon no other evidence than the Epistles called by the Apostle's name, which were thought not to be intelligible without it.[2] Our opinion on this pretended fact, as well as on all that goes beyond the limit set by the Acts, depends chiefly on the question how far the historical connection in which these later fortunes of the Apostle are embodied appears to be worthy of our confidence. We still find Peter and Paul inseparable from each other; even in their death they are not divided. This is very significant; we cannot fail to see here the mythico-traditional working out of the parallel which the author of the Acts has instituted between the two Apostles all along. The legend continues to expand in the direction of this definite idea; and this process does not cease till a belief is formed and takes possession of the mind of the period, that Peter and Paul, the most illustrious of the Apostles, had founded the Roman Church together, and after this common work had suffered a common martyrdom in the same city. Here the legend reaches

[1] In order to explain this conclusion of the Acts of the Apostles, Schneckenburger remarks, p. 126—"He came to Rome and there preached unmolested: μετὰ πάσης παρρησίας ἀκωλύτως. Is not this a fitting conclusion? Is it not quite in harmony with the design running through the whole history of Paul?" Certainly; it, that is to say, the author of the Acts had no more positive result to communicate; if Paul was not actually acquitted and released.

[2] H. E. ii. 22. Τότε μὲν οὖν ἀπολογησάμενον αὖθις ἐπὶ τὴν τοῦ κηρύγματος διακονίαν λόγος ἔχει στείλασθαι τὸν ἀπόστολον· δεύτερον δ' ἐπιβάντα τῇ αὐτῇ πόλει τῷ κατ' αὐτὸν (Νέρωνα) τελειωθῆναι μαρτυρίῳ ἐν ᾧ δεσμοῖς ἐχόμενος τόν πρὸς Τιμόθεον δευτέραν συντάττει ἐπιστολὴν, ὁμοῦ σημαίνων τήν τε προτέραν αὐτῷ γενομένην ἀπολογίαν καὶ τὴν παραπόδας τελείωσιν.

its completion. Its point of departure was simply what was known of the life of Paul; nothing more. Paul did actually come to Rome: his office as Apostle to the Gentiles led him thither, and we may also take it as a historical fact that he died there as a martyr. In the case of Peter, however, we can find no basis for the story but vague legends. It cannot be disputed that he laboured for the Gospel beyond the bounds of Judea. At least the Acts of the Apostles represents him as not only going into Samaria, but also as visiting the cities of Phœnicia; and, according to Gal. ii. 11, he also appeared at Antioch. But on this point further proof is wanting: nothing can be built on the passage 1 Cor. ix. 5. The Apostle Paul here says of himself, μὴ οὐκ ἔχομεν ἐξουσίαν ἀδελφὴν γυναῖκα περιάγειν, ὡς καὶ οἱ λοιποὶ ἀπόστολοι, καὶ οἱ ἀδελφοὶ τοῦ Κυρίου, καὶ Κηφᾶς, but this περιάγειν can only refer to the Apostle Paul himself, and the sense of the words can only be: Had he not the right to take with him on his missionary journeys an ἀδελφὴ γυνὴ as the rest of the Apostles had an ἀδελφὴ γυνή? In any case it may well be assumed that the foreign missionary activity of the Apostle Peter was directed exclusively to the Jews, according to the arrangements made Gal. ii. 9. The martyrdom of the Apostle Peter is certainly mentioned in the New Testament, but it is only in the apocryphal-looking appendix to the Gospel of John, xxi. 18, 19, and neither here nor in the fourth epistle of Clemens Romanus, ch. v., is the place specified. 1 Peter v. 13 shows, however, that when that Epistle was written, the legend had fixed his residence at Rome; the interpretation of Babylon by Rome agrees best with the whole tenor of the Epistle. Perhaps we may see a slight allusion to this legend in the two passages, Acts xix. 21 and xxiii. 11. Even at that time, when the Apostle Paul first took the resolve to travel from Ephesus by Macedonia and Achaia to Jerusalem, he is said to have declared emphatically ὅτι μετὰ τὸ γενέσθαι με ἐκεῖ, δεῖ με καὶ Ῥώμην ἰδεῖν, and when he had successfully passed through the trial before the Sanhedrim, and the stormy scene with which it ended, the Lord is represented as appearing to him on the following night, and encouraging him with the words, Θάρσει, ὡς γὰρ διεμαρτύρω τὰ περὶ ἐμοῦ εἰς Ἱερουσαλὴμ, οὕτω σε δεῖ καὶ εἰς Ῥώμην μαρτυρῆσαι. In both these passages there is so marked a suggestion, that the apostolate must reach its highest point, and receive its crown of glory in the εἰς Ῥώμην μαρτυρῆσαι, that there must be some special meaning in the phrase. In the case of an author who displays so distinct and so persistent an apologetic interest, it may not be too bold to suppose that the thought of the Apostle Peter, whom legend had already taken to Rome, may have been before his mind. Whether this be so or not, there was no doubt about the Apostle Paul's case; but the author wishes to make his claim to the honour as clear as possible, and makes him express beforehand his knowledge of his destination.

Starting from this, and seeking to trace the elements of the legend further, we find it divide into two different branches, one of which takes an Anti-Pauline, the other a Petrino-Pauline direction. The first of these forms is connected with Simon Magus, on whose account Peter is made to come to Rome. Even the Acts of the Apostles represents them as meeting in Samaria. When the Apostle perceived the perverse nature of the Magus from his design to obtain the Holy Spirit by impure means, he encountered the danger of corruption which threatened Christianity through the Magus. As for the question whether the Magus represents a real historical person, it is clear from the Acts that he is the reflection of a Samaritan popular deity. The religion of Samaria being considered a heathen one, he became the representative both of the heretical Christianity which was mingled with elements of heathenism, and of heathenism itself;[1] and the Apostle Peter travelled from place to place, from land to land, from east to west, hard on the footsteps of the Magus who went before him, to combat him in every place, and to refute the godless doctrine he promulgated. This is the form in which the legend appears in the pseudo-Clementine Homilies, and in the writings connected with them.

[1] Die Chr. Gnosis, p. 306. A more accurate and detailed account of Simon Magus will be found in "Christenthum der drei ersten Jahrh.," p. 87, sq.

In the same form Eusebius is also acquainted with it. As soon as the Magus had fled before the Apostle from the east to the west, and had attained so great success in Rome itself by means of his magic arts, that he was there honoured as a god and had a statue erected to him, Peter also appeared there. Παραπόδας γοῦν ἐπὶ τῆς αὐτῆς Κλαυδίου βασιλείας ἡ πανάγαθος καὶ φιλανθρωποτάτη τῶν ὅλων πρόνοια τὸν καρτερὸν καὶ μέγαν τῶν Ἀποστόλων, τὸν ἀρετῆς ἕνεκα τῶν λοιπῶν ἁπάντων προήγορον, Πέτρον, ἐπὶ τὴν Ῥώμην ὡς ἐπὶ τηλικοῦτον λυμεῶνα βίου χειραγωγεῖ ὅς οἶατις γενναῖος τοῦ Θεοῦ στρατηγὸς τοῖς θείοις ὅπλοις φραξάμενος, τὴν πολυτίμητον ἐμπορείαν τοῦ νοητοῦ φωτὸς ἐξ ἀνατολῶν τοῖς κατὰ δύσιν ἐκόμιζεν φῶς αὐτὸ καὶ λόγον ψυχῶν σωτήριον, τὸ κήρυγμα τῆς τῶν οὐρανῶν βασιλείας εὐαγγελιζόμενος. What is said here as well as by Justin Martyr in the lesser "Apology," of a statue erected to this Simon in Rome, on an island of the Tiber, with this inscription, "Simoni deo Sancta," is an evident mistake, a confusion of Simon Magus with the Sabine Roman god Semo Sancus (who may also have been originally allied with the ancient Eastern Sem, Semo); but the curious and important legend of the Magus and the Apostle Peter cannot have been derived altogether from this circumstance. This then was what brought the Apostle to Rome at so early a period. For the truth of this tradition Eusebius appeals at the close of his narrative (ii. 15) to Clement of Alexandria, who has related the history in the sixth book of his Hypotyposes, and to the similar testimony of Bishop Papias of Hierapolis. It is doubtful here whether Clement and Papias are cited as witnesses for the whole of the foregoing narrative about Simon Magus and Peter, or only for that part of it which refers to the Gospel of Mark. Eusebius is speaking about the reason why Mark composed his Gospel in Rome; he says: "the great impression which Peter had made on the Romish Christians by his brilliant victory over Simon Magus, had produced in them a strong desire to possess a written memorial of the Christian doctrine he had preached to them. So on their pressing entreaty, Mark, the companion of Peter, drew up the

Gospel which has been handed down under his name." As we see in Eusebius vi. 14, Clement did actually mention Peter's teaching in Rome, but whether the elder Papias did so too is doubtful, as Eusebius can only have referred to the passage quoted by him (iii. 39) from the works of Papias, in which it is only said that the Gospel of Mark arose out of the doctrinal teachings of the Apostle Peter. The Romish origin of the Gospel of Mark seems, moreover, to have been an ancient tradition, which may thus have been well known to Papias; and if he knew this, why should he not have been acquainted with the rest of the story which stood in close connection with it? Mark came to Rome only as the companion of Peter, but for what cause could Peter have come to Rome at so early a period, but that the presence of Simon Magus there made it necessary that he should be there also? It is very possible that even in this form the legend had a certain antithetical relation to the Apostle Paul.

Simon Magus being the personification of heathenism, the Apostle Peter, who followed him wherever he went, to combat him and convert the people everywhere from his false doctrine, is expressly described as the Apostle to the Gentiles, which he really was not, but is now made to have been, in order not to leave this renown exclusively to Paul. The pseudo-Clementine Homilies expressly ascribe this title to the Apostle Peter, as he himself says, iii. 59, " ὁρμᾶν εἰς τὰ ἔθνη τὰ πολλοὺς Θεοὺς λέγοντα, κηρύξαι καὶ διδάξαι, ὅτι εἷς ἐστιν ὁ Θεὸς ὃς οὐρανὸν ἔκτισε καὶ γῆν καὶ τὰ ἐν αὐτοῖς πάντα ὅπως ἀγαπήσαντες αὐτὸν σωθῆναι δυνηθῶσιν." This sphere, which we are accustomed to see occupied exclusively by Paul, as the Apostle to the Gentiles, is here described as being filled by Peter equally, and in this same Homily we are startled to find, by plain indications, that Simon Magus, whom the Apostle Peter overcomes, represents the Apostle Paul himself. It has already been shown what unequivocal attacks upon the Apostle Paul these Homilies contain; and especially how their theory of revelation is used to prove that he had forced his way among the number of the Apostles by illegitimate means, and was destitute of all true apostolic authority. This attack runs through the whole of these Homilies. The great charge brought against Simon Magus is that he had called Peter κατεγνωσμένος (Hom. xvii. 19). Now this applies to the Apostle Paul (Gal. ii. 11). There is the same reference when Peter, in the letter to James which is prefixed to the Homilies, chap. ii., speaks of a difference of doctrine which he not only knew of as a prophet, but because he could already see the beginning of the evil. "For some among the Gentiles," he says, "have rejected my preaching in accordance with the law, and have adopted the lawless and unworthy doctrine of a man opposed to me. Even in my lifetime some have undertaken, through artful interpretation of my teachings, to transform them into exhortations to the abolition of the law, as if that were my real opinion, and I were not straightforward in my teaching, which may God forbid. This conduct of theirs is nothing but opposition to the law of God, which was given by Moses, and testified to by our Lord when he said of its everlasting duration, 'Heaven and earth shall pass away, but one jot or one tittle shall not pass away from the law.' Thus he spoke that it might be kept in its entirety. But those persons who, I know not how, profess to be able to tell what I think, and to understand the teachings which I deliver better than I do myself, say of those teachings, that their doctrine and intention are such as I never intended them to be. If such persons dare to utter such lies in my lifetime, how much more will they dare to lie after my death!"

There can scarcely be any doubt that this ἄνθρωπος ἐχθρὸς, whose ἄνομος καὶ φλυαρώδης διδασκαλία the Gentiles accepted, is the Apostle to the Gentiles, Paul. He is also that πλάνος, of whom Peter says, Hom. ii. 17, that Simon Magus came to the Gentiles before him, but that he (Peter) followed him, ἐπελθὼν ὡς σκότῳ φῶς, ὡς ἀγνοίᾳ γνῶσις, ὡς νόσῳ ἴασις. οὕτως δὴ ὡς ἀληθὴς ἡμῶν προφήτης εἴρηκεν, πρῶτον ψευδὲς δεῖ ἐλθεῖν εὐαγγέλιον ὑπὸ πλάνου τινὸς καὶ εἶθ᾽ οὕτως μετὰ καθαίρεσιν τοῦ ἁγίου τόπου εὐαγγέλιον ἀληθὲς κρύφα διαπεμφθῆναι, εἰς ἐπανόρθωσιν τῶν ἐσομένων αἱρέσεων. The false gospel of this heretical teacher, on which the true one follows, is the Pauline gospel of the abolition of the law, and the words μετὰ καθαίρεσιν τοῦ ἁγίου τόπου are not merely a piece of chronology, but an allusion to Acts xxi. 28, according to which passage the Jews fell upon Paul with the cry, οὗτός ἐστιν ὁ ἄνθρωπος, ὁ κατὰ τοῦ λαοῦ καὶ τοῦ νόμου καὶ τοῦ τόπου τούτου πάντας πανταχοῦ διδάσκων, ἔτι τὲ καὶ "Ελληνας εἰσήγαγεν εἰς τὸ ἱερὸν καὶ κεκοίνωκε τὸν ἅγιον τόπον τοῦτον. With reference to the occurrence here narrated, Paul's conduct, aiming, as it was thought, at the violent abolition of the Mosaic law, and all the institutions of Judaism, is designated as a καθαίρεσις τοῦ ἁγίου τόπου. His wild and characteristically heathen attack upon the law was thus represented as a prelude to the destruction of Jerusalem and the temple, the ἅγιος τόπος, by the Romans. These charges show the genuine Ebionitish spirit and character of these Homilies. The Ebionites saw in the Apostle Paul nothing but an apostate from the law, and a false teacher, and they rejected all his Epistles.[1] Epiphanius could have mentioned, if he had chosen, many other particulars of their abuse of the Apostle Paul.[2] Men are apt to think that those whom they detest as heretics and innovators in religion have never been true members of the religion against which they have thus grievously transgressed, and so the Ebionites maintained that Paul was no Jew by birth, but a Greek or Gentile, born of Gentile parents, and who had only in later life become a proselyte to Judaism. To account for his inimical attitude towards Judaism a story was told which reminds us of many other charges originating in the same spirit. When Paul, the Ebionites asserted, came at a later period to Jerusalem and remained there for some time, he wished to marry a daughter of the High Priest. With this view he became a proselyte, and submitted to circumcision. Failing, however, to obtain his desire, he vented his wrath and vexation by writing against circumcision and the Sabbath, and the law generally.[3] It may be asserted that it

[1] Irenæus contra Haer., i. 26. Eusebius, H. E. iii. 27.
[2] Περὶ τοῦ ἁγίου Παύλου, ὡς βλασφημοῦντες αὐτὸν λέγουσιν, πόσα ἔχω λέγειν; Haer. xxx. 25.
[3] Epiphanius, cap. xvi.

was only in the extreme development of their heresy that the Ebionites took up so hostile an attitude towards the Apostle Paul; but we must not forget that the tendency which, as it increased, constituted Ebionitism a heresy, was present in it from the beginning. The Jewish-Christian teachers whom Paul combated in his Epistles afford the clearest evidence of the feeling with which the Jewish-Christians regarded the Apostle Paul even in the first age of the Church, in the period when the antagonism between Ebionitism and Paulinism was only beginning to arise. Wherever Ebionitism appeared, whether in a more or less advanced stage, the same views and feelings with regard to the Apostle Paul must to some extent have prevailed. Papias and Hegesippus belonged to the Jewish-Christian or Ebionite party, and we cannot be surprised to find, even in the few fragments of their writings which have been handed down to us, allusions which make us certain of their anti-Pauline tendency. Papias took a great deal of trouble (as he himself tells us in Eusebius, H. E. iii. 39) to collect together and keep in remembrance all the information about the disciples of the Lord that he could glean from living tradition, which he accounted of more value than written documents. For this end he made inquiries specially of those who had been in any way connected with the original disciples of Jesus. "$Oὐ\ γάρ$," he says, "$τοῖς\ τὰ\ πολλὰ\ λέγουσιν\ ἔχαιρον\ ὥσπερ\ οἱ\ πολλοί,\ ἀλλὰ\ τοῖς\ τἀληθῆ\ διδάσκουσιν,\ οὐδὲ\ τοῖς\ τὰς\ ἀλλοτρίας\ ἐντολὰς\ μνημονεύουσιν,\ ἀλλὰ\ τοῖς\ τὰς\ παρὰ\ τοῦ\ κυρίου\ τῇ\ πίστει\ δεδομένας\ καὶ\ ἀπ'\ αὐτῆς\ παραγινομένας\ τῆς\ ἀληθείας.$" Therefore he carefully inquired for what Andrew, Peter, Philip, Thomas, Matthew, or any other of the disciples of the Lord had said. Not only is there no mention made here of the Apostle Paul, but it is not improbable that a man who laid so much weight on tradition which went back directly to the doctrine and person of Christ, should have had the Apostle Paul and his adherents in view, when he spoke of those who $τὰς\ ἀλλοτρίας\ ἐντολὰς\ μνημονεύουσι$, in opposition to those who, in what they knew of the Lord, possessed the utterances of truth itself. Photius has preserved a remarkable fragment on Hegesippus, in his extracts from

HIS IMPRISONMENT AND MARTYRDOM.

a work of the Monophysite Stephen Gobarus.[1] The work of Stephen Gobarus consisted of a series of articles in which he collected together the contradictory declarations of the teachers of the Church. Thus he brings forward the statement, ὅτι τὰ ἡτοιμασμένα τοῖς δικαίοις ἀγαθὰ οὔτε ὀφθαλμὸς εἶδεν οὔτε οὖς ἤκουσεν, οὔτε ἐπὶ καρδίαν ἀνθρώπου ἀνέβη, and in contrast to this he goes on: Ἡγήσιππος μέντοι, ἀρχαῖός τε ἀνὴρ καὶ ἀποστολικὸς ἐν τῷ πέμπτῳ τῶν ὑπομνημάτων, οὐκ οἶδ' ὅτι καὶ παθὼν μάτην μὲν εἰρῆσθαι ταῦτα λέγει καὶ καταψεύδεσθαι τοὺς ταῦτα φαμένους τῶν τε θείων γραφῶν καὶ τοῦ κυρίου λέγοντος· μακάριοι οἱ ὀφθαλμοὶ ὑμῶν οἱ βλέποντες καὶ τὰ ὦτα ὑμῶν τὰ ἀκούοντα. The first extract is taken from 1 Cor. ii. 9, and the charge of false doctrine seems therefore to point to the Apostle Paul. He is said to have made an untrue statement in these words, and to have contradicted the words of the Lord, Matt. xiii. 16. In this passage Jesus calls his disciples blessed, because they see and hear what many prophets and righteous men had desired to see and hear, but had not seen nor heard. The reason why they are called blessed, is the direct personal intercourse with Jesus, which the Apostles were privileged to have. This utterance of the Lord seems to Hegesippus to conflict with what the Apostle Paul says, 1 Cor. ii. 9, "ἀλλὰ καθὼς γέγραπται· ἃ ὀφθαλμὸς οὐκ εἶδε, καὶ οὖς οὐκ ἤκουσε, καὶ ἐπὶ καρδίαν ἀνθρώπου οὐκ ἀνέβη, ἃ ἡτοίμασεν ὁ Θεὸς τοῖς ἀγαπῶσιν αὐτόν. ἡμῖν δὲ ἀπεκάλυψεν ὁ Θεὸς διὰ τοῦ πνεύματος αὐτοῦ," and as Hegesippus undoubtedly understands these words to refer to the manner in which Paul asserted that he had been called to the apostolic office, namely, by a special revelation, we have here the same contention as is set up in the pseudo-Clementine Homilies, when these deny the true characteristics of apostleship to the Apostle Paul, because he had become an Apostle only by a revelation in a vision, and not, as the other Apostles, by immediate intercourse with Jesus. Because this qualification for the apostolic office was wanting to him, Hegesippus, speaking in the spirit of Ebionitism, declares him to be a liar, and his asser-

[1] Bibl. Cod., 232.

tion that a man may become an Apostle as he had, without any outward hearing or seeing, to be a groundless one (μάτην εἰρῆσθαι ταῦτα). There is no reason whatever why we should take the words of Hegesippus in any other sense than that which they so obviously suggest, and which satisfies so well the requirements of the argument in which they occur. All that we know of Hegesippus leaves us in no doubt of his Ebionitism.[1] It will not help us much to suppose with Neander that he may have said this not as against Paul, but in the vehemence of his zeal against the opponents of the material millennium, which the Pauline passage already quoted, and others like it, might be used to discredit, as they are opposed to sensuous ideas of the happiness of the future.[2] Such zeal for the material millennium would simply stamp him as a genuine Ebionite, and warrant us in looking for the usual Ebionite view of the Apostle Paul.[3] It is just a strong expression of these views, when it is said of the Apostle Paul that he is no Jew but a Gentile, a Samaritan—that very Simon Magus who was conquered by the Apostle Peter. It may reasonably be supposed that this form of the legend, according to which Peter's controversy with the Magus made him follow that personage even to Rome, originated in the anti-Pauline tendency of Ebionitism.

[1] Cf. my remarks on this subject in the Theol. Jahrb., 1844, p. 571.
[2] Neander's Church History, ii. 431 (Bohn's edition).
[3] The only objection that can be made to this reference of the passage of Hegesippus to the Apostle Paul, is that according to another passage from the same work of Hegesippus (Eusebius, H. E. iii. 32) the Church up to the time of the first Gnostics had remained a pure untainted virgin, and only after the holy company of the Apostles was broken up did the ἄθεος πλάνη begin. But it must not be forgotten that the Church at that time remained so only ἐν ἀδήλῳ που σκότει φωλευόντων εἰσέτι τότε τῶν, εἰ καί τινες ὑπῆρχον, παραφθείρειν ἐπιχειρούντων τὸν ὑγιῆ κανόνα τοῦ σωτηρίου κηρύγματος. At that time, then, ὑπῆρχόν τινες, as Peter speaks of such τινες in the epistle to James in the Homilies, chapter ii., ἔτι μου περιόντος ἐπεχείρησάν τινες, etc. Although Hegesippus attached no further importance to these τινὲς, it was only because the immediate presence of the Apostles seemed to him so overpowering that a heretical element, even did it exist, could not flourish. The expressions αὐτὴ ἡ ἀλήθεια, ἡ ἔνθεος σοφία, which Papias and Hegesippus use of the person of Christ, are very characteristic of their Ebionite position. The expressions are used in the Homilies to point out the true prophets. Papias thought he heard the living voice of this truth in the traditions which he collected.

The other form of the legend represents the two Apostles as in fraternal agreement instead of being at enmity. They work together in their vocation, share the same martyr-death, and the scene of their common and glorious martyrdom is Rome, the Eternal City of the world. The comparison of the different witnesses on this legend shows clearly how it concentrated itself more and more on the common work and end which the two Apostles had found in Rome. Clement of Rome, the oldest witness on this side, merely speaks of the martyrdom with which the two Apostles ended the great work of their life. In his first Epistle to the Corinthians (chap. iii. *sqq.*), he reminds this church, which was again divided into parties, of the great mischief which is excited by envy and malevolence, and exhorts it to order and unity. After quoting some Old Testament examples in support of his exhortations, he continues (chap. v.) : Ἀλλ' ἵνα τῶν ἀρχαίων ὑποδειγμάτων παυσώμεθα, ἔλθωμεν ἐπὶ τοὺς ἔγγιστα γενομένους ἀθλητάς· λάβωμεν τῆς γενεᾶς ἡμῶν τὰ γενναῖα ὑποδείγματα. Διὰ ζῆλον καὶ φθόνον οἱ μέγιστοι καὶ δικαιότατοι στύλοι ἐδιώχθησαν καὶ ἕως θανάτου ἦλθον. Λάβωμεν πρὸ ὀφθαλμῶν ἡμῶν τοὺς ἀγαθοὺς ἀποστόλους. Ὁ Πέτρος διὰ ζῆλον ἄδικον οὐχ ἕνα, οὐδὲ δύο, ἀλλὰ πλείονας ὑπήνεγκεν πόνους, καὶ οὕτω μαρτυρήσας ἐπορεύθη εἰς τὸν ὀφειλόμενον τόπον τῆς δόξης. Διὰ ζῆλον ὁ Παῦλος ὑπομονῆς βραβεῖον ὑπέσχεν, ἑπτάκις δεσμὰ φορέσας, ῥαβδευθείς, λιθασθείς, κῆρυξ γενόμενος ἔν τε τῇ ἀνατολῇ καὶ ἐν τῇ δύσει, τὸ γενναῖον τῆς πίστεως αὐτοῦ κλέος ἔλαβεν, δικαιοσύνην διδάξας ὅλον τὸν κόσμον, καὶ ἐπὶ τὸ τέρμα τῆς δύσεως ἐλθών, καὶ μαρτυρήσας ἐπὶ τῶν ἡγουμένων, οὕτως ἀπηλλάγη τοῦ κόσμου, καὶ εἰς τὸν ἅγιον τόπον ἐπορεύθη ὑπομονῆς γενόμενος μέγιστος ὑπόγραμμος. It may be reasonably doubted here whether the μαρτυρεῖν of Peter is to be understood in a special sense, of martyrdom, or in a general sense, of his witness to the truth throughout his apostolic labours. But, even irrespective of this, there is little advantage conceded to Peter over Paul; he rather holds the second place. Not only are the long and checkered labours of Paul described in detail, but it is specially mentioned that he was a herald of the faith in the west as well as in the east, and when he arrived at the end of his career was the teacher of the whole world. Nor is there a word to show that the two Apostles suffered martyrdom together; we are led rather to infer the contrary, since it is said only of Paul and not of Peter, that he worked in the west as well as in the east. They are merely mentioned together as μάρτυρες in the wider sense; and a distinction is drawn between them, as Paul, having come ἐπὶ τὸ τέρμα τῆς δύσεως καὶ μαρτυρήσας ἐπὶ τῶν ἡγουμένων, is called the great example of steadfast endurance. At a later period, when the martyrdom of Peter was an established fact, there was still some variety of opinion on the point whether both the Apostles suffered martyrdom at the same time. We find in the transactions of a Roman Synod, held under Bishop Gelasius I., the following sentence in reference to Peter, "Cui data est etiam societas S. Pauli, qui non diverso sicut hæretici garriunt, sed uno tempore, eodemque die, gloriosa morte cum Petro in urbe Roma cum Nerone agonizans coronatus est."[1] It is true that the difference mentioned here is only one of date, but if the two Apostles did not suffer at the same time as well as at the same place, it makes a very different affair, and so the "garrire" that is charged to the heretics probably covers a wider difference, and rests on some old tradition. The tendency, however, which led to the Apostles being placed in the relation to each other which we find in the passage quoted from Clemens Romanus (it is rather juxtaposition than identification with each other in this passage) tended increasingly in the further development of the legend to represent them as having everything in common. They not only suffered a common martyrdom at the same time and in the same place, that is to say in Rome, but it is no accidental meeting that unites them here; they had entered on the journey to Rome from the same point of their common labours, as if with a view to the same martyrdom. This fact is specially dwelt on in the testimony of the Corinthian Bishop Dionysius, who lived soon after the middle of the second century. Eusebius quotes him as a witness of the common Roman martyr-

[1] Cf. Valesius in Eusebius, Eccl. Hist. ii. 25.

dom of the two Apostles in the words (ii. 25), ὡς δὲ κατὰ τὸν αὐτὸν ἄμφω καιρὸν ἐμαρτύρησαν, Κορινθίων ἐπίσκοπος Διονύσιος ἐγγράφως 'Ρωμαίοις ὁμιλῶν ὧδέ πως παρίστησιν· ταῦτα καὶ ὑμεῖς διὰ τῆς τοσαύτης νουθεσιὰς τὴν ἀπὸ Πέτρου καὶ Παύλου φυτείαν γενηθεῖσαν 'Ρωμαίων τε καὶ Κορινθίων συνεκεράσατε. Καὶ γὰρ ἄμφω καὶ εἰς τὴν ἡμετέραν Κόρινθον φυτεύσαντες ἡμᾶς, ὁμοίως δὲ καὶ εἰς τὴν Ἰταλίαν ὁμόσε διδάξαντες ἐμαρτύρησαν κατὰ τὸν αὐτὸν καιρόν. Not merely did the two Apostles suffer the same martyrdom in Rome—they were also the common founders of the Corinthian as well as of the Roman Church. From this time forward it is a standing tradition that the Roman Church, as Irenæus says in the well-known passage,[1] was the "maxima et antiquissima et omnibus cognita, a gloriosissimis duobus Apostolis Petro et Paulo Romæ fundata et constituta ecclesia." The two Apostles now stand side by side like brothers, united together in death as in life; both share the same renown. But this equilibrium is soon lost in the preponderance of one over the other. For it is something else than the simple truth of history which places them so fraternally side by side, and in the growth of the legend there is a rivalry working between them. In the earliest form of the legend Paul had been treated as an adversary, and now he has to yield precedence at least to Peter, who is gaining the upper hand of him. If both Apostles, as Tertullian says,[2] in the "felix ecclesia totam doctrinam cum sanguine suo profuderunt," it is only Peter who "passioni dominicæ adæquatur," whilst Paul "Johannis" (the Baptist) "exitu coronatur." With Origen this story has grown.[3] After preaching the Gospel in Pontus, Galatia, Bithynia, Cappadocia, and Asia, Peter had at last come to Rome, and ἐν 'Ρώμῃ γενόμενος ἀνεσκολοπίσθη κατὰ κεφαλῆς, οὕτως αὐτὸς ἀξιώσας παθεῖν, on which Rufinus gives the following commentary in his translation of the Ecclesiastical History of Eusebius : " Crucifixus est deorsum, capite demerso, quod ipse ita fieri deprecatus est, ne

[1] Contra Hær. iii. 3.
[2] De Præscr. Hær. c. 36. Compare Adv. Marc. iv. 5. Petrus passioni dominicæ adæquatur.
[3] In the passage in Eusebius, H. E. iii. 1. Compare Dem. Ev. 37; H. E. ii. 25.

exæquari Domino videretur," although Tertullian takes no objection to the "adæquari passioni dominicæ." Their graves even were not allowed to be in the same place. The Presbyter Caius, living under the Roman Bishop Zephyrinus, was the first to speak, as Eusebius states, of the martyr-graves of the two Apostles. In his work against the Montanist Proclus he is said to have mentioned the place, "ἔνθα τῶν εἰρημένων ἀποστόλων τὰ ἱερὰ σκηνώματα κατατέθειται," with the words, "'Εγὼ δὲ τὰ τρόπαια τῶν Ἀποστόλων ἔχω δεῖξαι. Ἐὰν γὰρ θελήσῃς ἀπελθεῖν ἐπὶ τὸν Βατικανὸν, ἢ ἐπὶ τὴν ὁδὸν τὴν Ὠστίαν, εὑρήσεις τὰ τρόπαια τῶν ταύτην ἱδρυσαμένων τὴν ἐκκλησίαν," and Eusebius states, in proof of the trustworthiness of the traditions concerning Peter and Paul, that the places where the two Apostles were buried were generally known at this time, and were called by this name.[1] Caius does not indeed give the names of the Apostles in connection with these τρόπαια, but there can be no doubt that at this time the legend had already assigned to the Apostle Peter the more distinguished place in the Vatican, and to Paul that outside the city on the road leading to Ostia. Still more striking is the subordination of Paul to Peter in the narrative of Lactantius: "Quumque jam Nero imperaret, Petrus Romam advenit, et editis quibusdam miraculis, quæ virtute ipsius Dei, data sibi ab eo potestate faciebat, convertit multos ad justitiam, Deoque templum fidele ac stabile collocavit. Qua re ad Neronem delata, quum animadverteret, non modo Romæ, sed ubique quotidie magnam multitudinem deficere a cultu idolorum et ad religionem novam, damnata vetustata, transire, ut erat execrabilis ac nocens tyrannus —Petrum cruci affixit et Paulum interfecit."[2] Here Paul is only casually mentioned; the legend confines itself to Peter; he alone is the original and true founder of the Roman Church.

As for these miraculous deeds which excited so much attention, there is no doubt that the reference is to Simon Magus, and so

---

[1] Πιστοῦται τὴν ἱστορίαν ἡ Πέτρου καὶ Παύλου εἰς δεῦρο κρατήσασα ἐπὶ τῶν αὐτόθι κοιμητηρίων πρόσρησις. H. E. ii. 25.
[2] De Mort. Persecut. cap. 2.

this story indicates to us that stream of tradition which appears in the full development of legend in the Acta SS. Pauli et Petri.[1] In these Acta, when Paul came to Rome Peter was already there with Simon Magus. The greater part of the people was converted by the preaching of the two Apostles. (Peter even converted Nero's wife Livia, and Agrippina the wife of the Prefect Agrippa; Paul converted many soldiers and members of the Imperial household.) But the Magus, working against them out of envy, also obtained followers by his magic arts, although Peter strove against his sorcery by the miracles which he worked, by healing the sick, casting out demons, and raising the dead. The contest of the two Apostles with the Magus was carried on before the Emperor Nero, and ended by the Magus being struck dead to the earth by the prayer of the Apostles, as he was about to ascend flying to heaven. After his death, he was divided into four parts and changed into a stone consisting of four flints; while the two Apostles were put to death as martyrs by Nero's command. Paul was beheaded outside the city, Peter was crucified, and by his own desire, on a reversed cross; for as the Lord who had come down to earth from heaven had been raised up on a cross standing upright, so he who was summoned from earth to heaven ought to turn his head to the earth and his feet to heaven. We may remark here the relation which Paul bears to Peter, as it is given us in the declaration made by Peter before Nero. "Everything that Paul has said is true. For a long time I have received many letters from our Bishops all over the world about what Paul has said and done. When he was a persecutor of the law[2] the voice of Christ called to him from heaven and taught him the truth, because he was not an enemy of our faith through malevolence but through ignorance. For there

---

[1] First edited by Thilo in the two Halle Osterprogrammes, 1837, 1838.

[2] Διώκτου γὰρ αὐτοῦ ὄντος τοῦ νόμου, φωνὴ αὐτὸν Χριστοῦ ἐκ τοῦ οὐρανοῦ ἐκάλεσε. If Paul was converted as a persecutor of the law, then his conversion to Christianity is represented as a conversion from his enmity to the law. The law and truth, or Christianity, are here identified. From this standpoint, the original Ebionitish one, the Apostle's persecution of Christianity was the same thing as his Christian Antinomianism. He had therefore to be converted from his Antinomianism if he were to be counted an Apostle.

were before us false Christs such as Simon, and false Apostles and Prophets, who attacked the sacred writings and sought to abolish the truth. Against these there could only be opposed a man who from childhood had devoted himself to nothing else than the investigation of the secrets of the Divine Law, and the defence of truth and the persecution of falsehood. But as his persecution did not arise from malevolence but only from a wish to defend the law, the Truth himself appeared to him out of Heaven, and said, I am Jesus whom thou persecutest : cease from persecuting me, for I am the truth, for whom and against whose enemies thou must now be seen to fight." Here mystical tradition has carried its conciliatory tendency to the utmost extent possible. All the elements of the legend are incorporated, and the two Apostles are brought as near each other as was compatible with maintaining the primacy of Peter. Peter and the Magus are in Rome together, but the scene is now laid in the reign of Nero, in order to allow of Paul's taking his part in it. The Ebionite identification of him with the Magus has entirely disappeared : he is converted by Christ for the purpose of confuting the Magus. But though he is now acknowledged as a brother and Apostle side by side with Peter, he holds distinctly the second place. When the two Apostles prepare for the last and crowning act of the defeat of the Magus, the Acta makes Paul himself say to Peter : " It is my part to pray to God on my knees, but yours to bring to nothing what you see the Magus do, because you were first chosen by the Lord." Peter was the true miracle-worker and conqueror of the Magus.[1]

[1] The form in which these Acta have come down to us cannot be very ancient, but the traditional elements which they contain are much older. Even Origen is acquainted with both the crucifixion κατὰ κεφαλῆς, and the appearance of Christ, related also in these Acta, as having been vouchsafed to Peter before his martyrdom, when Christ told him he was being crucified again. For these facts Origen refers to πράξεις Παύλου. Joh. T. xx. c. 12, compare De Princ. 1, 2. Fortasse hæc Acta, remarks Thilo, part ii. p. 24, fuerunt Petri et Pauli, sicut probabile est prædicationes Petri et Pauli fuisse unum idemque scriptum quod modo sub alterutrius modo sub utriusque nomine allegatur. I regret not having been able to make use of the critical discussion of these Acta which Thilo announces at the close of his Programme.

Taking a comprehensive view of the legend in its various forms and modifications, we cannot but see that Peter is the favourite. The direction in which the legend moves is sufficient to show this. The actual achievements on which it is based belong directly and indubitably to Paul; yet Peter eventually gets all the credit of them; he leaves Paul scarcely any share in the foundation of the Roman Church. This evident bias not only makes us suspicious of the legend, but produces a disregard of well-established historical facts which nothing but the presence of the bias can explain. The Acts of the Apostles, which bears the character of an original document in the part where the Apostle's journey to Rome is narrated more than anywhere else, says nothing of a meeting of Peter and Paul in Rome, and we should thus have the indirect testimony of the Acts for the assumption which is usually made, that the meeting of the two Apostles in Rome took place after the time at which the Acts concludes. If the two Apostles really (as the Corinthian Bishop Dionysius says was the case) travelled from Corinth to Italy and Rome in company, this must have been a different journey from that described in the last chapters of the Acts of the Apostles, since not the least trace is found either in the Acts, or in the Epistles reputed to have been written during Paul's imprisonment at Rome, of his having been in company with the Apostle Peter during his journey (which besides did not touch at Corinth) or during his stay in Rome at that time. In this case he must have been liberated from this imprisonment and have undergone a second with Peter afterwards. Now is there anything to make this probable? The testimony of Eusebius rests (as has been already remarked) merely on an inference drawn from the second Epistle to Timothy; and thus this Epistle itself comes to be the sole support of the theory. But the genuineness of the Pastoral Epistles has long been called in question for weighty reasons, and the justice of the doubt has been acknowledged to such an extent that they cannot be held to afford a good foundation for any certain conclusion. We should thus be led to lay the more weight on the passage of Clemens Romanus, quoted above.

Neander asserts without hesitation that the τέρμα τῆς δύσεως, the limit of the west, which Paul is there said to have reached, cannot mean Rome, and would naturally suggest Spain. If, he says, we infer from this statement of Clement that Paul carried out his design of visiting Spain, or at least that he went farther west than Italy, we are obliged to suppose that he had been liberated from his imprisonment at Rome.[1] This, however, is a very unfounded conclusion, and in spite of all Neander's protestations I must still maintain that the much-vexed phrase τέρμα τῆς δύσεως must be taken differently. The question, as Schenkel very correctly observes, is whether Clement speaks of a τέρμα τῆς δύσεως in an objective sense, as being the τέρμα for the whole world, or in a subjective sense, as a τέρμα for Paul only. For the world the τέρμα τῆς δύσεως could only be the extreme west; for Paul it would be the place that set the last limit to his progress westwards. If this limit to his apostolic labours was reached at Rome, why should Rome not have been called a τέρμα in reference to the Apostle, and, as it lay in the west, why should it not be further described, from that circumstance, as τέρμα τῆς δύσεως?[2] "He came εἰς τὸ τέρμα τῆς δύσεως" would then mean, as I have already interpreted the words, he came to his appointed goal in the west. As it was situated in the *Occident*, it was the natural place of his *occidere*. The words suggest this latter idea without stretching. No further objections have been raised against this explanation, and I may thus refer the reader to what I have already said on the subject.[3]

If these two points of support are withdrawn from the theory of a second imprisonment, it at once falls to pieces. But a positive argument may be raised against it, namely, the improbability that the Apostle, under the circumstances as they then existed, was

---

[1] Planting and Training, I. 332.

[2] Schenkel, Theol. Stud. u. Krit. 1841, p. 71. Die Zweite Gefangenschaft des Apostels Paulus.

[3] Compare Tüb. Zeitschrift für Theol. 1831, No. 4. Die Christus-Partei, etc., p. 149, and Die sogenannten Pastoral-Briefe, p. 63. Tüb. Zeitschrift f. Theol. 1838. 3. Ueber den Ursprung des Episc. p. 46.

released from one imprisonment and underwent another. If, in accordance with the most probable calculation, we place the arrival of the Apostle Paul in Rome in the spring of the year 62, and add the two years of his imprisonment, of which the Acts of the Apostles speaks, what can be more natural than to suppose that the Apostle fell a victim to the Christian persecution under Nero in the year 64, which is described by Tacitus (Annal. xv. 44)? How unlikely is the assumption that after an imprisonment of two years' duration, he was liberated just at that crisis of misfortune for the Christians, and how can we believe that the same scene was repeated, so short a time afterwards, under circumstances so nearly identical? The wildness of the combinations in which those writers involve themselves who attempt the very least arrangement of the data which are thought to point to a second imprisonment,[1] certainly does nothing to diminish our confidence in placing the catastrophe of the Apostle's life at the conclusion of the first.

If the second imprisonment of the Apostle Paul be thus full of improbability, the martyrdom of the Apostle Peter at Rome becomes problematical also, depending, as it does, mainly upon the former. It loses its connection with history. The statement is that the two Apostles were in Rome and died there together, but they cannot have been there together unless we fix the date of their visit after the time covered by the Acts. Now our information about the Apostle Paul does not warrant us to overstep this limit. If then we consider the martyrdom of the Apostle Peter at Rome as a separate question, what historical evidence have we in favour of it, and what degree of probability does it possess? The oldest and most reliable testimony we have, that, namely, of the Epistle written by Clemens Romanus at Rome itself, can scarcely be held to say anything at all of the Apostle's martyrdom. Dionysius of Corinth is the first to mention the fact distinctly. But what a low

---

[1] We may compare, for example, the combinations (which are not the worst of their kind) made by the author of the treatise in the Theol. Quartalschr. Ueber den Aufenthalt des Apostels Petrus in Rom. 1820, p. 623, cf. 1830, p. 636.

conception must we form of his trustworthiness as a historian, if we only consider this one fact, that in direct contradiction to the Apostle's own Epistles he makes not only Paul, but Paul and Peter together, the founders of the Corinthian Church? This is enough to justify us in thinking that as Peter was not the founder of the Corinthian Church, so neither was he ever at Corinth. It must have been the Petrine party in Corinth, who, wishing to claim for themselves the merit of the foundation of the Church, caused it to be asserted that Peter himself had been at Corinth. The testimony of Dionysius of Corinth has been thought worthy of greater credit than that of Caius of Rome, not only because he lived half a century earlier, but also because he is thought to have been less biassed. Caius naturally wished to enhance the glory of the Church of Rome by the fact which he reports, but Dionysius plainly states that the two great Apostles died not in his Church, but at Rome.[1] Dionysius lived, it is true, half a century before Caius, but even he was separated by an interval of more than a century from the circumstances to which he bears witness. He can only testify therefore to the legend, current in his time, of the common journey of the two Apostles from Corinth to Rome and their martyrdom which there ensued. He does not enable us to judge whether this is merely a legend or the account of a real historical fact. The bias which Caius of Rome must have had for his own Church, is of course not likely to have operated with Dionysius; but the question is not whether the one or the other is the originator and author of the legend in a special interest, but only whether an unhistorical legend current in their day was believed and related by them as historically true. It certainly cannot be disputed that this is possible, and if the readiness with which such legends were believed would seem to argue a certain interest in them, how easily can we imagine such an interest as existing in the case of Dionysius of Corinth! Legends tending to the glorification of the Apostles were in general readily believed,—most readily, it is true, in cases where they also served to enhance the glory of the Church to

[1] Cf. Olshausen, Introduction to his Comm. über den Brief an die Römer, p. 39.

which the hearers belonged. But was not this the case here? Was it not highly honourable to the Corinthian Church that the two great Apostles should be represented as having been at Corinth together, before the most glorious moment of their lives arrived; that they had met here either by common agreement or by a higher call, to set out from here on the journey to their martyrdom in the capital of the world—to that death which was to reflect glory on their whole lives? And does not this interest to place the city of Corinth on the same footing as the city of Rome, and to make the light proceeding from the two Apostles shed its glory on both cities alike, appear very clearly in the Epistle of the Corinthian Bishop? "Thus have ye also (he writes to the Roman Christians), by your exhortation (the Epistle of the Roman Bishop Soter to the Corinthians, which Dionysius was answering)[1] brought into union what Peter and Paul founded" (τὴν ἀπὸ Πέτρου καὶ Παύλου φυτείαν γενηθεῖσαν Ῥωμαίων τε καὶ Κορινθίων συνεκεράσατε, i.e. ye have renewed the connection which exists between the Churches founded by the same Apostles—the Corinthian Church and the Roman). " For after the two Apostles had planted for us our Corinth" (εἰς τὴν ἡμετέραν Κόρινθον φυτεύσαντες ἡμᾶς, founded our Corinthian Church), " they proceeded to Italy, still teaching together, and suffered martyrdom there at the same time." Does not a special interest betray itself in this transformation of facts, where, contrary to all history, Peter is represented as the founder of the Corinthian Church as well as Paul?

In the case of the third in our list of witnesses, Caius of Rome, the possibility of a special interest is readily granted; but we have also to remember that he wrote in Rome itself, that he gives the precise localities at the Vatican and on the road to Ostia, and that there can scarcely be any error in this statement, because thousands would at once have corrected him. Caius indeed speaks of the τρόπαια of the two Apostles in Rome, with an exact description of the localities; but what can the testimony of an author prove, who is separated by the interval of nearly a century and a half from the

[1] Cf. Eusebius, Eccl. Hist., iv. 22.

occurrence of those deaths of which the graves are to serve as evidence? His testimony is only of value as showing that what he states about the two Apostles was told and believed in Rome at the time when he wrote. To this extent, of course, it is not to be thought that there can be any error in this statement; thousands would have immediately contradicted him, if he had stated, as the current Roman tradition, a thing of which no one in Rome knew anything. Only let us not confound fact with legend. There can be no doubt of the existence of the legend; but that proves nothing with regard to its historical basis.

Nor do the contents of the legend enhance its historical trustworthiness. Neander himself acknowledges that the later tradition of the crucifixion of Peter, according to which his humility was so great that he thought it too much honour to suffer in the same manner as the Holy One had done, and prayed to be crucified with his head downwards, bears the stamp of a later and more sickly piety, rather than that of the simple apostolic humility.[1] How dearly bought is the theory of the Apostle Peter's presence in Rome, which, for Protestants, is a purely historical question, and has no further importance whatever, if it is only to be gained at the price of sacrificing the genuine apostolic character, the humility that is free from all display and vanity! But if we only take our stand on Tertullian's "adæquari passioni dominicæ," what probability can even this have, when we consider the circumstances under which the Apostles are said to have died?[2] If the two Apostles were put to death together in a Roman persecution of the Christians, it is not likely that there was any difference made between them in respect to the manner of their execution, least of all such a difference as would so exactly have corresponded to the rivalry between them which the legend everywhere suggests. Even the localities of the two graves betray the same rival interest, since Paul, as a more outward preacher of Christ, was allotted a grave on the road

[1] Page 473; Bohn, 377.

[2] If we believe Tertullian's "Petrus passioni dominicæ adæquatur," we must also believe his account of the martyrdom by oil of the Apostle John, which is given in the same passage.

to Ostia, whilst Peter was glorified by the highest honour of a martyr's grave given him in the famous theatre of the persecution in the garden of Nero. In the Epistle of Clement of Rome, we hear merely of the glory of martyrdom, without particulars: in the growth of the legend this has grown into a tradition of a definite form, and with its local attachments and corroborations.[1]

It has been necessary to enter so far into the bearings of the legends affecting the two Apostles, in order to determine with some accuracy what facts lie at their foundation. It appears from the foregoing investigation, that the history of Paul is the only historical foundation and point of departure from which the web of tradition has been spun in different directions. Everything which is stated as an actual occurrence can be traced to Paul and not to Peter. What is related of Peter is only the traditional reflex of the historical reality which belongs to the life of Paul. Starting in this way, the legend proceeded to take from Paul the whole actual contents of his life and transfer it to Peter; while what undeniably belonged to Paul, and could not be robbed from him, was given back to him in such a form as to appear to be merely the reflected splendour shed on him by Peter's superlative glory. The legend has thus made free use for its own purposes of the three historical facts that had to be considered: the apostolic mission to the Gentiles, the residence in Rome, and the martyrdom there. We have thus to distinguish three stages in the formation of the legend. First Paul is displaced from the position of Apostle to the Gentiles,

[1] The circus of Nero was at the foot of the Vatican. Tacitus, Annal. xiv. 14. The gardens of Nero were in the same neighbourhood. Peter was said to have been buried there, where a church was afterwards built to him. Compare Roma antica di F. Nardini, Ed. iv. di A. Nibby, T. iv. Rom. 1819, page 358, where the Italian antiquarian asks, forse Nerone immanissimo in far strage di Christiani usò poi pietà in distruggere il suo circo per concedervi loro la sepoltura? In the description of the city of Rome by E. Plattner, C. Bunsen, etc., ii. 1, 1832, page 52, it is remarked on the words of Caius quoted above, 'Ἐγὼ δὲ τὰ τρόπαια, etc.: "When we look into this statement, we find that it affirms merely that the Apostle suffered here in that persecution: the town where the martyrdom took place is the Christian's trophy, even though not his tomb." But Eusebius evidently understands the words of Caius as referring to the graves of the Apostles.

which he was the first to occupy. Peter is set up as the true Gentile Apostle, and Paul takes the *rôle* of a false Apostle, preaching a heathen doctrine. Scarcely had historical truth re-asserted itself so far as to leave Paul in possession of his historical claims, and let the two Apostles stand side by side in equal dignity, when another inroad is made upon Paul's distinctions. There was much that no one either could or would deny to him; the foundation of the most important churches, especially those at Corinth and at Rome, the honour of martyrdom which he had met at Rome, and of having been buried there. Yet in all these particulars he was made to yield precedence to Peter. Who can fail to see in all this the reflex of the varying forms of the relation in which the two great parties stood over against each other in the apostolic and post-apostolic ages? It cannot be doubted that the Jewish-Christians saw in the Apostle Paul only the opponent and enemy of the law, and of Jewish-Christianity as it depended on the continuance of the law, and that they sought to oppose him by all the means at their disposal in all the Gentile-Christian Churches. But the greater the progress was which Christianity made among the Gentiles through the efforts of the Apostle Paul and his followers, the more certain did it become that there must be many who would not be deterred by all that the Jewish-Christians could do from maintaining the principles of Pauline Christianity. Thus there arose a conflict of interests and views which could not continue to exist in its harsher form, if there was ever to be such a thing as one Christian Church. That this one Church did emerge is a historical fact, but it is incorrect to suppose that it was Pauline Christianity alone which everywhere won the victory over the Jewish-Christianity which opposed it. Concessions were made on each side, and the two parties melted gradually into each other : yet there are not wanting traces that Judaism was still by far the stronger of the two. The concessions to which the Paulinists submitted, whether of their own motion or from the pressure of circumstances, are to be seen in works such as the Acts of the Apostles, and many of the post-apostolic Epistles of the canon. Thus in the legend concerning the fate of the two Apostles, we have a picture of what they did not live to see, not of them individually but of the parties in whom their influence survived, with their respective fortunes. So considered, and taken for what they really are, these legends possess, notwithstanding the unhistorical nature of their contents, a true historical value. They are living pictures of the age, its motives and its aims. They certainly show, in a striking manner, how seriously history is changed, when not only is legend treated as history, but when, in order to eke out the connection between legends which refuse to fit into each other, new facts are invented and added to the unhistorical facts already rashly received. Thus the assumption of a second imprisonment of the Apostle Paul is one which it would be well to get rid of once for all, that we may no longer be confused and misled by it in our attempts to form a clear conception of the relation which existed in that early time when the Church was preparing to appear.

SECOND PART.

THE EPISTLES OF THE APOSTLE PAUL.

SECOND PART.

THE EPISTLES OF THE APOSTLE PAUL.

INTRODUCTION.

THE foregoing inquiry shows what a false picture of the personality of the Apostle Paul we should form if the Acts of the Apostles were the only source we had to draw from. The Epistles of the Apostle are thus the only authentic documents for the history of his apostolic labours, and of the entire relation in which he stood to his age; and in proportion as the spirit that breathes through them is great and original, we see that they present the truest and most living mirror of what that spirit was. The deeper we go in the study of the Epistles the richer and the more peculiar do we find that life to be which the Pauline spirit developed. Yet on this ground also we find that double of the Apostle making his appearance at his side, who in the Acts completely supplanted him. That all these thirteen Pauline Epistles, which Christian antiquity unanimously recognised, and handed down as the Epistles of the Apostle, cannot make equal claim to authenticity, and that several of them labour under an overwhelming suspicion of unauthenticity, is a result of recent criticism, which is steadily making its way to general acceptance. In view of the present state of the criticism of the subject, it cannot be thought premature to sum up the investigations that have been made with regard to the various Epistles, in a classification similar to that in which Eusebius, in his classical passage on the canon, recorded his verdict on the various writings which claimed to be admitted to it, as the historical evidence before him seemed to require. The Pauline Epistles fall into the two classes of Homologoumena and Antilegomena.

In the Homologoumena there can only be reckoned the four great Epistles of the Apostle, which take precedence of the rest in every respect, namely, the Epistle to the Galatians, the two Epistles to the Corinthians, and the Epistle to the Romans. There has never been the slightest suspicion of unauthenticity cast on these four Epistles, and they bear so incontestably the character of Pauline originality, that there is no conceivable ground for the assertion of critical doubts in their case. All the rest of the Epistles, which are commonly ascribed to the Apostle, belong to the class of Antilegomena; but this does not amount to a positive assertion that they are spurious, any more than Eusebius meant this by his use of the phrase; it is simply a statement of the fact that their genuineness has been and may be called in question,— since among all these lesser Pauline Epistles there is not a single one against which, from the standpoint of the four chief Epistles, some objection or other may not be raised. In their entire nature they are so essentially different from the four first Epistles, that even if they be considered as Pauline, they can only form a second class of Epistles of the Apostle. In fact they profess for the most part to have been composed at a later period of his apostolic career. Eusebius makes a further division of his Antilegomena, and selects from that class a certain number of Notha, the doubt regarding which amounts to more than merely a suspense of judgment, and passes into an overwhelming probability of actual spuriousness. Among these deutero-Pauline Epistles there are not wanting some, the verdict of criticism on which inclines more and more to this side. In my opinion, and in that of other critics, the so-called Pastoral Epistles must be placed in this subdivision of the Pauline Antilegomena. Thus we have three classes of Pauline Epistles. This classification can also appeal to an ancient authority. The Marcionite Canon, whose Ἀπόστολος is the most ancient collection of Pauline Epistles known to us, does not contain the generally received thirteen Epistles of the Apostle, but only ten; the three Pastoral Epistles being excluded. For the Canon of Marcion then, the Pastoral Epistles are a class by themselves; so much is certain, and the distinction that was drawn was probably the reason for their being omitted. If they were absent because they were not in existence at the time, of course they would not be afterwards included as Notha in a collection which was to contain only genuine Pauline Epistles. If they were in existence at the time, but unknown to Marcion (and this is scarcely credible if they had been long current as genuine Pauline Epistles), their relation to this Canon remains the same; they were not included because they were not known as Pauline writings. But if the compiler of the Marcionite Canon knew of their existence when he excluded them, then they were excluded as being writings which were held by the compiler of this Canon not to be Pauline; and by this exclusion the verdict was pronounced on them that even if not notoriously dating from a later period, they were at least wanting in the genuine Pauline character, and could not be considered as Pauline writings. From the standpoint of the Marcionite Canon, these Epistles must in any case be considered as composing the last class of the Epistles generally ascribed to the Apostle Paul. If we proceed from the Epistles which were wanting in that Canon to those which it contained, we find two classes which agree with the above classification, namely, a series of Pauline Epistles of the first order, and another of the second order. According to Epiphanius (Hær. 42. 9.), the Canon of Marcion arranged the Pauline Epistles in the following order:— Galatians, 1 and 2 Corinthians, Romans, 1 and 2 Thessalonians, Ephesians (Marcion's title to this Epistle, however, was "To the Laodiceans"), Colossians, Philemon, and Philippians. In this arrangement of the Pauline Epistles it is usual to consider little more than the prominence given to the Epistle to the Galatians, the reason of which is held to be the importance which this Epistle must have held in the teachings of so decided an anti-Judaistic Paulinist as Marcion. But if this be so, we should expect to find the rest of the Epistles arranged from the point of view of their greater or less importance with regard to the teachings of Marcion, and we fail to understand why the two Epistles to the Corinthians should precede that to the Romans, and still less why the rest should follow precisely in the order they do. If we assume that the arrangement follows the order of time in which the Epistles were held to have been written, the two Epistles to the Thessalonians seem to be out of place, as in this case they ought not to come just after the Epistle to the Romans, but ought to come first of all, as they were the first written. And yet we must recognise a certain reference to the order of time in the fact that the Epistles to the Thessalonians follow immediately the four principal Epistles. If we consider all these different points, we can only explain the Marcionite Canon by the supposition that it consists of two separate collections. The first collection is composed of four Epistles; Galatians, 1 and 2 Corinthians, and Romans, which could only be so placed by following a chronological order. The second collection must also have been arranged chronologically—it would be hard to explain on any other theory how it commenced with 1 and 2 Thessalonians, and why the Epistle to the Philippians follows that to Philemon. Whatever may be the origin and history of these two collections, it must certainly be considered a very remarkable feature of this Canon, that in it we find all those lesser Pauline Epistles placed in a second series, which in many respects differ so much from the principal Epistles as to raise grave doubts about their origin; and the supposition very naturally presents itself, that if weighty reasons should be forthcoming against their unauthenticity, the secondary position of these collected Epistles may be due to the fact that they appeared as deutero-Pauline writings, after the collection of genuine Pauline Epistles had been closed. As they professed to be Pauline Epistles, they were indeed added to the original genuine Epistles of the Apostle; but the manner in which they are arranged along with the latter betrays their later origin, and it is just as natural that they should be distinguished from the others as being later Epistles, although still held as Pauline, as it is natural that the Pastoral Epistles which were opposed to the Marcionite teaching, and so must have followed it in point of time, should be entirely wanting in that Canon. Marcion is a name of critical importance in the history of Pauline Christianity: to him Paulinism was the only true and genuine Christianity, and this fact entitles him to a consideration which has hitherto been denied to him, the so-called heretic. As we have seen, he provides us with a piece of information which the criticism of the Pauline Epistles cannot, at the stage it has now reached, afford to disregard.[1]

[1] As the weight of the reasons which are adduced against the authentic origin and character of the lesser Epistles, as compared with the four Epistles which stand first, will not, according to all probability, be diminished by the further free exercise of criticism, but, on the contrary, rather strengthened, it is even at this stage the simplest and most natural way of proceeding, to divide the Epistles standing in the Canon, under the name of the Apostle, into authentic and unauthentic, Pauline and pseudo-Pauline, and to arrange the later ones according to their probable chronological order.

THE FIRST CLASS OF THE PAULINE EPISTLES.

THE GENUINE EPISTLES OF THE APOSTLE.

CHAPTER I.

THE EPISTLE TO THE GALATIANS.

IT is generally assumed that the Galatian Churches (αἱ ἐκκλησίαι τῆς Γαλατίας, Gal. i. 2) were founded by Paul himself. The passages i. 8, iv. 13, 19, in which the Apostle speaks of his preaching the Gospel among the Galatians, would seem to leave little doubt on this point, but the Acts of the Apostles gives us no details about the time and occasion. If we try to find a place for the founding of these churches in the Acts, we are shut up to the second journey of the Apostle (xvi. 6, *sq.*) as he visited Galatia at that time, and on the third journey which led him to Galatia again, he only "confirmed" the disciples who were already there (Acts xviii. 23). But it is remarkable that the author of the Acts says nothing at xvi. 6 of the founding of a Christian Church, and represents the Apostle as merely travelling through Phrygia and Galatia, and, it is suggested, passing through these countries rapidly, so as to preclude the idea of any lengthened stay. This is certainly the conclusion to which we are led by the Acts of the Apostles. With regard to the members of this church, the general opinion is that they consisted partly of Jewish and partly of Gentile Christians. That there were Jewish Christians among them is thought to be likely in itself, as many Jews lived in Asia Minor generally, and therefore also in Galatia (compare 1 Peter i. 1). It is also thought that the Apostle would not have spoken of the Law and of the Old Testament as he does in Galatians iii. 2, 13, iv. 5, 31, if there had not been Jews among the readers of his Epistle. This last consideration, however, does not carry much weight, as a knowledge of the Old Testament might be presupposed on the part of Gentiles who were inclined either to Judaism or Christianity. It thus remains doubtful whether there were any Jewish Christians in the Galatian Churches, and although this is not in itself improbable, yet it cannot be taken as certain, as the Epistle itself shows undeniably in many places (compare iv. 8, v. 2, vi. 12) that the Apostle was addressing Gentile Christians.

What led the Apostle to write this Epistle to the Galatian Churches we learn very clearly from the Epistle itself. The Galatian Christians were very near falling away from the Gospel as it had been preached to them by the Apostle (i. 6, iii. 1, 3, iv. 9, *sq.*, 21, v. 2, *sq.*, 7). This was due to the influence of strange teachers who had visited these churches after the Apostle, and destroyed the confidence of the Galatian Christians in their newly acquired Christianity by suggesting that they could not be saved by a doctrine like that of the Apostle Paul. These teachers represented to them that, as a first step to the Christian salvation, they must submit to circumcision (v. 2, 11). Here we first meet with those Judaising opponents with whom the Apostle had to maintain so severe a struggle in the churches which he founded, and they appear here quite in the harsh and uncompromising Judaistic character which marks them as opponents of Pauline Christianity. Their opposition to the apostolic work of the Apostle Paul did not indeed go so far as to deny that the Gentiles were called to partake in the Messianic salvation; in this respect the limits of Judaism are for them also broken through, but they were the more zealous to assert the principle that in this wider sphere salvation could only be obtained in the form of Judaism. The absolute right of Judaism could not be relinquished; the Gentiles must acknowledge that right. It was therefore simply impossible that a man could be saved by Christianity unless he professed Judaism, and submitted to everything that Judaism prescribed as a condition of salvation. Whilst they asserted this principle in every country alike, they made it their special task to repair the injury which the Apostle Paul had done; and where he had preached his gospel of freedom from the law, they insisted energetically on the necessity of observance of the law; they sought, in fact, rather to Judaise than to Christianise the Gentiles whom Paul had converted. The Apostle Paul having, according to their views, played the part of an innovator and revolutionary, they desired to interpose with their conservative principles to repair the evil, and to found the new ideas and doctrines in which the salvation of mankind was comprised entirely on the positive foundation of Judaism. It lay in the very nature of the case that they should appear as opponents of the Apostle Paul, and that wherever they came in contact with him, they should present the most obstinate and thoroughgoing opposition to him; but this opposition does not warrant us to regard them as mere heretics, impostors, and corrupters—persons who from bad motives made it their business to interfere everywhere with the beneficent work of the Apostle, and introduce hindrance and confusion where it had been begun. It is true that the Apostle Paul himself thus represents them, but we must not forget that party is here opposed to party, and each side takes up the question and discusses it from a party point of view. We have no reason for assuming that these opponents of the Apostle were not thoroughly in earnest in the views and principles of which they were the champions, or that they did not act on conviction in what we see them to have done; in fact, the whole impression which they make on us is that they were men so firmly wedded to the opinions and principles for which they contended, that they could not separate themselves from them or raise themselves above them. In one word, they were Jews or Jewish Christians of the genuine old stamp, who could so little understand the more liberal atmosphere of Pauline Christianity that they would have thought the very ground of their existence was cut from under them if Judaism were no longer to have its absolute power and importance. We certainly do not deny that they permitted themselves to employ the most unjust accusations and most malicious calumnies against the Apostle Paul; these are never wanting in any party struggle; but if we look steadily and fairly at the main facts of the case, we must allow so much to the Apostle's opponents, that the chief reason why their Judaistic position was so narrow was just their natural incapacity to raise themselves from a lower state of religious consciousness to a higher and freer one.

This determines the point of view from which this Epistle of the Apostle as a whole is to be considered. It takes us to the very ferment of the strife between Judaism and Christianity, at the point when it had just come in sight of its critical issue; to the debate of the momentous question whether there was to be a Christianity free from Judaism and essentially different from it, or whether Christianity was to exist merely as a form of Judaism, was to be, that is to say, nothing but Judaism modified and extended. But all that Christianity was or was yet to become as a thing radically different from Judaism had been first brought to historical reality by the Apostle Paul, and had no existence yet apart from his person; the peculiar theme of the Epistle is the vindication of Pauline Christianity, which was necessarily at the same time the personal vindication of the Apostle. In this conflict with Judaism and its champions he found himself obliged to enter into a defence of his position as an Apostle; and he could only do this by appealing to his own immediate Apostolic consciousness. Thus the first point that he takes up is the proof of his immediate apostolic calling, or his peculiar standpoint, showing that he had not arrived at this standpoint by means of any communication from man, but entirely by means of an immediate act of his own self-consciousness, by which he became aware of his inner divine call, i. 6-16. This independence of the principle on which his apostolic call rested he maintains as against the elder Apostles— first, negatively, inasmuch as he became an Apostle of Christ quite independently of them, and what he was as an Apostle he was in the fullest sense before he ever came in contact with them at all, i. 17, 18; and then, positively, inasmuch as when he did come in contact with them he not only surrendered nothing of his principle and held his own against them, but was able to win for it the most unequivocal and triumphant recognition. This was done in three different particulars, forming a sort of ascending scale, in which he maintained his principle against them in a manner perfectly convincing, and even went so far as to carry it out in acts to which it applied. For, in the first place, at the time of his journey to Jerusalem, no one had anything to allege against his peculiar standpoint, i. 18, 19; in the second place, when matters came to an open difference, he put the case before them in such a way that they were obliged to recognise his co-ordinate sphere of apostolic activity, ii. 1-10; and, in the third place, when Peter in Antioch acted in disregard of the principles which had formerly been acknowledged, he was so distinctly in the wrong, that he had to submit to be rebuked, ii. 11, *sq.* The personal vindication here passes over naturally to the dogmatic, to the proof of the great proposition that the principle of the justification which alone brings salvation to man lies only in faith in Christ, and not in the works of the law. In proof of this proposition it is first alleged that it is an immediate affirmation of the Christian consciousness, iii. 1-5; and then that it underlies the whole of the Old Testament, inasmuch as the substance of what the Old Testament contains is the promise given to Abraham, to which the law was added as in fact merely an accident, iii. 6-18. Thereupon follows a further discussion of the nature of the law, in which the subordinate relation of the law to the promise is further insisted on, together with the merely relative importance which the law possesses in its position between the promise and faith as a merely mediating element, though by no means an unimportant one. The Apostle's argument then moves forward in the antitheses of preparation and fulfilment, the carnal and the spiritual minds, the servitude of the "heir as long as he is a child," and his freedom when he becomes of age. Christianity is the absolute religion, the religion of the spirit and of freedom, with regard to which Judaism belongs to an inferior standpoint, from which it must be classed with heathenism under the $\dot{a}\sigma\theta\epsilon\nu\hat{\eta}$ καὶ πτωχὰ στοιχεῖα τοῦ κόσμου. The proof of this is given (1.) partly objectively from the inner nature of Christianity as compared with the nature of Judaism, partly subjectively from the Christian's own experience of the life of spirit and freedom, iv. 1-11 (what next follows, iv. 12-20, is an expression of the Apostle's sorrow and displeasure at the falling away of the Galatians); (2.) from the Old Testament, through an allegorical use of the two sons of Abraham, Isaac and Ishmael, who hold to each other the relation of freedom and bondage. The hortatory and practical part of the Epistle contains (1.) an exhortation to perseverance in the freedom of the spirit, by means of the true faith, and a warning against relapse into Judaism, v. 1-12; (2.) a description of that moral conduct by which the true freedom and the life of the spirit approve themselves, and a warning against the abuse of freedom. This moral conduct is considered generally, v. 13-15, and in particular with reference to the circumstances of the Galatians, v. 26-vi. 10. Finally, in vi. 11-18, we have the conclusion of the Epistle, consisting of a brief emphatic summary of what had been said before, with a benediction. The Epistle may accordingly be divided into three parts: the first, personal and apologetic; the second, dogmatic; and the third, practical. All three are intimately interwoven with each other. The dogmatic part of the Epistle proceeds, on the one hand, on the vindication that has been given of the writer's apostolic authority, and on the other, it passes naturally over to the practical part, inasmuch as the νόμος is one of the chief ideas of the dogmatic part. It was necessary to show that freedom from the law does not by any means do away with the obligations of moral conduct.

The composition of this Epistle is placed by many at a very early, and by others at a much later date. The general opinion is that it was written soon after the Apostle's second journey, Acts xviii. 2, 3; and Rückert, Credner, and others have sought to find circumstantial evidence for this opinion in combinations of a very subjective kind. To give the Epistle its proper place in the chronology of the Pauline Epistles, we need only consider its relation to the two Epistles to the Corinthians and to the Epistle to the Romans. In this respect we have certainly an important piece of evidence in the opponents with whom the Apostle had to contend among the Galatians as well as among the Corinthians. The Judaising opponents are the same; but there can be little doubt, from the manner in which the Apostle attacks them in the Galatian Epistle, that this is the first brunt of the conflict. What is discussed in this Epistle is the very first question that would be raised; the Apostle finds it necessary to give an account, first of all, of how he came to his apostolic office, and he speaks of it in a manner which he could not have employed if he had ever come in contact with these opponents in the same way before. He wants to get to the very root of the matter with them; he sets to work in a spirit which we do not find except when opposition has for the first time revealed to a man the full importance of the principle on the assertion of which the whole work of his life depends. This same impression of a party contest only just arisen, in which each party puts forth all its power to attain its one definite object, is shown also in the conduct of the opposition. Circumcision, the most direct and unmistakable recognition of the value of the Mosaic law, is the point at issue. It is certainly remarkable that in the Epistles to the Corinthians there is no longer any mention of this subject. The opponents against whom the Apostle contends are the same Judaising propagandists; but the relations of parties, which in the Galatian Epistle are quite simple and undisguised, have now undergone some modification, and the conflict has entered on another stage. On this account the Epistle to the Galatians must be placed before the three other Epistles, and this is the place it holds in the

Marcionite Canon. In regard to the opponents with whom the Apostle had to contend, it is closely related to the two Epistles to the Corinthians; in regard to its dogmatic contents, it is closely connected with the Epistle to the Romans. But here also the relation is a perfectly analogous one. The ideas which appear in the Epistle to the Romans as the complete system of Pauline doctrine, worked out in all its particulars, appear in the Galatian Epistle in their first outlines, yet distinctly and clearly traced. We can thus start from this Epistle to trace the development of the Pauline doctrinal system through the various stages at which we meet it in the four great Epistles. It has already been shown in our former inquiry, for which the Epistle to the Galatians was the chief authority, what importance this Epistle possessed as an historical document. It gives us what knowledge we have of the original relation in which our Apostle stood to the other Apostles, and thus shows us the process of development by which the struggle with Judaism led to a more distinct perception and appreciation of the essential principle of Christianity.

CHAPTER II.

THE TWO EPISTLES TO THE CORINTHIANS.

THESE two Epistles stand in chronological order between the Epistle to the Galatians on the one hand, and the Epistle to the Romans on the other, and they thus introduce us to the very centre of the Apostle's busy and many-sided activity as the founder of Gentile Christian churches. That which is presented in its simplest elements in the Epistle to the Galatians, and which in the Epistle to the Romans passes over to the abstract sphere of dogmatic controversy, opens out in the Epistles to the Corinthians into the full reality of concrete life, with all the complicated relations which must have existed in a Christian Church of the earliest period. The Corinthian Church was the peculiar creation of the Apostle; it was, as he himself says (1 Cor. iv. 15), a child begotten by him and lovingly fostered, but such a child also as needed, in every way, his fatherly correction and educating care. With no other church did he stand in so close and confidential a relation; to none did he address so many and such important Epistles; in none did he undergo so many experiences of different kinds; above all, in none had he such a difficult and important problem to solve. All this arose naturally from the fact that the Corinthian Church was the first Christian Church which existed on the classic ground of ancient Greece. How could the Greek spirit disown its original nature, even when new-born into Christianity? There is nothing more natural than that Christianity should break out into phenomena of a peculiar kind at its first application to a people like the Greeks, whose activity and versatility of mind, and whose political party spirit had a new theatre before them, in the newly-opened sphere of action. Especially must this have been the case in a city like Corinth, where Greek culture and Greek sensuality were so intimately allied with each other. Add to this, what is of peculiar importance in considering the personal relation of the Apostle to the Corinthian Church, and what gave him so many an opportunity of showing us the underlying, purely human element of his many-sided character, namely, that the same Judaising opponents, with whom we are already acquainted, introduced a new and most disturbing element into the life of this Greek Christian Church, when still in the first stage of its development. But these opponents now appear in a more polished and refined guise; they have less of the Jewish national tone; they seem to have perceived that they must take up a different line in this altogether Greek Church from that which they had taken up in the churches of Asia Minor: or it may be that their religious views had made some progress, and that they had become less rigid. Their opposition to Pauline Christianity no longer proceeds from the purely Jewish standpoint, where circumcision is the great thing to be insisted on: it has become Christian, and the main point urged is the true Christian notion of apostolic authority; but it has gained in intensity by applying itself to this one principle, and is all the more personally dangerous to the Apostle.

In the first Epistle, the Apostle takes up a series of subjects which at that early period had a special interest for a church still in its infancy. The chief matter with which he was concerned was the party spirit which had sprung up in the Corinthian Church through the influence of the Judaising opponents. The Church had split into several parties, which were called by names denoting their several tendencies, i. 12. The names Paul, Apollos, Cephas, and Christ denote, as it seems, so many different parties. The party of Paul is, very naturally, placed first. The Corinthians had not fallen away from the Apostle, they had only divided themselves into parties; and those members of the Church who had remained most faithful to the Apostle still continued to form, as we see from both the Epistles, the overwhelming majority. Nor can we be surprised that when parties were formed in Corinth, one of these should be called by the name of Apollos. Apollos had immediately succeeded the Apostle at Corinth as his lieutenant in the cause of the Gospel, and if, as is related of him, Acts xviii. 24, he had attained great eminence in Alexandrine culture and knowledge of the Scriptures, it may easily be understood how there might be many persons in Corinth, who, owing to the attractiveness of his discourses for the Greek mind, became so fond of him that they even preferred him in some measure to the Apostle Paul. But how was it that the favourable reception which other teachers, like-minded with himself, met with from a portion of the Church, appears to the Apostle to indicate such a dangerous party spirit, and one so earnestly to be opposed? There must be something more in the circumstances of the Church to explain how this predilection for Apollos could have been considered by the Apostle as a subject for anxiety. The true cause of division and schism is to be sought in the names of the other two parties. The name of Peter naturally suggests an opposition to Paul. As far as we know, Peter himself had never been at Corinth; but under the authority of his name a Jewish-Christian element had been introduced into a Church which, there can be no doubt, consisted almost entirely of Gentile Christians. In this sense only can the Apostle affix the name of Cephas or Peter to one of these parties. We do not find, however, what we might have expected, that the Apostle addresses himself to a confutation of the principles promulgated by Judaising opponents : the Epistles contain nothing of this kind. The Jewish doctrines of the absolute value of the Mosaic law, and the necessity of its observance for salvation, are nowhere combated in these Epistles, as they are in the Epistles to the Galatians and the Romans ; there is no mention made of the law and its place in Christian doctrine. Throughout the whole of both the Epistles to the Corinthians we look in vain for any trace to show that that party still existed : it is only in the last chapters of the second Epistle that we obtain clear information that the old dispute is by no means at rest. At the close of the Epistle (xi. 22) the Apostle denounces the Judaism of his opponents so unreservedly, and describes them so bitterly as false teachers of Christianity, vain of their privilege of Jewish birth, that we easily understand the reason of his polemic against them; but we are no nearer to the desired information about their principles. The Judaism of his opponents thus appears here in a new form, and we are led to ask whether the fourth party named by the Apostle, the party of Christ, will not throw some light on these party relations. Here, however, we come to a most difficult question, which we must endeavour as far as possible to answer if we are to reach any clear understanding of the circumstances of the Corinthian Church, and the position of the Apostle in it.

Who were οἱ τοῦ Χριστοῦ?[1] Amongst the modern commentators and critics who have directed their attention to this question, Storr and Eichhorn have advanced theories which are opposed to each other to this extent, that the one adheres too closely to one special point, and the other loses itself in generalities; though in this they are agreed, that they neither found on any statement of the Epistles, nor succeed in making the subject clear. According to Storr,[2] οἱ τοῦ Χριστοῦ were those members of the Corinthian Church who had made the Apostle James the chief of their party as being the ἀδελφὸς Κυρίου, in order that through this outward relationship of the head of their sect to Jesus they might claim for it a precedence which would exalt it over even the Petrine party. This would explain the Apostle's expression, Χριστὸν κατὰ σάρκα γινώσκειν, 2 Cor. v. 13; it would then be a reference to this carnal

[1] I first discussed this question in a treatise in the Tübinger Zeitschr. für Theologie, 1831, pt. 4, p. 61, Die Christus-partei in der korinthischen Gemeinde, der Gegensatz des petrinischen und paulinischen Christenthums, der Apostel Petrus in Rom.

[2] Notitiæ historicæ epistolarum Pauli ad Corinthios, interpretationi servientes. Tub. 1758, p. 14. Opusc. acad. vol. ii. p. 246. The same opinion is supported by Flatt, Vorlesungen über die beiden Briefe Pauli an die Cor., p. 15; by Bertholdt, Hist. Krit. Einl., p. 339; by Hug, Einleitung in die Schriften des N. T., 3d ed., p. 360; and by Heidenreich, Comment. in 1 Corinth., vol. i., 1825, p. 31.

mode of establishing relations with Christ; but if Storr cannot bring forward anything else in support of his theory than that the Apostle speaks of the "brethren of the Lord," 1 Cor. ix. 5, and mentions James in connection with Peter, xv. 7, what is the value of such an hypothesis? According to Eichhorn,[1] οἱ τοῦ Χριστοῦ were the neutrals who differed from the other conflicting parties in asserting that they did not attach themselves to Paul, nor to Apollos, nor to Peter, but only to Christ. That these neutrals might not be entirely colourless, Pott[2] pressed into the service of Eichhorn's view the passage 1 Cor. iii. 22, where Paul, after denouncing the schisms in the Corinthian Church, is held to state his own position in the words πάντα ὑμῶν ἐστιν, εἴτε Παῦλος, εἴτε Ἀπολλὼς, εἴτε Κηφᾶς, πάντα ὑμῶν ἐστιν· ὑμεῖς δὲ Χριστοῦ, the views and doctrine of the Χριστοῦ ὄντες being those which the Apostle himself approved of. "These same τοῦ Χριστοῦ are meant in i. 12. In exhorting the Corinthians, 1 Cor. iii. 22, τοῦ Χριστοῦ εἶναι, the Apostle, it is held, wished to direct the adherents of the sects to that teaching of the true teachers, to which οἱ τοῦ Χριστοῦ already adhered. The source from which they derived their Christian doctrine was just the teaching of Paul, Apollos, and Peter; but in order to avoid any appearance of sectarianism, they did not call themselves by the name of the teacher who first enunciated the principle τοῦ εἶναι Χριστοῦ, but simply called themselves τοῦ Χριστοῦ." Both the passages quoted do indeed speak of a Χριστοῦ εἶναι, but, as a more correct comparison will easily show us, in two very different senses. In the passage i. 12, the words ἐγὼ δὲ Χριστοῦ serve to denote a sect, just as the three clauses immediately preceding them denote so many other sects. The words must be taken as describing those who belonged to the so-called Christ-party; but the Apostle cannot be held to be referring to the divine unity that is found in Christ, and lies beyond all the sectarian divisions and distinctions, a thing greater than them all. If οἱ Χριστοῦ were the neutrals, the neutrals themselves were nothing

---

[1] Einleitung in das N. T. vol. iii. p. 107.
[2] Epist. Pauli ad Cor. Partic. 1, 1826. Proleg. p. 31.

but a sect, as Neander also supposes them to have been.[1] "They may indeed have maintained, in a false sense, that they were Christ's men ; very probably the conceit of the Corinthians caused some to come forward in these disputes as to whether the teaching of Paul, or of Peter, or of Apollos, were the true and perfect doctrine, who asserted that they understood Christianity better than Paul, or Peter, or Apollos. From verbal or written tradition, which they interpreted to suit their own foregone theories and opinions, they made a Christ and a Christianity for themselves. In their arrogant zeal for freedom they declared themselves to be independent of the authority of the chosen and inspired witnesses of the Gospel, and professed to have as perfect a system of doctrine as they had. In their presumption they called themselves disciples of Christ as a distinction from all others, as if they alone had a good title to the name." This view can only be regarded as a modification of that of Eichhorn. What, after all this, are we to consider the peculiar characteristics of this so-called party of Christ to have been ? If they wished to set up a Christ and a Christianity of their own in opposition to the chiefs of the other sects, to whose authority the adherents of those sects appealed,[2] their relation to Christ must have been brought about in some way similar to that which had been the case with the other sects, and we cannot see if they claimed to have a more perfect doctrine than others and to know Christianity better than Paul, Apollos, and Peter, how they could have thought to justify their claim to this distinction on any higher grounds than were open to all the sects alike. Therefore either οἱ Χριστοῦ were not a sect to be classed with the other sects which are mentioned along with them, or they did form a sect, but one of whose tendency and peculiar position none of the views hitherto advanced enables us to form any satisfactory conception.

Having arrived at this point, it seems to me that in making our next step we must take into account the suggestion made by J. E.

[1] Kleine Gelegenheitschriften praktisch-christlichen, vornehmlich exegetischen und historischen Inhalts, 3d. ed., Berlin, 1829, p. 68. Der Apostel Paulus und die Gemeinde zu Korinth.

Chr. Schmidt, in a treatise on 1 Cor. i. 12, namely, that there were really but two parties, one that of Paul and Apollos, while the Petrinists and Christ-ians, as Schmidt expresses it, also formed one party. In view of the well-known relation in which Paul and Peter, one the Apostle to the Gentiles, the other to the Jews, really stood towards each other, or at least the relation in which they were thought to stand towards each other by the chief parties of the early Christian Church, there can be no doubt that the chief difference lay between the two sects which called themselves after Paul and Cephas. It follows from this that the differences which gave rise to the existence of the other two parties, that of Apollos and that of Christ, were much less important; and the relation of the party of Paul to that of Apollos confirms us in this opinion. We see from many passages that Paul identified Apollos completely with himself, and considered him as a true fellow-worker with himself in the preaching of the Gospel; and we find nothing in the contents of either of these Epistles of the Apostle which would lead us to suppose that there was any important difference between them. I do not mean to deny, what is generally assumed, that in the passage in which he speaks of the distinction between the σοφία κόσμου and the σοφία Θεοῦ, the Apostle had the party of Apollos in view; but, on the other hand, it must be admitted that the attitude here described must have been more or less the ruling one in the Corinthian Church as a whole. The Apostle represents this taste for the σοφία τοῦ κόσμου, this want of faculty to penetrate to the inner regions of the Christian life, as a quality characteristic of the Corinthians as a whole at the stage of spiritual life which they had then reached. The greater prevalence of this spirit among them may have been what distinguished the party of Apollos from that of Paul, and this may have shown itself in attaching more value to the graces of delivery than to the nature of the doctrine preached. It may also have been that the adherents of these parties placed the teachers under whose names they enrolled themselves in a relation to each other which they themselves disclaimed. At all events the difference cannot have been so essential or so connected with doctrine as to prevent the two parties from being one party as against the party of Peter. It is also very conceivable that the relation of the Cephas-party and the Christ-party to each other was of a similar nature. Even if these two parties should be considered as in the main one and the same party, this would not prevent us from considering the relation between the parties of Paul and Apollos to have been what we have stated above. The Apostle may be trying, 1 Cor. i. 12, to give as many names as possible, as a way of portraying the prevailing party spirit in the Corinthian Church, which delighted to multiply sectarian names, which might indicate different colours and shades of opinion, although not exactly different parties.

Let us, then, first investigate the question wherein the opposition between the parties of Peter and Paul chiefly consisted.[1]

In the above-named treatise, Schmidt finds the chief cause of the difference between the two parties in the presumption which led the Jewish Christians to consider themselves true Christians, and denied that the Gentile Christians were real Christians at all. Among the first Christians there was a party who might (in one way) claim Christ as peculiarly their own: this was the Jewish Christian party. Christ, the Messiah, came in the first place for the sake of the Jews, to whom alone he had been promised; the Gentiles had to thank the Jews that Christ had come into the world. "Among such proud men as these Jewish Christians, would not the presumption arise that Christ, the Messiah, belonged to them alone? We find the presumption, 2 Cor. x. 7, exactly in this form. They called themselves τοὺς τοῦ Χριστοῦ—adherents of Christ—adherents of the Messiah,—or, changing the name slightly, Χριστιανούς. If these Christians were Jewish Christians, there can be no doubt that they formed one party with the adherents of Peter." But suppose this to have been the case, something else must have lain at the root of such a presumption on the part of the Jewish Christians; they must

---

[1] In the first edition there followed here a refutation of the views of Storr, Heidenreich, and Flatt on the Peter and Christ party, especially of the theory that the Christ-party contained elements of Sadduceeism. The Editor has not thought it necessary to include this discussion in the second edition.

have had something further to appeal to, since it is quite incredible that, as Jewish Christians, putting forward a claim which excluded the Gentile Christians from participation in the Messianic salvation, they should have gained entrance into a Church consisting for the greater part of Gentile Christians. Therefore, however right Schmidt may be in seeing the ground of this opposition between the parties of Peter and of Paul, in the claim that encouraged the Petrine party to call themselves also οἱ τοῦ Χριστοῦ, we have still to inquire for some clearer and exacter information on this point than has as yet been discovered.

In attempting to solve this problem, we shall certainly not be proceeding on an arbitrary assumption, if we suppose that the chief point of the attack made on Paul by the opposite party will be recognisable in one way or another in the Epistles. Now a great deal of space is devoted in both of the Epistles to a vindication of his apostolical dignity, which his opponents refused to concede to him to its full extent. May not the reason of their not recognising him as a real and genuine Apostle, have been that he was not, in the same sense as Peter and the rest of the Apostles, τοῦ Χριστοῦ; that he had not like these stood in direct connection with Jesus during his life on earth? Peter himself had no share in the party which went by his name in Corinth; in fact he was never in Corinth at all; but everything tends to show that travelling pseudo-apostles had come to Corinth, who made use of Peter's name. In the second Epistle, in which Paul expresses his views of these opponents with less reserve, and proceeds to a direct attack upon them, he calls them plainly, xi. 13, ψευδαπόστολοι, ψευδάδελφοι, ἐργάται δόλιοι, μετασχηματιζόμενοι εἰς ἀποστόλους Χριστοῦ. They also claimed to be the true ἀπόστολοι Χριστοῦ, or to be in the closest connection with them, and in this sense to be Χριστοῦ ὄντες. That zeal for the Mosaic law, which was a characteristic of Jewish Christians, was probably their real motive in this case as well as in others; but in a Church of Gentile Christians, such as that of Corinth, they could not expect a favourable reception, if they brought forward their principles openly, and so they fell back on the more special ground of their Judaistic opposition; they attacked the apostolic authority of the Apostle, and endeavoured in this way to counteract him. According to this supposition, we have a very simple and natural explanation of the relation of the party of Peter to that of Christ. Just as those of Paul and of Apollos did not essentially differ, so these two were not different parties, but only one and the same party under two different names, each name alike suggesting the claim which that party made for itself. They called themselves τοὺς Κηφᾶ because Peter held the primacy among the Jewish Apostles, and τοὺς Χριστοῦ because they asserted direct contact with Christ to be the chief token of genuine apostolic authority; and on this account they would not recognise Paul, who had been called to be an Apostle at a later time and in a quite unusual and peculiar manner, as a genuine Apostle, enjoying the same privileges as the others, but considered that he must at least be placed far below the rest of the Apostles.[1] On this account also their designation, evidently chosen with a purpose, was οἱ τοῦ Χριστοῦ, not τοῦ Ἰησοῦ or τοῦ Κυρίου. The idea of the Messiah was to be made prominent, as if to suggest that only those could be reckoned true media for the communication of the Messianic happiness and blessing, of the higher life that flows from Christ, who had received that charge by the most immediate transmission, by an outward, well-attested connection with the person of Jesus as the Messiah.

We have now to bring what evidence we can in support of the view here brought forward, by an examination of some important passages in the two Epistles. Perhaps even the first section, in which the Apostle gives a vindication of his apostolic authority and work (chaps. i.-iv.), contains some statements, in making which he had before his mind those adherents of the party of Peter who

[1] Some scholars, notably Zach. Pierce (Pott, Proleg. p. 25), argue from a passage in the first Epistle of Clemens Romanus (c. 47, ἐπ' ἀληθείας πνευματικῶς ἐπέστειλεν ὑμῖν (ὁ μακάριος Παῦλος ὁ ἀπόστολος) περὶ αὑτοῦ τε καὶ Κηφᾶ καὶ Ἀπολλὼ, διὰ τὸ καὶ τότε προσκλίσεις ὑμᾶς πεποιῆσθαι) that the words, 1 Cor. i. 12, ἐγὼ δὲ Χριστοῦ are probably spurious. I do not know if the passage from Clement is entitled to much weight; but if it were, I would rather draw from it an argument in support of the theory stated above, that the Cephas-party and the Christ-party were identical.

claimed to be considered as οἱ τοῦ Χριστοῦ. When the Apostle asserts so emphatically, ii. 16, ἡμεῖς δὲ νοῦν Χριστοῦ ἔχομεν (inasmuch as the divine πνεῦμα is the principle of his Christian consciousness); when, iv. 1, he desires his readers to remember that they have to regard him as a ὑπηρέτης Χριστοῦ; when, iv. 10, he asserts that he, as the least of the Apostles, is willing to consider himself as a μωρὸς διὰ Χριστοῦ, if at least they are right in considering themselves as φρόνιμοι ἐν Χριστῷ; when, verse 15, he reminds them that it is of less importance to have μυρίους παιδαγωγοὺς ἐν Χριστῷ than πολλοὺς πατέρας; in all passages such as these where there is evidently some hint implied, it is most natural to think of the party he has already mentioned, of those who called themselves οἱ τοῦ Χριστοῦ in a peculiar sense, which was meant to be offensive to our Apostle; though, of course, these special references retire behind the general apologetic tendency of the whole passage. An important passage for our purpose is at all events to be found in ix. 1, *sq.* The Apostle suddenly changes his subject here, and begins to speak of his own personal affairs; yet the section beginning ix. 1 is clearly related to the subject of the previous chapter; the opening for a personal discussion is very judiciously taken advantage of. In the eighth chapter the Apostle had taken up the question which had been laid before him, of participation in the heathen sacrificial feasts, and of the use of meat offered to idols; and had gone on to say that there might be cases in which, from tender consideration for others, a man might see it to be his duty to abstain from what in itself and for him was perfectly lawful. He turns this idea in such a way as to show that many of the things which his opponents interpreted to his disadvantage were acts of voluntary renunciation, undertaken for the sake of his apostolic calling. As an Apostle, he also had certain rights of which he, as well as the other Apostles, might avail himself; but he had never done so, because higher considerations had commanded him to make no use of them, Οὐκ εἰμὶ ἐλεύθερος; οὐκ εἰμὶ ἀπόστολος; οὐχὶ Ἰησοῦν Χριστὸν τὸν Κύριον ἡμῶν ἑώρακα; am I not free? am I not an Apostle? (an

Apostle as much as any other Apostle?) have I not seen the Lord Jesus Christ? Why the appeal to the ἑωρακέναι Ἰησοῦν Χριστὸν, τὸν Κύριον ἡμῶν, as a vindication of the ἀπόστολος εἶναι, if his opponents did not deny him the real apostolic character, because he had not seen the Lord as they, or rather, as the Apostles at the head of their party had done, and had not lived in direct contact with him? This, then, was held to be the genuine token of Χριστοῦ εἶναι. But that these opponents of the Apostle belonged to one class with the adherents of the party of Peter is clear from the following words, verse 5: μὴ οὐκ ἔχομεν ἐξουσίαν ἀδελφὴν γυναῖκα περιάγειν, ὡς καὶ οἱ λοιποὶ ἀπόστολοι, καὶ οἱ ἀδελφοὶ τοῦ Κυρίου, καὶ Κηφᾶς; the Χριστοῦ εἶναι held good of all these men in the sense already discussed; it held good of the whole circle of the Apostles, who had enjoyed communion with Jesus; it was true even in a sense of the ἀδελφοὶ Κυρίου, inasmuch as they stood in a still nearer connection to the Lord as his relatives; and it applied most directly to Peter, inasmuch as Jesus himself had given him a certain precedence over the other Apostles, and he was in his own person the most complete representative of the whole relation between Jesus and his apostles. But Paul thought that he himself, in the full consciousness of his apostolic dignity, and the rights and claims connected with it, ought not to take a secondary place even to Peter. In token that he possessed the same rights as the other Apostles, and especially the right to live at the expense of the churches to whom he preached the Gospel, the Apostle appeals, first, to what holds good in law and custom in common life (verses 7, 8); secondly, to a precept of the Mosaic law, which indeed primarily referred to animals needed for the use of man, but which warranted the conclusion *a minore ad majus* (9-12); and thirdly, to the custom prevailing in the Mosaic sacrificial worship (13). But however well grounded his claim on this score might be, he being an Apostle as well as the rest, still he had never made any use of it, because it seemed to him to be better for the cause of the Gospel and more satisfactory for himself not to do so. Accordingly, living constantly in the consciousness of the great aim to which he had devoted himself, he subordinated his whole personality to the interests of others and the regard to be paid to them, and his carnal nature he held in such subjection that it served the needs of his spirit absolutely and exclusively (15-27). This whole section is best explained by supposing that the opponents of the Apostle had interpreted the humility and unselfishness with which he preached the Gospel in the churches, as an obvious admission by the Apostle himself that he did not dare to place himself on a level with the other Apostles, by making use of a right which was universally conceded to their office. As a contrast to this supposed weakness and want of confidence, they thought they themselves had the less cause to keep within bounds the selfish and self-seeking πλεονεξία (2 Cor. xii. 17) of which the Apostle elsewhere accuses them. But as these charges were a part of the great attack on his apostolic dignity, the Apostle must have felt it necessary to vindicate himself from them, and to place his behaviour in its true light. In this passage his apology is founded mainly on the ἑωρακέναι Ἰησοῦν Χριστὸν, τὸν Κύριον ἡμῶν. Without explaining more clearly the peculiar nature of this ἑωρακέναι, he insists upon the main fact which places him on a level with the other Apostles: he can certainly maintain that the Lord has appeared to him individually. When he asserts (xv. 8) that the Lord appeared to him as well as to the other Apostles, the intention of the statement is probably the same. The great exposition of the doctrine of the resurrection which follows might certainly seem to require what we may call evidence at first hand for the main proposition on which it proceeds, namely, that Jesus rose from the dead, and was really seen as so risen. Yet this does not prevent us from supposing that the Apostle took care not to neglect the opportunity which thus arose of vindicating his claims to what his opponents chose to declare to be the chief mark of apostolic authority, placing himself on one line with the disciples who had been connected with Jesus during his lifetime, and maintaining that he, as well as they, possessed an immediate vision of the Lord as the seal of his mission.

The polemical references for which the Apostle had so frequent occasion in both Epistles are more open and more direct in the second than in the first; yet it is only at the end of the Epistle that the Apostle openly attacks his opponents, casts away all reserve, and subjects them to a keen and trenchant cross-examination.

In the earlier part of the Epistle, the passage v. 1-16, a most important one in itself, receives an added interest from its reference to his opponents. At the outset the Apostle assures the Corinthians in different ways of his love to them, which should call forth their confidence, and seeks to convince them of the purity of his views and efforts. In answer to the reproaches of his opponents, he points to the success which had attended his teaching through the ability given him by God as a minister of the διακονία τῆς καινῆς διαθήκης. The greater the superiority of the καινὴ διαθήκη, the greater also is the superiority of the διακονία. But in striking contrast to this, the Apostle continues, iv. 7, "are the sufferings of all kinds with which I, as a weak failing man, have to struggle—sufferings which threaten every moment to overwhelm my strength—still gloriously am I preserved through them all by that might which conquers death through life, by which Jesus was raised from the dead. Therefore I do not allow my sufferings to hinder me in the duties of my office. Sufferings only serve to educate the inward man, the true real man, for future glory." This idea makes the Apostle speak, in chapter v., of the moment at which the earthly body, under the burden of which we now groan, will be changed into a glorified heavenly body, v. 1-4. This confident expectation, which belongs essentially to our Christian consciousness, of a condition in which, after departing from the body, we shall be present with the Lord, or enter into the most intimate connection with him, should even now impart to all our acts and efforts the most conscientious reference to Christ, for indeed it is he who will pronounce the judgment which our moral conduct shall have deserved (5-14). "This consciousness accompanies me in my apostolic labours, and you yourselves must bear me this witness; you may boldly assert against my opponents, and maintain against them, for my honour, what my inmost heart declares, namely, that it is not in the least my own person or my own interest that I serve. I labour in the spirit of that love in which Christ so offered himself up for us, that we can only live for him, and all our former ties and relationships have ceased to exercise any determining influence on us, wherefore we see ourselves placed in a perfectly new sphere of consciousness and life. The principal actuating cause by which we are raised to this completely new order of things is the reconciliation which God has effected through the death of Christ between himself and man. This reconciliation is the great burden of my apostolic preaching, the object of my labour; and it is really only Christ in whose name I work—only God, whose voice is heard through me. How then can I be so interested about my own person that my opponents should have any right to accuse me of a vain self-praise and of self-seeking views?" In this connection the Apostle uses the remarkable expression, Χριστὸν κατὰ σάρκα γινώσκειν.[1] The Χριστὸς κατὰ σάρκα can only be the Christ or Messiah of Judaism, and accordingly the Apostle says, in a sense which is as grammatically natural as it is satisfactory: "If it were the case that formerly I knew no other Messiah than the Messiah of Judaism—such an one as left me under all the peculiar prejudices and materialistic tendencies of my nation, and who could not raise me to the new stage of spiritual life on which I now stand, where I live for the Christ who died for me, as for all—yet now I do not any longer acknowledge this conception of the Messiah as the true one. I have freed myself from all prejudices, from all the material ideas and expectations which had naturally passed into me from my nationality, which had devolved upon me as a Jew by birth." If this is the sense of the passage, it can scarcely be denied that in the expression Χριστὸν κατὰ σάρκα γινώσκειν, the Apostle cast a glance at his opponents who prided themselves as being specially τοὺς τοῦ Χριστοῦ. Was it not exactly a κατὰ σάρκα Χριστὸν

[1] In the first edition, pp. 284-288, there was a discussion of this phrase. The author did not intend it to appear in a second edition.

γινώσκειν, did it not indicate that those who brought the allegation were still at the standpoint of Judaism and of the Jewish conception of the Messiah, when his opponents gave it as their reason for denying to Paul the true apostolic character that he had not been in that direct outward contact with Jesus during his life on earth, of which those Apostles could boast who were originally called to the apostolic office by Jesus himself. The true point, the Apostle then says, from which alone εἶναι ἐν Χριστῷ could be deduced, was not so much the earthly and national appearance of Jesus, in which the σάρξ in the above sense had still its share, but rather the death of Jesus, in so far as it is in that death that the old life dies, and the new life which is to be awakened in us takes its beginning. That which essentially distinguishes the national Jewish Messiah from the Christ of the true Christian consciousness, is the sufferings and death of Christ—the great significance of the death on the cross which the Apostle everywhere represents as the central point of Christian doctrine, and on which he emphatically and very necessarily insists as against his opponents in these two Epistles. Therefore if the earthly life of Jesus as the Messiah and visible contact with him during his life on earth be taken as a thing of value in itself, and if his whole appearance on earth be not looked at in the light of his death on the cross, and thus stripped of what of it is earthly, then this is still a Χριστὸν κατὰ σάρκα γινώσκειν, we are still contenting ourselves with a thing given us from the outside, and conditioned by its natural relations, to which we must first die. But if we look at the death of Christ as the great turning-point, in which the καινὴ κτίσις appears—in which old things vanish away and all things become new—then everything falls to the ground that seemed to give the opponents, or rather the Apostles on whose authority the opponents relied, their peculiar lofty precedence, owing to their direct contact with Jesus during his earthly life. It had its foundation merely in relations into which the Apostles had entered as Jews by birth. He also then, the Apostle called so late, may place himself in the same rank with the witnesses of the resurrection of the Lord. He also has beheld Jesus as the person who, having died and risen to life again, has caused the full meaning of the Christian consciousness and life to dawn in us, and established in us the true Χριστοῦ εἶναι.

Another passage, x. 7, is very nearly allied to those we have above examined. In chap. x. the Apostle enters on the consideration of the charge made against him by his opponents, that he was wanting in personal energy. He declares that he will show, on the contrary, that when it comes to the main issue, he will know how to act with all necessary decision and energy, and with the greatest confidence as to the result. And this he says is itself an answer to the charge that he is without the true sign of a Χριστοῦ ὤν. Unless we look only on the outward appearance, what better proof of Χριστοῦ εἶναι can there be than the ἐξουσία εἰς οἰκοδομὴν—the strength and energy with which a man labours in the furtherance of the cause of Christianity? He says τὰ κατὰ πρόσωπον βλέπετε, not so much of the opponents themselves as of certain members of the Corinthian Church who had already given heed to them, and were in danger of being misled by them still further. "If in respect to my person you consider merely what I am κατὰ πρόσωπον—this is a proof that the outward appearance is the chief thing in your eyes, that you judge only by what is outward" (πρόσωπον, as ver. 12). These words are generally considered as referring to the so-called party of Christ, and Storr and Flatt understand them according to their view of what that party was, of circumstances of outward relationship. As the Apostle is speaking of the Χριστοῦ εἶναι, the reference to those who considered themselves specially τοὺς τοῦ Χριστοῦ is certainly very natural, only I can find nothing in this passage either, which would justify the conclusion that οἱ τοῦ Χριστοῦ were what could be called a party. It is the general body of his opponents that the Apostle is here dealing with: with all who boasted of their closer outward connection with Jesus or with the immediate disciples of Jesus, and especially with Peter, the first of the Apostles, and found in this the true criterion of Χριστοῦ εἶναι. But that these Χριστοῦ ὄντες belonged to one and the same class as the party of Peter, and the whole Judaising party of opposition, is clearly shown by the connection with what follows, where the Apostle speaks of the ὑπερλίαν ἀπόστολοι. What he advances against his opponents in reference to the Χριστοῦ εἶναι, ver. 7, appears to me to amount to this: "If any one maintains so confidently of himself that he is a genuine disciple of Christ, and stands in the true relation towards him, and according to his subjective opinion—since this is the view of the matter he feels himself obliged to take (this lies both in the word ἑαυτῷ and in πρόσωπον, which contains the notion of the subjective element which is determined by personal considerations)—considers outward connection with Christ to be the proper criterion of true connection with Christ, then such a man must on the other hand concede to me the right of defining the true connection with Christ by another criterion which I judge to be the true one. Looking at the matter in this light I feel that I have at least as good a right as my opponents to assert the Χριστοῦ εἶναι of myself." What token of Χριστοῦ εἶναι the Apostle means to indicate in reference to himself is seen by what follows. "This right, that of considering myself as Χριστοῦ ὄντα, from my own standpoint cannot be denied me, in fact there would be no good grounds for refusing to acknowledge it, even if I founded much larger claims upon it than I do. Even should I claim a higher official position than I do, my claims would still be true and well-founded; I should have no fear of being brought to shame; for I employ my privilege of working as an Apostle only εἰς οἰκοδομὴν and not εἰς καθαίρεσιν ὑμῶν; I seek to work only in furtherance of the true welfare of the Church. With such good right do I believe that I am justified in maintaining that I am Χριστοῦ." Thus what the Apostle wishes to set up as the true token of Χριστοῦ εἶναι, in opposition to the κατὰ πρόσωπον βλέπειν, is the aim of οἰκοδομή, the genuinely Christian nature of his apostolic activity with its public spirit and zeal for edification; as he further says in verse 13: "I am certainly very far from placing myself in the same class with those who recommend themselves with empty ambition and after an arbitrary standard which they have made themselves, and seek to exalt their own glory by detracting from the merits of others. My glory lies in those things which I have been actually enabled to effect for the cause of Christianity in my apostolic calling, within the bounds of the circle of action which God has appointed me, insomuch as I was the first who brought Christianity to Corinth, and planted it there, in such a way, I hope, that this may open up to me a yet wider circle of action. So little is it necessary for me to seek my glory in the sphere of others, and so little can anything else than real work done be of any value in the cause of Christianity." The Apostle's antitheses in this passage give rise to a presumption that his opponents not only tried to undermine his authority, but even went so far as to claim the merit of having been the true founders of the Corinthian Church. They came to Corinth after the Apostle indeed, but as they did not acknowledge Paul as a true Apostle, as $X\rho\iota\sigma\tau o\hat{u}$ $\check{o}\nu\tau a$, they assumed to themselves the glory properly belonging to him, at least in so far as they pretended to have been the first to plant true Christianity there.

The section in which the Apostle turns round upon his opponents, and delivers himself of all his feelings with regard to them, and his relation with them, may be said to begin at x. 7. The tone which he uses against them becomes stronger and more vivid at ver. 11. There is a cutting irony in his words, and the picture which he draws of his opponents becomes more and more distinct and repulsive. "You do not want patience at other times," he says, xi. 1, "to listen to what fools have to say (my opponents who would exalt themselves with vain presumption), you will surely give me a moment's hearing when I speak to you in the same language as a fool. (For my vindication and my praise can only appear as folly from the high standpoint from which my opponents look down upon me.) I am jealous over you with a godly jealousy (I am seized as by a holy jealousy when I think how you transfer the love, to which I as the founder of the Christian Church in Corinth have the justest claim, to others who only oppose all my aims). I have espoused you to one husband, to present you as a chaste virgin to Christ. But I fear, as the serpent beguiled Eve through deceit, that your thoughts also may be turned away from your simple faithfulness to Christ. Indeed, if one were to come who preached another Christ whom I have not preached, or if you could receive another spirit or another gospel than that which you have received (*i.e.* if there could possibly be another Christianity, which you were obliged to regard as the real and true one, and which I had never made known to you, which you learned only now from these teachers; if, that is to say, I had either not declared the truth to you at all, or had done so incompletely and impurely), then indeed you would be quite right to welcome him. (This, then, is the secret of the Apostle's direct and unqualified hostility to his opponents: the question between the two parties amounted to nothing less than that of a true or a false Christianity. When they accused the Apostle that what he preached was not true, the opponents of the Apostle were actually preaching another Jesus and another Christianity.) But this is a perfectly impossible supposition. That Christianity which I have preached to you is the only true one, which deserves to be believed. For I think that I stand in nothing behind the 'very chiefest Apostles.'" The ὑπερλίαν ἀπόστολοι may have been the opponents of the Apostle themselves, those who are afterwards called ψευδαπόστολοι. But as these ψευδαπόστολοι, who in Corinth appealed especially to the authority of the Apostle Peter, came to Corinth from Palestine—and doubtless stood in some connection with the Jewish Apostles of Palestine—the ὑπερλίαν ἀπόστολοι may well have been the Apostles themselves whose disciples and delegates the ψευδαπόστολοι claimed to be. The expression ὑπερλίαν ἀπόστολοι may therefore refer simply to the over-estimate which was attached to the authority of these apostles as against that of Paul. This is also indicated by the expression οἱ δοκοῦντες στύλοι εἶναι used, Gal. ii. 9, in reference to James, Peter, and John, which says no more than that this was the estimation in which they were held by a certain party, and which that party wished to impose upon the public as well. "However much," the Apostle accordingly says, "the authority of these apostles may be quoted against me, that proves nothing against the truth of the Christianity which I teach." In what follows, the Apostle declares that he thinks he has every right to feel assured of his apostolic calling, both on account of his true insight into the essence of Christian doctrine, and on account of the disinterested zeal for the cause of Christianity which he had shown in all his relations with the Corinthian Church, as indeed through his whole life. "For," he declares firstly, "I have in the most disinterested manner never once made any claim upon you for my support, while my opponents use all the deceitful and seductive arts with which they are so well acquainted (οἱ τοιοῦτοι ψευδαπόστολοι, ἐργάται δόλιοι, μετασχηματιζόμενοι εἰς ἀποστόλους Χριστοῦ, as he calls these false teachers who assumed nothing but the name of Apostles of Christ, verse 13) to make gain out of you, and use you as tools for their selfish plans," verses 7-20. Secondly, he says, "My whole life has been a series of hardships, sacrifices, and dangers, which I have undertaken for the cause of Christianity," 20-33. This passage sets it beyond doubt that these opponents were born Jews, of genuine Israelite descent. They belonged therefore to the party of Peter, and doubtless appealed to Peter's authority in support of their own claims. Keeping up his ironical tone, the Apostle allows for the moment his enemies' charge of ἀφροσύνη, to use it as a mask for confronting his presumptuous and vain opponents on their own ground, in their assertion of empty distinctions, and enable himself to say things which sounded like foolish and vain self-praise, but which were best put before the Corinthians, accustomed as they were to the speeches of his overbearing opponents, in this tone (compare 19, 20, 21). He asks the question (22), Ἑβραῖοί εἰσι; κἀγώ· Ἰσραηλῖταί εἰσι; κἀγώ· σπέρμα Ἀβραάμ εἰσι; κἀγώ. If, he says, there is to be such a καυχᾶσθαι κατὰ τὴν σάρκα, (18) a καυχᾶσθαι referring to mere inherited and fortuitous distinctions, I can rival my opponents even on this ground. But they do not only claim to be genuine Israelites, but also as such, διάκονοι Χριστοῦ. If it appears to them to be mere folly on my part that I venture to claim equality with them with respect to the above-mentioned advantages, they will consider it to be nothing short of madness (παραφρονεῖν here plainly means much more than the former expression ἀφροσύνη) that I even claim to surpass them, appealing as I do to something far more real than these advantages of theirs, namely the facts of my apostolic ministry, by which its reality is abundantly attested. Here we see that those persons who had so high an opinion of themselves as born Jews, also asserted that they were the true διάκονοι Χριστοῦ. In the following chapter, xii., also, the Apostle carries on the vindication of his apostolic authority, and now he adds a third reason to the two he has already mentioned in chap. xi., in proof of the right he has to feel sure of his apostolic calling. This third reason consists in the extraordinary revelations which he had received, especially an ecstasy into which he had been thrown during the first period of his apostolic career. Still he does not appeal to these revelations, he says, for the sake of boasting. On the contrary, he bears about in his body a trouble which ever keeps alive in him the feeling of his human weakness as a corrective of any exalted opinion of himself, and which causes him to put his whole trust in divine help. He had been induced to say what he had said in his own praise, only because the Corinthians had not said what they should properly have said in vindication of him against his opponents. How far he was from being behind the other Apostles they themselves had the best means of judging, as he had approved himself among them by all the signs of a genuine apostolic mode of activity ; and no benefit that Christianity had conferred on other churches had failed to be conferred on them. There cannot be anyreasonable doubt that the mention of the ὀπτασίαι and ἀποκαλύψεις to which the Apostle here appeals has a very close connection with his apologetic aim and the character of the opponents with whom he is dealing. If, as Judaising teachers of Christianity, and in accordance with the view which must have been that of the Petrinists or of the Christ-party, they held an outward connection with Jesus, and intercourse with him, such as had been enjoyed by those disciples whom Christ had called and educated expressly for their office, to be the true criterion of the $Χριστοῦ εἶναι$ and the apostolic calling, then the Apostle Paul, when he came to the last and highest point of his argument in defence of his apostolic office, naturally appealed to an inward spiritual experience instead of the outward material experiences of the rest of the Apostles. This inward experience consisted in those extraordinary phenomena which, as inward visions and revelations of the Divine, as facts of his immediate consciousness, had awakened faith in Christ within him—that $ἑωρακέναι\ \text{'}Ιησοῦν\ Χριστὸν\ τὸν\ Κύριον\ ἡμῶν$, to which he had already appealed, 1 Cor. ix. 1, and which must certainly be classed together with the $ὀπτασίαι$ and $ἀποκαλύψεις\ Κυρίου$ which he speaks of here, although it is not probable that the ecstasy described in verse 2 is the same with the phenomenon related in the Acts of the Apostles (chap. ix.), which brought about the Apostle's conversion. Such $ὀπτασίαι\ καὶ\ ἀποκαλύψεις$ might appear to the opponents of the Apostle to be mere imaginary visions which could make no claim to objective truth, in comparison with the actual outward relations in which the other Apostles had lived with Jesus, and according to the principles which Peter had laid down, Acts i. 21, on the occasion of the election of the Apostle Matthias. But for the Apostle himself the phenomena which had thus transpired in his inner life were none the less solid and incontestable facts; and willingly as he would have avoided speaking of them at all, in order to escape every appearance of vain self-exaltation, yet here it behoved him to be silent on nothing which might serve for the vindication and establishment of his apostolic authority, and he could not omit appealing to them. But he could not conceal from himself that this evidence to his apostolic call belonged only to the sphere of his own immediate consciousness; and this made him insist the more pointedly, as he does again and again throughout the whole of these two Epistles, on that witness of facts to which the character of objective reality could be least denied—

namely, the great experiment in which his apostolic calling had been verified, and the great success which had attended his efforts to further the cause of Christianity. Compare 1 Cor. iii. 8-15; ix. 15, *sq.*; xv. 10 (περισσότερον αὐτῶν πάντων ἐκοπίασα) 2 Cor. x. 12, *sqq.*

That this controversy turned on a question of principle, in which it was necessary to trace the difference between our Apostle and the older Apostles up to its origin and its true grounds, is shown in a noteworthy way in the passage 2 Cor. iii. 1, *sq.* In this passage we hear of ἐπιστολαὶ συστατικαί, of letters of commendation which certain persons (τινὲς as the τινὲς ἀπο Ἰακώβου—Gal. ii. 12, opponents of the Apostle) had brought with them to Corinth. The object of these letters must have been to afford evidence that the bearers were genuine, trustworthy preachers of Christianity, and bore the seal of an acknowledged authority. Under what other names then can these letters have been drawn up but those of the elder Apostles? and what could make it seem necessary to issue such letters of commendation and authentication, but the fact of the parties in the Church being so suspicious of each other, that it was necessary for any one who wished to appear as a teacher, in order not to be taken for a false teacher, to provide evidence to which party he belonged, and to which principles and teachings he adhered? The more considerable the authority was to which such missionaries referred, and the more universally acknowledged it was, the more certainly could they reckon on their reception and influence. From what other place then could they bring with them so satisfactory a legitimation as from Jerusalem?[1] The ἐπι-

[1] That such a legitimation belonged to the principles of the Judaisers, and was customary among them, we see from passages of the pseudo-Clementine writings, which also afford a satisfactory explanation of the ἐπιστολαὶ συστατικαί. In the 4th Book of the Recognitions, C. 34, the Apostle Peter says the devil sends abroad into the world false prophets, and false apostles, and false teachers, who indeed speak in the name of Christ, but do the will of the devil; he exhorts them therefore to use caution, "et nulli doctorum credatis nisi qui Jacobi fratris Domini ex Hierusalem detulerit testimonium vel ejus quicunque post ipsum fuerit. Nisi enim quis illuc ascenderit, et ibi fuerit probatus quod sit doctor idoneus et fidelis ad prædicandum Christi verbum, nisi, inquam, inde detulerit testimonium, recipiendus non est; sed neque propheta, neque apostolus in hoc tempore speretur a vobis aliquis alius præter nos." Compare Homily ii. 35.

στολαὶ συστατικαὶ thus point to a higher authority standing in the background, behind the opponents with whom the Apostle is contending, and which he saw went to discredit his own; he therefore takes occasion from those letters to explain fully the principle of his apostolic authority. This he does in chapter iii. If no one were admitted to be a real, authenticated teacher of Christianity except he were recommended from Jerusalem and brought with him thence a "letter of commendation," this could only be on the principle that there were no other Apostles but the elder ones. This the Apostle could not concede, and yet with regard to his apostolic office and apostolic authority he could only appeal to that εὐδόκησεν ὁ Θεὸς ἀποκαλύψαι τὸν υἱὸν αὑτοῦ ἐν ἐμοί, Gal. i. 15, that is to say, to a mere fact of his own consciousness. Starting then from these ἐπιστολαὶ συστατικαί, and seeking for some objective fact to bring in proof of his own claims, he maintains that he has an epistle of commendation as well as his opponents, although a very different one. His letters of commendation are the Corinthians themselves, and written indeed in his own heart. What they are as Christians concerns him so nearly, that it is an essential part of his own self-consciousness. But as he has to show not only what they are to him, but also what they are objectively as recommending and authenticating him to others, he adds that this letter written in his inmost heart is also lying open before the eyes of the world, legible to every one, laid before the general consciousness of the world, composed by him under the commission of Christ, written not with ink but with the Spirit of the living God, not on tables of stone, but on the fleshly tables of the heart; *i.e.* the legitimation of his apostolic authority is the fact of the success of his preaching of the Gospel, the fact that through him the Corinthians have become a Christian Church. He who founds Christian Churches may with justice consider himself to be an Apostle of Christ, because he cannot do such work except by Christ working in him. The argument is one from result to cause, it is an appeal to the principle which we must conclude to be present where a certain movement takes place.

In the same way the Apostle says to the Corinthians, 1 Cor. ix. 2, in arguing against those who were not willing to allow his claim to be an Apostle: εἰ ἄλλοις οὐκ εἰμὶ ἀπόστολος, ἀλλά γε ὑμῖν εἰμί· ἡ γὰρ σφραγὶς τῆς ἐμῆς ἀποστολῆς ὑμεῖς ἐστε ἐν Κυρίῳ· ἡ ἐμὴ ἀπολογία τοῖς ἐμὲ ἀνακρίνουσιν αὕτη ἐστί. In the same way also, in Gal. ii. 7, he grounds his εὐαγγέλιον τῆς ἀκροβυστίας on the fact that he who had wrought in Peter εἰς ἀποστολὴν τῆς περιτομῆς, has wrought effectively in himself εἰς τὰ ἔθνη—i.e. the existence of Gentile Christian Churches is the result of this ἐνεργεῖν. But the greater and more evident the success of his ministry, the more certain is it that he derived the apostolic commission which it presupposes only from God and Christ, whose servant he is—and he derives it from Christ as the founder of a new διαθήκη of which the πνεῦμα is the principle. The more perfectly this principle is realised in him, the more able he is to produce a result corresponding to this principle. The question therefore can only be what it comprises and how it acts in him. Thus the whole stage of development at which the religious consciousness of the Old Testament stands is the subject in opposition to which the Apostle develops the idea of the πνεῦμα as the Christian principle, iii. 11-18. He defines the essential difference between the two διαθῆκαι by the two ideas γράμμα and πνεῦμα, the ἀποκτείνειν on one side, and the ζωοποιεῖν on the other; he then considers the subjective side of this objective difference, in the light of the question, what is the attitude of the religious consciousness in each of the two διαθῆκαι? He works this out by means of the Old Testament narrative of the glory on the face of Moses. This glory is a symbol of the character of the old διαθήκη, as well with regard to its advantages as to its defects. Its advantages consisted in having a glory in which the majesty of God reflected itself in such a manner, and from this we may conclude that if the old διαθήκη had such a glory, the new one will be infinitely more glorious and splendid. The defect of the old διαθήκη consisted first in the transitory nature of the glory on the face of Moses; and even more in the fact that on account of the veil which covered the face of Moses in order to hide the glory from their eyes, the Israelites did not perceive its extinction when that happened, and therefore believed that it still continued after it had become extinct. This veil, the symbol of Mosaism, still lies on the consciousness of the Jews, this is the limitation in their religious consciousness, that they do not realise the finite nature of the old διαθήκη. In contrast to this concealment and constraint which belongs to the character of Judaism, is the πνεῦμα as the Christian principle, the Christian consciousness certain of itself in its unity with Christ, identical with itself and absolute, which unfolds to the full knowledge of the truth, and has no need of any merely outward medium. If where the Spirit is, the Lord is also, then the Lord himself is the Spirit, iii. 16; then he who has the Spirit in the sense meant by the Apostle is in the διακονία τοῦ πνεύματος, iii. 8, and is also a διάκονος Χριστοῦ, xi. 23. The opponents whom the Apostle encountered at Corinth also considered themselves to be διάκονοι Χριστοῦ. As they were not Apostles themselves, but were forced to rest their claims on some apostolic authority, they must have considered those to whose authority they appealed to be specially ἀποστόλους Χριστοῦ, in the same sense, that is to say, in which they themselves claimed to be διάκονοι Χριστοῦ. They were not Apostles, but if, as the Apostle says, they were μετασχηματιζόμενοι εἰς ἀποστόλους Χριστοῦ, this ἀπόστολοι Χριστοῦ suggests that they called the Apostles, on whose authority they relied and whose representatives they desired to be considered, Apostles of Christ in the same emphatic sense in which they themselves claimed to be διάκονοι Χριστοῦ, and in which the Apostle himself speaks of the Χριστοῦ εἶναι, x. 7. In what else could the distinguishing criterion of their Χριστοῦ εἶναι consist, as against the Apostle Paul, but in this, that the elder Apostles, on account of the direct companionship which they had with Jesus during his earthly life, must be the only authenticated preachers and ministers of the Messianic salvation? And what other standpoint could the Apostle himself take up in maintaining his own apostolic authority than that which we see him take up in these two Epistles, opposing to the external considerations urged by his opponents the inward and the spiritual, and making the Spirit, which is the Lord himself, the principle of true communion and of true apostolic activity? Thus it is evident how he could not justify himself to those who were his opponents on this occasion in Corinth without referring to the Apostles whose representatives they claimed to be. That he was in no whit behind them, that he could claim for himself the same rights as they did, and bore in himself the same apostolic consciousness,—this is the assumption on which he proceeds when he comes to close quarters with them, xi. 5; and to this he adheres throughout his whole discussion, as is shown by the repetition of this statement, xii. 11. Whilst far removed from doing anything to discredit their apostolic dignity, yet he cannot tolerate the exclusive claims set up on their behalf by his opponents. The admirably chosen phrase οἱ ὑπερλίαν ἀπόστολοι is meant to show that he had no fault to find with themselves, but only with the exaggerated view of them held by others. They are confronted with him as the "grand Apostles," as if he were nothing in comparison with them (οὐδέν εἰμι he says, xii. 11, in a sense that was true for him, but not without allusion to this), and as if he were not to count as an Apostle of Christ at all. If in maintaining his apostolic authority he had only said that he was in no respect behind such opponents as he characterises in chap. xi., those ψευδαπόστολοι, ἐργάται δόλιοι, μετασχηματιζόμενοι εἰς ἀποστόλους Χριστοῦ, what a mean opinion must he have entertained of himself and of his apostolic dignity? He could only have meant to measure himself with the Apostles themselves, and the σημεῖα τοῦ ἀποστόλου of which he speaks, xii. 12, cannot be understood of any other comparison.

Our exposition of the principal passages concerned has thus shown us that all the points of the Apostle's controversy with his opponents may be reduced to the idea of Χριστοῦ εἶναι, that being the main criterion of apostolic authority, and the question being as to the real meaning of the term. If we be correct so far, it will follow that those who claimed to be specially οἱ τοῦ Χριστοῦ asserted of themselves that Χριστοῦ εἶναι against which the

Apostle Paul found himself obliged emphatically to assert and to defend his own view of the principle.

We might suppose that the question of the party of Christ is here answered with as great a measure of probability as the available data allow; but since this view was first propounded certain objections have been raised to it which it will be well to consider before we go further.[1]

It is granted that my view does justice to the phrase οἱ τοῦ Χριστοῦ, that it is corroborated by many antithetical references in both Epistles, and might even appear as the only correct solution of the difficulty; but it is thought that by this theory the difficulty is not overcome, that the party of Christ is distinguished from the party of Peter only in name, whilst the name clearly stands for a party which was one of several; or, what is the same thing, that the identity of the party of Peter with that of Christ is nowhere indicated. Till this be proved we cannot see in 1 Cor. x. 7 any dispute with the party of Christ, but only the assertion which the Apostle brings against his opponents of Peter's party, namely, that if they were Christians so was he.[2] Now if we could find a passage in which it was said clearly and decidedly that the Petrinists and those of Christ were one and the same party, then the matter would be very easily decided. But as no such passage is to be

[1] Compare Neander, Gesch. der Pflanzung u. Leitung der christl. kirche, 1832, 1 Thl. p. 298, Bohn 234. Billroth, Commentar zu den Briefen des Paulus an die Korinthier, Leipzig, Einl. p. xix. Rückert, Der erste Brief Pauli an die Korinthier, Leipzig, 1836, Appendix, p. 435. Schenkel. De Ecclesia Corinthia primæva factionibus turbata. Disquisitio critico-historica ad antiquissimum ecclesiæ Christianæ statum illustrandum pertinens, Basil. 1838. Goldhorn, Die Christuspartei zu Korinth im Zeitalter der Apostel, in Illgen's Zeitschr. für hist. Theol. 1840. Dähne, Die Christuspartei in d. Apost. kirche zu Korinth. Halle, 1841. Compare with these my replies in the Tübinger Zeitschr. für Theol. 1836, H. 4. p. 1, und in den Jahrb. für wissensch. Kritik. 1839, No. 88. In the commentaries of Olshausen, Meyer, De Wette, Osiander, etc., the views of their predecessors are merely repeated, and combined now in one way, now in another, which only tends to convince one more of the necessity of escaping from this maze of curious and conflicting hypotheses, and reaching some firm ground of fact. This of course cannot be done without framing a consistent theory of the history of the whole period.

[2] Neander, Billroth, Rückert.

found, we are obliged to resort to combination; by comparing together all the data which appear to bear on the subject, and by paying strict attention to the main tendency of the author, we must seek to arrive at a more or less probable result. What a different light is shed upon the passage when we remember, what cannot be denied, that in the passages which deal with the personal relations of the Apostle to his opponents, the point at issue is not Christianity but apostolicity, the criterion of apostolic authority which the Apostle maintains against his opponents. If we can only approach the facts of the case by a process of combination, it is evident that the theory here adduced can only claim relative probability, and then we must ask, what other theory can be brought forward with a greater show of probability than this one?

According to Neander, the adherents of the party of Christ were those who, disregarding the Apostles, professed to hold only to Christ, to recognise him only as their teacher, and to receive direct from himself, without any mediation, the truth which he taught. This was such a manifestation of self-will, such an arrogant departure from the historical process of development ordained by God for the delivery of divine revelation, as could not but lead to an arbitrary treatment of the Christian doctrines themselves. It might easily happen, that where one party was disposed to attach itself especially to Paul, another to Apollos, and a third to Peter, persons might at last appear who would not be called by any of these party names, but formed for themselves, and in their own way, a Christianity independent of and different from what the Apostles proclaimed. Their subjective procedure in this may have taken a more mystical or a more rationalistic direction.[1] Neander himself thinks that the rationalistic was the more prevailing tone, as according to his view the party of Christ was a philosophical sect, which made of Christ only a second, perhaps a more exalted, Socrates.[2] This is the prin-

[1] Op. cit. p. 236.
[2] In his first edition, Neander gives this account of the view of Christ's person as that which the Christ-party must have held. It is an admirable and appropriate feature in his discussion of this party, and it is difficult to see why it is omitted in the subsequent editions. Of course this parallel shows most distinctly

cipal view that has been set up against mine : its distinctive feature is that it endeavours, instead of identifying the parties of Christ and of Peter, to find as far as possible a specific difference between them. But what this idea leads to when it is carried out, and how much it is wanting in even probable grounds, is shown by the modification which it has received from Rückert. He maintains that the party of Christ was not, as Neander says, composed of persons of philosophical culture who had made for themselves their own philosophical view of Christ; the alternatives are, he says, that either the party of Christ took its stand as a party among the other parties, or set itself up as the only true Church, which the rest of the sects ought to join. The first idea he decides cannot be entertained, as Christ could not have been looked upon as a mere teacher such as Paul, Apollos, or Cephas; the second alternative must therefore be accepted. The party of Christ placed itself above the others, maintained that it did not adopt the views either of Paul, or of Apollos, or of Cephas, but acknowledged Christ alone as its Lord and Master; but it did not do this in the sense in which Paul certainly desired that all men should be $Χριστοῦ$.[2] In what sense then did it do this? The party of Christ must naturally have been a separate party, or it would not have been reckoned by the Apostle along with the rest; further, it must have recognised Christ as Lord and Master, or it would not have designated itself by his name, but it cannot have acknowledged him in the right way, or else Paul would not have described it as a mere party. But what is all this but a series of purely abstract definitions, out of which we can get no concrete idea of what this party actually was. Till we can say what made it a party, not only negatively but positively, we cannot conceive of it as a party at all? It cannot have been a philosophical sect, as Rückert expressly declares; but can it have been a mystical one,

that these disciples of Christ who placed Christ on the same level as Socrates, no longer stood upon the platform of Christianity. Then the very name οἱ τοῦ Χριστοῦ contradicts the theory of Neander. Whilst the name would have marked them as a sect who specially pretended to possess the true Christianity, this view of Christ which is attributed to them would have made them a sect completely unchristian.   [1] Op. cit. p. 446.

according to Neander's distinction? Schenkel, Goldhorn, and Dähne consider the adherents of the party of Christ to have been visionaries, in a sense which raises a further difference between their theories and my own. In my view the Christ of the party of Christ was the bodily Christ who was connected with his disciples through the intercourse of outward physical life; but in the view of these critics he was a spiritual Christ revealing himself in visions from heaven. The disciples of Christ boasted, it is said, of a mainly inward union with Christ, on the strength of which they declared themselves independent of all the autocratic authority of the Apostles, but this boast of theirs they did not rest on a special outward relation with Christ, but only on an inward one, on heavenly revelations made to them in visions, which they set in competition with the transmission of doctrine through the Apostles. To this Schenkel refers what is said by the Apostle, 2 Cor. xii. 1, of his ὀπτασίαι and ἀποκαλύψεις, as the Apostle speaks of his ὀπτασίαι and ἀποκαλύψεις only in this place and nowhere else, and, as he himself says here, only because his opponents forced him to do so. His opponents must have been boasting of their special visions and revelations of Christ, and, since they had these to glory in, have thrown off all apostolic authority. This therefore clearly shows that the party of Christ had called themselves by the name of Christ and not by that of an Apostle, because they did not recognise the Apostles' authority. The reason of this must have lain in what happened at the feast of Pentecost. From the quite immediate manner in which the Divine Spirit descended from heaven on that occasion, it must have been concluded that the apostolic instruction was of no great importance, and this conviction must have been strengthened by the sudden conversion of the Apostle Paul by means of a heavenly vision. We cannot accordingly wonder that after that time there arose men who asserted that they were called only by the Spiritual Christ. But what are we to think of this Spiritual Christ?[1] With the precarious suppositions on which the hypothesis rests, he floats before us so completely in the air

[1] Schenkel, op. cit. p. 91.

that in neither Epistle does he stand on the firm ground of a real existence. How can we assume that the Apostle shared those visions and revelations of which he speaks, with those very opponents with whom he was contending? It is true that this Christ-party, characterised now in one way and now in another, those neutrals, independent of all apostolic authority, those adherents of a philosophical or Spiritual Christ (all simply modifications of one and the same view), do present that specific difference from the party of Peter which the words of the Apostle seem to require. But we cannot get any clear and definite idea of the party in question; nor is it kept in mind that if it was so characteristically different from all the other parties, this difference must have appeared in the Apostle's treatment of the subject. Where does he speak of a party so peculiarly and so essentially different from all the rest? or how can it be supposed that he attacked the others, but passed over in complete silence that one which stood in the plainest antagonism not only to Pauline but to Apostolic Christianity, and threatened to destroy its very foundations? If we say with Neander, that what the Apostle says in the first chapter of the first Epistle, in condemnation of the Corinthian party-spirit, applies to the party of Christ as well as to the rest, we can indeed appeal in confirmation of this to the Apostle's own declaration, iv. 6, where he speaks of a μετασχηματίζειν in reference to himself and Apollos; this can only be understood as implying that what had just been said in immediate reference to the parties of Paul and Apollos, was perfectly applicable to the two others as well. But the same difficulty presents itself here also. If what is said of one applies also to the others, they must all be reducible to the same category. But how could this be if the party of Christ differed from the three other parties in refusing to recognise an apostolic authority? This distinction is not made by the Apostle, and in the passages of the two Epistles where the subject is dealt with, we find very naturally that the point at issue is not the recognition of an apostolic authority in general, but the recognition of that special authority which the Apostle Paul asserted for himself as against the other Apostles.

Now if all these modifications of the view which has been set up as against mine still fail to give a clear and distinct idea of what the party of Christ was, and are not founded on data contained in the two Epistles, we find ourselves again face to face with the question, whether it is impossible, on the supposition of the identity of the parties of Christ and of Cephas, still to distinguish them and hold them separate in such a way as to explain how the Apostle came to speak of them as of two separate parties. This is in fact the only objection which can be advanced against my theory, and I can see no difficulty in it which does not vanish as soon as we go closer into the relations of the parties in the Corinthian Church. The chief opposition undoubtedly concerned the Apostle Paul. The authority of the Apostle Peter was set up against his. But this relation of opposition may have had a double aspect. The one party called itself after Paul, the other after Peter; so far there was nothing disparaging to or excluding the Apostle Paul: party stood over against party; each one held to its own Apostle as its head; but as soon as we go a little further, and ask for the argument that may have been used why Peter should be followed and not Paul, why the preference was to be given to him over Paul,—if this reason can only be found on looking at the matter from the Jewish standpoint on which the chief opponents of the Apostle in Corinth stood, and found only in the fact that Peter had been an immediate disciple of Christ, while Paul had not, then this relation of opposition does become exclusive; a principle is established involving as a necessary consequence that Paul was not to be considered as a true Apostle, because devoid of the most essential qualifications of true apostolic authority. This extreme of opposition against the Apostle was represented by those persons whom he refers to under the name of the party of Christ; and the nature of the case shows that the party of Christ in this sense was composed of those from whom this whole opposition to the Apostle Paul on this principle proceeded, namely, those Judaising false teachers who had come to Corinth with their letters of recommendation (2 Cor. ii. 1). For the whole party the name of the Apostle Peter was used; it concealed the principle of the opposition, and formed a natural counterpart to the name of the Apostle Paul. This view of the relation between the party of Peter and the Christ-party not only agrees with the passage 1 Cor. i. 12, but is even confirmed by it. For as the Apostle here mentions first himself, then Apollos, then Cephas, and lastly Christ, this is clearly an ascending scale: Apollos stands nearer to him than Cephas, and the party of Christ is further from him than that of Cephas. The Apostle then lays hold of this name of Christ, and, in his peculiar manner, at once puts the question in its extreme form; beginning his reply boldly with the words, μεμέρισται ὁ Χριστός; is this name (Χριστοῦ, as a party name) not the most undoubted proof that ye are tearing Christ in pieces with your parties? Each party must as a Christian party desire to have a share in Christ; if then there was a peculiar "party of Christ," how was the one Christ divided in whom all ought to find their unity, and all differences to disappear? This would be the more forcible if the party of Christ were the head-quarters of the opposition against him, and the focus of all the party troubles in Corinth.

If this be allowed I do not see what more can be alleged against the view in question. The whole contents of both Epistles agree with it admirably. Though no further reference to the name of the party of Christ should be brought forward, the matter itself on which it alone depends agrees in the most complete manner with all that this view implies. Both names indicate the same party, so that what is said against the party of Peter holds good with regard to the party of Christ. Indeed, only if both parties together formed the opposition to the Apostle Paul in the Corinthian Church can we fully comprehend and enter into the earnest and trenchant polemics against an anti-Pauline Judaising Christianity, which run through both Epistles. But the name is not so completely absent from the Epistles that our theory should not receive its due confirmation from this side as well. Billroth remarks, not without reason, that among the passages in which I find a reference to the party of Christ, only the passage 2 Cor. x. 7 distinctly supports my theory; yet this passage renders further doubt superfluous, and the want of more passages containing express mention of the party of Christ is very simply explained by the name of the party itself. It is true, that if once our foundation be firmly laid, many passages will be found to contain unmistakable allusions to the name of the party of Christ, but such passages cannot be used as direct proofs, because the name Χριστὸς has its own clear meaning in every case, whether the further reference be in it or no. But the name of the party of Christ appears all the more remarkable in the passage above quoted. We see plainly that the Χριστοῦ εἶναι is a phrase which the opponents and false teachers, against whom the Apostle contended, were in the habit of using, as one which they had a special right to appropriate to themselves as against the Apostle (εἴ τις πέποιθεν ἑαυτῷ Χριστοῦ εἶναι, τοῦτο λογιζέσθω πάλιν ἀφ᾽ ἑαυτοῦ, ὅτι καθὼς αὐτὸς Χριστοῦ, οὕτω καὶ ἡμεῖς Χριστοῦ). How fitting is the allusion which the Apostle, in pursuance of his former argument, here makes to the name of those who maintained that they were especially and exclusively οἱ τοῦ Χριστοῦ. In this name the whole of the opposition against the Apostle was gathered up to a point, in this name a principle was advanced against him, which in the eyes of those who used it no protest that he could make could in the least invalidate. With great reason therefore does the Apostle call this name to his own mind and to that of his readers, when he is proceeding on the one hand to assert that fact which he considers as the most direct and undeniable token of his apostolic authority, and on the other, to attack his enemies without any further reservation or evasion, in the most open and decided manner, and to represent them in all their nakedness, as ψευδαπόστολοι, ἐργάται δόλιοι, μετασχηματιζόμενοι εἰς ἀποστόλους Χριστοῦ. Thus the polemic of the Apostle contained in the foregoing passages, against both the party of Peter and the party of Christ, reaches its natural climax in the assertion that his opponents were what they claimed to be only in appearance, falsely and deceitfully: that they were not true but only false ἀπόστολοι Χριστοῦ.

We must now direct some attention to the fact that according to this theory of the relations of the Corinthian parties, the whole polemic of the Apostle, and the whole arrangement and composition of both these Epistles to which it gave rise, appear as a great and well-harmonised whole. Each of the parties named in 1 Cor. i. 12 is duly considered in the polemic of the Apostle, each has its proper place according to the enumeration in this passage, and to each there is said what is appropriate and needful for it. The first section bearing on this polemic, 1 Cor. i. 12—iv. 21, is directed against the party of Paul and that of Apollos, and on this account does not touch upon the difference between Pauline and anti-Pauline Christianity. In discussions like these, it is the Apostle's way to take as wide and general a view as possible; and so what he rebukes in these two parties is the sensuous tendency which lies at the root of all such partisanship, and which is wholly inconsistent with all deeper insight into the true spirit of Christianity. That in this he had the two other parties in view as well, he himself indicates, iv. 6, ταῦτα μετεσχημάτισα, etc. This is commonly taken as referring merely to iii. 4, *sq.* But in iii. 22 the Apostle mentions Cephas along with Apollos and himself, and why did he not mention Cephas also in iii. 4, 5 ? I am therefore inclined to refer this μετασχηματίζειν to the whole section from i. 12 onwards. All that the Apostle says in this section of the relation of the σοφία τοῦ Θεοῦ to the σοφία τοῦ κόσμου, refers most naturally to the difference existing between the party of Paul and that of Apollos. Whilst the Apostle traces the love of the Corinthians for the σοφία κόσμου to their sensuousness, to the fact that they were σαρκικοὶ and not πνευματικοὶ, iii. 1, and points out, as the source of their divisions and party strife, the carnal mind that still dwelt in them, and kept them on so low a level of Christian life, that they might be expected to see for themselves how little they were fitted to set up as judges of their teachers, all these exhortations naturally applied also to the party of Peter. The sectarian spirit showed itself also in that party in the same carnal tendency arising from egotistical interests; and the excessive self-appreciation which flatters itself with haughty, empty speeches, and which the Apostle lays to the charge of party spirit in general, must have applied with special force to the party of Peter. But besides this it must not be overlooked how in 1 Cor. iii. 5, as well as in 2 Cor. xi. 15, the Apostle speaks of διάκονοι Χριστοῦ. Without doubt the party of Peter arrogated to itself the name διάκονοι Χριστοῦ, and with regard to this it must not be considered as accidental that the Apostle takes up the question of διάκονοι, the true ministers of the Lord, in the course of his strictures on the Corinthian parties, 1 Cor. iii. 5. We thus see from the section 1 Cor. i. 12—iv. 24, how from the beginning the Apostle never lost sight of this opposition, but deals with it at first with a certain forbearance and self-restraint, and only gradually passes from the indirect to the direct refutation of his opponents.

This transition he makes 1 Cor. ix. 1, for here his polemic, having treated hitherto of the parties of Paul and Apollos, turns to that of Cephas. Nor does he avoid indicating this party by its name, nor taking up his ground against it with the assertion that he had the same rights with the rest of the Apostles, with the brethren of the Lord, and specially with Cephas, ix. 5.

The polemic passes from the indirect to the direct, 1 Cor. ix. 1, *sqq.*, but does not reach its full severity till the second part of the second Epistle, x.—xiii. Even here the Apostle has various things to say before he comes to the direct attack on his opponents : we see that it costs him a certain inward struggle to take this extreme but also necessary step. He first discusses all he has to say to the Corinthians themselves, though in all this he has his opponents before his mind. Then when everything else is said, and everything is ready, he attacks his opponents in the way we have already seen. As this discussion proceeds to its climax, the peculiar position of the Christ-party, with which it deals, comes prominently forward. This partly is dealt with in its proper place, as assigned to it at 1 Cor. i. 12, so far at least as it is distinguishable from the party of Peter.

Besides the existence of parties, which is the chief point of which the Apostle never loses sight throughout the two Epistles, there were in the Corinthian Church several other peculiar phenomena of a nature more or less disturbing to the regulation of the Christian life. With respect to these phenomena the Apostle explains himself for the most part in a very explicit manner, being led to do so by questions which had been addressed to him in a letter he had received from the Corinthians before his Epistle was written. The chief subjects of this kind were the following: the unchaste relations in which a member of the Corinthian Church lived with his stepmother, giving rise to great scandal (chap. v.) Connected with this was the immorality which was prevalent among the Corinthian Christians, which the Apostle denounces more than once, v. 9, *sqq.*, vi. 15, *sqq.*, 2 Cor. xii. 21; the practice of bringing law disputes before Gentile judges, and even of prosecuting Christians in their courts, vi. 2; the question as to the superiority of married or celibate life (chap. vii.), as well as that of participation in Gentile sacrificial feasts and the use of meat offered to idols, chap. viii.; the liberty which the women of the Corinthian Church permitted themselves with regard to their head-dress in the Christian assemblies, chap. xi. 1,[1] *sqq.*; an abuse connected with the celebration of the Lord's Supper, xi. 17, *sqq.*; the difference of opinion as to the value of the so-called λαλεῖν γλώσσαις,[2] especially in its relation to the προφητεύειν, chap. xii.—xiv.; and finally the question as to the resurrection from the dead, which was denied by some of the members of the Corinthian Church. All these phenomena, and the questions stirred by them, give us a very clear and vivid picture of the condition of the Corinthian Church; yet it would be most interesting to know more distinctly than we do how the various parties were related to these various phenomena, and how the state of parties in Corinth bore on them. All that we can be sure of is this, that the Gentile Christian element had a great

---

[1] Cf. my "Beiträge zur Erklärung der Korintherbriefe" in the Theol. Jahrb. 1852, p. 1. Der Zusammenhang von cap. vii. mit v. 1—vi. 20, p. 15. Die Ansicht des Apostels von der Ehe und der Sklaverei, cap. vii. p. 563. Die Frauen der Korinthischen Gemeinde und die Schleiersymbolik des Apostels, 1 Cor. xi. 2-16.

[2] Compare the treatise mentioned at p. 16.

predominance, which was everywhere felt. And yet the Judaising opponents of the Apostle were able to force their way into this Church, and take up a strong position in it, so as to form this energetic opposition which he himself considered so formidable.

The relation of the second Epistle to the first deserves to be carefully attended to. It has been already remarked that the polemic of the Apostle against those opponents with whom he contends in the first Epistle is continued in the second, and that the very strongest utterances with which he makes his directest and most vehement attack on them are found in the last chapter of the second Epistle. But all the stronger is the contrast between the sharp and vehement tone of this last chapter, and the tone of the first part of the Epistle, in which the Apostle betrays the greatest uneasiness and apprehension about the reception of his former letter, and about his whole relation to the Corinthians, and labours with the utmost anxiety to secure for himself, by repeated assurances of his love and sympathy, the confidence of the Corinthians, which he fears is growing cold towards him. Different theories have been advanced to explain this striking change of tone in the second Epistle, but the chief question is, what reason the Apostle could have had to bear such great uneasiness and anxiety as to the impression made by his first letter. The contents of our first Epistle are thought not to furnish a sufficient reason for this anxiety. This circumstance, as well as what is found in the two Epistles about a mission not only of Timothy but also of Titus, a matter in which they do not very well agree, has given rise to the suspicion that our second Epistle does not stand in that close connection with the first which is commonly supposed. "Our second Epistle," it is maintained,[1] "does not refer to the impression which may have been produced by the first, but to the reception of a letter which Titus conveyed, and which we no longer possess. In fact there occur in our second Epistle several passages, such as ii. 3, 4, vii. 12, which, although they are generally referred directly to

[1] Compare Bleek, Erörterungen über die Cor. Briefe, Theol. Stud. u. Krit. 1830, iii. 627.

the circumstances treated of in 1 Cor., still on closer inspection are difficult to explain upon this theory, and of themselves would plainly lead us to suppose that in the relations of the Apostle to the Corinthians something more intervened between our two Epistles than merely the news brought to the Apostle by Titus about the effect produced by the first Epistle. The whole tone and character of the reproof in 1 Cor. are not such as Paul's expressions here would lead us to think of. It is therefore highly probable that in the Epistle mentioned in 2 Cor. ii. 3, the special matter here referred to occupied a larger proportion to the whole Epistle than the passage in 1 Cor. about the incestuous person to the whole of that Epistle. If therefore the τοῦτο αὐτὸ, 2 Cor. ii. 3, really referred to something which the Apostle had written with respect to this matter, which of course is highly probable, we are led to conclude that it does not apply to the first Epistle, but to a subsequent one, in which Paul had expressed himself on this subject with much greater vehemence. It is also possible, of course, that this verse does not refer to that incestuous person and the Apostle's expression regarding him at all, but to some other matter of which Paul had heard through Timothy, and of which he had then spoken indignantly and sternly in his Epistle. What comes afterwards, 2 Cor. iii. 5, does not necessarily oblige us to think of the incestuous person; but if we give up the idea of this reference we must also resign the possibility of ascertaining exactly what the special matter was, and can only surmise in general that some of the commands of the Apostle had been flagrantly disregarded."

I cannot consider this opinion to be well grounded, and it seems to me that what we know of the Apostle's character affords no adequate reason for taking the relation of the two Epistles to each other to be different from what has been commonly supposed. We need only remember with what vehemence and indignation he speaks of the occurrence mentioned in 1 Cor. v. 5, and how, as soon as he has said what he had to say on the chief subject of his letter, this is the first of the more special subjects to which he addresses himself. The Apostle takes up this matter seriously enough, and at the same time it so notoriously concerns one particular individual, that it is against all probability that the individual who is spoken of in the same pointed way, 2 Cor. ii. 5,[1] should have been any other than the one referred to, 1 Cor. v. If we consider, further, what the Apostle writes to the Corinthians with regard to this individual, in the most solemn manner, with all the emphasis of his apostolic authority, as his judicial sentence, we can well understand what anxiety and care this affair must soon after have occasioned him. To speak plainly: he had taken a step which he himself must have regarded as a rash and overhasty one, and which, as it failed of its intended result, simply laid him open to his opponents. Indeed, he afterwards retracted what he had done, and adopted a course which was exactly the opposite of what he had formerly distinctly said ought to be done. The most natural sense of the passage in question, 1 Cor. v. 3, I can only consider to be that given by the most recent commentators, namely, that the Apostle thought he had the power, by virtue of the strength of Christ which was present with him, to give over the criminal to the disposal of Satan; his sentence was to take effect by means of a disease which should smite the offender at that moment in which he should be solemnly expelled from the Christian communion by the assembled Church, in which the Apostle himself would be present in spirit to work the miracle. However we may take the expression $\pi\alpha\rho\alpha\delta o\hat{\upsilon}\nu\alpha\iota$ $\tau\hat{\omega}$ $\Sigma\alpha\tau\alpha\nu\hat{q}$, the Apostle certainly declares a double sentence, first a bodily sickness miraculously inflicted (for nothing else than this can be meant by $\ddot{o}\lambda\epsilon\theta\rho o\varsigma$ $\tau\hat{\eta}\varsigma$ $\sigma\alpha\rho\kappa\grave{o}\varsigma$), and the excommunication spoken of in verses 2 and 13, for which the Church was to be assembled. But neither of these two things, as we see from the second Epistle, had happened. Neither had the miraculous punishment occurred which the Apostle had threatened,[2]

[1] He is called ὁ τοιοῦτος 2 Cor. ii. 7, as well as in 1 Cor. v. 5.

[2] The passage 1 Cor. v. 4 contains a criterion of some interest by which to judge of the alleged miracles of the Apostles. The consciousness of miraculous power, the δύναμις τοῦ Κυρίου, was certainly felt by the Apostles, and in this consciousness they may have looked upon the specially remarkable results of their ministry, the operations of their energy in action, as σημεῖα, τέρατα, and δυνάμεις.

nor had the Corinthians proceeded to the exclusion of the offender from the Church. I feel myself obliged to agree with Rückert's explanation of the second passage touching on this matter, 2 Cor. ii. 6 ; that the Apostle declares himself content with the punishment decreed by the Corinthians, and says he does not require any graver punishment to be inflicted, which he could not have said if the punishment which he had demanded had already taken place. From ver. 10 it is clear that the χαρίζεσθαι did not now originate with him, but had already been put in force without his being consulted, so that now he could only acquiesce in what had taken place in order not to put himself in open conflict with them by persistence in his former demands. The Corinthians then had confined themselves to a mere reproof, and even this mild punishment had been inflicted on the man not by the Church as a whole but only by a part of it. If this was the state of affairs, Rückert very justly remarks, Paul must have found himself in a very awkward position. His command had not been carried out; only a part of the community, although it may be the larger part, had taken the matter to heart, the remainder, as might have been expected from the feeling of the Church towards him, had not even done this—his authority was greatly impaired. What was he to do now ? Insist on his former orders ? He might be sure that he should find no more obedience than before, and the scandal would be all the greater. He could not enforce obedience, and the affair would only make a bad impression on all sides. There was nothing for it but what prudence dictated in similar cases : to give the matter another turn, by which an open breach might be avoided, and the evil not indeed cured, but concealed until in better times he should recover his proper position. This turn was to approve of what had been done, even although it had been done without his consent, to represent it as his own wish, and to bring the whole matter under a Christian point of view. This is

Compare 1 Cor. xii. 10, 28, 2 Cor. xii. 12. But as in the case of 1 Cor. v. 4 this conviction was distinctly expressed, and no miracle actually ensued, the same may have taken place in other cases too.

what he now does, partly through the concession that the punishment which the man had undergone may have been sufficient, partly through the admonition to forgive him. This account of the Apostle's position is undoubtedly correct; and the whole tone in which he wrote our Epistle to the Corinthians, the restlessness and anxiety which it betrays, are thus very naturally explained. He had taken a step the consequences of which he only now clearly perceived.[1] It must now have appeared very questionable to him what its effect would be on his opponents.[2] As we see from the Apostle's own Epistle, they did not fail to use the occurrence as a handle to depreciate his authority. When he is absent, said they, he can indeed make severe speeches and be full enough of boasting and vain-glory, but when it comes to real action he does not trust himself to be personally present (x. 10, 11; compare iii. 1, v. 12.) Without doubt this was the reason which made the Apostle so solicitous to vindicate himself, as he does in the beginning of his Epistle, on account of his delay to undertake his long-contemplated journey to Corinth. An Epistle written under such circumstances must of course have a mainly apologetic tendency, but the apology is by no means a merely personal one; it passes at once into more general considerations, and becomes an apologetic examination of his apostolic office, which he represents in its two aspects, as it brings salvation to some, and works ruin to others, and shows to be superior to the ministry of the Old Covenant, as the lofty experience which he himself had had of it had taught him. Having worked out these ideas, and conceived new confidence in the Corinthians, he turns with fresh spirit and incisive logic to his opponents, with a view to arriving

[1] Rückert has no hesitation in saying with regard to 1 Cor. v. 5, "The Apostle's line of conduct is simply passionate; and, like other passionate acts, could never hear any good result. And that he issued, to a Church in which his authority was much lowered, dictatorial commands which he had no means of enforcing—this was not wise." Who will blame the unprejudiced critic for saying this?

[2] The Apostle gives marked expression to this in 2 Cor. ii. 11: ἵνα μὴ πλεονεκτηθῶμεν ὑπὸ τοῦ Σατανᾶ, οὐ γὰρ αὐτοῦ τὰ νοήματα ἀγνοοῦμεν. He is aware, then, that his παραδοῦναι τῷ Σατανᾷ has harmed no one but himself.

at a thorough clearing up of his relations to them. In no other of the Apostle's Epistles are we allowed to look deeper into the pure humanity of his character, and into the peculiarities of his relations to the Churches, than in his second Epistle to the Corinthians. No other Epistle teaches us so much of his character, if at least we do not suffer the genuine human traits which it contains to be glozed over by false ideas of what we ought to find in it. If we have traced the relation of 2 Corinthians to 1 Corinthians correctly, there is no reason for supposing another lost Epistle to the Corinthians besides that mentioned in 1 Cor. v. 9.[1]

The Apostle had written to the Corinthians before the two Epistles which we possess, as he himself says, 1 Cor. v. 9; but we do not know anything further of this lost Epistle than what we may gather from this passage. This missive cannot have been of equal importance with our two Epistles—as the way in which the Apostle discusses the subjects which fill up our first Epistle does not allow us to suppose that there had been much communication between him and the Corinthians on these points before. The composition of our two Epistles is commonly placed in the years 57-59, in the period in which the Apostle, after leaving Corinth, Acts xviii. 18, took up his residence for some time at Ephesus, Acts xix. 1, xx. 1. There seems no doubt that in his journey to Greece, Acts xx. 2, he visited Corinth again, and during his residence there wrote the Epistle to the Romans; but whether this visit was the second or third is not so easily decided, as in the passages in the Epistles where the Apostle speaks of a journey to Corinth, it is left doubtful whether the "third time" of which he speaks is to be understood as referring to the journey, or to the intention of taking it. In my opinion the latter is the more probable, if we consider the connection in which the passages which bear on the question stand to one another. When he says, 2 Cor. xii. 14, ἰδού τρίτον τοῦτο ἑτοίμως ἔχω ἐλθεῖν πρὸς ὑμᾶς, τρίτον τοῦτο may

---

[1] What follows was added for the second edition. Compare the author's essay, Beiträge zur Erklärung der Korintherbriefe 1. Die Reisen des Apostels Paulus nach Korinth. Theol. Jahrb. ix. 139 sq.—*Editor.*

apply either to ἐλθεῖν or to ἑτοίμως ἔχω, and therefore we do not know whether the Apostle now for the third time resolved to go to Corinth, or whether he was setting out on his third journey. To clear up this point we must go back to the beginning of the Epistle, where he also speaks of a visit to the Corinthians. Ἐβουλόμην, he says, i. 15, πρὸς ὑμᾶς ἐλθεῖν πρότερον, ἵνα δευτέραν χάριν ἔχητε, etc. When he says he wished to go πρότερον, he must mean that he had already formed a distinct plan of travel, but wished to visit them before the occasion which it provided; and if the Corinthians were to have a δευτέρα χάρις, there must have been one already, with reference to which this one would be the second, and on which they might count in any case, even apart from a δευτέρα χάρις. If the Apostle journeyed direct from Ephesus to Corinth, and from thence to Macedonia, the only way in which he could add a δευτέρα χάρις was by taking Corinth again on his way back from Macedonia. He could not have done it if he went to Macedonia first, and from Macedonia to Corinth, since his route embraced only the three points, Ephesus, Corinth, Macedonia. Thus we reach the result that the πρότερον ἐλθεῖν could only be the δι' ὑμῶν διελθεῖν εἰς Μακεδονίαν. It was a δευτέρα χάρις, since the ἐλθεῖν ἀπὸ Μακεδονίας of which he speaks afterwards (though not as πάλιν ἀπὸ Μακεδονίας, still as ἐλθεῖν ἀπὸ Μακεδονίας) was already a part of the Apostle's plan, quite in accordance with 1 Cor. xvi. 5. He still adheres to the original plan of a journey by Macedonia to Corinth, only he intends, without giving that up, to come at once straight from Ephesus to Corinth and to go from there to Macedonia. Thus he had already resolved twice to go to Corinth, and had indeed arranged for two visits there (a δευτέρα χάρις) without either of these plans and intentions having been carried out at the time of his writing to the Corinthians, and this is the very reason which induces him to speak of it. He wishes to remove the idea that it was owing to his fickleness and want of purpose that he did not perform what he undertook, and that his opponents could thus justly accuse him (as they doubtless did) of a want of sincerity and of interested motives, which must go far to impair the confidence the Corinthians might be disposed to have in his discharge of the apostolic office. He protests against all those injurious inferences which might be drawn from his non-appearance. We do not learn from him here how often he had been in Corinth, or how many journeys this one would have made; he is not speaking of an actual journey, but only of an intended one of plans and travel. It is thought that precise information on this point is certainly given where he gives his reasons for not going to Corinth. "Ἔκρινα δὲ ἐμαυτῷ τοῦτο, says the Apostle, 2 Cor. ii. 1, τὸ μὴ πάλιν ἐν λύπῃ πρὸς ὑμᾶς ἐλθεῖν; and nothing seems more simple than to conclude that as the Apostle had already once been to Corinth ἐν λύπῃ, and this cannot have been the case at his first visit, he must have been twice at Corinth when he wrote our second Epistle. But where can we find an appropriate time to which we may assign this second journey? If he had been in Corinth for the second time, for a reason which made his visit one ἐν λύπῃ, before our Epistle was written, we should expect to find some allusion to the circumstance in our first Epistle, where the fact of a prior letter having been written is not left unmentioned. For we must remember that the question is not merely whether the Apostle visited Corinth twice or three times altogether, but further, what was the nature of the second visit here alluded to. If he was in Corinth between the time of his first visit and the despatch of the first Epistle, it must have been ἐν λύπῃ, that is, under circumstances which obliged him to use some severity, and in fact to depart with the threat of taking still harsher measures against the Corinthians if they did not improve. But this theory makes the whole contents of our first Epistle to the Corinthians, and the tone in which the Apostle speaks of the whole condition of the Church and of its various failings, simply impossible. Of what nature can those irregularities have been, which had already taken place and had disturbed the good understanding between the Apostle and the Church? We have no alternative but to suppose that they were irregularities of the same kind as those which he had to deal with in such detail in our first Epistle. The detail and the earnestness of his discussion of the various failings and weaknesses of the Church in this Epistle, make it difficult to suppose that he had already been dissatisfied with the Corinthians for a reason not here mentioned. The subjects that he deals with in our first Epistle appear to have been just brought under his notice for his advice; indeed he says that this was the case. The circumstances and relations have just arisen; he is speaking of them to the Corinthians evidently for the first time. Of the parties into which the Church was divided, he had first heard through the household of Chloe (1 Cor. i. 11). He had only heard of the prevailing immorality, and the particular case which seemed to require a special intervention on his part, v. 1. The misunderstanding which he has to correct, v. 9, in regard to the μὴ συναναμίγνυσθαι πόρνοις, an instruction which he had addressed to the Corinthians in a letter previous to our first Epistle, could scarcely have arisen if the subject had been treated of before by word of mouth. The questions relating to married life, which he discusses in detail in chap. vii., had been first raised in a letter from the Corinthians, vii. 1. And as we may clearly see from the whole of the Apostle's discussion of the subject that there has been no mention of these things between him and the Corinthians before, so this is likewise obvious with regard to all the other subjects on which, in the rest of his Epistle, he either expresses his anger and disapprobation, or lays down rules and directions. Nowhere do we meet with the slightest indication that the Apostle had previously had cause to find fault with the Corinthians on these or similar subjects; that any differences had arisen between him and them; that he had given any advice which had not been followed, or uttered any threats which had not been heeded. Still less can we imagine a journey of this kind to have taken place between our two Epistles. Our first Epistle gives no hint of such an interval in the time preceding it as would necessitate the supposition of a journey made by the Apostle, in addition to those we are already acquainted with; and the second Epistle follows so hard on the first, that nothing that took place between them, and is essential to the understanding of the second, can have escaped our knowledge. But it must be asked, is it so essential to make the words, 2 Cor. ii. 1, ἐν λύπῃ and πάλιν refer so directly to each other, that we must think of a prior journey ἐν λύπῃ, to be followed by a second one ἐν λύπῃ? May we not suppose that the Apostle should properly have written ἐλθὼν after πάλιν, but omitted it, including it in the following ἐλθεῖν? No great exactness of expression is expected in a letter, especially when the readers are familiar with the circumstances treated of, and do not need to have it all explained to them. After what we have said, there appears to be no reason of much weight why we should not take the τρίτον τοῦτο, 2 Cor. xii. 14, thus:—" Twice already have I proposed to myself to come to you, but it was not possible to me to fulfil my intention, but now that my thrice-formed design is about to be realised, I will declare to you what attitude I shall assume towards you." On a casual glance the passage xiii. 1, which begins with the words τρίτον τοῦτο ἔρχομαι πρὸς ὑμᾶς, would seem to silence all doubts on the subject of a third journey, but on a closer examination we find that it gives the information about this journey of which we are in quest. Why should we not construe those words to mean that the Apostle is now for the third time on the point of visiting them? And if the passage where he speaks of his journey does not necessarily suggest a second journey already made, but merely an intention of making it, while the Epistle as a whole is meant to excuse the Apostle for having meant to visit Corinth and not having done so, does not all this show us at once what is to be attested by the word of two or three witnesses? In their literal sense, these words are unintelligible; but it is not unnatural to suppose that the Apostle wishes to add strength to his statement and says:—" If the principle of the Mosaic law be a sound one, that what is attested by two or three witnesses is true and stands before the law, then as I have now three times resolved to come to you, it will now be true, it is the case, that my resolution will soon be carried out." Those who have been able to accept my exposition of the subject up to this point as not only possibly, but probably correct, will now be in a position to receive the last statement in the passage, the Apostle's own assertion that he has only been once at Corinth before, and is now coming for the second time, as the authentic confirmation of the result to which the other evidence has pointed. Even in point of grammar, the words ὡς παρὼν τὸ δεύτερον must be taken not of an actual presence but of one imagined (cf. 1 Cor. v. 3). The Apostle is so eager to exclude all room for doubt of his coming to Corinth immediately, and to create the impression that his word is now to be realised without fail, that though absent from them he seems to himself to be present with them; he is in Corinth for the second time, and tells them, as present with them for the second time, yet absent, what will infallibly take place.

Let us then reject the idea of a journey which has nowhere any basis of evidence. When we have got rid of it, this whole episode will appear to us much clearer and simpler, more natural, and more a living part of history.

CHAPTER III.

THE EPISTLE TO THE ROMANS.

It is not merely in the order of time that the Epistle to the Romans comes immediately after those to the Corinthians : there is also an inner progress from the latter to the former. Only from the standpoint of the Epistle to the Romans do we survey the rich treasures of the spiritual life of which the Apostle was the depositary and the organ, and see how severe and well-reasoned is the system in which he develops his Christian principle, how large the world in which he moves, and the subjects that he deals with. We have already had occasion to remark the relation in which the Epistle to the Galatians and that to the Romans stand to each other, the one being the first sketch of a bold and profound system as conceived in its characteristic and essential features, the other the completed system, developed on all sides, and provided with all necessary argument and illustration. This character of the Epistle to the Romans as a systematic work, dealing with a massive body of thought, marks it off from the two Corinthian Epistles, which are distinguished rather for the variety of their contents, and their richness in suggestive and spiritual ideas, arising out of, and illuminating, various relations of life. But in the Epistle to the Romans, we mark also an advance in the Apostle's attitude towards that great opposing force, to resist and conquer which became more and more the task of his apostolic activity. His mission as Apostle to the Gentiles was not fulfilled till the absolute importance which Judaism claimed, a claim in which Jewish Christianity sympathised with it, had been wrested from it, both in principle and in all the consequences involved, and Judaism shown to be of merely relative value. In the Epistle to the Galatians he had emancipated Christianity from Judaism to the extent of casting off the outward symbol of bondage, the rite of circumcision, which the latter sought to impose upon the former as the necessary condition of salvation. In the two Epistles to the Corinthians, he had asserted the principle that the call to, and the possession of, the Messianic salvation, were not conditioned by the authority of the Apostles, who had been called by Jesus himself: that he, the Gentile Apostle, was an Apostle quite as much, and to as good effect as they. In the Epistle to the Romans his task is to remove the last remnants of Jewish particularism, by showing that it is but a stage, a stepping-stone to the universalism of Christianity, in which all nations should be embraced. Jewish Christianity, which still maintained the absolute importance of Judaism, had not been able to prevent the rise in Gentile Christianity of a religious realm which lived upon its own resources, and was free and independent of Judaism. But the idea that Jewish Christianity and Gentile Christianity were not only to exist side by side, that the latter was to assume an immense preponderance over the former—this idea was one which the religious consciousness of the Jewish Christians scarcely allowed them to take in. And this seemed likely to be the ultimate result of the apostolic activity among the Gentiles. As the universalism of Christianity, in which all nations were embraced without distinction, was realised in fact, the Messianic salvation appeared to go altogether to the Gentiles; and the contrast between the Jews, who continued in their unbelief, and the Gentiles, who were more and more converted to the faith, seemed to point to no other conclusion than that the Jews were rejected and the Gentiles called. This is the Apostle's position in the Epistle to the Romans; this is the theme which he works out in that Epistle. To show this, however, we have to advance a view of the occasion and the purpose of his writing the Epistle, which is radically different from the common one.[1]

The origin and aim of the Epistle are generally determined from the purely dogmatic point of view. Scholars have failed to inquire carefully into the historical occasion and the circumstances in the Roman Church on which the Epistle proceeds, and to make these the starting-point of their discussions; as if the Apostle had had no other motive for writing than a desire to give a connected and comprehensive view of his whole scheme of doctrine, to furnish, as it were, a compendium of the Pauline dogmatics in the form of an Apostolic Epistle. With those who have given more pains to the proper understanding of the Epistle, the opinion has prevailed that there is no sufficient ground to believe that the Apostle intended his Epistle mainly to put an end to local disputes, such as Eichhorn[2] and Hug[3] suppose to have taken place between the

[1] I follow here my essay, Über Zweck und Veranlassung des Römerbriefs, which appeared in the year 1836 in the Tüb. Zeitschrift für Theologie, H. 3, p. 54. I adhere to the view there advocated, as I first conceived it, and still hold it, the more that I feel that those scholars who have noticed it have not estimated it thoroughly or impartially. Rückert (Com. über den Br. P. au die R., second revised edition, 1839, ii. 366) spoke of devoting to it an examination in detail; but I have never heard of the appearance of such a work. Fritzsche (Pauli ad Rom. Ep. ii. 1839, p. 238) noticed it, at least on Romans ix., but very cursorily. Nor did Neander deal with the question thoroughly in his Planting and Training. Mere expressions of dissent, such as those of de Wette (Kurze Erkl. des Röm. B., third edition, 1841, p. 3, cf. Einleitung, p. 247), are of little value. If the Apostle's indication of the occasion and purpose of his writing, i. 8-16, were as clear, and the line of thought—of which the theme is given i. 17, and the discussion occupies i. 18-viii. 39—as distinct, as de Wette asserts, there would not be room for much difference of opinion. But my essay shows that these passages prove nothing against my view. Thus an essay in which an original view is propounded and furnished with proof, is simply thrown aside. Some outside features are laid hold of and criticised, and that is all; the verdict is passed that the whole view is incorrect. But such a verdict can only be passed by such as take a superficial view and do not see the difficulties which lie deeper; and who can, without compunction, neglect the more important bearings of an Epistle altogether. (Thus the author in the first edition. For the second he subjected this whole chapter to a thorough revision, making use of his second essay, " Über Zweck und Gedankengang des Römerbriefs (Theol. Jahrb. xvi. 60-108, 184-209).—*Editor.*)

[2] Einl. in's N. T. p. 214.

[3] Einl. in's N. T. vol. ii., second edition, p. 361.

Judæo- and the Gentile-Christians. But the character and arrangement of the first part of the teaching has been thought to unquestionably indicate a general aim, which did not arise from the special circumstances of the Roman Church, and which was to point out the great importance of Christian doctrine, and to show how it alone meets the needs of human nature, which neither heathenism nor Judaism can satisfy.[1] De Wette and Olshausen agree with Tholuck in this view of the aim of the Epistle. De Wette's position is, that the Apostle desired to exert what influence could be transmitted in writing, on this Church, which must have been so important in his eyes, and to set before it in a connected form the doctrine which was the distinguishing feature of his gospel, namely, that salvation was to be attained only through faith, and not through the works of the law. He wished to set forth the Christian faith before the eyes of the capital of the world, as the only way of salvation for the whole world, both Gentile and Jew; to represent the Christian revelation as the revelation for the whole world. The Epistle to the Romans is the only epistle of the Apostle in which he sets himself to expound his doctrine connectedly, and in detail, while in the other epistles he is concerned with special circumstances, with doubts, errors, questions, that had come before him, and merely presupposes his doctrinal system. This doctrine of faith as the only way of salvation is here expounded, not as opposed to the errors of Judæo-Christianity, as in the Epistle to the Galatians, but as opposed to Judaism. He had less opposition to expect from the Gentile Christians; what he had to contend with was the self-assertion of Judaism, which was much in favour at the time, and had sufficient influence to prejudice the Gentiles against Christianity.[2] Olshausen insists still more than De Wette that the representation of the nature of the Gospel in the

[1] Compare Tholuck in the first four editions of his Commentary. This exposition, with continuous extracts from the exegetical writings of Fathers and Reformers, first appeared in 1824, and marks an epoch in the history of the exposition of the Epistle.

[2] Kurze, Erklärung des Briefs an die Römer. Leipzig, 1841. Third edition Introduction, p. 2.

Epistle to the Romans is a purely objective one, and has in view not the special question between Judæo and Gentile Christianity, which had arisen within the Church itself, but the larger question between Jew and Gentile. According to him the whole exposition is objective in tone, and there is no more than a merely cursory reference to any minor point : the great object before the writer's mind is the truth of the Gospel. But this truth found itself by its very nature in contradiction with all kinds of errors, and to this extent these do appear in the Epistle ; yet the Apostle's wisdom as a teacher led him to begin with presenting such a view of the Gospel that the corrective of the errors which Christians must encounter was suggested spontaneously and at once.[1] There is no special aim whatever, but a desire to present the Gospel to the Roman Christians in its natural relation to the law, and in its practical consequences. The Judæo-Christians are not attacked ; points of difference with them, such as are clearly referred to in the Epistle to the Galatians, are not taken up here.[2] Multitudinous as the recent commentaries on the Romans are, we find in none of them any account of the object of the Epistle further than this general one, which is necessarily blind to the special circumstances of the case. Differences of expression do occur ; one writer, for example, says that "the main object of the Epistle was to confirm the Roman Christians in their new faith, and to exhort and encourage them to work out the Christian ideal on all its sides, by contemplating the necessity and grandeur of the scheme of salvation revealed in the Gospel, its harmony with the divine character and with the earlier revelations, and also the sad results of heathen superstition, and of the abuse of the law through sin, in contrast with the ideal life in the Spirit of the true Christian."[3] Some have

[1] This is the extreme point of the purely dogmatic view. De Wette allows the contention against Judaism, but here no direct antithetical reference whatever is allowed.

[2] Der Brief des Ap. P. au die Römer. Königsberg, 1835, p. 50, 44.

[3] Thus Reich, Versuch einer ausführlichen Erklärung des Briefs P. an die R. Göttingen, 1833, p. 73. Compare Köllner, Comm. zu dem Br. des Ap. P. au die R. Darmstadt, 1834, p. xliv. Glöckler, der Br. des Paulus au die R. Frankfort a. M., 1834, p. xxii. Fritzsche, Pauli ad Rom. epist. Hal. Sax., 1836, i. p. xxx.

felt that some concessions were due to the opinion advanced by me in a contrary direction, or at least that it ought to be mentioned, yet in these cases the dogmatic point of view is not in the least departed from. On the contrary, the greater pains are taken to smoothe down and gloze over all the points and corners, which one might suppose to afford some clew to the Epistle's connection with the concrete circumstances in which it originated. The dogmatic view is not to yield one step to the historical, lest the position of an Epistle such as that to the Romans should be impaired, and the Lutheran forensic process of justification, which it is of such moment to maintain in its integrity, suffer from the shaking of its great buttress.[1]

Whether this theory is intrinsically probable, or whether the Epistle does not, with all its seeming want of any distinct indication of its historical occasion, yet afford some data which may be sufficient to shed some light on it in this respect, this is the question to which we have first of all to address ourselves.

The analogy of those Epistles with which alone the Epistle to the Romans can be properly compared, does not favour the common view. The Epistle to the Galatians and those to the Corinthians, the only ones which we are at liberty to regard as types of what Pauline Epistles are, give us a very different notion of how the Apostle came to write an Epistle. What led him to

[1] In this sense hear Philippi, the chief representative of the stiffly orthodox dogmatic view of the Epistle, in his Commentary, second edition, p. 14 :—" We can conceive no other opposition to the Pauline universalism but that which we know to have been conducted by the Judæo-Christian false teachers and sects. This is the only opposition with which the Apostle contends in the Epistle to the Romans ; he contends with the Jewish righteousness by works, not against the exclusion of the heathen world from Christianity ; and against the *Jewish* righteousness by works, not that of the Judæo-Christian portion of the Roman Church. Had the Jewish Christians of Rome been guilty of this tendency, he would have attacked them on that ground, as he attacked the false teachers of Galatia, and rebuked the Galatian Churches ; and no considerations, of whatever kind, would have induced the Apostle of the Gentiles to pass lightly over this tendency, one which gnawed at the very root of the Gospel." But this would still be true if the Roman Church had been addicted not to the errors of Galatia but to the Jewish particularism which I have described.

write these ones were special circumstances and needs. Nor was it that he used these as a peg on which to hang a doctrinal treatise which he had in his mind already; it is the imperious pressure of circumstances which calls and forces him to write, at the risk of seeing his work destroyed. We cannot but suppose that there was something of this sort in the case of the Epistle to the Romans; and here we must wonder at the bias which commentators have displayed in estimating the relation of the two great sections of the Epistle, chaps. i.-viii. and ix.-xi., to each other. If we set out with supposing that the main drift of the Epistle and the Apostle's aim in writing it are to be discovered in the dogmatic part with which he begins it, that the order of thought, that is to say, in which the Epistle originated in his mind, has been exactly reproduced in its outward form, that is just placing ourselves from the very beginning at the dogmatic point of view for the interpretation of the Epistle. It is thought that the dogmatic contents, as presented to us in the first eight chapters, must have been what the Apostle started from; this was the germ from which the whole system of the Epistle was developed. Everything else, and particularly what we find in the chapters ix.-xi., is secondary and subordinate to that, the main part of the Epistle, and was added to it after the true theme had been fully discussed, as an inference resulting from it, and a practical application. Thus the Epistle would be a complete whole even without this second part, its main idea being already fully worked out, and the end attained which the Apostle designed it to further. By some commentators, specially Tholuck, p. 341, and De Wette, p. 4, this section is expressly called a historical corollary, an appendix in which the Apostle sought to show the consequences which naturally arose from the doctrine he had already propounded, namely, the exclusion of the unbelieving Jews from the Christian salvation; and this idea may have suggested itself to him at this point, when his discussion was completed and he cast his eye over it again. This is the ordinary view of the relation of the two parts of the Epistle to each other, and the question may well be asked whether the very reverse of this relation may not be more correct, and whether this view of the Epistle would not give us a much more satisfactory account both of the aim and drift of the work, and of the historical relations out of which it arose. On this view we should find in these three chapters the germ and centre of the whole, from which the other parts sprang; and we should take our stand on these three chapters in order to enter into the Apostle's original conception, from which the whole organism of the Epistle was developed, as we have it especially in the first eight chapters. For this purpose we have first to examine the contents of the three chapters, ix.-xi.

In these chapters the Apostle finds an answer to the question, how it has come to pass that so great a part of the Jewish people, the people chosen by God of old and the object of all the divine promises, did not participate in the Messianic salvation, how it was that the Gentiles occupied the place which should have been filled by God's own people? The Apostle's answer to this question consists in the following propositions:—1. In these things the important point is not natural descent, but spiritual sonship of God and election by his free grace. As not all who are born Jews belong to the true people of God, so God calls his people from among the Gentiles as well; for the extending of salvation is a free gift of divine grace, and thus the way to obtain the salvation that is in Christ is not that $\nu \acute{o} \mu o \varsigma$ $\delta \iota \kappa a \iota o \sigma \acute{u} \nu \eta \varsigma$ which the Jews followed after, but the $\delta \iota \kappa a \iota o \sigma \acute{u} \nu \eta$ $\acute{\epsilon} \kappa$ $\pi \acute{\iota} \sigma \tau \epsilon \omega \varsigma$ which is as open to the Gentiles as to the Jews (chap. ix.) 2. In respect of the $\nu \acute{o} \mu o \varsigma$ $\delta \iota \kappa a \iota o \sigma \acute{u} \nu \eta \varsigma$ which God has set up, which is $\delta \iota \kappa a \iota o \sigma \acute{u} \nu \eta$ $\acute{\epsilon} \kappa$ $\pi \acute{\iota} \sigma \tau \epsilon \omega \varsigma$, the Jews cannot claim the divine salvation as a right, and it is their own fault that they do not participate in it. For salvation can only come through faith in the preaching of the Gospel, in which respect there is no difference between Jew and Gentile (x. 12), but the Jews have not all listened to the Gospel nor believed it (chap. x.) 3. In spite of all this the promises made by God to the Jewish nation are not absolutely unfulfilled, and God has not absolutely cast away his people. Not only is there already a remnant by the election of grace ($\lambda \epsilon \hat{\iota} \mu \mu a$ $\kappa a \tau$' $\acute{\epsilon} \kappa \lambda o \gamma \grave{\eta} \nu$

χάριτος, xi. 5) in those who do believe, but more, the hardness and blindness in which so many Israelites still remain with respect to the Gospel is to be regarded as a merely temporary thing, and God does not repent his calling; all Israel will still be saved some time. The rejection of a part of the Israelites, or their present unbelief of the Gospel, serves only to exalt the divine grace. The place of the unbelieving Jews has in the meantime been occupied by the believing Gentiles; their παράπτωμα is ἡ σωτηρία τοῖς ἔθνεσιν, their παράπτωμα is πλοῦτος κόσμου, their ἥττημα, πλοῦτος ἐθνῶν (xi. 11, 12). Divine grace is glorified with regard to the whole, as it becomes more manifest how it is part of God's plan to admit the Gentiles to his grace (πώρωσις ἀπὸ μέρους τῷ Ἰσραὴλ γέγονεν, ἄχρις οὗ τὸ πλήρωμα τῶν ἐθνῶν εἰσέλθῃ, ver. 25). Thus what is loss on the one side is on the other gain. On this view, moreover, it is still open to hope that though now departed from God the Jews will yet be saved. For if the Jews are jealous of the grace of God which the Gentiles have obtained, this jealousy must provoke them to seek that grace themselves (xi. 11, 14).

When we look at this whole section and the points of the argument as we have stated them, and reflect that the subject of which it treats is both the relation of Judaism and heathenism to each other, and the relation of both to Christianity, and when we further consider the force and earnestness which the Apostle expends upon the subject, as is very manifest even in the touching words with which he takes up the question (. . . λύπη μοί ἐστι μεγάλη, καὶ ἀδιάλειπτος ὀδύνη τῇ καρδίᾳ μου· ηὐχόμην γὰρ αὐτὸς ἐγὼ ἀνάθεμα εἶναι ἀπὸ τοῦ Χριστοῦ ὑπὲρ τῶν ἀδελφῶν μου, τῶν συγγενῶν μου κατὰ σάρκα), it certainly appears that he cannot have devoted so large a part of his Epistle to answering this question without some special outward reason prompting him to do so, such as may have arisen out of the circumstances of the Church at Rome. And what can this occasion have been? We cannot but think that it must have been what was opposed to the Apostle's great idea in this section, the objection that was raised to the participation of the Gentiles in the grace of the Gospel, or against the Pauline universalism considered in the results to which it led. It must have been the great religious difficulty which had such deep root in the consciousness of both Jews and Judæo-Christians, that as long as Israel did not enter upon this grace as a nation, as God's chosen people, the admission of the Gentiles to it was an encroachment on their rights, a positive injustice to them, and a falsification of the promises which God had made to the Jews, his own people. The leading idea of the whole discussion, the object in which both sides alike are interested, is the theocratic primacy of the Jewish nation, the absolute superiority which they claimed to possess above all other nations, and which they saw passing away from them irrevocably under the influence of the Pauline universalism. In order to grasp the significance of this question, we must make clear to ourselves the stage which Paulinism had now reached in the development of its anti-Judaistic contest, and how different the position is which the Apostle occupies here from that which he occupied when he composed his Epistles to the Galatians and Corinthians. We have here no longer the earliest conflict where no compromise seemed possible, where the opposition offered by Judaism was put forward in its most material and repulsive form, in an absolute demand of circumcision. Nor have we the personal question of the Corinthian Epistles, where the Apostle had to defend himself against attacks on his apostolic authority. In the Epistle to the Romans all this is past and settled, and the question appears in a totally different form. In fact the Apostle writes here in a different tone; he is no longer contending with opponents whose hostility excites him to bitter attacks on them; he turns to his readers with confidence, to speak to them of a question which he knows that they regard as he does, as a very serious matter, closely pertaining to salvation, and not to be thought of without deep concern. He knows that in them he is addressing a Church which is more likely than others to understand him and agree with him. Every subordinate, special, personal question being left out of view, the ultimate and by far the most important problem was simply, What is Judaism? What advantage does it possess, if the distinction between heathenism and Judaism be completely removed in the universalism of Pauline Christianity? As things then were, this must have been a matter of most serious consideration for the more liberal class of Judaists. We have to remember that this is the last of the apostolic epistles, and was written at a time when the Apostle was just about to take a step which could not fail to have momentous consequences, by travelling to Jerusalem. The time called for a decision. The Apostle had resolved to bring the controversy between Judaism and Paulinism to a point, and to make a bold cast for reconciliation and unity by being personally present at Jerusalem, where Judaism had its headquarters. At such a time, and with such plans working in his head, he felt himself impelled to lay his views before the Church at Rome, not merely as the most considerable church of the western world, but as that one in which he thought he would find most appreciation for his views, and most readiness to attend to discussions such as the position of affairs suggested. After the many years of the Apostle's ministry, great numbers of Gentiles had embraced the Christian faith, while the number of Jews who were converted formed a very trifling proportion to the nation as a whole; and thus the very condition on which the Messianic faith of the Jewish Christians was based, namely, that the fulfilment of the old promises made to their nation had come about in Jesus, appeared not to have been fulfilled. How could he be the Messiah of the nation if the nation did not believe in him, nor seem at all likely to do so, and if the respective proportions of Gentile and Jewish Christianity made it clear that what the Messiah was to bring had gone far more to the Gentiles than to the Jews? Let it not be forgotten that though they did not desire the exclusion of the Gentiles from the Messianic fellowship, the Jewish Christians could never consent to abandon the primacy which as Jews they possessed over the Gentiles. Either, then, this glaring disproportion which so conflicted with the old promises must lead them to renounce their faith in Jesus as the Messiah altogether, or they must have serious scruples as to the mode in which the Gentiles had been called to Christianity. What had swollen the numbers of the converts from heathenism to such an extent that all the advantages of the Messianic community appeared to accrue to the Gentiles at the Jew's expense, but the easy terms of admission to that community which had followed the Apostle's declaration of the abolition of the law? Though circumcision was no longer demanded, there should not have been such a complete dispensation from all the requirements of the law as the Apostle's doctrine of faith involved. The more liberal-minded Jewish Christians would argue in this way, who had given up many of the prejudices of Judaism to which others still clung, but could not get over the formidable difficulty which arose from the collision of that conception of the world, which was based on the old national promises, with the actual state of the world as it then appeared. And the liberal and conciliatory attitude of the Jewish Christians, so different from that of their party generally, made it the more incumbent on the Apostle to do something to meet their difficulties, which certainly struck at the very root of the relation between Judaism and Christianity, and had the closest bearing on his conception of the latter.

The view that the great point on which the controversy between Judaism and Paulinism turned, was the claim of primacy with which the Jewish Christians, as born Jews, confronted the Gentiles and Gentile Christians; and that this was the great stumbling-stone which lay between even the best of them and any friendly approach to Paulinism, this view is not without direct evidence. It is confirmed by a curious phenomenon in the Acts, which is closely connected with the peculiar Paulino-apostolic tendency of that work. How is it that in its apologetic narrative of the Apostle Paul's labours, it is always careful to remark that the Apostle preached the Gospel to the Jews first, and only after the Jews had rejected him and his Gospel, as they everywhere did, turned to the Gentiles? It is certainly very striking to observe the consistency with which the Acts give the Jews the priority, and makes the Apostle's practice conform to the maxim put in his mouth, xiii. 46, where he says to the Jews, ὑμῖν ἦν ἀναγκαῖον πρῶτον λαληθῆναι τὸν λόγον τοῦ Θεοῦ· ἐπειδὴ δὲ ἀπωθεῖσθε αὐτὸν, καὶ οὐκ ἀξίους κρίνετε ἑαυτοὺς τῆς αἰωνίου ζωῆς, ἰδοὺ στρεφόμεθα εἰς τὰ ἔθνη. Even in Damascus the Apostle at once appears in the synagogues after his conversion, and seeks with all his might to convince the Jews of Damascus that Jesus is the Messiah; the consequence is, however, that he is obliged to escape from Damascus in order to avoid the machinations of the Jews (Acts ix. 20, *sq.*) How this is to be harmonised with the Apostle's own statement, 2 Cor. xi. 32, that he fled from the persecution of the ethnarch of king Aretas, we need not inquire; but it will scarcely be altogether fortuitous that the author of the Acts names the Jews as the party whom the Apostle had to fear. That on his first visit to Jerusalem after his conversion, the Apostle spent his time there in public preaching, is inconsistent both with his own assertion that he went to Jerusalem for a totally different purpose, and with the short duration of his stay there (Gal. i. 18). But the Acts represents him as preaching the Gospel with all boldness, and especially holding disputations with the Hellenists. The Jews, however, laid plots against him here too, and this was the reason of his removing to Tarsus (Acts ix. 28). In another passage of the Acts (xxii. 18), in the speech which the Apostle delivers to the Jews just before his arrest, we are told of an ecstatic vision which he had in the temple on the occasion of that visit to Jerusalem, in which Jesus appeared to him and commanded him to leave Jerusalem at once, because the Jews there would not receive his, their former persecutor's, testimony for Jesus. On this account Jesus says he is sent far off to the Gentiles. At that time then, according to the Acts, he did not regard himself as an Apostle to the Gentiles. When he made his first missionary journey some time afterwards, he everywhere visited the synagogues of the Jews first (xiii. 5, 14, xiv. 1), and though he met Gentile proselytes there, his discourses were addressed exclusively to the Jews (xiii. 15-41), and he did not go to the Gentiles till something happened which determined him to do so. This dutiful regard for the Jews appears most strikingly in xiii. 42-52. In the synagogue of Antioch in Pisidia, Paul and Barnabas had preached the Gospel with good effect to the Jews and proselytes. When the Jews saw the whole people crowding to the Apostles, they raised an opposition to them. The Apostles then boldly declared that it was necessary that the Word of God should be preached first to the Jews; but seeing they put it from them and judged themselves unworthy of eternal life, they now turned to the Gentiles. When the Gentiles heard this, it is said they were glad, and glorified the Word of the Lord, and those who were ordained to eternal life believed. We must conclude from this passage that if the Jews had not taken up a position of hostility to the Apostles, the Gentiles would not have received the Gospel, eagerly as they were looking for it (48), and Paul would have remained an Apostle of the Jews (the fact that there were proselytes from heathenism in the Jewish synagogues would not have made him an Apostle of the Gentiles, the opposition of ἔθνη to προσήλυτοι shows us this: compare vv. 46 and 47 with 43). Now is it credible that the Apostle's ἀποστολὴ εἰς τὰ ἔθνη originated in a fortuitous occurrence like this, that this was needed in order that the Gospel should reach the many Gentiles who were prepared to receive it? Yet this scene repeats itself again and again, as in the section immediately following this one. The Gospel was preached to the Gentiles in Lystra of Lycaonia, but only because the Apostles had been expelled from Iconium by the unbelieving Jews, chap. xiv. This strikes us even more in xviii. 1, *sq.*, where we are told of the foundation of the Church at Corinth. The Apostle first attached himself to the Jew Aquila, who, with his wife Priscilla, had just come to Corinth from Italy, and spoke in the synagogue every Sabbath, so as to convert both Jews and Greeks. But when the Apostle's companions, Silas and Timothy, who had remained behind in Macedonia, arrived, he began to insist upon the evidence that Jesus was the Messiah. As the Jews opposed themselves and blasphemed, he shook the dust off his raiment (cf. xiii. 51), and said to them, "Your blood be upon your own heads; I am clean: from henceforth I will go unto the Gentiles," and with these words he took up the other side, and entered into the house of a certain Justus who worshipped God, and whose house adjoined the synagogue. Here, as well as in the former passage, it is obviously the opposition of the Jews that gives the signal for the bold resolution to preach the Gospel to the Gentiles. Though Gentiles had been converted previously, as well as Jews (ver. 4), yet this was done in the synagogue, and in such cases the Jewish synagogue did not cease to be the road through which the Gentiles approached the Gospel. It was felt that some warrant must be found in external circumstances for discarding this troublesome restriction, and so Paul becomes pressed in spirit after the arrival of Silas and Timothy in Corinth, and devotes himself to the preaching of the Gospel with redoubled energy, for no apparent end but to excite that opposition which would make it permissible to disregard the Jews altogether and carry the Gospel directly to the Gentiles. What good purpose could be served by such a mode of action? It could have no effect, of course, on the unbelieving Jews, and as for the Jews who believed, it might very easily, especially if the preaching of the Gospel to the Gentiles was offensive to them, cause them to fall away again from the faith altogether. And if there was no fear of this, why wait for an occasion to be given by the unbelieving Jews? Surely the view of his ἀποστολὴ εἰς τὰ ἔθνη, which this would imply, is not worthy of the Apostle. Either he was convinced that it was according to God's will that he should preach the Gospel to the Gentiles, or not. If he had this conviction, he could never leave the question, whether he should enter on his apostleship to the Gentiles or not, to be decided by the accident of certain Jews raising opposition and strife against him. Even if no act of open hostility occurred, there could be no doubt that the great majority of Jews regarded the Gospel with the utmost aversion. If he had not this conviction, no chance occurrence could have formed it for him. And when we consider how firmly the Apostle held his principles, and his thorough-going decision in applying them, how can we ever imagine that in the most important question of his apostolic career he could content himself with such half measures as this ? The author of the Acts must have thought this a somewhat important point for the end he has in view, as he comes back to it again and again. The procedure of Corinth is repeated at Ephesus, where the Apostle went after leaving Corinth, and made a considerable stay, xix. 8, *sq*. He visited the synagogue and spoke boldly, in order to convert men to the kingdom of God. But when some (or perhaps τινὲς means more definitely certain persons, namely, Jews, their mode of action being now so well known that it is not necessary to specify them by name) were hardened, and would not believe, but spoke evil of the movement before the multitude, he departed from them and separated his disciples, and spoke daily in the school of one Tyrannus, for two years, with such success that all the inhabitants of Asia, both Jews and Greeks, heard the doctrine of the Lord. In this case also we find a σκληρύνεσθαι καὶ ἀπειθεῖν, a κακολογεῖν τὴν ὁδὸν, even ἐνώπιον τοῦ πλήθους, before the public, as if to certify to all men and provide incontrovertible evidence against the Jews : all this takes place before the Apostle enters upon his full apostolic activity and begins to work as an Apostle of the Gentiles. This scene repeats itself once more at the close of the Acts. This time it is in Rome, a circumstance which makes the line of action so steadily attributed to the Apostle of more moment for our present purpose. When the Apostle arrived at Rome, xxviii. 17, the first thing he did was to summon the chief men of the Jews, in order to put himself right with them as to the cause of his imprisonment. The reason of his becoming a prisoner in the hands of the Romans at Jerusalem was not, he says, that he had committed any offence against his people or the customs of their fathers. The reason of his imprisonment was the hope of Israel (*i.e.* the belief in a Messiah, which he held in common with all his fellow-countrymen). The Jews assure him that they have heard nothing against him from Judea, and express a wish to hear his opinion of this sect (Christianity) which, they knew, was everywhere spoken against. On an appointed day they came to his lodging; and the Apostle sought to persuade them concerning Jesus out of the law of Moses and the prophets, in a discourse which lasted from morning to evening. Some believed his words, and some did not believe. As they were leaving him in this divided state of opinion, the Apostle addressed to them this one word:—" Well spake the Holy Ghost by the prophet Esaias to our fathers, saying, Go unto this people, and say, Hearing ye shall hear, and not understand; and seeing ye shall see, and not perceive: for the heart of this people is waxed gross, and their ears are dull of hearing, and their eyes have they closed; lest they should see with their eyes, and hear with their ears, and understand with their heart, and should be converted, and I should heal them. Be it known therefore unto you," the Apostle concludes, "that the salvation of God is sent unto the Gentiles, and that they will hear it." The practical point to be led up to by this whole conference with the Jews at Rome is evidently this last declaration. The step which the Apostle was about to take in preaching the Gospel to the Gentiles was to be justified by the opposition of the Jews which had preceded it. But there is an obvious want of logic in the sequence of the story; the opposition of the Jews is not even represented as consisting in obstinate unbelief, it is merely that they were not yet convinced by the arguments they had heard, and is obviously a mere pretext to give some colour of justice to a step which seemed to be unjustifiable without it. And this representation of what took place is manifestly irreconcilable with what we learn from the Epistle to the Romans of the state of the Roman Church.

One of the great merits of Olshausen's Commentary on this Epistle is that it draws attention to the great difficulty which this passage of the Acts presents when regarded in the light of the Epistle. Olshausen very properly remarks that this has not been sufficiently considered in discussing the aim of the Epistle. "If," he says,[1] " we adopt the common view of the condition of the Church of Rome at the time when the Epistle was written, then Paul's experience in the capital is quite unintelligible. The Roman Church is

[1] Op. cit., Introd. p. 45.

CHAP. III.]   *THE EPISTLE TO THE ROMANS.*   325

held to have been divided into the two parties of Gentile and Jewish Christians. The stricter Jewish Christians are said to have wished to keep up the outward observance of the Mosaic law, with its circumcision, its Sabbath, etc. The Gentile Christians, on the contrary, had asserted their freedom from all this. If this was the case, must we not assume that the Roman Jewish Christians remained attached to the Roman synagogue? The Jewish Christians in Jerusalem frequented the Temple and did not renounce the Jewish religion, and neither would the Jewish Christians of Rome separate themselves from the synagogue. But is not this supposition completely disproved by the story of the Acts, xxviii. 17, *sq.*, where the chiefs of the synagogue are entirely ignorant of Christianity? They could have no reason for concealing their knowledge of it if they did know of it, and the only conclusion left is that the heads of the Jews actually knew nothing about the Christians in Rome. Paul's speech, xxviii. 17-20, is evidently given in a condensed form; he had doubtless spoken of his faith in Christ, and the ἐλπὶς τοῦ Ἰσραὴλ refers to this. The Jews reply: περὶ τῆς αἱρέσεως ταύτης γνωστόν ἐστιν ἡμῖν ὅτι πανταχοῦ ἀντιλέγεται. Could people speak in this way of a sect which they saw before them, and of the struggles and divisions of which they themselves were witnesses? It will be hard to make this seem probable. And then the interview with Paul, xxviii. 23, *sq.*, when he expounds the Scriptures to them the whole day long, in order to convince them of the Messiahship of Jesus, and the division which arose among the Jews in consequence. On the ordinary theory this must have been the merest juggle; the Jews must have known of Jesus and decided against him long before. Only in towns where no churches existed do we find the Jews so open to conviction as they appear here; where a Church had been formed and they had become acquainted with the Gospel, they would listen to no Christian preaching. But there must have been a Church at Rome, and we have to seek for some explanation of this curious attitude which the Jews assumed towards it."

The question is boldly and distinctly put, and we look for the solution with great interest. The only possible explanation of the phenomenon is said to be this :—" We must assume that the persecution of the Jews under Claudius led the Christians to insist strongly on their difference from the Jews, which was probably owing to the influence exerted on the Roman Church by men of Pauline views. Paul wrote the Epistle to the Romans four or five years after that persecution, in the beginning of the reign of Nero. It is not probable that many Jews had ventured at this date to return to Rome; those who did return must have kept themselves quiet, and the Christian Church would naturally wish to have as little as possible to do with them. Even three years later, when Paul appeared at Rome himself, the Jewish colony was probably still weak, and consisted not of its former members, but of new arrivals, who were not aware of the existence of the Christian Church. It may thus have come about in these eight or ten years that the Christian Church was entirely separate from the Jewish colony: and this is the state of matters in the narrative at the end of the Acts." But if this be the only possible solution of the problem, how can we fail to see that it is strikingly contradicted by the Epistle to the Romans itself? What do we find here? A Church which had for some time attracted the Apostle's attention to such a degree (i. 13, xv. 22) as to make him anxious to visit Rome; a Church, the state of which interested him so much that he addressed to it this lengthy and important Epistle; a Church of which he goes so far as to say that their faith was spoken of throughout the whole world (εὐχαριστῶ τῷ Θεῷ μου . . . ὅτι ἡ πίστις ὑμῶν καταγγέλλεται ἐν ὅλῳ τῷ κόσμῳ, Rom. i. 8, cf. xvi. 19 : ἡ γὰρ ὑμῶν ὑπακοὴ εἰς πάντας ἀφίκετο). And such a Church was so completely unknown, even to the Jews of Rome, who must surely have been led by every natural consideration to inquire about a Christian Church consisting in great part of their own countrymen, and contained in the same city with themselves, that they could speak of Christianity as the Acts reports, as a thing about which they had still to learn, with which they had not yet come in contact, which was known to them only by hearsay? Can we not meet this assertion with the same question which

Olshausen uses to confute the ordinary view :—" Could people speak in this way of a sect which they saw before them, and of the struggles and divisions of which they themselves were witnesses? It will be hard to make this seem probable." It will be as hard to make it seem probable that the Jews in Rome were the only people who did not see what every one in possession of his senses must have seen, since it lay open to the eyes of the whole world and must have been a matter of notoriety. Only two years later (according to the ordinary assumption) there occurred the great Neronian conflagration, and the persecution of the Christians consequent on it. How well known the Christians of Rome were at that time is attested not only by the event itself, but by the express statement of the historian :—Nero subdidit reos, et quæsitissimis pænis affecit, quos per flagitia invisos, vulgus Christianos appellabat." (Tacitus, Annals, xv. 44.) How then is it possible that two years earlier, Christianity could be so unknown in Rome as we must assume it to have been according to the narrative in the Acts of the Apostles, or how is it possible to suppose that the Jews alone were ignorant of what every one else in Rome was acquainted with? As for the Jewish persecution under the Emperor Claudius, on which Olshausen relies for his statement, the importance so often attached to it is not entirely warranted. That it included not only Jews, but Christians also, we must of course assume, as at that time no distinction could be made between Jews and Christians, and the nearer the existing Christian Church in Rome was then to the time of its origin, the more would it consist of Jewish-Christian members. There is no doubt that by the "impulsor Chrestus," who, according to Suetonius in the life of Claudius (chapter xxv.), was the cause of the incessant tumults of the Jews, we must understand nothing else than the Christianity which was then becoming known in Rome, which was received with acceptance by a part of the Jews residing there, and which thus gave occasion to the disturbances and disputes which had arisen within the Jewish population of Rome. It would then be all the more natural that the two contending parties, the Jews and the Christians, should both be expelled from the city; and we find that Aquila and Priscilla, who met with the Apostle Paul in Corinth, in consequence of this banishment, were by no means entirely unacquainted with the Christian faith. (Acts xviii. 2, *sq.*) But however this may be, the prohibition of the Emperor Claudius can only have been of short duration, and cannot have been attended by any important results. Such prohibitions were never very strictly observed in Rome, especially when a change in the government occurred soon after their issue. What Tacitus says of the mathematicians, who were so often expelled not merely from Rome but from Italy, that this "genus hominum in civitate nostra et vetabitur semper et retinebitur,"[1] allows us to infer that the Jews were not very severely dealt with, the mild treatment they received being also observable in the fact that both Suetonius and the author of the Acts of the Apostles agree in stating that they were only banished from the city of Rome, and not from Italy. How easy must it have been for them to return from the neighbourhood into the city itself, where they always had powerful patrons and protectors, and at that very time had such in Nero and Poppæa.[2] Though some individuals, like Aquila and Priscilla, withdrew to a greater distance than the prohibition required, and went not only out of Rome but out of Italy, yet their absence from

[1] History, i. 22. Under the reign of the Emperor Claudius, Tacitus speaks of a "de Mathematicis Italia pellendis factum Senatus Consultum," which is often compared with this prohibition against the Jews as being "atrox et irritum."

[2] Compare on this the Programme of Professor C. Cless. Quæritur de Coloniis Judæorum in Ægyptum terrasque cum Ægypto conjunctas post Mosem deductis. Part I. Stuttgart, 1832, page 32, *sq.*, where it is shown that many Jews lived at the courts of princes as slaves and freedmen, and in high offices. "Ita in Cæsarum ædibus Acmen quandam, genere Judæam, Liviæ servisse, Thallum, Samaritanum, Tiberii libertum fuisse scimus ; Poppæam, Neronis, qui et ipse Judæum quendam mimum in deliciis habuit uxorem Judæis sacris deditam, gentisque Judææ fautricem hujus mimi vel famulæ Judææ impulsu mentem hunc in modum flexisse, veri non est dissimile." Cless here follows Josephus, Antiq. xvii. 5, 7, xviii. 6, 4, xx. 8-11 (where Poppæa is designated as a proselyte to Judaism by the expression $\theta\epsilon o\sigma\epsilon\beta\dot{\eta}s$). Josephus relates in his Life, chapter iii., that he had become acquainted with the Empress Poppæa through a Jewish $\mu\iota\mu o\lambda\acute{o}\gamma os$, who was in great favour with the Emperor Nero, and that through her he speedily obtained the release of the Jewish priests who had been sent to Rome by the Procurator Felix, and that she had even made him rich presents before he returned home.

Rome at a later date does not warrant us to conclude that this prohibition was still maintained in its full stringency. It may well be imagined that the more intimately Aquila and Priscilla became connected with the Apostle Paul, the less desirous would they be to return again to a Church in which without doubt an anti-Pauline tendency had early begun to develop itself. And finally, how distinctly does the undeniable existence of a Roman Church, not only at the time of the composition of the Epistle to the Romans, but (as we cannot but suppose) for a series of years before, speak for the fact that the residence of Jews in the city of Rome was no longer attended with any difficulty at that time. It is therefore opposed to all historic probability, that in consequence of an interdict issued under Claudius (which does not in any way warrant us to speak of Jewish persecutions under Claudius, such as Olshausen supposes) the number of Jews in Rome was very small, even at the time when Paul came there, and that that interdict had led to such a separation of the Christian Church from the Jewish population, that the Jews and the Christians in Rome were in fact quite unknown to each other. If the enigmatical phenomenon presented in the account in the Acts of the Apostles cannot be explained in this way, another way must be tried. If it be simply impossible that such relations existed in Rome at that time, then this representation of the matter can only be explained by a special design on the part of the author. What this design was we can have little doubt after what has been said above. The author of the Acts of the Apostles represents the Apostle Paul as working with great success in the cause of Christianity, even during his Roman imprisonment (xxviii. 30, 31). Now, if he preached Christianity to the Gentiles in Rome, he must have done so as an Apostle to the Gentiles. But it seemed necessary for him to gain a right to do this, by means of an act in which the unbelief of the Jews and their rejection of the Gospel were strikingly declared. Accordingly we find that the affair is represented in such a manner as if the Jews in Rome now for the first time came to know of Christianity, and took up the attitude of unbelief towards it. Thus we have here a clear proof that the author of the Acts of the Apostles was determined by a special interest to give a representation which is wholly inconsistent with the real facts of the case; and we shall be obliged to make allowance for this same interest in the analogous cases where the Apostle is said to have acted in the same way towards the Jews. We have already seen in detail that these narratives are not in themselves probable, and cannot be reconciled with the sharp distinction which the Apostle draws in his Epistle to the Galatians (chapter ii.) between his $\mathring{α}ποστολὴ\ εἰς\ τὰ\ ἔθνη$ and the $\mathring{α}ποστολὴ\ περιτομῆς$. Now if the author of the Acts never loses an opportunity of asserting that it was owing to the Jews' own fault, that it was in consequence of their unbelief, that the Gospel was preached to the Gentiles,—if he allows this aim of his to dominate his narrative; if it be therefore indisputable that he works out in his narrative an apologetic aim with reference to Paul in his character of Apostle to the Gentiles, then it is impossible to avoid the conclusion that he was led to this out of consideration for the outward circumstances with which he found himself surrounded. This is accordingly the point where the Acts meets the Epistle to the Romans. Both pre-suppose the same circumstances, and in the same Church, since the Acts of the Apostles was in all probability written at Rome. The Pauline author of the Acts of the Apostles, like the Apostle himself in the Epistle to the Romans, states with the same apologetic intention that the Gospel is given to the Gentiles owing to the fault of the Jews themselves, and in consequence of their unbelief. But in order to place this fault of theirs in a clearer light, and completely to clear the Apostle Paul from every reproach that could be brought against him in this respect, the author of the Acts of the Apostles represents the case as though the Apostle had respected the Jewish national claim to priority so far that he turned to the Gentiles only when he considered that the unbelief of the Jews gave him a right to do so. Thus the testimony of the Acts agrees with what we have learned from other quarters, that the cardinal point, which the Jew could never consent to relinquish, and any questioning of which awakened his most anxious and conscientious scruples, was the primacy of his nation over other nations. His becoming a Christian did not make him indifferent to this prerogative; he still resented any attack on its permanence or its integrity.

Before proceeding to discuss the Apostle's attack on this last stronghold of Judaism, we must try to settle the question who the readers of the Epistle were. After all that we have said, it seems scarcely possible to doubt that they consisted principally of Jewish Christians. And yet the traditional view is still upheld that they must have been Gentile Christians. Neander says in his usual style:[1]—" It is not improbable that the seed of the Gospel was brought at an early period by the Jewish Christians to the Jews at Rome, as at that time, if we may judge from the salutation at the end of the Epistle, persons who were among the very earliest Christians lived at Rome; but those certainly did not form the main body of the Church, for the greater part evidently consisted of Christians of Gentile descent, to whom the Gospel had been preached by men of the Pauline school, as a thing independent of the Mosaic law. As an Apostle to the Gentiles, Paul felt himself under an obligation to write to those men, and the relation in which he felt he stood to them in virtue of that office, enabled him to speak to them with a considerable amount of freedom. The condition of this church was similar to what generally obtained in the churches where the Gentile-Christian element was predominant, but not without some admixture of Jewish Christianity," etc.

All this is said to be perfectly evident, but not only is it destitute of all historical foundation: the conclusion to be drawn from the Epistle as a whole, as well as from all the indications to be found in it which bear on this subject, is exactly the opposite. I think we are entitled to take it for granted that the section of the Roman Church to which the Epistle is addressed, must have been the preponderating element in the Church; and if this be so, then the Church consisted mainly of Jewish Christians. This is what we

[1] Planting and Training (Bohn), p. 280.

might have expected; for the early existence of a Roman Church is traceable simply to the large number of Jewish residents in Rome. The last chapter of the Epistle does not warrant the conclusion that those who had preached the Gospel in Rome had been men of the Pauline school; the conclusion which this chapter, whether genuine or not, suggests, is that the Roman Church came into existence at a time when there was no such thing as Pauline Christianity. Andronicus and Junia, the ἐπίσημοι ἐν τοῖς ἀποστόλοις, are said to have been Christians before Paul (ver. 7). In fact the notion, which was set afloat mainly by Eichhorn, that those who had most to do with the formation and development of the Roman Church were disciples of the Apostle Paul, rests on nothing but the common idea that as Rome was the centre of the Gentile world, a Christian Church existing there must have been composed mainly of Gentile Christians, and that the Apostle would not have written to the Romans at such length or with such emphasis had he not been in some special way related to them. This relation seemed to be that the Christians of Rome were Gentile Christians, and if so, who could have converted them to Christianity but disciples of the Apostle? All this falls to the ground as soon as we regard the Epistle from the point of view which the work itself suggests. The Epistle to the Romans certainly leaves no doubt as to the fact that when it was written the Roman Church comprised Gentile as well as Jewish Christians, but we do not know in what way the latter had been converted, and for the main contents and the main object of the Epistle they are clearly of subordinate importance. The very fact that when the Apostle turns to the Gentile Christians, he makes it appear that he does so, and addresses them specially (xi. 13-24), shows that in the rest of the Epistle he had Jewish much more than Gentile Christians before his mind. The main argument being concluded, they are singled out as a part of the community, they are addressed specially (ὑμῖν γὰρ λέγω τοῖς ἔθνεσιν, xi. 13), and thus appear as subordinate to the general body, in addressing which no special designation is required. The whole section which concludes this part of the

Epistle, xi. 13-36, is certainly devoted to the Gentile Christians (this is shown by the repeated ὑμεῖς, vv. 28, 30, 31, and by the drift of the passage 25-29, when correctly understood; the idea that in spite of the πώρωσις ἀπὸ μέρους in regard to Israel, and in spite of the πλήρωμα τῶν ἐθνῶν, yet the time is coming when οὕτω πᾶς Ἰσραὴλ σωθήσεται, being here insisted on in its application not to the Jewish but to the Gentile Christians). But this section is of the nature of a digression, and the argument then returns to its proper object.[1] There are also many minor points in which we recognise the main tone and drift of the Epistle, such as the opening, where Old Testament ideas are studiously introduced (εὐαγγέλιον Θεοῦ, ὃ προεπηγγείλατο διὰ τῶν προφητῶν αὐτοῦ ἐν γραφαῖς ἁγίαις, περὶ τοῦ υἱοῦ αὐτοῦ, τοῦ γενομένου ἐκ σπέρματος Δαβὶδ, i. 2, 3), and which show that the Apostle had Jewish-Christian readers in his eye when he addressed himself to the composition of the Epistle. As for what he says at the beginning of the Epistle, of his vocation to proclaim the Gospel to the ἔθνη, this is not to be understood, as Neander takes it, as an intimation that his being the Apostle of the Gentiles had made him feel it his duty to write to the Romans. It must not be overlooked, and the better commentators have drawn attention to the fact, that the ἔθνη of vv. 5 and 13, are not the Gentiles, but the nations generally. The Apostle refers to the obligation attaching to his apostolic office of preaching the Gospel to all men, without distinction of race or culture, as the reason why he writes to the Christians of Rome. If he had had Gentile Christians in his mind he need not have done more than simply announce himself as an Apostle to the Gentiles. But in respect of the Jewish Christians, he speaks of the universality of his calling; it extended to all nations alike, and the Jewish Christians of Rome were not beyond its scope. In order to meet the objection that he was an Apostle of the Gentiles

[1] Olshausen's assertion, Introduction, p. 48, is incorrect, that the section, chaps. ix.-xi., is addressed solely to the Gentile Christians. They are addressed only in xi. 13-35. How a commentator on the Romans like Olshausen can maintain that chaps. ix.-xi. are intended only for Gentile Christians, I am at a loss to understand.

and had nothing to do with Jewish Christians, he speaks of the Jews as one people under the general term of the ἔθνη. He shows his credentials with regard to the Jewish Christians, to justify the Epistle which he is going to write.

We now pass on to the question which has still to be answered, how, if the drift of the Epistle be what we have said, the preliminary doctrinal discussion is related to the whole ? We have here simply to inquire whether this part of the Epistle can be regarded as anti-Judaistic; and we think it can. The last and gravest argument which Judaism had to bring against Paulinism was comprised in the claim of primacy, which it regarded as the inalienable advantage which the Jews as a nation possessed over all other nations, as its theocratic birthright and privilege. The Apostle Paul does not shrink from examining this question and probing it to the very bottom, and the dogmatic discussion of his Epistle thus comes to be the most radical and uncompromising refutation of the claims of Judaism and of Jewish Christianity. How distinctly does the dominant anti-Judaistic tendency of the Epistle appear even in the first chapters, where, after announcing his great theme, the δικαιοσύνη Θεοῦ ἐκ πίστεως εἰς πίστιν, the Apostle at once contrasts with the righteousness of God the unrighteousness of men, and establishes it as a notorious historical fact. The result to which this leads him is that not only do Jews and Gentiles stand completely parallel with each other in this respect, but that, what his argument is evidently intended from the very beginning to demonstrate, the unrighteousness of the Gentiles presses home the fact of their own unrighteousness on the consciousness of the Jews. He depicts in the strongest colours the idolatry and all the sinful abominations of the Gentile world; but then he turns sharply round upon the Jews, and says to them, ii. 1, that they who judge the Gentiles and condemn them as sinners, do the same things as the Gentiles do, not perhaps in point of matter, by committing the same sins and crimes, but certainly in point of form, since what makes such actions deserving of punishment is that in spite of higher knowledge (which the Gentiles also possessed, or else they would not have been morally accountable, i. 19), things are done which, it is felt, cannot be done without making the doer worthy of death. In this respect Gentiles and Jews stand side by side; if there be any difference it must consist simply in the measure of light against which the things are done which ought not to be done; and in this respect the Jews are the greater offenders. The Gentiles are not entirely without law, they have the law of their conscience; and if the Jew has the advantage of a further law in addition to this law of nature, then all that he boasts of with regard to his law confirms the sentence against him. The great advantage of the law is simply that one knows the divine will and can judge what is right or wrong; and so the Jew is simply the more deserving of punishment, the more clearly and completely he knows from the law what he ought to do, while he does the contrary nevertheless. The true moral worth of a man consists in his act and in that alone, in his doing what he is conscious that he ought to do, and in this regard the difference between heathenism and Judaism disappears; uncircumcision is as circumcision, circumcision as uncircumcision; the question is not what the Jew is outwardly, but only what he is inwardly, in his heart before God, ii. 1-29. At iii. 1 a new position is advanced, with the question, what advantage the Jew has, if these things are so, as if there must necessarily be some advantage which circumcision gives him over the Gentile. But the Apostle meets this argument with a new humiliation for the Jew, bringing the dicta of his own law to convince him of his criminality. He has no advantage whatever; the charge remains true which has already been advanced, that Jew and Gentile are alike under sin; Scripture itself confirms the charge. We know that what the Scripture or the law says, it says to those who are under the law. Thus all those passages of Scripture which declare the wickedness of men apply first of all to the Jews, and so everything combines to show that by the deeds of the law no one can be justified before God; the law does not justify—on the contrary, it merely introduces the knowledge of sin, iii. 1-20. If there be a righteousness at all, it cannot depend on the law, it is the righteousness of God which is by faith in Jesus Christ, towards which, as it is a free gift of God, man's attitude can only be that of faith. Faith alone answers to the universal notion of God. If it were possible to obtain righteousness and salvation by the works of the law, as the Jews think it is, since they hold circumcision itself to be a saving work of the law, then only the Jews would have this righteousness, and God would be the God of the Jews alone. But God is the God of the Gentiles as well as of the Jews. Under faith, then, the difference between the uncircumcised and the circumcised disappears; faith, and nothing else but faith, is the essential point, iii. 20-31. Now if faith stands over against works, works being of no value, the law itself seems to lose its value along with the works of the law, and the question arises, What is the use of the law at all? In this question the Apostle arrives at a point where he cannot continue to argue against Judaism in the same trenchant and uncompromising style as hitherto, or to take up a purely negative position with regard to it. The Jew, who can never be driven out of the belief that he must have some advantage over the Gentile, can here appeal to the absolute importance of the law, which cannot be simply abrogated. Thus in speaking of the law the Apostle is obliged on the one hand to acknowledge and uphold its absolute character, and on the other to show that in relation to faith the law possesses a merely subordinate, relative, and negative importance. This is the ruling idea of the discussion which now follows. In chap. iv. he shows that even in the cases of Abraham and David there was a $νόμος$ $πίστεως$ which stood above the $νόμος$ $ἔργων$ (iii. 27), a righteousness mediated by faith which was a way of salvation indicated in the law itself. In v. 1-11, where the transition is made to the great and cardinal passage, v. 12-21, he gives a general view of the great blessings which flow from the justification that is by faith. Then in v. 12-21 he rises to the very highest point of view, that of the contemplation of the development of religion. Looking down from this vantage-ground, he examines and refutes the claim of Judaism to absolute importance, and suggests to the Judaists a point of view from which their Old Testament ideas may most easily be harmonised with the new doctrine. The Jewish theory of the religious history of the world contains, when rightly understood, all the momenta out of which the Apostle's doctrine is constructed. If the course of the history of humanity from Adam to Christ be regarded in the light of its great principles as these are indicated in the passage v. 12-21, it is at once seen that it requires to be supplemented by a way of salvation such as that of δικαιοσύνη. It is an absolute postulate of the history of the world and of revelation, that there is not merely a condemnation to death, but also a justification to life; and in the view of the world which thus arises, the whole history of humanity falls into two opposed and mutually complementary periods, each with its own characteristic principle by which all the details are determined. But it is a further and equally necessary result of this objective historical view, that the law and the salvation founded upon it belong to a subordinate stage of religious development, is thus of merely relative importance, and occupies a merely negative relation to the era which succeeds it. In the following section, in which a new train of ideas appears, vi. 1, it is still the notion of the law round which the Apostle's argument moves. The law can only be fulfilled by works, and the works which the law asks for are a moral requirement. Now the Apostle has shown that where the requirement of the law ought to be met by works of the law this is not the case, that the very opposite takes place,—immorality, unrighteousness, sin; so that, as no man can become righteous through the works of the law, the unrighteousness of man is simply confronted by the righteousness of God. Here his opponents who founded the absolute importance of Judaism upon the law might charge his doctrine of faith as opposed to works with subverting the idea of the law, and being prejudicial to morality. To meet this charge the Apostle takes up, chap. vi., a different standpoint from that of the former chapters, and asserts that so far is this from being the case, that the destruction of sin in its principle and from its very roots is only to be found in the salvation which he preached. That unity with Christ in which the Christian is already dead to sin, and sin in fact no longer exists for him, makes it practically and morally impossible for him to serve sin, vi. 8-23. And the connection with which man was bound to sin being absolutely severed through the death of Christ, his connection with the law is also absolutely severed. For if the Christian as such stands no longer under sin, then neither does he stand under the law. Sin and law are entirely parallel; what is said of sin applies to the law as well; so far is the law depreciated. The Apostle had already said of the law that the works of the law had no power to justify; that by the law came the knowledge of sin, iii. 20; that the law increased sin in the period between Adam and Christ, v. 20; and that the reign of the law had now been succeeded by the reign of grace; and throughout his discussion the notions of sin and law had been so closely interwoven that they might almost appear to be identical. At vii. 7 the Apostle himself is led to put the question, What shall we say then? Is the law sin? The question on which he has to explain himself to his readers is thus put in the sharpest form that controversy could give it, and it now becomes necessary for the Apostle to state his view of the nature of the law. The identity of the two notions, law and sin, which his words suggest, is shown not to be a real one by the distinction which he draws between what the law is objectively, in itself, and what it is subjectively, for man. In drawing this distinction the Apostle enters fully into the psychological process in which, though Judaism and Christianity approach each other ever so nearly, there is yet a barrier which cannot be broken through, separating the Jew as such from Christianity, and excluding him from its blessings.

If we look back on the Apostle's whole line of thought, as we have traced it in the first eight chapters of his Epistle, it seems impossible to suppose that he had any other readers than Jewish Christians before his mind. The whole section is evidently meant to bear on the scruples and objections which deterred the Jewish

Christians who were to read the Epistle from a full acceptance of Pauline universalism. And as for these scruples and objections, must not the great stone of stumbling, which it was impossible to surmount, just have been the notion to which the Apostle's whole argument refers, that the Jews were no better than the Gentiles, that they had no privileges which the Gentiles did not equally possess, that even the law did not warrant the assertion of that absolute importance which they ascribed to Judaism? We see how warmly he threw himself into these questions which possessed such interest for his readers as well as for himself, when, after concluding the first part of his Epistle with expressions of the highest joy, with a rapturous description of the infinitely blessed fellowship which Christians enjoy with God and Christ, he goes on in words of the deepest sorrow and pathos to express his deep concern at the fate of his fellow-countrymen. The fact before his mind, which forms so sad a contrast with what goes before, is that all those blessings are lost to those for whom they were first of all designed. They are Israelites; all the goods and blessings of the religious polity of the Old Testament belong to them, the adoption, and the glory, and the covenants, and the giving of the law, and the service of God, and the promises; theirs are the fathers, Abraham, Isaac, and Jacob; of them, according to the flesh, Christ came, on which account God who is over all is to be blessed for ever. We must assume that this idea which the Apostle here expresses with such a gush of sympathy, was present to him from the beginning, determined the whole scope and conception of the Epistle, and was never lost sight of during the elaboration of the theme. Only on this hypothesis can we see into the motive and origin of the Epistle in such a way as to be able to understand its historical position. What connects the two parts of the Epistle with each other is, more than anything else, that in both the Apostle is controverting Judaism in its radical principles. That no righteousness can be attained in the way of works of the law, that in justification by faith the Jews have not the slightest advantage over the Gentiles, that on the side of the law there is nothing but unrighteousness and sin, this is the gist of the first eight chapters; and in the next three we find a refutation of the same claims of Jews and Jewish Christians which the first part presupposed, only that now there is more direct reference to the arguments which could still be brought to support these claims, and the Apostle argues with greater emphasis and power, as he stands more directly face to face with the concrete facts of the case. The particularism of Judaism had been to a great extent overcome; yet the question was still asked as a pertinent one, whether ἐκπέπτωκεν ὁ λόγος τοῦ Θεοῦ; ix. 6. The old national promises of God cannot have become entirely meaningless, which would be the case if the Jews had no advantage as a nation over the Gentiles. This is the mildest form of Jewish particularism, which simply appeals to the theocratic ideas, to the truth and faithfulness of God. Yet even in this form it is to be shown to be destitute of all warrant whatever. Even this form of the idea claims some advantage for the Jew over the Gentile, and this can be nothing but a righteousness founded upon works. But there is no such righteousness; the only righteousness is that of God which excludes all human works. The Apostle thus presents the idea which is the subject of his Epistle in its extreme form, discusses it dogmatically, and then expresses his view of the subject in his profound regret that the new way of salvation set up by God does nothing for the Jews, in spite of all their national advantages. They are rejected; and though God's word cannot indeed prove untrue, nor his promise remain unfulfilled, yet this will be in a way quite independent of all human co-operation. What right then has any one to complain of the rejection of the nation as if that were inconsistent with the old national privileges, and to take offence and complain against God on this account? God can do what he will, and the Jews have no one but themselves to blame if they have no part in this salvation; they have failed to consider that the life under the law has come to an end in Christ, and to submit themselves to the new order set up by God.

Is not the connection of the two parts of the Epistle perfectly satisfactory as we have traced it, both externally and internally? The fundamental idea which runs through the whole, is the absolute nullity of all the claims advanced by Jewish particularism. The Apostle aims at refuting Jewish particularism so thoroughly and radically, that it shall appear to the age to have been plucked up by the very roots. When we understand the intimate connection of the two parts of the Epistle to each other, we see how clearly and perfectly this purpose was attained in it.

In the hortatory part of the Epistle, which begins with chap. xii., we find general moral precepts, especially in chap. xii., and then more special exhortations to obedience to the authorities and to mutual toleration in respect of certain sumptuary abstentions and regulations. As for this latter point, the commentators, as is well known, are in great uncertainty as to who the "weak" were, of whom the Apostle thought it necessary to speak in chap. xiv. It is correctly assumed that this section must be understood to refer to the relations between the liberal Gentile Christians and the more prejudiced and anxious Jewish Christians. To come nearer the point, however, it is necessary to seek more light from history on the Judaising character of the Roman Church. Like the Jewish Christians of the early Church generally, the great majority of those at Rome held more or less Ebionite principles.[1] The characteristics of this party at Rome, as suggested to us by chap. xiv., are such as are found nowhere else but with the Ebionites. Those whom the Apostle designated as weak, refrained from eating meat, and ate only herbs (λάχανα, verse 2, as distinguished from κρέας—vegetables generally). They also drank no wine (καλὸν τὸ μὴ φαγεῖν κρέα, μηδὲ πιεῖν οἶνον, xiv. 21). We are told by Epiphanius that the Ebionites on principle refused to eat meat,[2] because, as they themselves explained, all meat is the result of copulation. They held the eating of meat to be polluting,

---

[1] Epiphanius, Haer. xxx. 18, makes Ebion, the pretended founder of the Ebionites, appear with his κήρυγμα in Rome as well as in Asia.

[2] Haer. xxx. 15. Καὶ κρεῶν, καὶ πάσης ἄλλης ἐδωδῆς τῆς ἀπὸ σαρκῶν πεποιημένης Ἐβίων καὶ Ἐβιωνῖται παντελῶς ἀπέχονται, διὰ τὸ ἐκ συνουσίας καὶ μίξεως σώματα εἶναι αὐτά.

and in this light it must also have been considered by the Roman Jewish Christians, as the Apostle finds himself obliged to remind them, ὅτι οὐδὲν κοινὸν δι' αὐτοῦ· εἰ μὴ τῷ λογιζομένῳ τι κοινὸν εἶναι, ἐκείνῳ κοινόν (verse 14); and πάντα μὲν καθαρὰ ἀλλὰ κακὸν τῷ ἀνθρώπῳ τῷ διὰ προσκόμματος ἐσθίοντι (verse 20). If they held flesh to be in itself impure, what other reason could they give for this impurity but that mentioned by Epiphanius? According to the pseudo-Clementine Homilies also, the unnatural eating of meat is of demoniacal origin, and was introduced by those giants who, from their bastard nature, took no pleasure in pure nourishment and only lusted after blood, Hom. viii. 15. Therefore the eating of meat is as polluting as the heathen worship of demons, with its sacrifices and sacrificial feasts, through participation in which a man becomes an ὁμοδίαιτος of demons. Having rejected animal flesh as food, the Ebionites had to take to vegetables (λάχανα). There is some direct evidence of this. In the Homilies the Apostle Peter describes his way of living to Clement (xii. 6), and says ἄρτῳ μόνῳ καὶ ἐλαίαις χρῶμαι καὶ σπανίως λαχάνοις. It was a lofty degree of holiness that Peter cultivated, and he permitted himself the use of λάχανα but seldom: for ordinary Jewish Christians they were well fitted for ordinary use. According to certain passages in the fathers,[1] Matthew the Apostle and James, the brother of the Lord, also subsisted entirely on vegetable food. And we can understand why these two men are credited with this mode of living. Both of them are prominent examples of the character of the primitive Jewish-Christian Church into which the strict Ebionite element entered much more largely than is commonly supposed. There is no express statement about abstinence from wine, but the two things generally went together, and we are warranted in assuming that the stricter Ebionites held

---

[1] Clement of Alexandria, Pædag. ii. 1 :—Ματθαῖος, ὁ ἀπόστολος σπερμάτων, καὶ ἀκροδρύων καὶ λαχάνων, ἄνευ κρεῶν, ἐλάμβανε. Augustine Adv. Faustum, xxii. 3 :—Jacobus, frater Domini, seminibus et oleribus usus est, non carne nec vino. The description also which Hegesippus (Eusebius, H. E. ii. 2, 3) gives of this James, has quite the Ebionite stamp of thought and manners, and it is specially said of him, οἶνον καὶ σίκερα οὐκ ἔπιεν, οὐδὲ ἔμψυχαν ἔφαγε.

the use of wine to be unlawful, by the fact that, according to Epiphanius (*loc. cit.* 16), they celebrated their annual mysteries, *i.e.* the Eucharist, with unleavened bread and pure water. The Roman Ebionites must have had the same custom, as Peter celebrated the Eucharist, which followed after baptism, with nothing but bread and salt (Hom. xiv. 1). We see from xiv. 5 that the Jewish Christians of Rome also regarded certain days as peculiarly sacred. This appears natural when we remember the importance which the Jews ascribed to Sabbaths, and new-moons, and other such days. We further find it expressly mentioned about the Ebionites that, after the rite of circumcision, they regarded the keeping of the Sabbath as the most sacred ordinance of the Jewish religion.[1] It thus seems then extremely probable, that the Apostle had in his eye the custom of observing the Sabbath and the Passover in the Jewish fashion, which kept its ground so long in the Jewish-Christian churches.

In connection with the exhortation which the Apostle gives (chap. xiii. 1) to obedience to authority, the commentators do not fail, in order to explain the persistency and detail with which this is enforced and made into a duty, to call to mind the position of the Christians with regard to the power of the State, which from the beginning was mistrustful of the new religious community, and under the incessant appeals of its immediate opponents, the Jews and priests (Acts xvii. 7, xix. 26), was likely to turn any illegal act of its members into a pretext for measures of oppression. They also refer to the very intelligible anxiety which certain prejudices and misconceptions on the part of new converts might give rise to. The ordinary Jew, it is said, "held the Jewish theocracy to be the only legitimate form of government (Deut. xvii. 15), and held the Gentile states to be founded and governed by diabolic agency. (Luke iv. 6, Apoc. xi., Eph. vi. 12, John xii. 31.) His obedience was rendered only on compulsion, and he regarded the raising of taxes as a direct robbery of the temple at Jerusalem (Matt. xxii. 17). These fanatical ideas, gathering strength from the Messianic

---

[1] Epiph. Haer. xxx. 2, xvi. 17.

hope, and from the oppressive policy of government, made the people in Gentile lands inclined to lawless and seditious conduct; and an example of this had just been witnessed in the capital (Acts xviii. 2, and Suet. vita Claud. 25)." There is some show of reason for these observations, though they are advanced without sufficient historical basis. It certainly confirms the view we have taken up to find that it throws light both on the occasion the Apostle may have had for issuing such exhortations, and on the direct bearing these exhortations had. The point of the Apostle's exhortation is to be found in the statement, that every higher power, the governing authority in general, is of God. This assertion, put in so universal a form, seems to presuppose an antithesis equally universal, the view, namely, that the civil magistracy, not only in certain special cases, but generally, as such, is not of God, but from an ungodly source. This view the Ebionites actually held; in their dualistic way of thinking they regarded the whole present world, with all its earthly powers, as the opposite of the world to come, and the kingdom of the devil.[1] It is true that we must not take the form of Ebionitism which we find in the writings of Epiphanius and in the Clementine Homilies to have been the original and only form which the sect assumed. The harsher and more one-sided elements of Ebionitism must belong to its later

[1] Δύο τινὰς συνιστῶσιν, says Epiphanius, Hær. xxx. 16, ἐκ Θεοῦ τεταγμένους, ἕνα μὲν τὸν Χριστὸν ἕνα δὲ τὸν διάβολον καὶ τὸν μὲν Χριστὸν λέγουσι τοῦ μέλλοντος αἰῶνος εἰληφέναι τὸν κλῆρον, τὸν δὲ διάβολον τοῦτον πεπιστεῦσθαι τὸν οἰῶνα ἐκ προσταγῆς δῆθεν τοῦ παντοκράτορος κατὰ αἴτησιν ἑκατέρων αὐτῶν. In harmony with this, the author of the Clementine Homilies says, xv. 7 :—"The true Prophet teaches that God the Creator of all things assigned two realms to two beings, the one good, the other evil. To the evil being he gave the lordship of the present world, with the provision that he should punish those who do evil; to the good being the future, eternal world. But God leaves every man to choose with his own will whether he will have the present evil or the future good. Those who choose the present world may become rich, may be at ease, and may enjoy what they can, for in the good of the future world they have no part. But those who decide for the future world must regard nothing as their own in this one, which belongs to an alien ruler, but bread and water (according to xii. 6, also olives and cabbage, λάχανα), and even this provision they must procure with sweat, for no man has a right to deprive himself of life. Thus the children of the future world are, while they remain in this one, in the hostile realm of a foreign king" (xv. 6).

age, when opposition to the Church drew out and hardened its peculiarities. Thus with regard to our present point, we must not carry the comparison of the later Ebionites with the Jewish Christians of Rome too far. But while we do not overlook this caution, which the nature of the case obviously imposes on us, we cannot be blind to the agreement and family relationship between the Ebionite view of the world and that of the Jewish Christians of Rome. In the surrounding world, living as they did, at the seat and centre of the power which ruled the world, they only saw a hostile principle, opposed to God; and their submission to the ruling power was not due to their thinking that a government which in its outward manifestations was evidently undivine might yet be good and divine in principle, an order set up by God: it was rendered with an inward repugnance and resistance of heart, as a feature of their struggle against the opposing might of evil, which had not ceased but was repressed for the time by the force of necessity. Hence the Apostle's exhortation, that it is a moral necessity to be subject to the higher power, not merely from fear of its punishment, resistance being positively out of the question, but from an inner conviction of its inherent right (ἀνάγκη ὑποτάσσεσθαι, οὐ μόνον διὰ τὴν ὀργὴν, ἀλλὰ καὶ διὰ τὴν συνείδησιν, ver. 5); that the cause of fear is not in the magistracy itself, as if it were essentially a wicked, hostile power, but only in the moral conduct of the subject (οἱ γὰρ ἄρχοντες οὐκ εἰσὶ φόβος τῶν ἀγαθῶν ἔργων, ἀλλὰ τῶν κακῶν. θέλεις δὲ μὴ φοβεῖσθαι τὴν ἐξουσίαν; τὸ ἀγαθὸν ποίει, ver. 3, cf. 4); and that the magistracy should not be regarded as a thing evil, wrong, or abominable in itself, as a diabolical power absolutely hostile to what is good (οὐ γάρ ἐστιν ἐξουσία εἰ μὴ ἀπὸ Θεοῦ ... Θεοῦ γὰρ διάκονός ἐστι σοι εἰς τὸ ἀγαθόν, vv. 1, 4). We must assume that the view which the Apostle is here combating was the extreme view,— the position that the principle which governs the world, and exerts its power through the existing civil magistracy is not divine, but purely worldly, or even devilish; otherwise we shall scarcely understand how the Apostle could pass over all the other questions which he might have been expected to take up in dealing with the relation of the governed to the government, and limit himself to the one wide proposition which no one would deny as a general truth, οὐ ἐστιν ἐξουσία εἰ μὴ ἀπὸ Θεοῦ. The negative of his proposition naturally suggests the antithesis he had before him: the magistracy is not of divine, but of undivine origin. If this assertion can in no case be true, and leads to absolute dualism, where can the magistracy be from εἰ μὴ ἀπὸ Θεοῦ? Thus the negative proposition which had to be maintained in the face of the Roman Christians, 'the magistracy is not of the devil,' passes over into the affirmative, 'it is of God.' Only in this connection can we understand the unqualified universality with which the Apostle claims for every government actually existing, for a Nero on the throne, for example, the dignity of a divine ordination. The assertion is of equal truth with the unquestionable doctrine which it presupposes, that the power which rules over the visible world cannot be an evil, undivine, principle. Even the Ebionite system represented the devil as charged with the government of the æon only ἐκ προσταγῆς τοῦ παντοκράτορος,[1] but the lordship thus handed over to the devil was given him absolutely, and too great room was still left for dualism; how easily could the deeper idea which subordinated dualism to monotheism retire completely into the back-ground, at least in the mind of the ordinary Christian? It might further be objected to the comparison of the Jewish Christian view of the world which we find in the Epistle to the Romans with that of the Ebionites, that the author of the Clementines deduces from his dualistic philosophy itself a new support of the Christian law to suffer injustice rather than do it. Those, he says, who have made the future world their choice, are yet allowed to enjoy many things which do not properly belong to them in the present world where they live together with the evil; life and light, bread and water, and many things more: the children of the present world, however, have no part in the future world, and so those who suffer wrong are actually the doers of it, and the

[1] Cf. the passage of Epiphanius cited above.

doers of wrong the sufferers (Hom. xv. 8). If the Ebionites held this opinion, how could the Apostle feel it necessary to issue a warning against ἀντιτάττεσθαι τῇ ἐξουσίᾳ? But we can scarcely suppose that the view indicated in these words was worked out practically, and when we find the precept rather to suffer injustice than to do it thus illustrated and pressed home in the Homilies, we are naturally led to think that there was a reason for this. The prevailing spirit of the Ebionites may have led the author of the Homilies to think these exhortations were by no means superfluous, just as the Apostle felt in writing to the Christians of Rome. There is nothing more natural than that a spirit of opposition so deeply rooted and appealing to such principles should have threatened again and again to break out in actual violence. Considering the whole case, then, we see that it is extremely probable that the Jewish Christians of Rome entertained a dualistic view of the world nearly related to that of the later Ebionites. And this conclusion is not difficult to reconcile with other facts we learn about the Roman Christians. This dualism in regard to civil life, stands in a very natural connection with that view which sees in the life of Nature an unclean, demoniacal principle, which excites disgust and abhorrence (xiv. 14, 20).

But, it is objected, if the Apostle had this kind of opponents to deal with, his polemic ought to have been of a totally different nature. "We should have to assume," Neander says (op. cit. 287), "that these people had gone so far as to consider the eating of flesh to be absolutely sinful. But this could only have been held on the principles of a certain dualistic theosophy. Paul would not have treated such a position with so much tolerance. We cannot suppose that he would treat people holding such views as simply 'the weak,' and show them so much indulgence, or forbear from discussing the ideas on which this standpoint was founded. And though we should not assume that they openly avowed the principles of dualism (for had they done so, he must have attacked their position), yet we cannot believe that he would deal so gently and indulgently with an arrogant asceticism which was so obviously irreconcilable either with his doctrine of justification, or with the principles of Christian humility." This line of remark is carried still further, when it is said that this tendency was connected with a dualistic view of the world which referred the civil government to an evil principle. But the objection does not appear to me to possess much weight. It is very hazardous to attempt to lay down how the Apostle must have argued against his opponents in such and such a case. If we have sufficient historical evidence for concluding that the readers of his Epistle held certain views and principles, we must also take it for granted that his polemic contains what was most likely to be of use in the circumstances. The data which we can command in such a case are generally scanty; and who can see into the circumstances so clearly, and balance the different considerations which weighed against each other so accurately, as to enable him to say with confidence that the Apostle must have spoken thus, and not otherwise? The main point is to see that what the Apostle actually says is not inconsistent with the view of the circumstances which we have formed, and presents some one side of the question in a clear and life-like way. And how much is this the case with regard to the question before us! How clear are the correctives which the Apostle seeks to apply to the narrow views and perverted principles of his readers; how admirably is the practical bearing of the subject, as it appeared to the Christian consciousness, stated and insisted on! It is said that if the Apostle had such opponents to deal with, he would have applied himself more directly to their dualistic view of the world. But this is not merely asking for a thing which nowhere occurs in the Epistle, a discussion of speculative ideas which lie outside the immediate sphere of the Christian faith; it is also an assumption that the Jewish Christians of Rome held their dualistic view of the world as a theory, distinctly and consciously. It may have had its root even then in a certain vague and undeveloped philosophy of the universe, but in what we see of it, it appears simply on its practical side, in its bearing on certain relations of life. Now the Apostle does not conceal that he does not consider the view of the Jewish Christians who refrained from the use of animal food, and of wine, and held vegetables to be the only pure and permissible diet, to be objectively true : he expressly calls these Christians the "weak," and says they have no right whatever to condemn those who do not share their views about eating and drinking (xiv. 1, *sq.*) He also exhorts those who are stronger not to scorn their weaker brethren for their more circumscribed notions; nor treat them with contempt. These exhortations to the two parties were to show that the question, when regarded objectively on its own merits, is indifferent. No man has a right to assume the office of master or judge of his neighbours, thus intruding on a sphere in which he has no right whatever. Man is not even his own master ; he belongs to Christ, and the importance of matters like this depends entirely on the relation which they occupy to Christ in each man's mind. At ver. 13 he comes to the subjective aspect of the question, and shows how important it is to consider that no offence be given to a brother. This offence could be given only on the side of the more liberal Christians; they could show their disregard of the scruples and restrictions of their weaker brethren in such a way as to shock them, and either lead them to form harsh judgments, or bewilder their conscience. The Apostle admonishes the more liberal Gentile Christians :—εἰ δὲ διὰ βρῶμα ὁ ἀδελφός σου λυπεῖται . . . μὴ τῷ βρώματί σου ἐκεῖνον ἀπόλλυε . . . μὴ ἕνεκεν βρώματος κατάλυε τὸ ἔργον τοῦ Θεοῦ . . . καλὸν τὸ μὴ φαγεῖν κρέα, μηδὲ πιεῖν οἶνον, etc. He advises them that they should abstain from animal food, and from wine too, that they should accommodate themselves to the principles of the Jewish Christians in these particulars. Not that he wished to bind it upon the Gentile Christians as a duty, that they should conform to the Jewish Christians in eating and drinking; the object and the whole connection of his argument show us that he merely recommends abstention from such eating and drinking as might shock others. This did not by any means imply that the Gentile Christians were not to make use of their liberty where they were not in contact with Jewish Christians, and had no such results to fear. This is the Apostle's customary mode of dealing with such cases, and he must have been very anxious, when writing to the Roman Christians, to avert anything that might endanger those peaceable relations between Jewish and Gentile Christians on which the unity of the Church so much depended. He had most important truths to press upon the Jewish Christians; and his levelling of their claims and privileges seemed to be putting the Gentile Christians before them : so, on the other side, he had to guard against undue self-exaltation on the side of the Gentile Christians, and to remind them of the duties attached to the relation which they bore to the Jewish Christians. In xi. 18, *sq.*, he gave an emphatic warning against that arrogance into which the Gentile Christians might easily be betrayed in view of the advantage which their call to the kingdom of God appeared to give them. The passage xiv. 13-23 is to be regarded from the same point of view.

There is besides an ancient authority in favour of the theory of the Judaistic character of the Roman Church, that of a commentary which is appended to the works of Ambrose.[1] With the view of explaining the circumstances of the Roman Church from its establishment,—ut rerum notitia habeatur plenior, principia earum requirere,—the author of this Commentary remarks on the introduction to the Epistle to the Romans :—Constat temporibus Apostolorum Judæos propterea, quod sub regno Romano agerent, Romæ habitasse, ex quibus hi, qui crediderant, tradiderunt Romanis, ut Christum profitentes legem servarent. Romani autem, audita fama virtutum Christi, faciles ad credendum fuerunt, utpote prudentes nec immerito prudentes, qui male inducti (so far as they were converted by Jewish Christians) statim correcti sunt

---

[1] To the works of Ambrose (in the Benedict. Edition, vol. iv., appendix, p. 33 f.) there are added Commentaria in xiii. Epistolas Paulinas. Augustine, who cites a passage from this Commentary (contra duas Epist. Pelag. iv. 7), names as the author one Hilarius, who apparently was a deacon of the Roman Church in the time of the Roman Bishop Damasus in the middle of the fourth century. In any case the Commentary seems to be of very early date, and to have been written by an author acquainted with the circumstances of the Roman Church.

(through the Epistle of the Apostle) et permanserunt in eo. Igitur ex Judæis credentes et improbe sentientes de Christo legem servandam dicebant, quasi non esset in Christo salus plena. Ideo negat illos spiritualem gratiam consecutos. Hi ergo ex Judæis, ut datur intelligi, credentes Christo, non accipiebant, Deum esse de Deo, putantes uni Deo adversum,[1] quamobrem negat illos spiritualem Dei gratiam consecutos, ac per hoc confirmationem eis deesse. Hi (Jewish Christians of this kind), sunt, qui et Galatas subverterant, ut a traditione Apostolorum recederent, quibus ideo irascitur Apostolus, quia, docti bene, transducte fuerant, Romanis autem irasci non debuit, sed et laudare fidem illorum, quia nulla insignia virtutum videntes, nec aliquem Apostolorum, susceperant fidem Christi, ritu licet Judaico, in verbis potius quam in sensu, non enim expositum illis fuerat mysterium crucis Christi. (Here also the author shows how completely he was aware of the true point at issue between Pauline and Jewish Christianity. For Jewish Christians generally the death of Christ possessed no essential importance; in the pseudo-Clementine Homilies it is only mentioned once in passing, Hom. iii. 19.) Propterea quibusdam advenientibus, qui recte crediderant, de edenda carne, et non edenda (the author seems to refer this dispute not merely to the participation in the Gentile sacrificial feasts) : quæstiones fiebant, et utrumnam spes, quæ in Christo est, sufficeret, aut et lex servanda esset. In the same reference, pp. 38, 39, it is remarked on Romans i. 10 and 13 :—
Carnalem illos sensum assecutos significat, quia sub nomine Christi non illa, quæ Christus docuerat, fuerant assecuti, sed ea, quæ fuerant a Judæis tradita. Se autem cupere citius venire, ut ab hac illos traditione abstraheret, et spirituale illis traderet donum. Hinc datur intelligi, superius non fidem illorum laudasse sed facilitatem et votum circa Christum : Christianos enim se profitentes, sub lege

[1] For a long period afterwards the Jewish representation of the person of Christ was the prevailing one in the Roman Church. The Unitarians, at whose head stood Artemon, appealed for their doctrine to the ancient mode of teaching of the Roman Church, and the doctrine in the pseudo-Clementine Homilies, that Christ was God of God, was considered as in opposition to the Jewish Monotheism. Cf. Die Lehre von der Dreieinigkeit, Th. i. pp. 155, 279.

agebant simpliciter, sicut illis fuerat traditum. Propositum et votum suum ostendit quod quidem scire illos non ambigit per eos fratres, qui ab Hierusalem vel confinibus civitatibus causa suæ religionis ad urbem (this genuine Roman designation of the city of Rome indicates almost with certainty that the author of this Commentary was a Roman), veniebant, sicut Aquila et Priscilla, votum ejus insinuantes Romanis. Cum enim sæpe vellet venire et prohiberetur, sic factum est, ut scriberet epistolam, ne diu in mala exercitatione detenti, non facile corrigerentur. Et fratres eos vocat, non solum, quia renati erant, sed et quia inter eos licet pauci qui recte sentirent.

The author, as is clear from these last remarks, by no means holds the view which the more modern commentators have long taken for granted, namely, that the Apostle wrote to the Romans as to a Church with whom he was on friendly terms. He rather represents him as writing to them as to opponents, or as to those who were now for the first time to be brought to the true Gospel faith, and, according to the contents of the Epistle itself, and the entire position of affairs in the Roman Church, this must certainly have been the case.

The two last chapters of the Epistle require a critical discussion for themselves. Doubts have more than once been expressed regarding them, and several features in them have been thought strange. One of these is the doxology at the end of chap. xvi. where we find it stands very detached, after the concluding benediction, and old authorities place it at the end of chap. xiv. Another is the nature of the contents of chap. xvi., in connection with which we have to remember Origen's statement that with Marcion the two last chapters were wanting.[1] This may be attributed to the famous habit of wanton mutilation in which the

---

[1] At the end of the Commentary on the Epistle to the Romans (Libr. x. 43) on the Doxology, xvi. 25-27, he says :—Caput hoc (the Doxology) Marcion, a quo scripturæ evangelicæ atque apostolicæ interpolatæ sunt, de hac epistola penitus abstulit et non solum hoc, sed et ab eo loco, ubi scriptum est : Omne autem quod non est ex fide, peccatum est. (Romans xiv. 23), usque ad finem cuncta dissecuit.

fathers said that he indulged with regard to the Scriptures of the New Testament, yet it is quite as probable in itself that the MSS. which he used were without these chapters. But a much more important objection than these, and one which is taken from a totally different point of view from that of most scholars, is the contrast presented by these two chapters to the whole character and contents of the Epistle.

The section, xv. 1-13, contains nothing that has not been said better than here at xii. 1, *sqq*. To what end does the Apostle recur to exhortations he has already given, and how do they come to be in a tone such as we do not hear in the whole of the rest of the Epistle? Such an appendix, in which the interests of the Jewish Christians are too obviously pressed forward, could not appear desirable except to another writer. How palpably is the Messianic passage quoted in ver. 3 brought in, in order to claim the support of the Old Testament for the good doctrine here to be given? How can we believe that in an Epistle of such a nature, after all that has gone before, the Apostle could all at once make such a concession to the Jews as to call Jesus Christ a minister of circumcision, in order to prove the truth of God by the fulfilment of the promises made to the fathers.[1] The series of Old Testament passages which follows at ver. 9 is adduced for the sole purpose of soothing the feelings of the Jewish Christians with regard to the admission of the Gentile Christians, this being spoken of as on a different level from that of the Jewish Christians, and a matter of pure grace (τὰ δὲ ἔθνη ὑπὲρ ἐλέους δοξάσαι τὸν Θεόν, ver. 9). The author may have had before him the passage ix. 24-29, but the comparison brings out very strongly the difference in the mode of argument adopted in the two passages. At ix. 24 the grand sweep

[1] Olshausen remarks on xv. 7, 8:—"It is curious how the Apostle represents the relation of Christ to the Jews as one of obligation. In consequence of the promises made to the fathers, God was, as it were, obliged to send Christ to the Jews for the sake of his own truthfulness, while Christ was preached to the Gentiles merely out of mercy. All this is to be understood of course merely κατ' ἄνθρωπον, for in chap. x. Paul finds fault with the Jews for thinking that God's grace was theirs by right." Is it of course that the Apostle speaks κατ' ἄνθρωπον, *i.e.* says the opposite of what he said before?

of his discussion brings the Apostle to speak of the call of the heathen, and he justifies it, and the exclusion of a part of the Jews which was connected with it, from prophecies of the Old Testament. But here, at xv. 9-12, we have a mere congeries of Old Testament passages, which is to remind the Jewish Christians whose conduct so imperfectly answered to the $τὸ\ αὐτὸ\ φρονεῖν\ ἐν\ ἀλλήλοις\ κατὰ\ Χριστὸν\ Ἰησοῦν$, and to the $ὁμοθυμαδὸν\ ἐν\ ἑνὶ\ στόματι\ δοξάζειν\ τὸν\ Θεὸν,\ καὶ\ πατέρα\ τοῦ\ κ.\ ἡ.\ Ἰ.\ Χρ.$, that in the Old Testament itself the calling of the Gentiles to a common thanksgiving with the Jews had been the subject of prophecy. We wonder still more, in what follows, how the Apostle could think it necessary to apologise for writing to the Romans at all. If the Roman Christians, to whom the Epistle is addressed, were not merely so thoroughly well-intentioned, but also so filled with all knowledge, and so fitted to admonish themselves, as the Apostle declares his conviction that they are in ver. 14, it would certainly have been quite superfluous to write such an epistle to them. Nor could they have required that $πνευματικὸν\ χάρισμα$ which he says at i. 11 that he was anxious to communicate to them, in order to establish their faith, for the pneumatical is the essence of the deeper knowledge. We should then have to regard it as a mere *captatio benevolentiæ* that he uses such expressions in this passage, and it must have been with the same object that he calls his Epistle in some sort a great boldness, for which it is necessary to excuse himself—his excuse being that he writes as one who, because of the grace that is given to him of God, can put them in mind when he writes that, as a minister of Jesus Christ, he fills the priestly office of a preacher of the Gospel among the Gentiles. He appeals to his mission to the Gentiles, and when he says, ver. 18, that he will not dare to ascribe anything falsely to himself that Christ was said to have done through him, but which, in fact, had been done not by him but by others, his apology seems meant to meet the supposition that he had claimed something for himself unwarrantably, to which his preaching of the Gospel did not entitle him, his principle being never to interfere in the province of another (20). But that which made him seek to ward off the appearance of such an assumption is nothing else than the Epistle to the Roman Church itself, that τολμηρότερον ἔγραψα, to which he had been forced by the pressure of circumstances, and in the course of his missionary calling (23). This bold Epistle having once been written, it seemed to the author of chap. xv. that the only way to remove the bad impression it must make was to represent the Apostle as declaring that he is aware he ought to keep within the limits of his own missionary sphere, and that he had been trying to respect these limits when he formed this relation to the Roman Church. With this aim he speaks, ver. 19, of the sphere of activity over which he had travelled from Jerusalem to Illyricum. But how can we suppose that the Apostle himself could speak of Jerusalem as the starting-point of his career, and that, in order to put this strongly, he counted even Arabia, Syria, and Cilicia, where he himself declares, Gal. i. 22, that he entered on his career as a preacher of the Gospel, as being round about Jerusalem? Is not this too evidently a concession made to the Jewish Christians, according to whose views every preacher of the Gospel could only start from Jerusalem? Commentators do not know what to make of this Illyricum; there is no trace whatever of any journey of Paul's into that rude, inhospitable land, which at that time was still inhabited by barbarians. It seems easier to take the expression as a merely oratorical one—as if he had touched the extreme borders of this province on some minor Macedonian journey, perhaps—than to interpret it in the light of the political importance which attached to Illyricum in the Roman way of speaking, as the border-land between east and west. These two limits, Jerusalem and Illyricum, as well as the expression πεπληρωκέναι τὸ εὐαγγέλιον Χριστοῦ, which must mean that he had filled this space completely with the Gospel, are meant to represent the Apostle's task as having lain in the East, and being now completely discharged. This is also the meaning of what he says afterwards (ver. 23), that in these parts, *i.e.* in the East, he had no more room to preach the Gospel, as if the whole of these districts were so full of the Gospel he had preached that there was nothing more for him to do there. How the Apostle could say this is a question which no one can help asking, and after all that has been said no reasonable explanation has yet been found. But is it not clear that the reason why the Apostle is said to have so completely finished his work in the East is that his crossing the threshold of the West may appear to have been a step which circumstances forced him to take, and which would provide him with the best justification for writing to the Christians of Rome? He stands now on the border of the West; only in the West can he find a further sphere of action; but why does he here speak of being bound in honour only to preach the Gospel in those places where Christ was not yet named? And when he speaks of his long cherished wish to visit Rome, and sees it about to be fulfilled, why does he at once look beyond Rome to far-distant Spain? Does it not seem as if there were here drawn a geographical line between two apostolic spheres of action, and that Rome and Italy, with the countries near them, were reserved for an ecclesiastical province, in which the Apostle could only appear as a passing traveller, in order to avoid trespassing on the sphere of another? To the author of chap xv. Rome and Italy and the neighbouring countries were already under another apostolic authority, the sphere of which extended so far that not till he reached Spain could our Apostle feel himself upon a soil where he could freely exercise his mission as Apostle to the Gentiles without any fear of building on another's foundation, or encroaching on another's territory. Although Gaul was still at that time an unconverted country, it was considered, as we find in the later traditions respecting its conversion as a country so closely connected with, and belonging to the Roman Church, that the Apostle could merely pass through it on his journey. The writer who could make the Apostle speak and act in this way must have been a Paulinist of similar sentiments with the author of the Acts, who, like him, had no scruples in letting his Apostle make all possible concessions to the Jewish Christians. These allowed him to take his stand with the other Apostles, not as one of equal claims, but only as a preacher of the Gospel, or as a λειτουργὸς Ἰησοῦ Χριστοῦ εἰς τὰ ἔθνη, as he is called in verse 16, with an expression evidently chosen in order to avoid calling him by the name of "Apostle," which name they had not yet granted him. All this goes to excuse the τολμηρότερον ἔγραψα, but how could Paul himself ever think of making an excuse for his Epistle? If he really believed, according to the principle ascribed to him (verse 20), that his field of work lay only in the exclusively Gentile world, he would never have conceived the idea of writing an apostolic Epistle to the Romans. For what was it but an οἰκοδομεῖν εἰς ἀλλότριον θεμέλιον for him to write an Epistle of such a nature as this Epistle to the Romans to a Jewish-Christian Church not founded by him, and with the view of establishing it in Christianity by imparting to it such a πνευματικὸν χάρισμα, i. 11, or rather, of raising it from its attachment to Judaism to the really evangelical Christianity? Whether this instruction was conveyed by word of mouth or by letter, the essential principle was the same. In either case the Apostle would have acted in a manner which could not be reconciled with the principle of his apostolic labours, which he himself enunciates in this passage. Is this probable? and why does he express himself in this manner only at the conclusion of his Epistle, and not at the beginning? Is not the commencement of the Epistle in complete contradiction with the end, when in the commencement the Apostle not only does not express the least anxiety to justify himself in writing such an Epistle, but declares it to be his duty to work, without making any exception, and without regard to any distinction of nationality or cultivation, among the nations—the ἔθνη, an expression to which he gives the widest possible meaning? It is impossible that the Apostle himself should have appended such an excuse to his Epistle. A further ground of doubt with regard to the genuineness of this chapter, is the relation in which it stands to the second Epistle to the Corinthians, especially to the passage x. 13-18. Here we have the original, from which the unknown author has borrowed the material for his supplement to the apostolic Epistle. The two sections correspond to each other both in contents and expression in such a way that we can only ask whether it is probable that the Apostle here makes use of what he had at an earlier period said to the Corinthians, or whether, considering the tendency with which it is done here, it must be the work of another. As the subject of the whole passage, 2 Cor. x. 13-18, is καυχᾶσθαι, so in Romans xv. 17, the Apostle speaks of his καύχησις ἐν Χριστῷ Ἰησοῦ, with reference to τὰ πρὸς τὸν Θεόν, and as in 2 Cor. xii. 12, he says, τὰ σημεῖα τοῦ ἀποστόλου κατειργάσθη ἐν σημείοις καὶ τέρασι καὶ δυνάμεσι, so in Rom. xv. 18, he will not dare to say anything respecting ὧν οὐ κατειργάσατο Χριστὸς δι' ἐμοῦ λόγῳ καὶ ἔργῳ (compare 2 Cor. x. 11) ἐν δυνάμει σημείων καὶ τεράτων, ἐν δυνάμει πνεύματος ἁγίου. The chief point of the parallel, however, lies in Romans xv. 20, where the words of the Apostle that he is φιλοτιμούμενος εὐαγγελίζεσθαι οὐχ ὅπου ὠνομάσθη Χριστός, ἵνα μὴ ἐπ' ἀλλότριον θεμέλιον οἰκοδομῶ are very clearly borrowed from what he lays down as his rule, 2 Cor. x. 16, εἰς τὰ ὑπερέκεινα ὑμῶν οὐκ ἐν ἀλλοτρίῳ κανόνι εἰς τὰ ἕτοιμα καυχήσασθαι, or as he says in the same sense, in verse 15, οὐ καυχᾶσθαι ἐν ἀλλοτρίοις κόποις. In this last passage, the Apostle speaks of his καυχᾶσθαι, which was founded on the objective success of his labours, as contrasted with the vain, empty, immoderate, subjective, and arbitrary καυχᾶσθαι of his opponents, which is only a καυχᾶσθαι ἐν ἀλλοτρίοις κόποις. They make the labours of other men the subject of their own boasting—arrogantly intrude on his apostolic province, appropriate to themselves what he had achieved in the preaching of the Gospel, and give themselves out to be the true founders of the Corinthian Church, just as if he had never been in Corinth at all. In opposition to these men, he declares that it is not his way to boast of himself at the expense of others, or where others have already laboured to appropriate their work to himself; that he always adheres to his rule to remain within the measure of the sphere of action allotted to him by God, and that he hopes through the increase of the faith in the Corinthian Church to become so great in his own κανών that he may even have an abundance, so that he may preach the Gospel even beyond Corinth, without boasting "in another man's line of things made ready to his hand." In Romans xv. the Apostle is made to apply this rule of his apostolic labours in such a sense as to declare that he did not consider himself justified in going to Rome except in passing. He is made to say that he is only coming to Rome on his way, to be at once sent forward by the Romans on his further journey, as soon at least as he has enjoyed their company as much as is possible under the circumstances, verse 24 (. . . ἐὰν ὑμῶν πρῶτον ἀπὸ μέρους ἐμπλησθῶ).[1] He was going to Rome then, only as a traveller who was going further; but where was he going to? He was to make the shortest possible stay in the neighbourhood of Rome: he was going on to Spain. Now this journey of the Apostle into Spain is one of the most improbable events that we hear of in connection with him. No one else says anything about it, and if this passage is thus the only testimony in favour of its occurrence, nothing can be more doubtful than the supposition that the Apostle ever entertained even the idea of such a journey. We must consider what motive he could have had for it. Because the Apostle had so filled the East with his preaching, that he could not remain in it without being idle, and because in the West, if he went to Rome he would be in a place where he could not remain without building on another man's foundation, nothing remained but that he should go to Spain! How completely unnatural all this is. Why then had he so great a desire to go to Rome, if, as he himself is obliged to confess, he has nothing at all to do there, but must appear as a stranger, perhaps even as an unwelcome guest? If the author of chapter xv. did not invent this journey into Spain entirely out of his own head, we can only explain his idea by referring to the chapter of the Corinthian Epistle on which he founds. The Apostle writes to the Corinthians, x. 15, 16, "I hope εἰς τὰ ὑπερέκεινα ὑμῶν εὐαγγελίζεσθαι." He thus expresses his intention to extend his missionary journeys still further, and to preach the Gospel in the countries lying

[1] "Non quantum vellem, sed quantum licebit," as Grotius strikingly puts the sense of these words.

beyond Corinth and Achaia. The word ὑπερέκεινα, which indicates even more exactly than the word ἐπέκεινα that which lies beyond, on the other side, is very elastic, and may indicate a country at a distance as well as a nearer one. As Rome and Italy were reserved for another apostolic authority, and the missionary sphere of this latter was to be kept as large as possible, it might very easily occur to the writer that this ὑπερέκεινα must mean Spain. The translation of εἰς τὰ ὑπερέκεινα εὐαγγελίζεσθαι, into πορεύεσθαι εἰς τὴν Σπανίαν, shows beyond doubt that the author of chapter xv. had the second Epistle to the Corinthians before him, and that he utilised the principle enunciated by the Apostle himself for the purposes of the Judaising tendency (from which standpoint this alien appendix to the Epistle to the Romans has to be considered). Verses 25-27 contain a further proof of this dependence. The subject here treated of is the journey of the Apostle to Jerusalem, for the purpose of transmitting the contribution made in Macedonia and Achaia, to the Christians of that city; and this is spoken of in the same manner as the Apostle speaks of it himself in 2 Cor. The contribution is represented as a duty on account of the κοινωνία which should unite the Christians of those churches with that of Jerusalem, 2 Cor. viii. 13, 14, ix. 12, sq.[1] How clearly is the Jewish Christian interest of the author of chap. xv. expressed, when he recommends this contribution as only a labour of Christian love, and represents it as a token of thankfulness from the Gentile Christians, which they have reason to show, since the Christians of Jerusalem have caused them to participate in the πνευματικὰ, the blessings of Christianity. On this subject the Apostle says nothing

[1] The dependence on 1 and 2 Corinthians is especially obvious in Romans xv. 27, where ὀφειλέται αὐτῶν εἰσιν· εἰ γὰρ τοῖς πνευματικοῖς, etc., is only another expression for the thought in 1 Cor. ix. 11 . εἰ ἡμεῖς ὑμῖν τὰ πνευματικὰ ἐσπείραμεν. The author might also be led to this by 2 Cor. ix. 6, where there is mention of σπείρειν and θερίζειν. There is also an obvious agreement in expression as is generally the case with second-hand writers of this kind. Compare διακονεῖν τοῖς ἁγίοις, Romans xv. 25, and διακονία εἰς τοὺς ἁγίους, 2 Cor. ix. 1; κοινωνία εἰς τοὺς πτωχοὺς τῶν ἁγίων ἐν Ἱερ., Romans xv. 26, and κοινωνία τῆς διακονίας τῆς εἰς τοὺς ἁγίους, 2 Cor. viii. 4. The expression εὐλογία, Romans xv. 29, occurs repeatedly at 2 Cor. ix. 5.

in those passages of his Epistle in which this idea, if he had ever entertained it, must have been present to his mind, he does not even attach this sense to the κοινωνία of which he speaks ; there is not in any way the least hint that he had ever thought of the Church at Jerusalem as the Mother Church, as sustaining such a relation to the Gentile-Christian Churches. It is he himself and no one else, who introduced the Gospel to them. It would not accord with the independence on which he insists with so much emphasis as distinguishing his preaching of the Gospel, if we found him representing the Christian blessings which he had been the means of imparting to these Churches as a benefit conferred on them from Jerusalem. This account of the matter is due to a different man, the author of chap. xv. He shows himself to be a different man, who can look beyond the Apostle's time, when he speaks of the dangers by which the Apostle was menaced in Judæa, as standing before his mind in a manner which we do not trace elsewhere, except with the author of the Acts of the Apostles, xx. 22.[1]

[1] It may be worth while to mention that the passage Rom. xv. 28, and its journey to Spain, have been used as the key to the Epistle by a writer who admits the correctness of the method I have adopted in examining the aim and the line of thought of the Epistle, but advances a view directly opposed to mine. This is the main purport of a work by Th. Schott, Licentiat und Privatdocent at Erlangen: "Der Römerbrief seinem Endzweck und Gedankengang nach. Erlangen, 1858." The subject is regarded from the point of view of the Apostle's projected journey. He stands at the most important crisis in his missionary career, being about to pass from the East to the West. He sees himself already in the West, at the utmost limit of his career, but this limit is distant ; the ways which lead to it, and all the intermediate steps have to be seriously considered. This is the occasion which produced the Epistle to the Romans. So extensive a line of operations required to have its basis well secured, and that basis could be nowhere but at Rome, and in the Roman Church. This Church then had first to be won for his design ; this was what determined the character of the Epistle, and this gives us the point of view from which alone the contents of the Epistle can be correctly interpreted. Cf. p. 99, sq., the section on the results of the preliminary inquiry. "To come to terms with the Roman Church, it was necessary for Paul to set forth at length the nature of his apostolic activity, and the principles by which he was led in carrying out his calling. The Church which he wishes to make his point of departure for his new labours, which is to give him the key to his new field of activity and some hope of success in it,

The last chapter has been frequently impugned, and even apart from that which precedes it, it certainly produces the impression of a later origin. The long series of persons whom the Apostle greets has quite the appearance of a catalogue of those who were known at the time as the notabilities of the primitive Roman Church. As the relation of the Apostle Paul to the Roman Church became afterwards a subject of party strife, it might easily seem to a follower of Paul that it would be well to give a proof by such a document as this, that the Apostle stood in very close and confidential relations with the best-known members of the original Church, and that many of them had been of special service to him. This is particularly mentioned, verse 4, οἵτινες ὑπὲρ τῆς ψυχῆς μου τὸν ἑαυτῶν τράχηλον ὑπέθηκαν, and verse 6, ἥτις πολλὰ ἐκοπίασεν εἰς ἡμᾶς. To make the Apostle's connection with these

this Church must first of all be assured that the principles and views on which his apostolate to the Gentiles was based were in conformity with its own Christian faith." The writer deals mainly with this point in working out his view of the aim of the Epistle to the Romans. He says expressly, p. 101, "that the Apostle selects from the general body of the evangelical Christian doctrine, first what was important to him as the determining principles for his work among the Gentile Christians, and then what might serve to show that his apostolic procedure was in thorough agreement with the true principles of the gospel." But in this view it is clear that the contents of the Epistle are nothing but a confession of faith which the Apostle lays before the Christians of Rome in order to convince them that on the basis of such a belief they may well take up his cause and promote his work. This point shows as well as any other how destitute this writer's view is both of any true foundation in history, and of the true evangelical spirit which alone can appreciate Paulinism, and sympathise with its opposition to Judaism. On this subject two completely opposite views are current. According to the view which is opposed to mine, the importance of Paulinism consists in nothing more than this, that the Apostle traverses wide districts of the world as a wandering missionary, and that at last his apostolical pilgrim staff touches the soil of Spain. In my view the essential interest of Paulinism does not consist in its passage outwardly from East to West, to a Gentile world where missionary labour had not even the support of a Jewish diaspora, but in the deep-rooted opposition, in virtue of which the true gospel of Christianity overcame Jewish particularism, and proved able to break through a barrier which was absolutely irreconcilable with the absolute idea of the *One God*, who stood over Jew and Gentile alike. The outcome of Paulinism is that universalism which, at its highest point, as it appears in the Epistle to the Romans, towers so far above the particularism of Judaism, and declares that no national early Romans Christians appear more distinctly, mention is repeatedly made of relatives whom he had among them; verse 7, τοὺς συγγενεῖς μου; verse 11, τὸν συγγενῆ μου. Also verse 13, τὴν μητέρα αὐτοῦ καὶ ἐμοῦ, a word is used, to say the least, by which the idea of relationship is suggested. If we add verse 21, where συγγενεῖς of the Apostle are named amongst those greeting, we may justly ask in what other passage of his genuine Epistles does the Apostle speak so much of his relations? Besides, how suspicious is the mention and description of some of these persons? Aquila and Priscilla are in Ephesus, 1 Cor. xvi. 19; according to Romans xvi. 3 they are in Rome. It is possible that in the not very long interval between the composition of these two Epistles they may have returned from Ephesus to Rome; but this is only a mere possibility, of which there is no further proof. As there

advantages or privileges can be recognised as having any foundation in the idea of God.

It is the prevalent opinion that the Roman Church was more Gentile than Jewish Christian, but it is as clear as ever that the whole tenor of the Epistle points the other way. If the Roman Church was mainly Jewish Christian, we can easily account for its origin, from the intercourse of the large Jewish colony in Rome with the mother country. But how can a Gentile Christian Church have come into existence there? Paul the Apostle of the Gentiles knows nothing of the fact, and stands before the Church as a perfect stranger. And how lofty a pitch of Christian faith must this Gentile Christian Church have attained to, if the Apostle's object in the weighty discussions of his Epistle be merely to obtain their consent and sympathy with views which he supposes them to be already familiar with! If he wrote the Epistle when in the act of taking the momentous step from the East to the West, and with the view of having the Roman Church for his basis of operations in his remoter labours, what a grand mistake must he have made! At this interesting epoch of his life he devoted his energies to a plan which, whether or not the Apostle really thought of it, there is every reason for thinking was never executed. What evidence is there that the Apostle ever was in Spain? Thus the whole theory of the Epistle which we spoke of resolves itself into a mass of arbitrary and unsupported assumptions; and the more we understand the Apostle's thought, the more strange does it appear that this grand Epistle can have owed its origin to the project of a journey to Spain, which moreover is mentioned in a part of the Epistle which we have other reasons for suspecting. Such commentators should first of all seek to comprehend the genius of Paulinism; then instead of making Paulinism and Judaism walk together hand in hand, they would see that what is most characteristic of the Apostle is just his opposition to Judaism.

are many other suspicious things in this chapter, the supposition is forced upon us that they are only named because they would naturally be placed at the head of such a catalogue as this, in which the author designed to enumerate the original Roman Christians who were in close connection with the Apostle. It is justly remarked[1] that the words 1 Cor. xvi. 19, added to the mention of Aquila and Priscilla, σὺν τῇ κατ' οἶκον αὐτῶν ἐκκλησίᾳ, are precisely the same as those in Romans xvi. 5, καὶ τὴν κατ' οἶκον αὐτῶν ἐκκλησίαν. This suggests the answer to the question, how does Epænetus, the beloved of Paul, who is said to be the first-fruits of the Christians in Asia (verse 5) appear at Rome? This description is evidently taken from the conclusion of the first Epistle to the Corinthians, where it is said of Stephanas, verse 15, ὅτι ἐστὶν ἀπαρχὴ τῆς Ἀχαΐας. This is now transferred to one of the Roman Christians, only instead of Ἀχαΐας, (which is the reading of some MSS. at Rom. xvi. 5) we find Ἀσίας, since the honour of the ἀπαρχὴ of any particular district can only be applied to one person. But ἀπαρχὴ Ἰταλίας, which we might have expected, would not do: Epænetus, the ἀπαρχὴ, was to be the Apostle's own convert, like Stephanas, 1 Cor. xv. 15; and Andronicus and Junia had been converted to Christianity even before the conversion of the Apostle himself (verse 7). These two Roman Christians of so early a date could also be made συγγενεῖς of the Apostle, and thus placed in the closest relations with him; and the phrase ἐπίσημοι ἐν τοῖς ἀποστόλοις might suggest that they had stood on friendly terms with the older Apostles. How they could be called his συναιχμάλωτοι, at a time when the Apostle had not yet endured any lengthy imprisonment, is inexplicable (the earlier φυλακαὶ, 2 Cor. vi. 5, xi. 23, could not justify such a description); but it is a very natural prolepsis for a later writer to whom such traits possessed great interest. That in such

---

[1] D. Schulz, Theol. Stud. und Kritik. 1829, iii. page 609. Schulz urges several reasons against chap. xvi. in his Review of Eichhorn's and de Wette's "Einleitung," and thinks that Paul addressed it more probably to Ephesus than to Rome, as if Paul must have been the writer of it in any case.

a connection as this there follows a section respecting the Judaising false teachers, is quite in harmony with our theory, as the writer, placing himself in the person of the Apostle, would consider an argument against such opponents to be one of the chief criteria of an Epistle of Paul. The description has no bearing on the rest of the Epistle, and is not in the least characteristic; the expressions are the vaguest and most general that could be used on the subject. On the other hand there are certain phrases as verse 20, Θεὸς συντρίψει τὸν Σατανᾶν ὑπὸ τοὺς πόδας ὑμῶν, verse 18, δουλεύουσι τῇ ἑαυτῶν κοιλίᾳ, compare Phil. iii. 19, which are meant to give in intensity what is wanting in colour. To this category belongs the expression (ver. 4) ὑπὲρ τῆς ψυχῆς μου τὸν ἑαυτῶν τράχηλον ὑπέθηκαν. If we add to this the awkward way in which verses 17-20 are introduced between the greetings, verses 1-16, and 21-24, and the uncertainty of the position of the concluding doxology, we certainly possess sufficient grounds for considering this chapter as not written by Paul. The criticism of the last chapters leads to but one result: they must be held to be the work of a Paulinist, writing in the spirit of the Acts of the Apostles, seeking to soothe the Judaists, and to promote the cause of unity, and therefore tempering the keen anti-Judaism of Paul with a milder and more conciliatory conclusion to his Epistle.[1]

[1] If these two chapters be an appendix of later date, and if the above be a true account of the aim they were to serve, they afford us some evidence both about the reception which the Apostle's Epistle encountered at Rome, and about the continued preponderance of the Judaistic element in the Roman Church. Compare on this, and on the data furnished to the same effect by the Epistles which bear to have been written by the Apostle in his imprisonment at Rome, especially that to the Philippians, Schwegler, Nachap. Zeit. i. 297, ii. 123.

END OF VOL. I.

Edinburgh University Press:
T. AND A. CONSTABLE, PRINTERS TO HER MAJESTY.

CPSIA information can be obtained
at www.ICGtesting.com
Printed in the USA
LVHW111831280620
659227LV00005B/1347

9 789354 007750